The University of Chicago School Mathematics Project

TRANSITION MATHEMATICS

VOLUME 2 • CHAPTERS 7-12

Authors

Steven S. Viktora

Erica Cheung

Virginia Highstone

Catherine R. Capuzzi

Deborah Heeres

Neva A. Metcalf

Susan Sabrio

Natalie Jakucyn

Zalman Usiskin

Director of Evaluation

Denisse R. Thompson

Mc Graw Hill   **Wright Group**

The **McGraw·Hill** Companies

Authors

3RD EDITION AUTHORS

Steven S. Viktora *Mathematics Department Chair*
New Trier Township H.S., Winnetka, IL

Erica Cheung *Mathematics Teacher*
Stone Scholastic Academy, Chicago, IL

Virginia Highstone *Mathematics Teacher*
York H.S., Elmhurst, IL

Catherine R. Capuzzi *Mathematics Teacher*
Westfield H.S., Westfield, NJ

Deborah Heeres *Mathematics Teacher*
Northern Michigan Christian School, McBain, MI

Neva A. Metcalf *Mathematics Teacher*
Evanston Township H.S., Evanston, IL

Susan Sabrio *Lecturer, Department of Mathematics*
Texas A & M University-Kingsville, Kingsville, TX

Natalie Jakucyn *Mathematics Teacher,*
Glenbrook South H.S., Glenview, IL

Zalman Usiskin *Professor of Education*
The University of Chicago

AUTHORS OF EARLIER EDITIONS

Cathy Hynes Feldman *Mathematics Teacher*
The University of Chicago Laboratory Schools

Suzanne Davis *Mathematics Supervisor*
Pinellas County Schools, Largo, FL

Sharon Mallo *Mathematics Teacher*
Lake Park East H.S., Roselle, IL

Gladys Sanders *Mathematics Teacher*
South Junior H.S., Lawrence, KS

James Flanders
UCSMP

Lydia Polonsky
UCSMP

Susan Porter *Mathematics Teacher*
Evanston Township H.S., Evanston, IL

---

www.WrightGroup.com

 **Wright Group**

Printed in the United States of America.

Send all inquiries to:
Wright Group/McGraw-Hill
P.O. Box 812960
Chicago, IL 60681

ISBN 978-0-07-618580-1
MHID 0-07-618580-X

1 2 3 4 5 6 7 8 9 VHP 13 12 11 10 09 08 07

The **McGraw-Hill** Companies

UCSMP EVALUATION, EDITORIAL, AND PRODUCTION

Director of Evaluation
Denisse R. Thompson, *Professor of Mathematics Education*
University of South Florida, Tampa, FL

Evaluation Consultant
Sharon L. Senk, *Professor of Mathematics*
Michigan State University, East Lansing, MI

Evaluation Assistants
Gladys Mitchell, Zhuo Zheng

Executive Managing Editor
Clare Froemel

Editorial Staff
John Wray, Adam R. Shapiro, Gary Spencer

Manuscript Production Coordinator
Benjamin R. Balskus

Since the first two editions of *Transition Mathematics* were published, millions of students and thousands of teachers have used the materials. Prior to the publication of this third edition, the materials were again revised, and the following teachers and schools participated in evaluations of the trial version during 2005–2006.

Mike Whaley
Ft. Riley Middle School
Ft. Riley, Kansas

Kathy Kelly
Shorecrest Preparatory School
St. Petersburg, Florida

Jim Buyer
Rosemont Middle School
La Crescenta, California

Ann Battaglia
Greensburg Salem Middle School
Greensburg, Pennsylvania

Jennifer Baker
Emily Kallemeyn
Park Junior High School
LaGrange Park, Illinois

Thom Burke
Oneida Nation High School
Oneida, Wisconsin

Patrice Rademacher
Mary Torcaso
Mt. Baker Middle School
Auburn, Washington

The following schools participated in field studies in 1992–1993, 1985–1986, or 1984–1985 as part of the first edition or the second edition research.

East Junior High School
Colorado Springs, Colorado

Powell Middle School
Littleton, Colorado

Edison Middle School
Miami, Florida

16th St. Middle School
St. Petersburg, Florida

Osceola Middle School
Seminole, Florida

East Coweta Middle School
Senoia, Georgia

Kerr Middle School
Blue Island, Illinois

Kenwood Academy
Chicago, Illinois

Parkside Community Academy
Chicago, Illinois

Walt Disney Magnet School
Gale Community Academy
Hubbard High School
Von Steuben Upper Grade Center
Chicago, Illinois

Hillcrest High School
Country Club Hills, Illinois

Friendship Junior High School
Des Plaines, Illinois

Grove Junior High School
Elk Grove Village, Illinois

Lively Junior High School
Elk Grove Village, Illinois

Mead Junior High School
Elk Grove Village, Illinois

Glenbrook South High School
Glenview, Illinois

Bremen High School
Midlothian, Illinois

Holmes Junior High School
Mt. Prospect, Illinois

Sundling Junior High School
Winston Park Junior High School
Palatine, Illinois

Addams Junior High School
Schaumburg, Illinois

McClure Junior High School
Western Springs, Illinois

Wheaton-Warrenville Middle School
Wheaton, Illinois

Edison Junior High School
Wheaton, Illinois

Northwood Middle School
Woodstock, Illinois

Olson Middle School
Woodstock, Illinois

Northwest High School
Wichita, Kansas

Golden Ring Middle School
Sparrows Point High School
Baltimore, Maryland

McCall Middle School
Winchester, Massachusetts

Forest Hills Central Middle School
Grand Rapids, Michigan

Hillside Middle School
Kalamazoo, Michigan

Walled Lake Central High School
Walled Lake, Michigan

Columbia High School
Columbia, Mississippi

Oak Grove High School
Hattiesburg, Mississippi

Roosevelt Middle School
Taylor Middle School
Albuquerque, New Mexico

Gamble Middle School
Schwab Middle School
Cincinnati, Ohio

C.A. Johnson High School
Columbia, South Carolina

Tuckahoe Middle School
Richmond, Virginia

Shumway Middle School
Vancouver, Washington

Washington High School
Milwaukee, Wisconsin

⊳ Contents

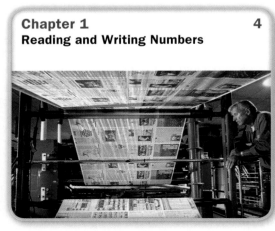

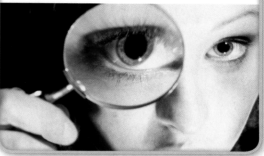

VOLUME 2

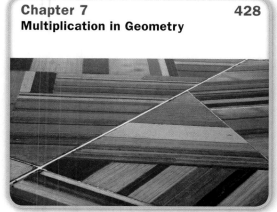 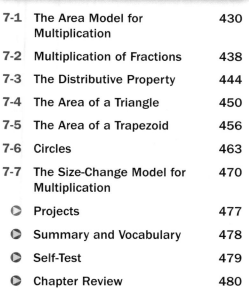

 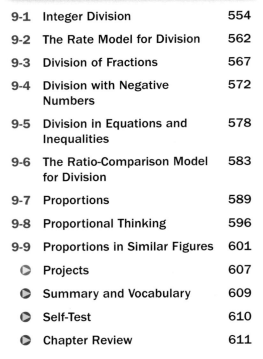

Chapter 11   672
Geometry in Space

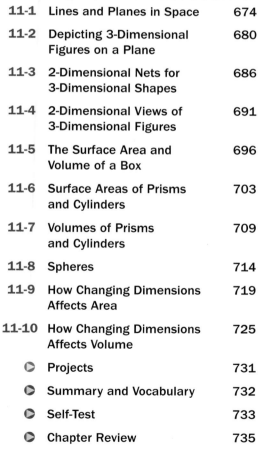

Chapter 12   738
Statistics and Variability

Acknowledgements

It is impossible for UCSMP to thank all the people who have helped create and test these books. We wish particularly to thank Carol Siegel, who coordinated the use of the test materials in the schools; Kathleen Anderson, Aisha Bradshaw, Jena Dropela, Meri Fohran, Solomon Garger, Lisa Hodges, Nurit Kirshenbaum, Alex Liu, Nathaniel Loman, Sarah Mahoney, Jadele McPherson, Emily Mokros, Currence Monson, Erin Moore, Jennifer Perton, Luke I. Sandberg, S.L. Schieffer, Sean Schulte, Yan Shen, Emily Small, John Stevenson, Yaya Tang, Erica Traut, and Alex Yablon.

We wish to acknowledge the generous support of the Amoco Foundation and the Carnegie Corporation of New York in helping to make it possible for the first edition of these materials to be developed, tested, and distributed, and the additional support of the Amoco Foundation for the second edition.

Chapter

7

Multiplication in Geometry

The title of this chapter may seem strange. Multiplication is arithmetic, isn't it? Yes; of course, most people think of arithmetic when they think of multiplication. But multiplication may have first become necessary to learn because of its importance in calculating how much land a person owned. Just as now, in ancient times land was often passed down from parent to child. If there were two or more children, then the land might be split among them. So, it was important to be able to calculate the area of a piece of property.

The basic operation in calculating area is multiplication. Every area formula gives an answer in square units, unit times unit, one dimension multiplied by another. The area of a square is the length of its side multiplied by itself. The area of a rectangle is length times width. By cutting and combining parts of these figures, we can find the area of any triangle. From triangles, the area of any polygon can be determined. And by cutting and approximating a circle with triangles, we get the area of a circle. The arrows show the logic by which one figure will be used to determine the area of others.

Area is more than an application of multiplication. Arithmetic (air ith MET ick) properties of multiplication can be pictured using area. The connections between multiplication and geometry show that what you learn in one part of mathematics is often helpful in understanding other parts of mathematics.

Lesson

7-1

The Area Model for Multiplication

Vocabulary

dimensions

rectangular array

ℓ-by-w or ℓ · w rectangle

▶ **BIG IDEA** Multiplication of any positive numbers *a* and *b* can be pictured as the area of a rectangle with dimensions *a* and *b*.

Recall that a plane figure encloses a given amount of *area*. The area of any figure is measured in square units. Any square that measures one unit on each side is called a ***unit square***. The area of the unit square shown below is actual size. Its area is 1 square centimeter, written either as 1 sq cm or as 1 cm².

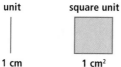

unit

square unit

1 cm

1 cm²

How to Find the Area of a Rectangle

Unit squares fit nicely inside the rectangle on the left below. Finding its area is easy. You can count to get 20 square centimeters. However, in the rectangle at the right, unit squares do not fit so nicely. (Some of the squares only partly overlap the rectangle.) The area cannot be found by just counting. But in both rectangles, the area can be found by multiplying the length of the rectangle by its width.

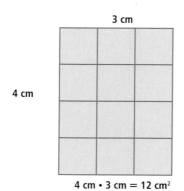

3 cm

4 cm

4 cm • 3 cm = 12 cm²

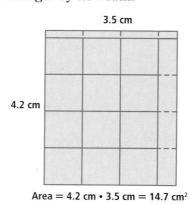

3.5 cm

4.2 cm

Area = 4.2 cm • 3.5 cm = 14.7 cm²

These examples are instances of a general pattern. The lengths of the sides of a rectangle are its **dimensions**. Its area is the product of its dimensions. This pattern is a basic application of multiplication, the *Area Model for Multiplication*.

Mental Math

Find the area of the shaded figure. All angles are right angles.

a.

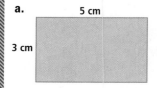

5 cm

3 cm

b.

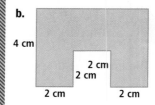

4 cm

2 cm
2 cm

2 cm

2 cm

c.

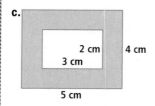

2 cm

4 cm

3 cm

5 cm

d.

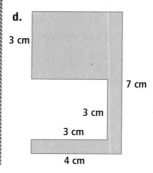

3 cm

7 cm

3 cm

3 cm

4 cm

Area Model for Multiplication

The area of a rectangle with length ℓ units and width w units is $\ell \cdot w$, or ℓw, square units.

Arrays

In the picture at the right, dots have been placed in the unit squares of a 4×5 rectangle. The result looks like a box of cans seen from the top. The dots form a **rectangular array** with 4 rows and 5 columns. The numbers 4 and 5 are called the *dimensions of the array*. It is called a 4-by-5 array. The total number of dots is 20, the result of multiplying the dimensions of the array.

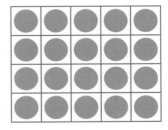

Dimensions and Area

In the physical world, a rectangle with dimensions ℓ and w is called an **ℓ-by-w or $\ell \cdot w$ rectangle**. A room that is 8 feet 9 inches long and 14 feet wide is often described as "8 feet 9 inches by 14 feet." Its area is $8\frac{9}{12} \cdot 14$, or 122.5, square feet. The room has the same area regardless of its orientation. Below are two possible pictures.

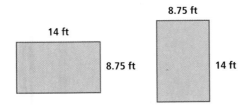

The two rectangles pictured above have the same dimensions. You could say the length and the width have been switched. You could also say that one rectangle has been rotated 90° to form the image of the other rectangle. You can see that the rectangles are congruent, so they have the same area. Because they have the same area, $14 \cdot 8.75 = 8.75 \cdot 14$.

The area is the same regardless of the order of the dimensions; that is, $\ell w = w\ell$. This describes a fundamental property of multiplication, the *Commutative Property of Multiplication*.

Commutative Property of Multiplication

For any real numbers a and b, $ab = ba$.

What Is the Area of a Right Triangle?

It is easy to see that the area of every *right* triangle is half the area of a rectangle.

Recall that the two sides of a right triangle that form the right angle are called the *legs* of the right triangle. The area of each right triangle is half the area of the rectangle.

Area Formula for a Right Triangle

Let A be the area of a right triangle with legs of length a and b.

Then $A = \frac{1}{2}ab$.

Example 1

Find the area of a right triangle with sides of length 7 centimeters, 24 centimeters, and 25 centimeters.

Solution The hypotenuse is the longest side. So its length is 25 centimeters. The legs, then, have lengths of 24 centimeters and 7 centimeters.

The formula for the area of a right triangle includes two multiplications.

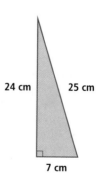

24 cm   25 cm

7 cm

Method 1	Method 2
Multiply $\frac{1}{2}$ by a first:	Multiply a and b first:
$A = \left(\frac{1}{2}a\right)b$	$A = \frac{1}{2}(ab)$
$\quad = \left(\frac{1}{2} \cdot 24 \text{ cm}\right) \cdot 7 \text{ cm}$	$\quad = \frac{1}{2}(24 \text{ cm} \cdot 7 \text{ cm})$
$\quad = 12 \text{ cm} \cdot 7 \text{ cm}$	$\quad = \frac{1}{2}(168 \text{ cm}^2)$
$\quad = 84 \text{ cm}^2$	$\quad = 84 \text{ cm}^2$

The area of the triangle is 84 square centimeters.

You can see in Example 1 that the order in which you multiply does not affect the calculation. This suggests that multiplication is *associative*. This is another general property of multiplication.

> ### Associative Property of Multiplication
> For any real numbers a, b, and c, $(ab)c = a(bc) = abc$.

Because multiplication is both commutative and associative, numbers can be grouped and multiplied in any order without affecting the product.

Areas of More Complicated Figures

By joining together or cutting out right triangles, you can often find areas of more complicated figures. The Commutative and Associative Properties can help to shorten such calculations.

GUIDED

Example 2

William Board is hired to repaint part of the exterior of a house. The side of the house faces a highway and has no windows. One of the first things Bill needs to do is find the area of the wall. How can this be done?

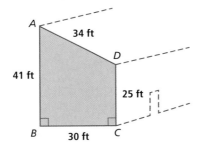

Solution 1 Think of region $ABCD$ as the union of a rectangle and a right triangle.

Step 1 Draw segment $\overline{DE}$ to create rectangle $BCDE$ and right triangle ADE.

Step 2 Determine the lengths of the sides of the right triangle and the rectangle and label them. The opposite sides of the rectangle have the same length, so

$EB = DC = $ __?__

$ED = BC = $ __?__

Since $AB = $ __?__, $AE + EB = $ __?__. (Why?)

So, $AE = $ __?__ $- $ __?__ $= $ __?__.

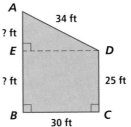

(continued on next page)

Step 3 Determine the area of the rectangle and triangle separately and then add.

Area of *EBCD* = _?_ • _?_

= _?_

Area of △*AED* = $\frac{1}{2}$ • _?_ • _?_

= _?_

Area of *ABCD* = Area of *EBCD* + Area of △*AED*

= _?_ sq ft + _?_ sq ft

= _?_ sq ft

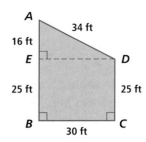

Solution 2 Think of the area as the difference of the areas of a rectangle and a right triangle.

Step 1 Draw $\overline{AF}$ and $\overline{DF}$ parallel to $\overline{BC}$ and $\overline{AB}$, respectively, to create rectangle *ABCF* and right triangle *FAD*.

Step 2 Label the sides with the appropriate measures.

Step 3 Find the area of *ABCF* and subtract the area of △*FAD* to determine area of *ABCD*.

Area of *ABCF* = _?_ • _?_

= _?_

Area of △*FAD* = _?_ • _?_ • _?_

= _?_

Area of *ABCD* = Area of *ABCF* − Area of △*FAD*

= _?_ sq ft − _?_ sq ft

= _?_ sq ft

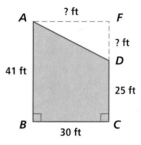

Questions

COVERING THE IDEAS

1. Make an accurate drawing of rectangles to show that the product of 4.2 and 5 is greater than the product of 4 and 5. Use 1 cm as the unit.

2. State the Area Model for Multiplication.

3. If the length and width of a rectangle are measured in feet, the area would probably be measured in what unit?

4. What is the area of a rectangle with dimensions 2.3 meters and 0.14 meter?

In 5 and 6, give the area of the rectangle.

5.

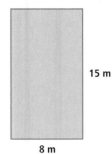

15 m

8 m

6.

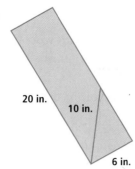

20 in.

10 in.

6 in.

7. Félix arranged some plates in the array shown below.

a. How many rows are there in this array?

b. How many columns are there in this array?

c. How many plates did he have in all?

8. Draw a rectangular array with 5 rows and 8 columns. How many elements are in the array?

9. **Fill in the Blanks** Make each equation an instance of the Associative Property of Multiplication.

a. $2.4(5.82 \cdot \underline{\ ?\ }) = (\underline{\ ?\ } \cdot 5.82) \cdot 3$

b. $(172 \cdot 6) \cdot \underline{\ ?\ } = 172 \cdot \left(\underline{\ ?\ } \cdot \frac{1}{2}\right)$

c. $m \cdot (\underline{\ ?\ } \cdot p) = (m \cdot n) \cdot \underline{\ ?\ }$

10. How is the Commutative Property of Multiplication related to area?

11. a. Draw a right triangle with sides of lengths 11 millimeters, 60 millimeters, and 61 millimeters.

b. What are the lengths of the legs of this triangle?

c. What is the length of the hypotenuse?

d. What is its area?

e. What is its perimeter?

12. Find the area of the trapezoid at the right using two different methods.

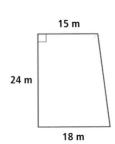

15 m

24 m

18 m

APPLYING THE MATHEMATICS

In **13** and **14**, three numbers are to be multiplied.

a. Place parentheses around the two numbers you would multiply together first to make it easy to multiply the numbers in your head. Then do the multiplication in that order.

b. Check by doing the multiplications in the other order.

13. $246.7 \cdot 8 \cdot \frac{1}{4}$

14. $0.82 \cdot 100 \cdot 4$

In **15–17**, tell whether the equation illustrates the Commutative or Associative Property of Multiplication, or both.

15. $5(3.2r) = (5 \cdot 3.2)r$

16. $\left(\frac{a}{3} \cdot 6\right) \cdot 9 = \left(6 \cdot \frac{a}{3}\right) \cdot 9$

17. $\left(10.26 \cdot \frac{1}{2}\right) \cdot m = 10.26 \cdot \left(m \cdot \frac{1}{2}\right)$

18. You are decorating a table for a class party with a runner, shown at the right. How much material is needed to make the runner?

19. Give the dimensions of two noncongruent rectangles each of which has area 25 square inches.

20. A rectangular picture measures 30 centimeters by 65 centimeters. It is mounted in a 3-centimeter-wide frame. Find the area covered by the picture and frame.

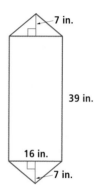

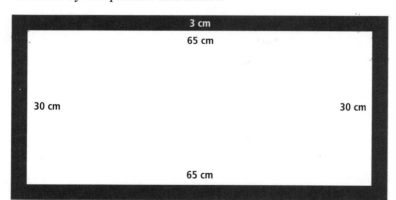

21. Rectangle $ABCD$ is drawn on the coordinate plane at the right. Each whole number on the graph represents one inch.

a. What are the dimensions of $ABCD$?

b. What is its area?

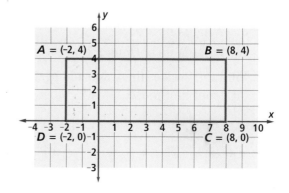

22. A rectangular array of dots has x columns, y dots, and z rows. Write a sentence relating x, y, and z.

23. One side of a rectangle has length 6 centimeters. The perimeter of the rectangle is 36 centimeters. Find the area of the rectangle.

24. A legal-size rectangular sheet of paper has dimensions $8\frac{1}{2}$ inches and 14 inches. The paper is cut in half along its diagonal. What is the area of each half?

25. If the dimensions of a rectangle are multiplied by 4, what happens to its area? Give three instances that support your answer.

26. The design at the right is made up entirely of squares. The little white square has side of length 1 unit. What is the area of rectangle $ABCD$?

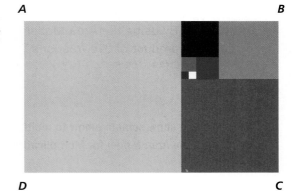

27. Find the distance between point $(-3, -4)$ and point $(-5, -6)$ on a coordinate grid. (**Lesson 6-9**)

28. A triangle has two congruent angles, each measuring $30°$.
    a. Find the measure of the third angle.
    b. What type of triangle is this? (**Lessons 6-8, 4-8**)

29. Identify the property of addition being used. (**Lessons 5-5, 5-2, 5-1**)
    a. $42.65 + 18.71 = 18.71 + 42.65$
    b. If $a + 7 = 10$, then $a + 7 + n = 10 + n$.
    c. $14 + (9 + w) = (14 + 9) + w$

30. Let A = the set of odd multiples of 3 and B = the set of multiples of 6.
    a. Describe $A \cup B$.   b. Describe $A \cap B$. (**Lesson 4-4**)

EXPLORATION

31. Is it possible for a rectangle to have a perimeter of 1 million miles but an area of less than 1 square mile? If so, give an example of such a rectangle. If not, explain why not.

Lesson

7-2

Multiplication of Fractions

Vocabulary

unit fraction

reciprocal,
  multiplicative inverse

> ▶ **BIG IDEA** By using the Area Model for Multiplication, you can show that the product of two fractions $\frac{a}{b}$ and $\frac{c}{d}$ is the fraction $\frac{ac}{bd}$.

Activity

How would you show someone how to multiply $\frac{1}{4} \cdot \frac{1}{8}$? This paper-folding activity uses the Area Model for Multiplication to illustrate multiplication of fractions.

Mental Math

Calculate.

a. $\frac{2}{3} + \frac{4}{3}$

b. $\frac{2}{3} - \frac{2}{9}$

c. $\frac{2}{3} + \frac{1}{4}$

d. $\frac{2}{3} - \frac{2}{5}$

Step 1 With a short side facing you, fold a sheet of notebook paper in half top to bottom. Then fold it in half top to bottom again. Unfold the paper. The folds should divide the sheet into four congruent sections. Each of the four sections represents $\frac{1}{4}$ of the sheet. Shade one of the sections with diagonals in one direction or with a colored pencil.

Step 2 Rotate the paper 90° and fold the paper in eighths top to bottom. Unfold the paper. Now the folds should indicate 32 congruent sections. Why?

Step 3 Each of the eight rows is $\frac{1}{8}$ of the sheet. Shade one of them with diagonals in a different direction or with a different-color pencil.

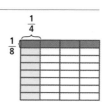

Step 4 What part of the paper is double-shaded? How does this show $\frac{1}{4} \cdot \frac{1}{8} = \frac{1}{32}$?

Multiplication of Unit Fractions

Here is a situation similar to the Activity.

Example 1

Selena's mother ordered a large cake for her birthday party. She cut the cake into 24 pieces of the same size. By the time the cake was served, the guests were not very hungry. So, Selena cut each piece into two smaller pieces of the same size. At the party, Sandi ate one of the smaller pieces. What fraction of the cake did she eat?

Solution 1 Because each of the 24 pieces was cut into two, there were 48 smaller pieces. Because all the pieces were of the same size, Sandi ate $\frac{1}{48}$ of the cake.

Solution 2 The original pieces were each $\frac{1}{24}$ of the cake. Sandi ate $\frac{1}{2}$ of $\frac{1}{24}$. To find $\frac{1}{2}$ of $\frac{1}{24}$, multiply the fractions.

$$\frac{1}{2} \cdot \frac{1}{24} = \frac{1}{48}$$

So, Sandi ate $\frac{1}{48}$ of the cake.

Fractions like $\frac{1}{2}, \frac{1}{3}, \frac{1}{4}, \frac{1}{5}$, and so on are *unit fractions*. A **unit fraction** is a fraction with 1 in its numerator and a positive integer in its denominator. The rule for multiplying two unit fractions is quite straightforward.

> ### Multiplication of Unit Fractions Property
>
> For all nonzero real numbers a and b, $\frac{1}{a} \cdot \frac{1}{b} = \frac{1}{ab}$.

Fractions and Division

The ancient Egyptians used unit fractions almost exclusively. The only fraction they used that is not a unit fraction was $\frac{2}{3}$. They used clever methods to write all other fraction as sums of unit fractions. For example, $\frac{5}{6} = \frac{1}{2} + \frac{1}{3}$.

Today we look differently at unit fractions. $\frac{2}{3}$ is thought of as $2 \cdot \frac{1}{3}$. In general, any fraction $\frac{a}{b}$ can be thought of as a times $\frac{1}{b}$. The fraction $\frac{a}{b}$ is also equal to the quotient $a \div b$. These fundamental relationships among fractions, multiplication, and division are sometimes grouped together in the *Algebraic Definition of Division*.

Algebraic Definition of Division

For all real numbers a and nonzero real numbers b,

$$a \cdot \frac{1}{b} = \frac{a}{b} = a \div b.$$

Multiplication of Any Fractions

You can multiply any fractions using the Area Model for Multiplication.

Example 2

A farm field is in the shape of a rectangle $\frac{3}{4}$ of a mile long and $\frac{5}{8}$ of a mile wide. What is its area?

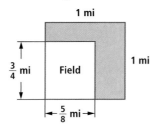

Solution Think of the field as being inside a square mile. Divide that square mile into rectangles that are $\frac{1}{4}$ mile by $\frac{1}{8}$ mile, as in the figure at the right. You can see that 32 of these rectangles fit into the square mile. So, the area of each small rectangle is $\frac{1}{32}$ square mile. The field, because it is $3 \cdot \frac{1}{4}$ mile wide and $5 \cdot \frac{1}{8}$ mile long, includes $3 \cdot 5$, or 15, of these rectangles. So, the area of the field is $15 \cdot \frac{1}{32}$, or $\frac{15}{32}$, square mile.

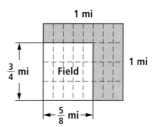

From Example 2, we see that $\frac{3}{4} \cdot \frac{5}{8} = \frac{15}{32}$. In general, the product of two fractions can be written as a fraction whose numerator is the product of the two numerators and whose denominator is the product of the two denominators. This pattern is easier to state with variables than with words. We call this the *Multiplication of Fractions Property*.

Multiplication of Fractions Property

For all real numbers a and c, and nonzero real numbers b and d,

$$\frac{a}{b} \cdot \frac{c}{d} = \frac{ac}{bd}.$$

 QY1

▶ **QY1**

Check that $\frac{3}{4} \cdot \frac{5}{8} = \frac{15}{32}$ by converting all three fractions to decimals.

What Are Reciprocals?

When 48 of the pieces of the cake from Example 1 were eaten, then $48 \cdot \frac{1}{48}$ of the cake was eaten. This is all of the cake.

$48 \cdot \frac{1}{48} = \frac{48}{48} = 1$ whole cake.

Two numbers whose product is 1 are called **reciprocals,** or **multiplicative inverses,** of each other. $\frac{1}{48}$ and 48 are reciprocals. This is one instance of a general pattern involving reciprocals.

> **Property of Reciprocals**
>
> For any nonzero real number a, a and $\frac{1}{a}$ are reciprocals. That is,
> $$a \cdot \frac{1}{a} = 1.$$

Notice that the reciprocal of a nonzero number is 1 divided by that number. All nonzero real numbers have reciprocals.

 QY2

▶ QY2

Find the reciprocal of 6.25.

Reciprocals of Fractions

It is easy to find the reciprocal of any fraction. Example 3 shows how.

> ### Example 3
>
> Find the reciprocal of $\frac{5}{12}$ in lowest terms.
>
> **Solution** The reciprocal of $\frac{5}{12}$ is $\frac{1}{\frac{5}{12}}$. Multiply both numerator and denominator by 12.
>
> $$\frac{1}{\frac{5}{12}} = \frac{1 \cdot 12}{\frac{5}{12} \cdot 12} = \frac{12}{5}$$
>
> The reciprocal of $\frac{5}{12}$ is $\frac{12}{5}$.
>
> **Check**
>
> $$\frac{5}{12} \cdot \frac{12}{5} = \frac{60}{60} = 1$$

 QY3

▶ QY3

Find the reciprocal of $\frac{2}{3}$.

 GAME Now you can play *Top-It: Fraction Multiplication.* The directions for this game are on page G11 at the back of your book.

Questions

COVERING THE IDEAS

1. Use paper-folding and a diagram to show how $\frac{2}{3} \cdot \frac{3}{4} = \frac{1}{2}$.

2. Consider the situation of Example 1. Suppose that each of the 24 pieces had been cut into 3 equal pieces. Then each smaller piece is what part of the original cake?

3. What is a unit fraction?

In 4–8, write the product as a fraction in lowest terms.

4. $\frac{1}{2} \cdot \frac{1}{3}$

5. $\frac{1}{5} \cdot \frac{1}{y}$

6. $\frac{1}{x} \cdot \frac{1}{y}$

7. $3 \cdot \frac{1}{12}$

8. $\frac{1}{a} \cdot 4$

9. A field is rectangular in shape, $\frac{1}{3}$ mile by $\frac{3}{4}$ mile. Use a drawing to explain why the area of the field is $\frac{1}{4}$ square mile.

In 10–13, simplify.

10. $\frac{5}{7} \cdot \frac{7}{5}$

11. $\frac{1}{5} \cdot \frac{5}{41}$

12. $\left(8 \cdot \frac{1}{15}\right) \cdot \left(3 \cdot \frac{1}{4}\right)$

13. $\frac{a}{b} \cdot \frac{x}{y}$

In 14 and 15, give the reciprocal of the number.

14. 11

15. 3.25

16. Write the reciprocal of 160 as a decimal.

17. Write the reciprocal of $\frac{9}{8}$ in lowest terms.

18. Janice has promised her parents that she will shovel the snow off their driveway. If the area of the driveway is 250 square feet and she has completed $\frac{1}{3}$ of it, how many square feet does she have left to shovel?

APPLYING THE MATHEMATICS

19. **a.** 10 seconds is what part of a minute?
    b. 10 seconds is what part of an hour?
    c. 10 seconds is what part of a day?

20. Write the reciprocal of $8\frac{2}{3}$ as a simple fraction.

21. Explain why 0 has no reciprocal.

In 22–25, write as a simple fraction or mixed number in lowest terms.

22. $4\frac{1}{4} \cdot 3\frac{1}{3}$

23. $\frac{x}{15} \cdot \frac{75}{x}$

24. $\frac{1}{2} \cdot \frac{2}{3} \cdot \frac{3}{4} \cdot \frac{4}{5} \cdot \frac{5}{6} \cdot \frac{6}{7} \cdot \frac{7}{8}$

25. $\frac{4}{5}$ of $\frac{80}{12}$

26. Without multiplying, explain why $\frac{1}{4} \cdot \frac{6}{7} \cdot \frac{7}{12} \cdot \frac{19}{50} \cdot \frac{61}{119}$ is less than 1.

27. Use the Multiplication of Fractions Property and the Property of Reciprocals to show that $\frac{5}{17}$ is the reciprocal of $\frac{17}{5}$.

REVIEW

28. Find the area of a right triangle with sides of lengths 40 centimeters, 42 centimeters, and 58 centimeters. **(Lesson 7-1)**

29. A calculator display has 64 rows and 96 columns of pixels. How many pixels does the display have in all? **(Lesson 7-1)**

30. If two angles of a triangle measure 88° and 87°, find the measure of the third angle. **(Lesson 6-8)**

31. Draw an example of a flag that has at least one line of symmetry in its design. **(Lesson 6-2)**

EXPLORATION

32. Examine this pattern that shows how to write some fractions as sums of unit fractions.

$$\frac{3}{4} = \frac{1}{2} + \frac{1}{4}$$
$$\frac{7}{8} = \frac{1}{2} + \frac{1}{4} + \frac{1}{8}$$
$$\frac{15}{16} = \frac{1}{2} + \frac{1}{4} + \frac{1}{8} + \frac{1}{16}$$

   a. Write the next two equations in the pattern.

   b. Use the pattern to write $\frac{1,023}{1,024}$ as a sum of unit fractions.

33. Draw a diagram to explain why $2\frac{3}{4} \cdot 1\frac{1}{5} = 3\frac{3}{10}$.

The state flag of Ohio is the only U.S. state flag that is not rectangular.

Lesson 7-3

The Distributive Property

▶ **BIG IDEA** The Distributive Properties of Multiplication over Addition and over Subtraction enable you to collect like terms and to rewrite some expressions without parentheses.

Gifford Trapp needs to wrap two presents. He has a roll of paper that is 30 inches wide. He cuts off a $12\frac{1}{2}$-inch-long piece of wrapping paper for the smaller present and a $25\frac{3}{4}$-inch-long piece for the larger present. What is the total area of the paper used to wrap the presents? Here are two ways to solve this problem.

Solution 1 Find the area of each piece and combine.

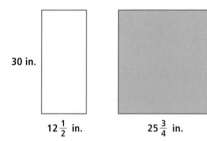

30 in.　　　　　　　30 in.

$12\frac{1}{2}$ in.　　　$25\frac{3}{4}$ in.

$$\begin{aligned}
\text{Area} &= 30 \cdot 12\frac{1}{2} \text{ sq in.} + 30 \cdot 25\frac{3}{4} \text{ sq in.} \\
&= 375 \text{ sq in.} + 772.5 \text{ sq in.} \\
&= 1{,}147.5 \text{ sq in.}
\end{aligned}$$

Solution 2 Combine the lengths of the two pieces and find the area.

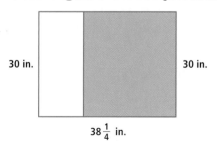

30 in.　　　　　　　30 in.

$38\frac{1}{4}$ in.

$$\begin{aligned}
\text{Area} &= 30 \cdot \left(12\frac{1}{2} + 25\frac{3}{4}\right) \text{ sq in.} \\
&= 30 \cdot \left(38\frac{1}{4}\right) \text{ sq in.} \\
&= 1{,}147.5 \text{ sq in.}
\end{aligned}$$

Mental Math

True or False

a. $6(\frac{1}{2} + 4) = 6 \cdot \frac{1}{2} + 4$

b. $6(\frac{1}{2} + 4) = 6 \cdot \frac{1}{2} + 6 \cdot 4$

c. $6(\frac{1}{2} + 4) = \frac{1}{2} + \frac{1}{2} + \frac{1}{2} + \frac{1}{2} + \frac{1}{2} + \frac{1}{2} + 4 + 4 + 4 + 4 + 4 + 4$

d. $6(\frac{1}{2} + 4) = 6 \cdot 4\frac{1}{2}$

Both solutions find the area of the same amount of wrapping paper. Either way you perform the computation, the area is the same.

$$30 \cdot 12\frac{1}{2} + 30 \cdot 25\frac{3}{4} = 30 \cdot \left(12\frac{1}{2} + 25\frac{3}{4}\right)$$

Because multiplication is commutative, the expressions could be written with the 30 at the right of each multiplication.

$$12\frac{1}{2} \cdot 30 + 25\frac{3}{4} \cdot 30 = \left(12\frac{1}{2} + 25\frac{3}{4}\right) \cdot 30$$

In this situation, two addends $\left(12\frac{1}{2} \text{ and } 25\frac{3}{4}\right)$ are multiplied by the same factor (30). The sum of the products is the same as if the sum $\left(38\frac{1}{4}\right)$ is multiplied by the factor (30). The general patterns are known as the *Distributive Property of Multiplication over Addition*.

> ### Distributive Property of Multiplication over Addition
> For any numbers a, b, and x:
> $$ax + bx = (a + b)x \quad \text{and} \quad x(a + b) = xa + xb.$$

The Distributive Property gets its name because it states that the same multiplications "distributed" over several quantities can be combined into one multiplication. In the situation above, 30 was distributed over the sum $12\frac{1}{2} + 25\frac{3}{4}$. In Guided Example 1 below, 6 is distributed over the sum of $3.35 and $1.75 as a common factor. The two multiplications can be written as one.

GUIDED

Example 1
A concession stand at a baseball game sold hot dogs for $3.35 each and sodas for $1.75 each. Dario bought one of each for himself and each of 5 friends. What was the total cost?

Solution Use the Distributive Property.

$$a \cdot x + b \cdot x = (a + b)x$$
$$\$3.35 \cdot 6 + \$1.75 \cdot 6 = (\underline{\ ?\ } + \underline{\ ?\ })\underline{\ ?\ }$$
$$= \underline{\ ?\ } \cdot \underline{\ ?\ }$$
$$= \underline{\ ?\ }$$

Using the Distributive Property to Calculate in Your Head

In Example 2, multiplication by 16 is distributed over parts of the $10.50. The Distributive Property enables you to do the calculation in your head.

Example 2

The soccer team wants to buy special soccer socks to celebrate their recent victory. They will buy 16 pairs for $10.50 each. In your head, calculate the total bill for the socks.

Solution Split the 10.50 into 10 and 0.50. Use these steps to calculate the answer in your head.

$16 \cdot 10.50 = 16(10 + 0.50)$ Separate 10.50 into 10 and 0.50.

$= 16 \cdot 10 + 16 \cdot 0.50$ Apply the Distributive Property of Multiplication over Addition.

$= 160 + 8$ Multiply.

$= 168$ Add.

The total bill for the socks is $168.

Soccer socks are larger than regular socks so they can fit over shin guards.

Remember, the Add-Opp property tells you that you can think of subtracting a number as adding the opposite of that number. It may not surprise you, therefore, that there is also a *Distributive Property of Multiplication over Subtraction*.

Distributive Property of Multiplication over Subtraction

For any numbers a, b, and x,

$$ax - bx = (a - b)x \quad \text{and} \quad x(a - b) = xa - xb.$$

Example 3

What will 7 pairs of earrings at $5.97 a pair cost? Calculate in your head.

Solution

$7 \cdot 5.97 = 7(6 - 0.03)$ Think of 5.97 as $6 - 0.03$.

$= 7 \cdot 6 - 7 \cdot 0.03$ Apply the Distributive Property of Multiplication over Subtraction.

(continued on next page)

$$= 42 - 0.21 \quad \text{Multiply.}$$

$$= 41.79 \quad \text{Subtract. You are taking 21¢ from}$$
42 dollars.

The earrings will cost $41.79.

Calculating one of the areas at the beginning of this lesson involved multiplying 30 inches by $12\frac{1}{2}$ inches. This arithmetic in itself illustrates the Distributive Property, because the mixed number is itself a sum: $12\frac{1}{2} = 12 + \frac{1}{2}$. Consequently, you might be able to do this multiplication in your head.

$$30 \cdot 12\frac{1}{2} = 30\left(12 + \frac{1}{2}\right)$$
$$= 30 \cdot 12 + 30 \cdot \frac{1}{2}$$
$$= 360 + 15$$
$$= 375$$

STOP QY

The Distributive Properties over Addition and Subtraction can be combined.

▶ **QY**

Multiply $25 \cdot 8\frac{1}{5}$ using the Distributive Property.

Example 4

Multiply $2(3x + y - 7)$.

Solution Use the Distributive Properties.

$$2(3x + y - 7) = 2 \cdot 3x + 2 \cdot y - 2 \cdot 7$$
$$= 6x + 2y - 14$$

Questions

COVERING THE IDEAS

In 1 and 2, refer to the situation at the beginning of this lesson.

1. How much more wrapping paper did Giff Trapp use to wrap the larger present than the smaller present? Find your answer two different ways.

2. Giff uses 3 pieces of $\frac{3}{4}$-inch-wide tape to wrap one of the gifts. The pieces are 4 inches, $4\frac{1}{2}$ inches, and $2\frac{1}{2}$ inches long. Use two methods to find the total area of the tape used.

3. Draw a picture of rectangles to show that
$7 \cdot (10 + 2) = 7 \cdot 10 + 7 \cdot 2$.

4. **True or False** Justify your answers.

a. $\frac{1}{2}(8 + 6) = 4 + 3$

b. $\frac{1}{2}(8 \cdot 6) = 4 \cdot 3$

c. $\frac{1}{2}(8 - 6) = 4 - 3$

d. $\frac{1}{2}\left(\frac{8}{6}\right) = \frac{4}{3}$

5. **True or False** For all values of x and y,

a. $7(2x - 2y) = 14x - 14y$.

b. $7(2x + 2y) = 28xy$.

In 6–9, multiply. Check by substituting for the variables.

6. $40(x + 2)$

7. $a(3b - c)$

8. $4(200 - 5t + u)$

9. $8\left(\frac{3}{4}p - \frac{1}{2}q\right)$

In 10 and 11, show how you can apply the Distributive Property of Multiplication over Subtraction to find the total cost in your head.

10. You buy four sweatshirts at $29.95 each.

11. You purchase 12 songs at $0.99 each.

In 12 and 13, use the Distributive Property to multiply.

12. $7\frac{4}{5} \cdot 6$

13. $60 \cdot 1\frac{2}{3}$

APPLYING THE MATHEMATICS

14. Verify that $3.27(863 + 261) = 3.27 \cdot 863 + 3.27 \cdot 261$ using a calculator. As you evaluate each side, write down the key sequence you use and the final display.

15. Provide a counterexample to prove that $a(b \cdot c) = ab \cdot ac$ is *not* true for all values of a, b, and c.

16. Suppose an acre of land will yield 200 bushels of corn. The Stalks have A acres planted. Mr. Ondacob planted B acres. Mrs. Muffin planted C acres. Find an expression to calculate the number of bushels of corn the three can expect to harvest altogether.

17. A pair of sneakers is bought at a 20% discount. The original price of the pair was $99.75. Use the Distributive Property to find the amount of the discount. Do not use a calculator.

In 18 and 19, combine using the Distributive Property.

18. $8x + 3x$

19. $4a - a$

20. Multiply 821 by 999,999,999,999,999. Do not use a calculator.

21. Find the area of the shaded region at the right.

22. Use the Distributive Property and the Commutative Property to show that $2d + 4v - 3d + v = 5v - d$.

23. Simplify $8n - 3z + 2n + 4z$.

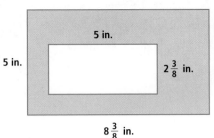

5 in.

5 in.

$2\frac{3}{8}$ in.

$8\frac{3}{8}$ in.

REVIEW

24. Jessica had $108.42 to spend during her vacation. She spent one-third of her money the first day and one-fourth of what was left on the second day. How much money did she have left after the second day? **(Lesson 7-2)**

25. Find the area of right triangle BCD in the picture below. **(Lesson 7-1)**

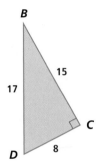

B

15

17

C

D   8

26. **Multiple Choice** For what real numbers is $6(5t) = 30t$ true? **(Lesson 7-1)**

    A   all real numbers

    B   some real numbers

    C   no real numbers

27. **True or False** If one of two vertical angles is acute, then the other is acute. Explain your answer. **(Lesson 6-5)**

EXPLORATION

28. Below is a worked-out multiplication of 362×481. Explain how this process is an application of the Distributive Property of Multiplication over Addition.

```
     481
  ×  362
     962
    2886
    1443
  174,122
```

29. Explain how to multiply two mixed numbers, such as $15\frac{2}{3} \cdot 7\frac{5}{6}$, using the Distributive Property.

Lesson

7-4

The Area of a Triangle

▶ **BIG IDEA** The area enclosed by any triangle is half of the area of a rectangle formed by a side of the triangle and the altitude to that side.

Using Altitudes to Find the Area of a Triangle

In the real world, you might need to find the area of a triangle. For example, behind your house you might have a triangular deck that needs to be stained. Then, knowing the area can help you decide how much stain to buy.

In $\triangle ABC$ below, $\overline{CF}$ is the segment from point C perpendicular to the opposite side $\overline{AB}$. It is called an **altitude,** or **height,** of the triangle. Recall that the shortest distance from a point to a line is along the perpendicular from the point to the line. So, the altitude gives the shortest path from a given vertex to the opposite side.

Every triangle has three altitudes, one from each vertex, perpendicular to the opposite side. The side to which the altitude is drawn is called the **base** for that

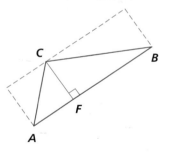

altitude. While you may be used to seeing the altitude drawn as a vertical line, the altitude is vertical only when the base is horizontal. When triangles are not drawn with a horizontal base, you may wish to rotate your book to change the orientation of the triangle.

On the next page are three copies of $\triangle MNO$. The three altitudes are drawn. Also drawn are three rectangles, using the base as one side of the rectangle. The area of the triangle is always half the area of the rectangle.

Mental Math

Find the area of the shaded part of the rectangle.

a.
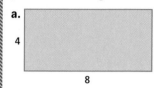

b.
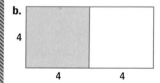

c.
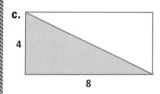

d.
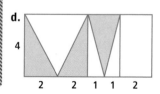

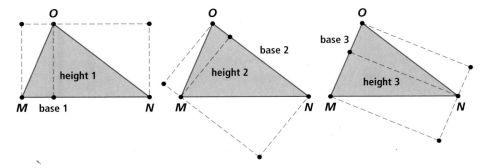

The area of a triangle is the same regardless of which vertex and altitude are used.

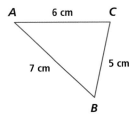

Activity 1

MATERIALS straightedge, compass, pencil

Step 1 Draw △ABC with side lengths 5 cm, 6 cm, and 7 cm. Your triangle should look like the one at the right.

Step 2 Pick a vertex of △ABC and draw an altitude from the vertex to the opposite side. Fold your paper so that the vertex lies on the crease and the opposite side lies on itself. The altitude lies along the crease.

Step 3 The altitude should form two right triangles. Measure the lengths of the legs of the right triangles.

Step 4 Use these lengths to calculate the areas of the right triangles.

Step 5 Add the two areas to get the area of △ABC. Did people in your class who chose a different vertex get the same area?

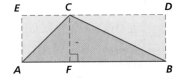

Any triangle can be inscribed in a rectangle whose base is one side of the triangle and whose opposite side contains the other vertex of the triangle. △ABC at the right is inscribed in rectangle EDBA. $\overline{CF}$ is the altitude from C to $\overline{AB}$ and has the same length as $\overline{EA}$ and $\overline{DB}$.

The areas of △ACF and △ACE are equal because each is $\frac{1}{2}$ the area of rectangle AFCE. The areas of △BCD and △BCF are equal because each is $\frac{1}{2}$ the area of rectangle BFCD. So the area of △CAB is $\frac{1}{2}$ the area of rectangle EDBA. Thus, the area of $\triangle ABC = \frac{1}{2}CF \cdot AB$. This argument gives us a formula for the area of any triangle.

Triangle Area Formula

Let b be the length of a side of a triangle with area A. Let h be the length of the altitude drawn to that side. Then,

$$A = \frac{1}{2}bh.$$

Altitudes That Lie Outside a Triangle

A triangle always has at least one altitude that lies inside it. But in some triangles, two altitudes lie outside the triangle. When this happens, you can still use the area formula $A = \frac{1}{2}bh$. You may also be able to find the area of the triangle by subtracting areas of right triangles.

GUIDED

Example

Find the area of $\triangle DRY$. $\angle K$ is a right angle.

Solution 1 Use the Triangle Area Formula. An altitude of the triangle is the perpendicular segment from D to $\overleftrightarrow{RY}$. That segment is $\overline{DK}$, which falls outside the triangle and intersects $\overleftrightarrow{RY}$ at K.

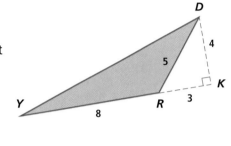

$$\text{area of } \triangle DRY = \frac{1}{2} \cdot bh$$
$$= \frac{1}{2} \cdot DK \cdot RY$$
$$= \frac{1}{2} \cdot 4 \cdot 8$$
$$= 16 \text{ square units}$$

Solution 2 Subtract the area of right triangle DKR from the area of right triangle DKY. Note that $KY = KR + RY = 3 + 8 = 11$.

$$\text{area of } \triangle DRY = \text{area of } \triangle DKY - \text{area of } \underline{\quad?\quad}$$
$$= \frac{1}{2} \cdot DK \cdot \underline{\quad?\quad} - \frac{1}{2} \cdot DK \cdot \underline{\quad?\quad}$$
$$= \frac{1}{2} \cdot \underline{\quad?\quad} \cdot \underline{\quad?\quad} - \frac{1}{2} \cdot \underline{\quad?\quad} \cdot \underline{\quad?\quad}$$
$$= \underline{\quad?\quad} - \underline{\quad?\quad}$$
$$= \underline{\quad?\quad} \text{ square units}$$

Activity 2

Find the area of the triangle drawn on the dot grid at the right. The distance between each consecutive horizontal or vertical dot is 1 unit.

Step 1 Find an altitude of the triangle. *Hint:* Look outside the triangle.

Step 2 Use the Triangle Area Formula.

Questions

COVERING THE IDEAS

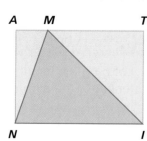

1. $\triangle MNI$ is inscribed in rectangle $TINA$.
   a. Write the area of $\triangle MNI$ in terms of the areas of $\triangle MNA$ and $\triangle MTI$.
   b. Write the area of $\triangle MNI$ in terms of the area of $TINA$.

2. Write the formula for the area of any triangle with base of length b and height h.

In 3 and 4, trace the triangle and draw its three altitudes. Extend a side of the figure if needed.

3.

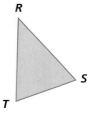

4.

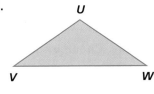

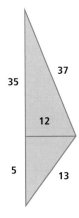

5. Adil used the Triangle Area Formula to calculate the area of the triangle at the right. His answer was marked wrong. Why?

$$A = \frac{1}{2} \cdot 35 \cdot 12 + 5 \cdot 12$$
$$= 210 + 60$$
$$= 270 \text{ units}^2$$

6. Find the area of $\triangle GIJ$.

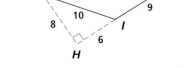

7. Find the area of $\triangle KLN$.

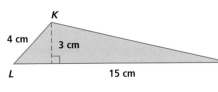

8. Find the area of $\triangle ABC$
   a. by using two right triangles.
   b. by using the Triangle Area Formula.

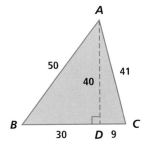

APPLYING THE MATHEMATICS

9. A standard yield sign is very close to an equilateral triangle with sides of about 30 inches each and a height of about 26 inches. Estimate the area of the sign.

10. In the figure at the right below, $AB = 10$ and $\overleftrightarrow{CH} \parallel \overleftrightarrow{AB}$. The perpendicular distance between $\overleftrightarrow{CH}$ and $\overleftrightarrow{AB}$ is 9.
    a. Find the area of $\triangle CAB$.
    b. **True or False** The area of $\triangle ABC$ is greater than the area of $\triangle ABG$.
    c. If $\triangle ABH$ were drawn, explain how you would find its area.
    d. Which distance is greater, AG or the perpendicular distance between $\overleftrightarrow{CH}$ and $\overleftrightarrow{AB}$? Explain.

11. Find the area of blue material, green material, and red and white material needed for the flag of Djibouti, a country in Africa, shown at the right.

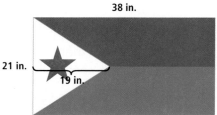

38 in.

21 in.

19 in.

12. Find the area of the triangle using a method different from the one used in Activity 2.

In **13–15**, find the area of each figure. Assume the sides of the squares in the grid are one unit long. Check by counting the squares inside each figure.

13.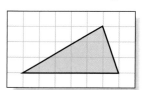

14.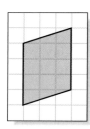

15.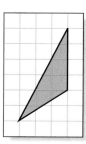

In **16** and **17**, a triangle is given.
a. Draw an altitude of the given triangle.
b. Use a ruler to measure the lengths of the altitude and the side to which it is drawn. Use the unit of measure that is indicated.
c. Find the area of the triangle. Round your answer to the nearest tenth.

16. Unit of measure: centimeters 17. Unit of measure: inches

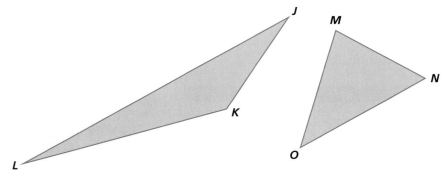

REVIEW

18. Lily bought a dozen roses at $3.75 each and a dozen tulips at $2.15 each. Explain how the total amount she spent can be calculated with one multiplication. (**Lesson 7-3**)

In **19–21**, simplify. (**Lesson 7-3**)

19. $x + 6x$

20. $3d - 2d + 4d$

21. $10v + 2w - 6w + v$

In 22–27, calculate. (Lessons 7-2, 3-3)

22. $\frac{2}{5} \cdot 5$

23. $\frac{1}{3} \cdot \frac{7}{9} \cdot \frac{3}{7}$

24. $\frac{1}{2} + \frac{1}{2} \cdot \frac{1}{4}$

25. $1.8 + \frac{6}{25}$

26. $a \cdot \frac{1}{a}$

27. $\frac{1}{n} \cdot \frac{1}{m}$

28. Write an algebraic expression for the following situation. Identify the variables you use. (Lesson 2-2)
Hugo earned 5 times as much as Phillip did.

29. Calculate in your head. (Lessons 1-5, 1-4)

   a. $96 \cdot 0.001$ **b.** $13.5 \cdot 10^4$

EXPLORATION

30. a. Here is a way to construct the perpendicular bisector of a line segment.

     Step 1 Copy line segment $\overline{AB}$ on your own paper.

     Step 2 Draw the circle with center A that contains B. Draw the circle with center B that contains A. Call the two points of intersection C and D.

     Step 3 Draw $\overleftrightarrow{CD}$. $\overleftrightarrow{CD}$ is the perpendicular bisector of $\overline{AB}$.

  b. In $\triangle GPI$, trace the triangle. Then construct the perpendicular bisector of each side. What do you notice?

31. a. Draw a $\triangle ABC$ that is not a right triangle.

  b. Follow the steps below to construct an altitude from A to $\overline{BC}$.

     Step 1 Construct circle A with radius $\overline{AB}$. Label the intersection of circle A with $\overline{BC}$ as point D. You may need to extend $\overline{BC}$ so it intersects with circle A.

     Step 2 Construct circle B with radius $\overline{AB}$. Construct circle D with radius $\overline{AD}$.

     Step 3 Circle B and circle D intersect at A and one other point. Call that point E.

     Step 4 Name $F = \overline{AE} \cap \overline{BC}$. Then $\overline{AF}$ is the altitude.

  c. With $\triangle ABC$, construct the altitude from point B to $\overline{AC}$.

  d. With $\triangle ABC$, construct the altitude from point C to $\overline{AB}$.

Lesson

7-5 The Area of a Trapezoid

▶ **BIG IDEA** The area enclosed by any trapezoid is the sum of the areas of two triangles with the same altitude and whose bases are the bases of the trapezoid.

Either diagonal of a trapezoid splits the trapezoid into two triangles. You can find the area of the trapezoid by adding the areas of the triangles.

Mental Math

Calculate.

a. $2 \cdot 6$

b. $2\frac{1}{2} \cdot 6$

c. $2\frac{1}{2} \cdot \frac{1}{2}$

d. $2\frac{1}{2} \left(6 + \frac{1}{2}\right)$

e. $2\frac{1}{2} \cdot 6\frac{1}{2}$

Activity

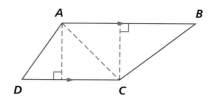

ABCD is a trapezoid with $\overline{AB} \parallel \overline{CD}$. Find the area of ABCD.

Step 1 Trace *ABCD* and draw $\overline{AC}$.

Step 2 In △*ACD*, draw the altitude from *A* to the base $\overline{CD}$. Measure that altitude and base in centimeters to estimate the area of △*ACD*.

Step 3 In △*ABC*, draw the altitude from *C* to the base $\overline{AB}$. Measure that altitude and base to estimate the area of △*ABC*.

Step 4 Add the areas of the two triangles to estimate the area of *ABCD*.

Step 5 Draw diagonal $\overline{BD}$ and repeat Steps 2–4 for the triangles formed by that diagonal.

You should notice in the Activity that the bases of the triangles are the bases of the trapezoid. The altitudes of the triangles are the height of the trapezoid. The height is the distance between the parallel lines.

To find a general formula, we can replace the specific lengths with variables. Let the bases of the trapezoid have lengths b_1 and b_2. (b_1 is read "b sub 1" and b_2 is read "b sub 2." The small 1 and 2 are *subscripts*.) b_1 and b_2 are different variables. b_1 means the "first base," b_2 means the "second base." Let the height be *h*.

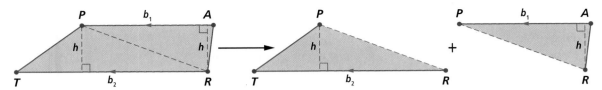

One triangle has area $\frac{1}{2}hb_1$. The other triangle has area $\frac{1}{2}hb_2$. The area of the trapezoid is

$$\frac{1}{2}hb_1 + \frac{1}{2}hb_2,$$

which, due to the Distributive Property, can be written as

$$\frac{1}{2}h(b_1 + b_2).$$

This is a formula for the area of any trapezoid.

Trapezoid Area Formula

Let A be the area of a trapezoid with bases b_1 and b_2 and height h. Then

$$A = \frac{1}{2}h(b_1 + b_2).$$

In words, the area of a trapezoid is one half the product of its height and the sum of the lengths of its bases.

GUIDED

Example

Approximate the area of Nevada from the map by using the formula for the area of a trapezoid.

Solution Examine the map. The bases are the almost parallel sides, $\overline{ND}$ and $\overline{EA}$. It doesn't matter which of the two we call b_1 and b_2. The height DV is the distance between the bases. Use the Trapezoid Area Formula:

$$\begin{aligned} \text{Area of NDAE} &= \frac{1}{2} \cdot h(b_1 + b_2) \\ &= \frac{1}{2} \cdot \underline{\ ?\ } (\underline{\ ?\ } + \underline{\ ?\ }) \\ &= \frac{1}{2} \cdot \underline{\ ?\ } \cdot \underline{\ ?\ } \\ &= \underline{\ ?\ } \cdot \underline{\ ?\ } \\ &\approx \underline{\ ?\ } \end{aligned}$$

The area of Nevada is approximately 113,000 square miles.

The actual area of Nevada is 110,561 square miles, so this is a fairly good approximation.

For What Figures Does This Formula Work?

Trapezoids come in many different sizes and shapes. Rectangles, squares, rhombuses, and parallelograms have two pairs of parallel sides, so they are trapezoids. This makes trapezoids important. Whatever is true for all trapezoids is true for all rectangles, squares, rhombuses, and parallelograms. So, the area formula for a trapezoid works for all these figures.

Here are some trapezoids with their bases drawn darker. We have labeled some of them with * because either pair of parallel sides can be bases. For example, since both pairs of sides of a parallelogram are parallel, you can choose either pair of sides to be bases, and we have picked one pair. Heights are dashed. In one trapezoid, the figure is quite slanted, so one base has to be extended to meet the height.

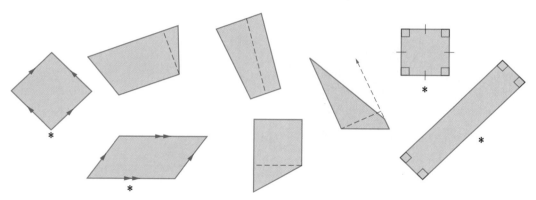

When the bases of a trapezoid have the same length, then the trapezoid is also a parallelogram.

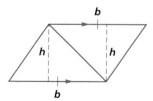

In this case, the diagonal splits the parallelogram into two congruent triangles. Each triangle has base length b and height h. So, each triangle has area $\frac{1}{2}bh$. So, the area of the parallelogram is $\frac{1}{2}bh + \frac{1}{2}bh = bh$.

Parallelogram Area Formula

Let A be the area of a parallelogram with base b and height h. Then:

$$A = bh$$

The four parallelograms drawn below, including the rectangle, have bases of the same length and the same height, so they all have the same area. Some people think that the longer, thinner parallelograms have more area, but that is because their eyes are misled by the greater perimeter of these figures.

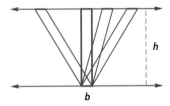

Questions

COVERING THE IDEAS

In 1–4, decide whether the statement is true or false.

1. Any side of a trapezoid can be a base.

2. The height of a trapezoid is the length of a line segment that begins at a vertex and extends perpendicular to the opposite side.

3. If a trapezoid has a height of 6 inches and its bases are 7 inches and 12 inches long, then its area is $6(7 + 12) = 6 \cdot 19 = 114$ square inches.

4. The bases of a trapezoid are parallel to each other.

5. Use the trapezoid at the right.
   a. Find the lengths of its bases.
   b. Find its height.
   c. Find its area.

6. a. Draw to actual size a trapezoid with bases of length 10 centimeters and 8 centimeters and height of 5 centimeters.
   b. Find the area of this trapezoid.

7. A trapezoid has bases m and n and height k. What is the area of the trapezoid?

8. In words, state the formula for the area of a trapezoid.

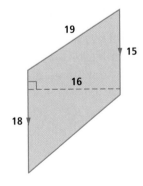

In 9 and 10, find the area of the shaded figure.

9.

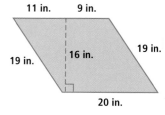

11 in. 9 in.

19 in.

16 in. 19 in.

19 in.

20 in.

10.

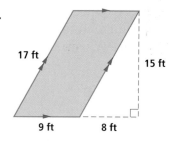

17 ft 15 ft

9 ft 8 ft

11. Find the approximate area of Arkansas by using the formula for the area of a trapezoid.

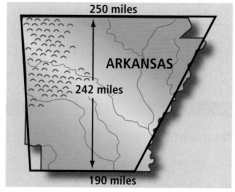

250 miles

ARKANSAS

242 miles

190 miles

APPLYING THE MATHEMATICS

12. Find the area of the parallelogram using two methods.

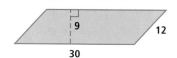

9 12

30

   a. the area formula for parallelograms

   b. the area formula for trapezoids

13. Find the area of the parallelogram on the coordinate grid.

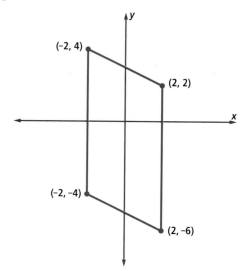

(-2, 4)

(2, 2)

(-2, -4)

(2, -6)

14. Calculate areas to find the percents of the flag of the Bahamas that are black, aquamarine, and gold.

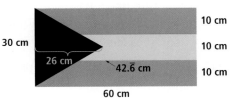

30 cm
26 cm
42.6 cm
60 cm
10 cm
10 cm
10 cm

15. The distance between horizontal or vertical dots at the right is 1 unit. Find the area of the trapezoid.

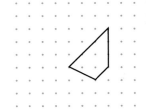

16. The John Hancock Center located in Chicago, Illinois, stands 1,127 feet tall, not including the height of the antennas. Its tapered design and strong steel beams and columns provide additional strength and stability against strong winds. The lower base of the front face of the building measures 265 feet. The upper base of this face is 105 feet across. The height of the face is 1,128 feet. What is the area of the front face of the building?

17. **a.** Find the area of parallelogram *PARL*.

   b. What must be the length of $\overline{AT}$, the height to $\overline{RL}$? How did you find your answer?

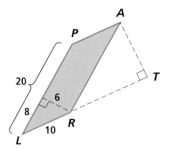

20
8
6
10
L
R
P
A
T

John Hancock Center

18. The Nazca Lines are giant ground drawings of figures and animals located in the Sechura Desert. They were created by the Nazca culture from 200 BCE to about 600 CE. One of the drawings is a large trapezoid similar to the drawing below. What is the total land area of the trapezoid?

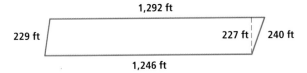

1,292 ft
229 ft
227 ft
240 ft
1,246 ft

Aerial view of some Nazca Lines

REVIEW

19. Find the area of △*CAT* below. **(Lesson 7-4)**

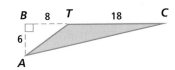

B   8   T   18   C
6
A

The Area of a Trapezoid   **461**

20. A triangle has a base with length 20 centimeters and an area of 250 square centimeters. What is the length of the altitude to that base? **(Lesson 7-4)**

21. **Multiple Choice** Which expression is equal to $y - \frac{1}{4}y$, for any value of y? **(Lesson 7-3)**

    A $\frac{3}{4}$ B $\frac{1}{4}$ C $\frac{3}{4}y$ D none of these

22. A spreadsheet contains data that show the heights of 5 different children over the past 12 months. If the columns of the spreadsheet represent each month and the rows represent each child, how many cells of data are in this spreadsheet? **(Lesson 7-1)**

23. m and n are parallel. Name all angles with the same measure as $\angle 1$. **(Lesson 6-6)**

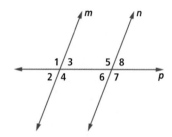

24. If you turn 46° counterclockwise and then turn 64° clockwise, where are you compared to where you started? **(Lesson 5-5)**

25. Picture the addition $-19 + 7$ using arrows on the number line and find the sum. **(Lesson 5-1)**

EXPLORATION

26. In June 2004, NASA's Spitzer telescope found a parallelogram-shaped image at the center of the galaxy Centaurus A. Find out about this parallelogram. How was the image obtained? How was the parallelogram found?

Centaurus A

27. Trapezoids are sometimes used to approximate the area under a curve. As the area under the curve is broken into more trapezoids, the approximation to the area under the curve becomes closer to the actual area. Find the area of the shaded region by adding the areas of the trapezoids shown.

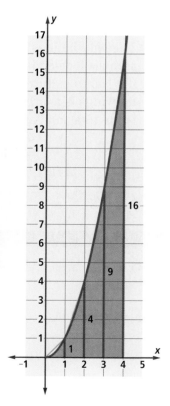

Lesson

7-6 Circles

> ▶ **BIG IDEA** The formulas $C = \pi d$ and $A = \pi r^2$ for the circumference C and the area A of a circle with radius r follow logically from the definition of π and the area formulas for triangles and parallelograms already mentioned in this chapter.

Vocabulary for Circles

A **circle** is the set of points that are all the same distance (its **radius**) from a certain point (its **center**). The plural of radius is **radii.** The distance across the circle through its center is twice the length of its radius. That distance is the circle's **diameter.** The words radius and diameter are used to name both distances and segments.

The circle below has center O and is named circle O. One radius of the circle is $\overline{OS}$. One diameter of the circle is $\overline{MN}$. If the radius of circle O is 7, then its diameter is 14.

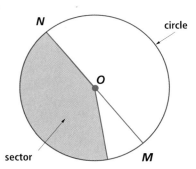

A part of a circle graph that looks like a slice of pie is an example of a *sector.* A **sector** is bounded by two radii and an *arc* of the circle. An **arc** is a part of a circle connecting two points (its endpoints) on the circle. The sector in the circle above bounded by $\overline{OS}$, $\overline{ON}$, and arc SN (written $\overset{\frown}{SN}$ or $\overset{\frown}{NS}$) is named sector SON or sector NOS.

Finding the Circumference of a Circle

Suppose you put a tape measure around your waist. Then you can measure the perimeter of your waist. You can do this even though your waist is curved.

Vocabulary

circle
radius (radii) of a circle
center of a circle
diameter of a circle
sector of a circle
arc of a circle
circumference

Mental Math

Find the area and perimeter of the rectangles below.

a.
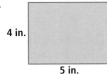
4 in.
5 in.

b.
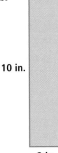
10 in.
2 in.

c.
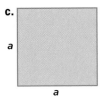
a
a

d.
$a - 2$
$a + 2$

The same idea works for circles. The perimeter of a circle can be measured. It is the distance around the circle, the distance you would travel if you walked around the circle. It is called the **circumference** of the circle.

The top of the aluminum can pictured below is a circle with diameter d. The circle's circumference can be estimated by rolling the can on a table.

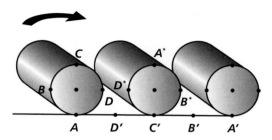

As the can rolls, the points D, C, B, and then A hit the table at D', C', B', and A'. The circumference of the can is the same distance as AA'. This distance around is just a little more than 3 times the diameter AC. In fact, the circumference of any circle is $3.1415926535\ldots$ times its diameter. You have seen this number before. It is called π (pi), an irrational number. Its decimal never repeats or ends.

Circumference of a Circle Formula

In a circle with diameter d and circumference C,

$$C = \pi d.$$

Example 1

Rounded to the nearest inch, what is the circumference of a can with a 6-inch diameter?

6 in.

Solution Let C be the circumference. Using the formula $C = \pi d$, $C = \pi \cdot 6 = 6\pi$ inches exactly.

To approximate C to the nearest inch, evaluate 6π on your calculator.

$6\pi \approx 18.84955\ldots$ Rounded to the nearest inch, the circumference is 19 inches.

Since the diameter d of a circle is twice its radius r, $d = 2r$. In the formula $C = \pi d$, you could then substitute $2r$ for d. The result is $C = \pi \cdot 2r$ or $C = 2\pi r$, which is another formula for the circumference of a circle.

Finding the Area of a Circle

You have now seen formulas for finding areas of rectangles, triangles, parallelograms, and trapezoids. Because circles are not polygons, you cannot use any of these formulas to find the area of a circle. However, you can use formulas for areas of polygons to develop an area formula for a circle.

Activity

MATERIALS thin paper such as patty paper, a compass, a centimeter ruler

Step 1 Use a compass to draw a large circle about 4 centimeters in diameter on the thin paper.

Step 2 Fold the thin paper along a diameter of the circle, making sure that the two halves of the circle coincide.

Step 3 Fold it in half again, making sure to overlap the circle. Repeat this one more time.

Step 4 Open the thin paper. The folds on the thin paper have formed eight sectors of the circle. Connect consecutive endpoints of the radii to form eight triangles.

Step 5 Draw an altitude from the center of the circle to the base of one triangle.

Step 6 Measure the altitude and base of this triangle. Calculate the area of this triangle.

Step 7 Multiply by 8 to approximate the area of this circle.

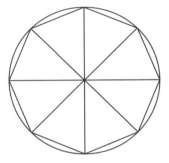

The idea in the Activity can be used to develop a general formula for the area of the circle. Suppose you take the 8 sectors and rearrange them.

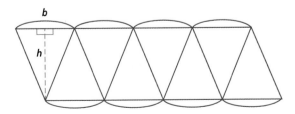

The figure resembles a parallelogram with height h. However, because the edges of the sectors are curved, the figure only *approximates* a parallelogram. But, if we imagine cutting the circle into a large number of sectors, the approximation becomes closer to a parallelogram that has the same area as the circle. Do you see why? Now we use the formula $A = bh$ for the area of a parallelogram.

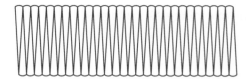

As the circle is split into more and more sectors, the height of each triangle becomes closer and closer to the radius r of the circle. The "parallelogram" becomes more and more like a rectangle with base πr. Since πr is half the circumference of the circle, the area of the rectangle is $\pi r \cdot r$, or πr^2, so the area of a circle is πr^2. This is a famous formula.

Area of a Circle Formula

Let A be the area of a circle with radius r. Then
$$A = \pi r^2.$$

Example 2

How many square miles are within 20 miles of the center of a city?

Solution Find the area of a circle with a radius of 20 miles.

$$
\begin{aligned}
A &= \pi r^2 \\
&= \pi (20 \text{ miles})^2 \\
&= \pi \cdot 400 \text{ square miles} \\
&\approx 1257 \text{ square miles}
\end{aligned}
$$

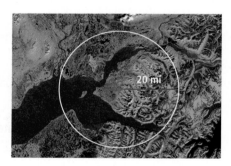

GUIDED

Example 3

What is the area of the shaded sector of the circle at the right?

Solution A formula for the area of the entire circle is __?__ .

The area of the entire circle is __?__ .

The shaded sector is $\frac{3}{4}$ the area of the entire circle, so multiply the area of the entire circle by $\frac{3}{4}$.

Area of shaded sector is __?__ .

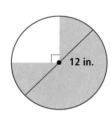

12 in.

Questions

COVERING THE IDEAS

1. Use the diagram of circle A at the right.

   a. Name at least two radii.

   b. Name at least three arcs.

   c. Name a diameter.

   d. Name at least two sectors.

2. **Fill in the Blank** The perimeter of a circle is called the ___?___ of the circle.

3. A calculator shows π to be 3.141592654.

   a. Is this an exact value or an estimate?

   b. Round this number to the nearest hundredth.

   c. Round this number to the nearest thousandth.

In 4–7, find the exact circumference and an approximation of the circumference to the nearest tenth for the circle with the given diameter or radius.

4. a diameter of 21 inches

5. a diameter of n meters

6. a radius of $\frac{1}{10}$ mile

7. a radius of m feet

8. The equator of Earth is approximately a circle whose diameter is about 7,920 miles. Find the distance around Earth at its equator, rounded to the nearest hundred miles.

In 9 and 10, find the exact area and an approximation of the area to the nearest tenth for the circle with the given radius or diameter.

9. a radius of 7 centimeters

10. a diameter of 32 meters

11. **Fill in the Blank** By approximating with triangles, you can show that the area of a circle with radius r is equal to the area of a figure that is almost a parallelogram with dimensions r and ___?___.

12. In the Midwest, it is common to irrigate crops with a very long sprinkler that rotates around a point. A farmer has a sprinkler with a watering-range radius of 320 yards. How many square yards of land, to the nearest square yard, will this sprinkler water?

In **13** and **14**, find the area of the shaded sector of a circle with radius *r*. Round your answer to the nearest hundredth.

13.

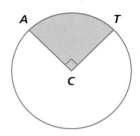

C is the center
of the circle

14.

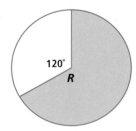

120°

R

R is the center
of the circle

APPLYING THE MATHEMATICS

15. The two circles shown at the right are called *concentric circles* because they have the same center. The radius of the smaller circle is 6.3 cm and the radius of the larger circle is 13.5 cm. Find the area of the shaded ring.

16. Curtis read that there were about 10 calories in each square inch of a cheese pizza. If he eats $\frac{1}{8}$ of a pizza with an 18-inch diameter, about how many calories would he consume?

17. The radius of a circle is 17 centimeters.
    a. Find the exact area of the circle.
    b. Find the exact circumference of the circle.
    c. If you double the radius of the circle, how many times as large is the area of the circle?
    d. If you double the radius of the circle, how many times as large is the circumference of the circle?
    e. Do the answers to Parts c and d depend on the size of the radius? Explain why or why not.

18. A CD has an outer diameter of 12 cm. You are making a label for the CD that reaches the edge of the disc and has a 2.5 cm diameter hole in the middle. Find the area of the label to the nearest tenth of a square centimeter.

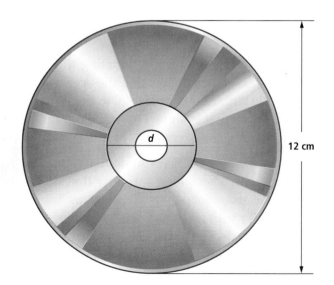

d

12 cm

19. Luanda is having a circular window pane cut from a square piece of glass with 5-foot sides. She wants the largest circle possible from the glass.
    a. What will be the circumference of the window pane?
    b. How much of the glass will be wasted?

REVIEW

20. Find the area of trapezoid *JKLM* below. (**Lesson 7-5**)

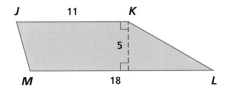

21. a. **True or False** If $x = 4.659$, then $2(x + 3) = (x + 3) \cdot 2$.
    b. **True or False** $\frac{3}{4} \cdot \frac{5}{6} = \frac{5}{6} \cdot \frac{3}{4}$.
    c. What general property is illustrated by Parts a and b? (**Lesson 7-1**)

22. **True or False** A polygon with an odd number of sides will not tessellate. Explain your answer. (**Lesson 6-4**)

23. Construct a triangle with side lengths of 3.5 centimeters, 2.4 centimeters, and 2.5 centimeters. (**Lesson 5-9**)

24. Give three solutions to the inequality $x - 4 < 3$. (**Lesson 5-6**)

25. Is the following statement *always, sometimes but not always,* or *never* true?
    A rational number is a real number. (**Lesson 4-9**)

EXPLORATION

26. Take two pieces of string of equal length. Form the first string into a circle. Form the second string into a square.
    a. Which figure has the greater area? Explain why you think so.
    b. Does the answer to Part a depend on the length of the string? Explain.
    c. Based on your answers to Parts a and b, why do you think the Native Americans of the Great Plains built tepees with circular floors?

Lesson

7-7

The Size-Change Model for Multiplication

Vocabulary

expansion

size-change factor

contraction

size change of magnitude k

▶ **BIG IDEA** Multiplying the coordinates of all points of a figure on the coordinate plane by a constant nonzero number creates an image similar to the original figure.

Activity 1

MATERIALS graph paper, a ruler, two colors of pencils

Step 1 On a grid, graph the following points: $P = (0, 1)$, $O = (1, 1)$, $I = (1, 0)$, $N = (3, 0)$, $T = (3, 1)$, $E = (4, 1)$, and $R = (2, 3)$. Connect the points to form an arrow.

Step 2 Multiply each coordinate of the points by 3. Call the new points P', O', I', and so on. Draw $P'O'I'N'T'E'R'$ in a color different from POINTER. $P'O'I'N'T'E'R'$ is the image of POINTER under a *size change of magnitude 3.*

1. Find the lengths of $\overline{PO}$, $\overline{P'O'}$, $\overline{IN}$, and $\overline{I'N'}$.

2. Make a conjecture: How do lengths on POINTER and $P'O'I'N'T'E'R'$ compare?

3. Draw $\overline{OT}$ and $\overline{O'T'}$. Find the areas of INTO and $I'N'T'O'$.

4. Make a conjecture: How do you think the area of POINTER compares with the area of $P'O'I'N'T'E'R'$?

Activity 2

Step 1 On a new grid, make another copy of POINTER from Activity 1.

Step 2 Multiply each coordinate of the points by 0.5. Call the new points $P*$, $O*$, $I*$, $N*$, $T*$, $E*$, and $R*$. Draw $P*O*I*N*T*E*R*$ in a color different from the one you used for POINTER. $P*O*I*N*T*E*R*$ is the image of POINTER under a *size change of magnitude 0.5.*

(continued on next page)

1. Find the lengths of $\overline{PO}$, $\overline{P*O*}$, $\overline{IN}$, and $\overline{I*N*}$.

2. Make a conjecture: How do lengths on *POINTER* and *P*O*I*N*T*E*R** compare?

3. Draw $\overline{OT}$ and $\overline{O*T*}$. Find the areas of *INTO* and *I*N*T*O**.

4. Make a conjecture: How do you think the area of *POINTER* compares with the area of *P*O*I*N*T*E*R**?

In Activities 1 and 2, coordinates of points are multiplied by a fixed number. The result is an image that is *similar* to the original figure. Similar figures have the same shape but often have different sizes. If the fixed multiplier is *k,* then the image and preimage have the same shape and the lengths of sides of the image are *k* times the lengths of the corresponding sides of the preimage. This is a geometric picture of a size change. Size changes can also be applied to other quantities.

Example

Megan earns $8.50 per hour. If she works overtime, she makes time and a half. How much does she make per hour when she works overtime?

Solution

Making time and a half means that you make $1\frac{1}{2}$ times your normal rate per hour.

Step 1 Change $1\frac{1}{2}$ to a decimal. $1\frac{1}{2} = $ __?__

Step 2 Perform the size change.   __?__ · __?__ = __?__

Step 3 Give your answer in words.   __?__

 QY1

When the final quantity is larger than the original value, we call the size change an **expansion.** Since this size change has a magnitude of 2, we say that 2 is the **size-change factor.** Activity 1 and the Guided Example show expansions.

Size-change factors can also be between 0 and 1, as in Activity 2. Since the products are less than the original values, these size changes are called **contractions.**

In each of the examples, there is a beginning quantity and a size-change factor. These numbers are multiplied to obtain a final quantity. This is the idea behind the Size-Change Model for Multiplication.

▶ **QY1**

Kendra normally charges $6 an hour to babysit, but she charges $1\frac{3}{4}$ times as much after midnight. How much is her hourly charge after midnight?

Size-Change Model for Multiplication

Let k be a nonzero number without a unit. Then ka is the result of applying a **size change of magnitude k** to the quantity a.

Picturing Size Changes

As Activities 1 and 2 show, a size change can be nicely pictured using coordinates. We began with a heptagon. In Activity 1, you performed an expansion of magnitude 3, so you multiplied both coordinates of all its vertices by 3. When you performed a contraction of magnitude 0.5 in Activity 2, you multiplied all the coordinates of the vertices by 0.5. A calculator can also show size changes on the coordinate plane.

Activity 3

Step 1 Begin by setting your window as shown at the right.

Step 2 Plot the polygon with these vertices. Remember to repeat vertex P as the last point in the list in order to complete the figure.

$$P = (0, 1) \qquad O = (1, 1) \qquad I = (1, 0) \qquad N = (3, 0)$$
$$T = (3, 1) \qquad E = (4, 1) \qquad R = (2, 3)$$

Step 3 Create a size-change image with magnitude 2.5. In the list titled **XIMAG**, multiply **XPRE** (the x-values of the preimage) by 2.5. Do the same multiplication of **YPRE** in **YIMAG** as shown at the right.

Step 4 To draw the preimage, choose a line graph for the lists named **XPRE** and **YPRE**. Use the + symbol to locate the vertices. Do the same for the lists named **XIMAG** and **YIMAG**, using the ¤ symbol for the vertices.

Step 5 Your screen should show a picture like the one shown at the right.

Trace to find the coordinates of the image.

$P' =$ __?__ $O' =$ __?__ $I' =$ __?__ $N' =$ __?__
$T' =$ __?__ $E' =$ __?__ $R' =$ __?__

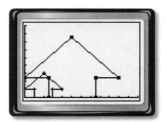

POINTER and its image
under an expansion of 2.5

This transformation is called a size change of magnitude 2.5. The image of any point (x, y) is $(2.5x, 2.5y)$. Because the image figure is larger than the preimage, this change is an expansion of magnitude 2.5. The number 2.5 is the size-change factor.

Step 6 On the same screen, create a second size-change image $P*O*I*N*T*E*R*$ of magnitude 0.8. In the lists labeled **XCON** and **YCON** (for an image that is a *contraction* of the figure), enter values formed by multiplying the preimage values (x, y) by 0.8. The *x*-coordinates are shown at the right.

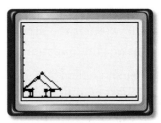

Fill in the **YCON** list and give the coordinates of $P*O*I*N*T*E*R*$.

$P* =$ __?__ $O* =$ __?__ $I* =$ __?__ $N* =$ __?__
$T* =$ __?__ $E* =$ __?__ $R* =$ __?__

Your preimage and image should look like the calculator screen at the right.

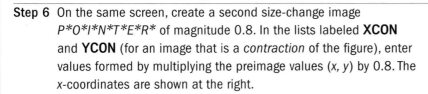

POINTER and its image
under a contraction of 0.8

In Activity 3, the calculator multiplied the vertices of the original figure by two values of k. Multiplying by $k = 2.5$ produced an expansion. Multiplying by $k = 0.8$ produced a contraction. You can use the results and experiment with other magnitudes for size changes to draw some conclusions. In each case, no matter what the magnitude of the size change, the figures will have certain characteristics.

1. The sides of the images are k times as long as the corresponding sides of the preimage.

2. The corresponding angles have the same measures.

3. Corresponding sides are parallel.

4. The shapes are similar.

5. The line containing any preimage point and its image also contains $(0, 0)$.

6. Any image point is k times the distance from $(0, 0)$ to its preimage.

The size changes of magnitude 2.5 and of magnitude 0.8 that were performed on heptagon *POINTER* are instances of 2-dimensional size changes.

2-Dimensional Size-Change Model for Multiplication

Under a size change of magnitude $k \neq 0$, the image of (x, y) is (kx, ky).

STOP QY2

If the magnitude of a size change is 1, then the image of (x, y) is $(1 \cdot x, 1 \cdot y)$, or (x, y). That is, each point is its own image. In this case, not only are the shapes similar, they are also congruent.

▶ **QY2**

The point $P = (3, 7)$ undergoes a size change of magnitude 1.75. What are the coordinates of its image P'? Is the size change an expansion or a contraction?

Questions

COVERING THE IDEAS

In 1 and 2, a situation is given.
a. Identify the size-change factor.
b. Tell whether the size change is an expansion or a contraction.
c. Answer the question.

1. Susan earns $9.00 per hour babysitting. After midnight, she charges time-and-a-half. How much does she earn per hour after midnight?

2. From 1994 to 2004, the average salary of a National Hockey League player tripled. So if players' salaries averaged $100,000 a year in 1994, what was the average salary in 2004?

3. Give the coordinates of the vertices of the images you found in Activity 3 for
   a. the expansion with $k = 2.5$.   b. the contraction with $k = 0.8$.

4. Find coordinates of the vertices of *POINTER* in Activity 3 under a size change of magnitude 50.

5. The image of (x, y) under a size change of magnitude k is __?__.

6. A size change having a magnitude greater than 1 is a(n) __?__.

7. A size change having a magnitude between 0 and 1 is a(n) __?__.

8. Find the image of the point $(12, 18)$ under a size change of the given magnitude.
   a. $1\frac{1}{3}$ b. $\frac{3}{4}$ c. 1   d. 0.5   e. 1.25

9. For each of the size changes in Question 8, tell whether the size change is an expansion, a contraction, or neither.

10. Consider a size change of magnitude 3.5 on a polygon.
    a. How do the lengths of corresponding sides compare?
    b. How do the measures of corresponding angles compare?
    c. **Fill in the Blank** Each image side is __?__ to the corresponding preimage side.
    d. **Fill in the Blank** The polygons are __?__.

APPLYING THE MATHEMATICS

11. A pair of jeans costing $34.97 is on sale at 15% off. If you buy now, how much will you save over the normal price?

12. At the time of the Declaration of Independence in 1776, about 1 in 5 people in the American colonies lived in Virginia. There were about 2.6 million people in the colonies then. About how many people lived in Virginia?

13. A model of a car is $\frac{1}{16}$ actual size. The actual car's rearview mirror is 12 inches long. How long is the model's mirror?

14. A magnifying glass magnifies objects to 4 times their actual size. Some ant eggs measure about 0.5 mm in length.
    a. How long will they appear under this glass?
    b. **Fill in the Blank** The size-change factor for the size change from the ant egg to the magnified image is __?__.
    c. If an object has length L, what will be its length through the lens?

Declaration of Independence

15. Marcus had a picture of his house that measured 10 inches high by 8 inches wide. He decided to make a photocopy of it that was a bit smaller. He set the copy machine to 80%, which means that all the measurements are reduced to 80% of their original sizes.
    a. What were the width and height of the photocopy?
    b. He decided that the picture was still a bit large, so he put the photocopy into the photocopier and kept the copy machine set on 80%. What was the size of the next copy?
    c. Compare the size of the final copy to the size of the original picture. What could the copy machine have been set on to get a picture the size of the final copy from the original by doing only one copy?

16. In Colleen Moore's miniature dollhouse, there is a 9″-tall replica of a sculpture. If her model is $\frac{1}{12}$ the size of the original, how tall is the original?

Colleen Moore's dollhouse at Chicago's Museum of Science and Industry

17. **Multiple Choice** A car was priced at $13,500.

   a. The salesperson offers a $540 discount. What size-change factor, applied to the original price, gives the discount?

   A 0.04   **B** 0.05   **C** 0.025   **D** 0.054

   b. The salesperson offers a $540 discount. What size-change factor, applied to the original price, gives the offered price?

   A 0.96   **B** 0.95   **C** 0.975   **D** 0.946

REVIEW

18. General Sherman, a Sequoia tree in California, is considered the world's biggest tree. It is 2,200 years old and 27 stories tall, and it has a diameter of about 11 meters at its base, and it is still growing. If Gina is standing on the opposite side of the tree from her mom, how far must she walk around the tree to get to where her mom is? **(Lesson 7-6)**

GENERAL SHERMAN

19. Find the radius to the nearest inch of a circle that has a circumference of 2 feet. **(Lesson 7-6)**

20. The boundaries of the ancient city of Nineveh are marked by the ruins of Kouyunjik, Nimrud, Karamless, and Khorsabad. If you were to draw lines to connect the ruins, a parallelogram would be formed that measured approximately 10 to 20 miles long by 12 to 14 miles wide. What might be the total area of this historic city? **(Lesson 7-5)**

21. **True or False** If one angle of a linear pair is an obtuse angle, then the other angle is obtuse. Explain your answer. **(Lesson 6-5)**

22. Otto wants to buy a new blue SUV. He calls a dealer who tells him that out of 60 available vehicles, 25 are SUVs. 30 of the 60 vehicles are blue. Can Otto be sure that there is a blue SUV? Explain your reasoning. **(Lesson 5-8)**

23. A CD has five songs on it. The length of the song times, in minutes, are 5:43, 3:15, 2:56, 5:12, and 3:19. What is the total length of the CD? **(Lesson 5-1)**

EXPLORATION

24. A home copy machine has 5 settings: 122%, 100%, 86%, 78%, and 70%. By using these settings as many times as you wish, show how you can make copies of 10 different sizes between 100% and 200% of the original.

QY ANSWERS

1. $10.50

2. $P' = (5.25, 12.25)$; expansion

Chapter 7 Projects

1 Perimeter and Area

If the perimeter of a rectangle increases, will the area also increase? Or, if the area of a rectangle increases, does the perimeter also increase? One way to find out is to use grid paper to try to draw rectangles that all have the same area but different perimeters. Then try to draw some rectangles that have the same perimeter but different areas. Use your drawings or some other method to create a display or report showing the relationship between perimeter and area of rectangles. Can you come to a conclusion that will always be true?

2 Hectares and Acres

In the metric system, land is often measured using a unit called the *hectare*. In the U.S. system, a commonly used unit of land area is the *acre*. Write a report describing how these units are related to other units of measure within their system. Determine how the hectare and acre are related.

3 Sir Cumference Book Report

Two short and entertaining books relate to the content of this chapter.

a. Read *Sir Cumference and the First Round Table* by Cindy Neuschwander to write a report on how Sir Cumference manages to make a table suitable for his knights. Find out why he chooses a round table instead of a rectangular or triangular table. What advantages does a circle have over other shapes when designing a table?

b. Read *Sir Cumference and the Dragon of Pi* by Cindy Neuschwander to write a report that explains the special relationship in a circle that Radius uses to rescue his father.

4 Mayan Temples

Research the ancient Mayan temples at Tikal, which from the front resemble a number of trapezoids stacked upon one another. Give an estimate of the area of the frontal face of Temple I, above, given that it has a height of 44 meters. Find this estimate by two different methods and describe them. Which estimate do you think is more accurate?

5 Tools for Multiplying

A variety of methods for multiplying two whole numbers have been developed over the centuries. Find out about one of the following methods of multiplication:

(a) using an abacus

(b) Napier's bones

(c) the Russian Peasant algorithm

Show how to multiply 239×47 using the method you have chosen.

6 Maps and Scales

Examine a large atlas or many maps. What are the scales of the maps? Why are different scales used for different maps? What scales are most common and why do you think they are the most common? Write an essay answering these questions using examples.

Chapter 7 Summary and Vocabulary

- Two connections between multiplication and geometry are discussed in this chapter: area and size change.

- A 2-dimensional figure encloses a given amount of area. The area of a rectangle is the product of its length and its width. Areas of rectangles provide pictures of the multiplication of fractions as well as the Distributive Properties that are true for all real numbers a, b, x, and y.

$$a(x + y) = ax + ay \qquad ax + bx = (a + b)x$$
$$a(x - y) = ax - ay \qquad ax - bx = (a - b)x$$

- A square is a special rectangle. The square provides the fundamental unit for measuring area. A rectangle can be split into two right triangles. Any triangle can be split into two right triangles. Any trapezoid can be split into two triangles. Parallelograms are special trapezoids. Circular areas can be approximated with parallelograms. Thus, from the area of any rectangle, area formulas for these other figures can be deduced logically.

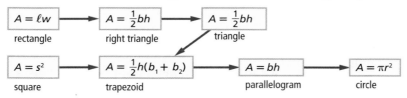

- A multiplication of the type "part of" or "times as many" can be pictured on a 2-dimensional coordinate system as a size change. Under **a size change of nonzero magnitude k**, the image of (x, y) is (kx, ky). Lengths of figures are multiplied by k. If k is between 0 and 1, then the size change is a **contraction.** If k is greater than 1, then the size change is an **expansion.**

Vocabulary

7-1
dimensions
rectangular array
ℓ-by-w or $\ell \cdot w$ rectangle

7-2
unit fraction
reciprocal,
   multiplicative inverse

7-4
altitude or height (of a
   triangle)
base of a triangle

7-6
circle
radius (radii) of a circle
center of a circle
diameter of a circle
sector of a circle
arc of a circle
circumference

7-7
expansion
size-change factor
contraction
size change of magnitude k

Theorems and Properties

Area Model for Multiplication (p. 431)
Commutative Property of Multiplication (p. 431)
Area Formula for a Right Triangle (p. 432)
Associative Property of Multiplication (p. 433)
Multiplication of Unit Fractions Property (p. 439)
Algebraic Definition of Division (p. 440)
Multiplication of Fractions Property (p. 440)
Property of Reciprocals (p. 441)
Distributive Property of Multiplication over Addition (p. 445)

Distributive Property of Multiplication over Subtraction (p. 446)
Triangle Area Formula (p. 451)
Trapezoid Area Formula (p. 457)
Parallelogram Area Formula (p. 458)
Circumference of a Circle Formula (p. 464)
Area of a Circle Formula (p. 466)
Size-Change Model for Multiplication (p. 472)
2-Dimensional Size-Change Model for Multiplication (p. 474)

Chapter 7 Self-Test

Take this test as you would take a test in class. You will need a calculator. Then use the Selected Answers section in the back of the book to check your work.

1. A lawn sprinkler sprays water 15 feet in all directions. To the nearest square foot, how much ground is watered by the sprinkler?

In 2–4, simplify the expression using the Distributive Properties.

2. $14(2m + 1 - 5n)$

3. $x + 3y + 3z - 3y + 3z$

4. $3x - 8y - 2x + 4(2y + x)$

5. Find the area of the triangle formed by connecting the cities of Los Angeles, Houston, and New York, as shown below.

In 6 and 7, evaluate.

6. $\frac{5}{12} \cdot \frac{3}{4}$

7. $360\left(\frac{1}{2} + \frac{1}{3}\right)$

8. Draw a picture of the multiplication in Question 6 using areas of rectangles.

9. The triangle pictured below has sides of lengths a, b, and c. The altitude to the side of length b has length h. Explain why the area of this triangle is $\frac{1}{2}bh$.

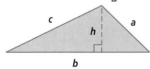

10. A map scale is 1:10,000, so objects 1 unit apart on the map represent real objects 10,000 units apart. If a town is 2 in. away from the nearest train station on the map, how far away is the actual town from the station? Express your answer in feet.

11. A circle has diameter 50. Find its area.

12. **True or False** If two trapezoids each have bases of length 5 centimeters and 8 centimeters with height 2 centimeters, they must have the same area.

13. **True or False** If two trapezoids each have bases of length 5 centimeters and 8 centimeters with height 2 centimeters, they must have the same perimeter.

14. An auditorium has 12 rows with 24 seats in each row and 6 rows with 28 seats in each row. How many seats are there all together in the auditorium?

15. Explain why $53x + 7.3x = 60.3x$ using areas of rectangles.

16. Give an example in which you use the Multiplication of Unit Fractions Property.

17. In the drawing below, $ABCD$ and $CDEF$ are parallelograms. Points A, B, E, and F all lie on the same line. Do the two parallelograms have the same area? Why or why not?

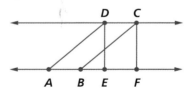

In 18–20, a triangle with vertices $A = (0, 10)$, $B = (0, 0)$, and $C = (20, 0)$ undergoes a size change of magnitude 2.5.

18. Is the size change an expansion or a contraction?

19. Graph triangle ABC and its image $A'B'C'$.

20. Find the area of the triangle ABC and its image $A'B'C'$.

Chapter 7 Chapter Review

SKILLS
PROPERTIES
USES
REPRESENTATIONS

SKILLS Procedures used to get answers

OBJECTIVE A Find the area of a triangle given appropriate dimensions.
(Lessons 7-1, 7-4)

In 1 and 2, find the area of the figure.

1.
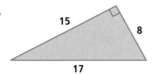

2.
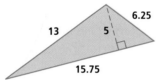

In 3 and 4, find the area of the shaded figure.

3.
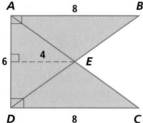

4.
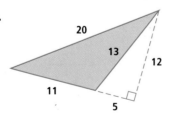

OBJECTIVE B Find the area of a trapezoid (including special types) given appropriate dimensions. (Lessons 7-1, 7-5)

5. Find the area of a rectangle that is 8 inches long and 1 foot wide.

6. Find the area of a trapezoid whose bases have lengths 5 centimeters and 7 centimeters and whose height is 20 centimeters.

In 7–9, find the area of the figure.

7.
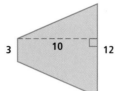

8.
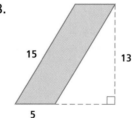

9.
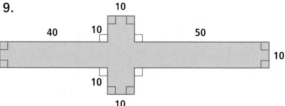

OBJECTIVE C Multiply fractions.
(Lesson 7-2)

In 10–17, write the answer as a whole number, simple fraction, or mixed number in lowest terms.

10. $\frac{2}{5} \cdot \frac{2}{3}$

11. $\frac{3}{8} \cdot \frac{4}{9}$

12. $28 \cdot \frac{7}{4}$

13. $11 \cdot \frac{11}{13}$

14. $1\frac{5}{6} \cdot 3\frac{1}{3}$

15. $2\frac{1}{100} \cdot \frac{200}{201}$

16. $\frac{1}{3} \cdot \frac{3}{5} \cdot \frac{5}{7}$

17. $8 \cdot \frac{2}{5} \cdot 7\frac{1}{4}$

OBJECTIVE D Find the area and circumference of a circle. (Lesson 7-6)

18. Find the circumference and the area of a circle with diameter 10 centimeters.

19. Find the circumference and the area of a circle with radius $\frac{2}{3}$ mile, to the nearest tenth.

20. A circle has circumference 16π.
    a. What is its diameter?
    b. What is its radius?
    c. What is its area?

PROPERTIES Principles behind the mathematics

OBJECTIVE E Recognize and use the Distributive Property and the Commutative and Associative Properties of Multiplication. (Lessons 7-1 and 7-3)

In 21–24, use the Distributive Property to remove parentheses.

21. $3(x + y)$

22. $5(a - 2b)$

23. $\frac{3}{4}(8c - 6d + 1)$

24. $100(t + 0.3)$

In 25–28, use the Distributive Property to simplify the expression.

25. $4x - x$

26. $v - 8v + 2v$

27. $a - b + 2a + 2b$

28. $5 + 3x - 7 + 9x$

29. Explain how the Distributive Property can be used to multiply $29.99 by 6 in your head.

30. Explain how the Distributive Property can be used to multiply 61 by 5 in your head.

In 31 and 32, identify the property that makes the equation true.

31. $6 \cdot (42 + 7) = (42 + 7) \cdot 6$

32. $8 \cdot (6 \cdot 5) = (6 \cdot 5) \cdot 8$

33. Explain how the Commutative and Associative Properties can be used to simplify the following expression in your head.
$$\left(\frac{1}{2} \cdot 7\right) \cdot \left(2 \cdot \frac{5}{8}\right) \cdot \left(\frac{1}{7} \cdot \frac{8}{5}\right)$$

OBJECTIVE F Recognize the differences between perimeter and area. (Lessons 7-1, 7-6)

34. Explain why the area of $\triangle ABD$ below is $\frac{1}{2}h(AE + ED)$.

35. Explain why the area of trapezoid $ABCD$ below is $\frac{1}{2}h(BC + AD)$.

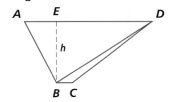

In 36 and 37, use these choices.

A its perimeter and its area

B its perimeter but not its area

C its area but not its perimeter

D neither its area nor its perimeter

36. A parallelogram has sides of length 11 meters and 3.7 meters. From this information, which can you determine?

37. A right triangle has a hypotenuse of length 61 and leg of length 60. From this information, which can you determine?

In 38 and 39, would you calculate perimeter or area to indicate the given characteristic of a lake?

38. how much room there is to water ski

39. how much room there is for houses to be built around the lake

USES Applications of mathematics in real-world situations

OBJECTIVE G Find areas of rectangles and the number of elements in rectangular arrays in applied situations. (Lesson 7-1)

40. A large classroom has 6 rows with 15 chairs in each row. How many chairs are there in all?

41. A camera can take pictures with a resolution of 2,048 by 1,536 pixels. How many pixels are there in a picture taken by this camera?

42. A football field is 160 feet wide and 120 yards long (including the end zones). What is the area of a football field in square feet?

43. How much area does the top of a desk have if it is 6 feet long and $2\frac{1}{2}$ feet wide?

OBJECTIVE H Find areas of triangles or trapezoids in real situations. (Lessons 7-4, 7-5)

44. Find the area of a triangular pennant that is 36 inches long from top to bottom, and whose top is 10 inches long.

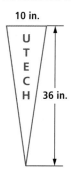

45. The shape of Egypt is roughly a trapezoid. The north border of Egypt is a coast of the Mediterranean Sea about 900 kilometers long. The south border of Egypt is about 1,100 kilometers long. The distance from north to south is about 1,100 kilometers. What is the approximate area of Egypt?

OBJECTIVE I Find the area and circumference of a circle in real-world situations. (Lesson 7-6)

46. The largest circular particle accelerator ever built was at the European Organization for Nuclear Research, the world's largest particle-physics center. It had a diameter of 8.5 kilometers and crossed the border of Switzerland and France.

    a. What was the circumference?

    b. What area did it enclose?

47. A dog is on a leash that is attached to a ring around the foot of a tree that has a radius of 1 foot. If the leash is 15 feet long and there is plenty of room around the tree, what is the area of the region in which the dog can roam?

48. Two circular pieces of metal are cut out of a 30-centimeter-by-60-centimeter rectangular metal sheet as shown below. To the nearest square centimeter, how much metal is left?

49. A wheel on a bicycle has a radius of 22 inches. In 100 revolutions of the wheel, how far, to the nearest foot, does the bicycle travel?

OBJECTIVE J Apply the Size-Change Model for Multiplication in real-world situations. (Lesson 7-7)

50. A second is $\frac{1}{60}$ of a minute. A minute is $\frac{1}{60}$ of an hour. So a second is what fraction of an hour?

51. In 2000, 11.5% of the population in Texas was classified as only African-American. The population of Texas then was about 20,852,000. About how many people were classified as only African-American?

52. A copy machine makes a copy of a picture that is $\frac{4}{5}$ as long and $\frac{4}{5}$ as wide as the original. How will the area of the copy compare to the area of the original?

53. If a picture is enlarged so that its length and width are 1.3 times what they were originally, how will the area of the larger picture compare with the area of the original?

54. If a $2,500 certificate of deposit is giving interest at an annual rate of 3.46%, how much interest is earned the first year?

55. When a person tithes, he or she gives one-tenth of his income to charity. If a person who tithes earns $640 a week, how much would be given to charity in a year?

REPRESENTATIONS Pictures, graphs, or objects that illustrate concepts

OBJECTIVE K Picture multiplication using arrays or area. (Lessons 7-1, 7-2)

56. Picture the multiplication $\frac{2}{5} \cdot \frac{2}{3}$ using area.

57. Without multiplying, explain why $\frac{87}{97} \cdot \frac{67}{77}$ is less than 1.

58. Picture 5 times 6 using an array.

59. Explain with pictures why $3,502 \cdot 1,625 = 1,625 \cdot 3,502$.

OBJECTIVE L Represent the Distributive Property with areas of rectangles. (Lesson 7-3)

In 60–63, use areas of rectangles to explain why the equation is true.

60. $30 \cdot 5 + 30 \cdot 6 = 30 \cdot 11$

61. $5 \cdot 7 + 0.2 \cdot 7 = 5.2 \cdot 7$

62. $24 \cdot \frac{5}{6} - 24 \cdot \frac{1}{3} = 24 \cdot \frac{1}{2}$

63. $20 \cdot 7 - 5 \cdot 7 = 15 \cdot 7$

OBJECTIVE M Perform expansions or contractions on a coordinate graph. (Lesson 7-7)

64. Graph $\triangle XYZ$ with vertices $X = (-2, 6)$, $Y = (0, 0)$, and $Z = (3, 4)$ and its image $\triangle X'Y'Z'$ under a size change of magnitude 1.5. How do lengths of sides of the two triangles compare?

65. Graph the triangle of Question 64 and its image $\triangle X^*Y^*Z^*$ under a size change of magnitude 3.

66. How are the triangles $X'Y'Z'$ and $X^*Y^*Z^*$ of Questions 64 and 65 related to each other?

67. What is the image of (x, y) under a size change of magnitude 10?

68. Is a size change of magnitude $\frac{5}{7}$ an expansion, a contraction, or neither?

69. Graph the quadrilateral $QUAD$ with $Q = (4, 1)$, $U = (4, 4)$, $A = (0, 4)$, and $D = (-5, 1)$ and its image under a size change of magnitude $\frac{1}{2}$. How do the lengths of sides of $QUAD$ and its image $Q'U'A'D'$ compare?

Chapter

8

Multiplication in Algebra

Multiplication has three important models or types of use: area, rate-factor, and size-change. In Chapter 7, you saw geometric applications of the area and size-change models. This chapter deals with situations stemming from arithmetic.

Suppose you buy four T-shirts at a store for $9.80 per shirt. To find the total cost, you multiply by 4. This is *rate-factor* multiplication. The quantity 9.80 dollars per shirt is a rate factor.

$$4 \text{ shirts} \cdot \$9.80/\text{shirt} = \$39.20$$

But because you paid the money, you can think of the cost to you as a negative quantity. Then the multiplication is

$$4 \text{ shirts} \cdot -\$9.80/\text{shirt} = -\$39.20$$

If the shirts were on sale for 25% off, then you would multiply $9.80 by 25% $\left(\text{or } 0.25 \text{ or } \frac{1}{4}\right)$ to find the discount on each shirt.

$$25\% \cdot \$9.80 = \$2.45$$

Or you could multiply the $9.80 by 75% $\left(\text{or } 0.75 \text{ or } \frac{3}{4}\right)$ to quickly find the sale price of each shirt.

$$75\% \cdot \$9.80 = \$7.35$$

These are examples of *size-change* multiplication. The 25% and 75% are size-change factors. Notice that this single everyday situation has positive and negative numbers, percents, decimals, and fractions.

Lesson 8-1

Multiplication as Shortcut Addition

Vocabulary

terms

coefficients

like terms

collecting like terms

▶ **BIG IDEA** When faced with a situation of adding *n* numbers that are alike, you can instead multiply the number by *n*.

Activity

On a trip to the store, suppose you buy a pair of socks, a cap, pants, and a shirt with prices *S*, *c*, *j*, and *T*, respectively.

Mental Math

Calculate in your head.

a. $5 + 5 + 5 + 4 + 4 + 4$

b. $6 + 6 + 6 + 6 + 6 + 6 + 6 + 6$

c. $9 + 7 + 9 + 7 + 5 + 4 + 5$

d. $10 + 8 + 12 + 10 + 13 + 7$

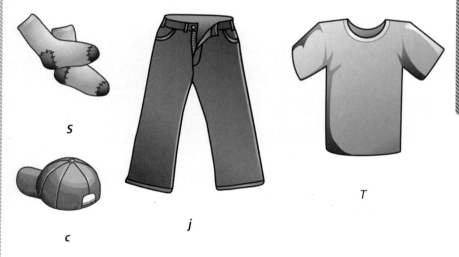

S

c

j

T

1. What will your total cost be?

2. Now suppose you buy 4 pairs of socks. Describe two ways the store clerk can arrive at your total cost.

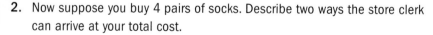

3. Suppose you change your mind and decide to buy 3 of each of the four different items. Describe three ways the store clerk can compute your total cost.

Multiplication can be a shortcut for addition when the addends are equal.

Specifically: $2x = x + x,$
$3x = x + x + x,$
$4x = x + x + x + x,$

and so on.

This property of multiplication is called the *Repeated-Addition Property*.

Repeated-Addition Property of Multiplication

If n is a positive integer greater than 1, then

$$nx = \underbrace{x + x + x + \ldots + x}_{n \text{ addends}},$$

What about $1 \cdot x$? You have long known that when any number is multiplied by 1, the number stays the same. This is the *Multiplicative-Identity Property of 1*.

Multiplicative-Identity Property of 1

For any number x,

$$1 \cdot x = x.$$

The Multiplicative-Identity Property of 1 is true regardless of the form of 1. Because $100\% = 1$, you know that 100% of a number x is equal to x. Also, for example, $\frac{15}{15}$ of a number is that number.

Some topics that you have seen in earlier chapters can be viewed as examples of repeated addition. For example, you have dealt with the perimeters of figures. Some formulas for perimeter are the result of repeated addition.

Example 1

What is the perimeter of an equilateral triangle with side length *s*?

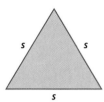

Solution

The perimeter is the sum of the length of the sides, $s + s + s$.

By repeated addition, $s + s + s = 3s$.

STOP QY1

> **QY1**
>
> What is the perimeter of a square with side length *s*?

Think again about the store situation. Suppose you buy 5 T-shirts and 3 pairs of jeans. Let *T* be the price of one T-shirt and *j* be the price of one pair of jeans. What is the total cost?

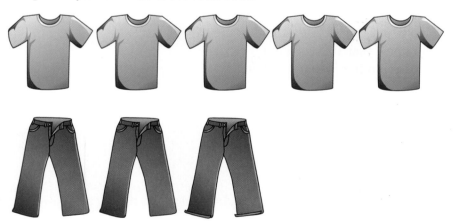

If you add, the total cost is
$$T + T + T + T + T + j + j + j.$$
This sum, by the Repeated Addition Property of Multiplication, is
$$5T + 3j.$$
The clerk can multiply the price of the T-shirts by 5 and the price of the jeans by 3 and add the products.

Collecting Like Terms

Terms in algebra are expressions that are added. The expression $6x + 3xy + y$ has the terms $6x$, $3xy$, and y. The numbers 6, 3, and 1 are **coefficients** of those terms.

Like terms are terms that contain the same variables raised to the same powers. Like terms may have different coefficients. In the expression $2m - 3n - m$, the terms $2m$ and $-m$ are like terms, while $2m$ and $-3n$ are unlike terms. In the expression $5y^2 + 2x + 3yx$, there are no like terms. Repeated addition can help you simplify expressions by *collecting like terms*.

For example, there are two ways to add $2x$ and $3x$. Think of $2x + 3x$ as repeated addition.

$$2x + 3x = \underbrace{x + x}_{\text{2 addends}} + \underbrace{x + x + x}_{\text{3 addends}}$$

$$= \underbrace{x + x + x + x + x}_{\text{5 addends}}$$

$$= 5x$$

You can also add $2x$ and $3x$ using the Distributive Property.

$$2x + 3x = x(2 + 3)$$

$$= 5x$$

You have seen that $2x + 3x = 5x$ and you know that $(2 + 3)x = 5x$. Because both expressions can be simplified as $5x$, $2x + 3x = (2 + 3)x$. This is a special case of the Distributive Property you saw in Lesson 7-3, such that $ax + bx = (a + b)x$ and $ax - bx = (a - b)x$ for all numbers a, b, and x. This use of the Distributive Property is sometimes called **collecting like terms.**

Example 2

Collect like terms to simplify $200x + 6y - 10y + 7.7 - x$.

Solution Reorder the terms to put like terms next to each other.

$200x + 6y - 10y + 7.7 - x = 200x - x + 6y - 10y + 7.7$

Use the Distributive Property.

$$= (200 - 1)x + (6 - 10)y + 7.7$$

$$= 199x - 4y + 7.7$$

 STOP QY2

> ▶ **QY2**
>
> Collect like terms.
>
> $m + m + 3m + 4n + m$

If you forget the Distributive Properties of Multiplication over Addition and Subtraction, you may use repeated addition to help you remember.

Example 3

Simplify $2 + 5(a + b)$.

Solution By repeated addition:

$$2 + 5(a + b) = 2 + \underbrace{(a + b) + (a + b) + (a + b) + (a + b) + (a + b)}_{\text{5 addends}}$$

By the Commutative and Associative Properties of Addition:

$$= 2 + \underbrace{a + a + a + a + a}_{\text{5 addends}} + \underbrace{b + b + b + b + b}_{\text{5 addends}}$$

$$= 2 + 5a + 5b$$

Check By the Distributive Property of Multiplication,
$2 + 5(a + b) = 2 + 5a + 5b$.

Questions

COVERING THE IDEAS

1. Suppose you have 5 quarters and 3 dimes.
   a. Find the total amount of money using repeated addition.
   b. Find the total amount of money using multiplication for the repeated additions.

In 2–4, simplify. Do not use a calculator.

2. $w + w + w + w$ 3. $\ell + w + \ell + w$

4. $5 + 10 + 15 + 5 + 5 + 10 + 15 + 15 + 25$

5. Find the perimeter of this arrow.

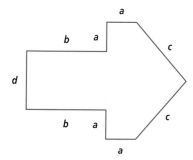

6. **a.** Use repeated addition to simplify $4x + 3x$.

   b. Use the Distributive Property to simplify $4x + 3x$.

7. **a.** Use repeated addition to simplify $10x - x$.

   b. Use the Distributive Property to simplify $10x - x$.

In 8–13, simplify.

8. $a + 5b + 4 + 3a + b + 3$

9. $7 + D + 8C + 4D + 2$

10. $12a - 22b - 32a + 42b - 52$

11. $\frac{3}{5}n + 1 + \frac{3}{5}n - 1$

12. $4e - e + 5f + 3f + 2e$

13. $11y - 42x + 3x - 15y$

14. For any number, 100% of the number is the number. $\frac{4}{4}$ of the number is also the number. These are instances of which property?

APPLYING THE MATHEMATICS

15. **a.** Write $5 \cdot -\frac{3}{5}$ as repeated addition.

    b. Calculate $5 \cdot -\frac{3}{5}$.

16. Suppose synthetic motor oil costs \$4.65 per quart in an auto-supply store.

    a. A shopper buys 6 quarts. Find the total cost using two methods.

    b. A shopper buys c quarts. What is the total cost?

17. Regular octagon and square tiles are used to tessellate a bathroom floor. Each octagon has an area of approximately 19.3 cm². Each square has an area of 4 cm². If h octagon tiles and s squares are used, what is the total area of the floor?

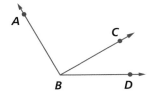

18. BC is 3 times AB. Let $AB = x$. What is AC in terms of x?

19. Monica believes that it is always true that $5m - m = 4m$. Kendra believes that it is always true that $5m - m = 5$. Is either person correct? How can you tell?

20. Explain why $3(ab) \neq (3 \cdot a) \cdot (3 \cdot b)$.

In 21 and 22, find an equivalent expression without parentheses.

21. $6(a - 3) + a + 18$

22. $3(a + b) - 3(a + b)$

23. $\angle ABC$ and $\angle CBD$ are adjacent angles that form $\angle ABD$. $m\angle ABC = 2 \cdot m\angle CBD$. If $m\angle CBD = x$, what is $m\angle ABD$?

REVIEW

24. From the top of a tall building, a person can see 40 miles in every direction. How many square miles are then visible? **(Lesson 7-6)**

25. What is the total area of the rectangles below? **(Lesson 7-3)**

26. **True or False** Every integer is a rational number. **(Lesson 4-9)**

27. The solution to what sentence is graphed below? **(Lesson 2-8)**

Looking northeast from the Sears Tower in Chicago, Illinois

28. Describe the pattern using variables.
    1 year on Mars is $1 \cdot 687$ Earth days.
    2 years on Mars is $2 \cdot 687$ Earth days.
    3 years on Mars is $3 \cdot 687$ Earth days.
    4 years on Mars is $4 \cdot 687$ Earth days.
    (Lesson 2-1)

29. **Fill in the Blanks** Complete these conversion formulas. **(Previous Course)**
    a. 1 foot = __?__ inches
    b. 1 mile = __?__ feet
    c. 1 yard = __?__ feet
    d. 1 mile = __?__ yards

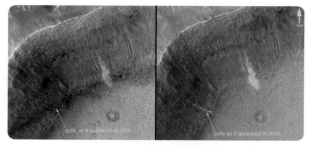

The change in these photos might be explained by the movement of water on the surface of Mars.

EXPLORATION

30. Pick a positive integer n. The next greater positive integer is $n + 1$. The next greater is $n + 2$ and so on.
    a. Add any five consecutive integers. Explain why the sum is divisible by 5.
    b. If you add six consecutive integers, is the sum always divisible by 6?
    c. Explore the idea of Parts a and b and make a generalization.

QY ANSWERS

1. $4s$

2. $6m + 4n$

The Rate-Factor Model for Multiplication

Vocabulary

rate factors

conversion factor

▶ **BIG IDEA** Rates such as 40 miles per hour, $2.99 per pound, and $1\frac{1}{2}$ minutes per page are often multiplied by quantities to obtain total amounts.

A quantity is a rate when its unit contains the word "per," "for each," or another synonym. Every rate has a *rate unit*. Rate units may be written with a slash, /, or horizontal bar, −. The slash or bar is read as "per." Here are some examples of rates.

<table>
<tr><th>Using the Slash</th><th>Using the Bar</th></tr>
<tr><td>90 km/hr
(speed limit)</td><td>$90 \frac{\text{km}}{\text{hr}}$</td></tr>
<tr><td>41.78 in./yr
(average rainfall in Seattle)</td><td>$41.78 \frac{\text{in.}}{\text{yr}}$</td></tr>
<tr><td>$3\frac{1}{2}$ pieces/student
(distribution of scratch paper)</td><td>$3\frac{1}{2} \frac{\text{pieces}}{\text{student}}$</td></tr>
</table>

Mental Math

Calculate.

a. $0 \cdot 1$

b. $-1 \cdot \pi$

c. $1 \cdot \pi - \pi \cdot 1$

d. $0 \cdot \pi + 1 \cdot \pi$

Multiplying by a Rate

Example 1

It is not uncommon for a person between the ages of 4 and 10 to grow about 2.5 inches per year. If the growth continues at this rate for 4 years, what is the total gain in height?

Solution The rate of growth is $2.5 \frac{\text{inches}}{\text{year}}$.

The total gain in height can be found by multiplying:

$$4 \text{ years} \cdot 2.5 \frac{\text{inches}}{\text{year}} = 10 \text{ inches}.$$

Look at the units in this multiplication. They work as if they were whole numbers and fractions. The units "years" at the left cancels the unit "year" in the denominator. The unit that remains is inches. The 10 comes from multiplying the numbers.

On the next page is a similar situation that requires multiplying by a rate.

GUIDED

Example 2

A motorist buys 10.2 gallons of gas at $3.499 per gallon.

a. What is the total cost?

b. Write a formula for the cost.

Solution

a. **Step 1** The rate is ___?___.

    Step 2 Multiply the rate by 10.2 gallons. ___?___

    Step 3 The total cost is __?__.

b. Regardless of the number of gallons or the cost per gallon, you would multiply to find the total cost.

    Step 1 Let n be the number of gallons, c be the cost per gallon, and T be the total cost.

    Step 2 Then, __?__ · __?__ = __?__.

In the previous examples, the quantities $2.5 \frac{\text{inches}}{\text{year}}$ and $3.499 \frac{\text{dollars}}{\text{gallon}}$ are rates that are multiplied, so they are **rate factors.** The general idea behind these examples is the Rate-Factor Model for Multiplication.

Rate-Factor Model for Multiplication

The product of (a unit$_1$) and $\left(b \frac{\text{unit}_2}{\text{unit}_1}\right)$ is (ab unit$_2$), signifying the total amount of unit$_2$ in the situation.

$$a \text{ unit}_1 \cdot b \frac{\text{unit}_2}{\text{unit}_1} = ab \text{ unit}_2$$

Converting Units Using Rates

Start with a conversion formula. Here is an example.

$$1 \text{ mile} = 5{,}280 \text{ feet}$$

Because the quantities are equal, dividing one by the other results in the number 1.

$$\frac{1 \text{ mile}}{5{,}280 \text{ feet}} = 1 \text{ and } \frac{5{,}280 \text{ feet}}{1 \text{ mile}} = 1$$

You could say there is 1 mile for every 5,280 feet or there are 5,280 feet per mile. The quantities $\frac{1 \text{ mile}}{5{,}280 \text{ feet}}$ and $\frac{5{,}280 \text{ feet}}{1 \text{ mile}}$ are *conversion factors.* A **conversion factor** is a rate factor that equals the number 1. Because of the Multiplicative-Identity Property of 1, multiplying by a conversion factor does not change the value of the number being multiplied. Instead, it changes the unit.

Example 3

Suppose you are in an airplane flying at an altitude of 32,000 feet. How many miles above sea level are you?

Solution Multiply 32,000 feet by the conversion factor with miles in the numerator and feet in the denominator. The mile unit is needed in the product, so feet must be in the denominator to cancel.

$$32,000 \text{ feet} = 32,000 \text{ feet} \cdot \frac{1 \text{ mile}}{5,280 \text{ feet}}$$
$$= \frac{32,000}{5,280} \text{ miles}$$
$$= 6.\overline{06} \text{ miles} \approx 6 \text{ miles}$$

 QY

The image is of Nice, France, and the French Riviera.

Multiplying Two or More Rates

In some situations, two or more rates can be multiplied. Again the units are multiplied as you would multiply fractions.

> ▶ **QY**
>
> How many miles above sea level is a weather balloon flying at 80,000 feet?

Example 4

Absalom has been absent and has 5 chapters of a book to read. Each chapter is about 20 pages long. Each page takes about $1\frac{1}{2}$ minutes to read. About how long will it take him to read these 5 chapters?

Solution Think of rates. There are 20 pages per chapter. It takes $1\frac{1}{2}$ minutes per page.

$$5 \text{ chapters} \cdot \frac{20 \text{ pages}}{1 \text{ chapter}} \cdot \frac{1\frac{1}{2} \text{ minutes}}{1 \text{ page}}$$
$$= 5 \text{ chapters} \cdot 20 \frac{\text{pages}}{\text{chapter}} \cdot 1\frac{1}{2} \frac{\text{minutes}}{\text{page}}$$
$$= 100 \text{ pages} \cdot 1\frac{1}{2} \frac{\text{minutes}}{\text{page}}$$
$$= 150 \text{ minutes}$$

If you wish to know how many hours this is, you can use a conversion factor relating hours and minutes.

$$150 \text{ minutes} = 150 \text{ minutes} \cdot \frac{1 \text{ hour}}{60 \text{ minutes}}$$
$$= \frac{150}{60} \text{ hours}$$
$$= 2\frac{30}{60} \text{ hours} = 2\frac{1}{2} \text{ hours}$$

Rate-factor multiplications can also be used to determine new conversion factors.

Questions

COVERING THE IDEAS

In 1 and 2, a sentence is given.

a. Copy the sentence and underline the rate.

b. Write the rate with its unit in fraction notation using the slash.

c. Write the rate with its unit in fraction notation using the fraction bar.

1. Only 6 tickets per student are available for the graduation ceremony.

2. The pitcher for the home team gives up about 2 earned runs per game.

3. Consider the multiplication

   $4 \text{ cans} \cdot 1.99 \frac{\text{dollars}}{\text{can}} = 7.96 \text{ dollars}$

   a. Identify the rate factor.

   b. Identify the unit of the rate factor.

   c. Make up a situation that could lead to this multiplication.

   d. Write a general formula for the total cost T, identifying each variable.

4. Explain why you are allowed to cancel the unit "years" in Example 1.

In 5–8, multiply.

5. $3 \frac{\text{apples}}{\text{day}} \cdot 5 \text{ days}$

6. $6 \text{ hours} \cdot 55 \frac{\text{miles}}{\text{hour}}$

7. $40 \text{ hours} \cdot \frac{\$15}{\text{hour}}$

8. $15 \text{ teachers} \cdot \frac{5 \text{ classes}}{\text{teacher}} \cdot \frac{28 \text{ students}}{\text{class}}$

9. a. Multiply. $10{,}000 \text{ feet} \cdot \frac{1 \text{ mile}}{5{,}280 \text{ feet}}$

   b. Make up a question that could lead to this multiplication.

10. An animal gained 2.5 kilograms per month for 9 months and then 1.75 kilograms per month for 4 months. How many kilograms did it gain in the 13 months?

11. A typist can type 80 words per minute.

    a. At this rate, how many words can the typist type in 40 minutes?

    b. Write a general formula for this situation.

12. Name the two conversion factors for converting between centimeters and inches.

13. Madison is 60 centimeters tall. How many inches is this?

Many grocery stores have deli counters where you can buy freshly sliced meats and cheeses, as well as a variety of salads.

APPLYING THE MATHEMATICS

14. A new car is advertised to get 24 miles per gallon of gas. If gas costs $3.29 per gallon, how much would a person pay for enough gas to drive 120 miles?

15. Roast beef costs $3.49/pound. Matt estimates that a pound will provide 4 servings. How much will 9 servings of roast beef cost?

16. **a.** By definition, 1 inch = 2.54 cm. Find out how many kilometers are in one mile by completing each method.

Method 1

1 mile

$$= \left(1 \text{ mi} \cdot 5{,}280 \frac{?}{?}\right) \cdot \frac{? \text{ in.}}{? \text{ ft}} \cdot 2.54 \frac{\text{cm}}{\text{in.}} \cdot \frac{? \text{ m}}{? \text{ cm}} \cdot \frac{1}{1{,}000} \frac{?}{?}$$

$$= \left(\underline{\ ?\ } \cdot \frac{? \text{ in.}}{? \text{ ft}}\right) \cdot 2.54 \frac{\text{cm}}{\text{in.}} \cdot \frac{? \text{ m}}{? \text{ cm}} \cdot \frac{1}{1{,}000} \frac{?}{?}$$

$$= \left(\underline{\ ?\ } \cdot 2.54 \frac{\text{cm}}{\text{in.}}\right) \cdot \frac{? \text{ m}}{? \text{ cm}} \cdot \frac{1}{1{,}000} \frac{?}{?}$$

$$= \left(\underline{\ ?\ } \cdot \frac{? \text{ m}}{? \text{ cm}}\right) \cdot \frac{1}{1{,}000} \frac{?}{?}$$

$$= \underline{\ ?\ } \cdot \frac{1}{1{,}000} \frac{?}{?}$$

$$= \underline{\ ?\ }$$

Method 2

Now perform this calculation by first canceling the units.

1 mile

$$= 1 \text{ mi} \cdot \frac{?}{\text{mi}} \cdot \frac{?}{\text{ft}} \cdot \frac{2.54 \text{ cm}}{\text{in.}} \cdot \frac{?}{?} \cdot \frac{?}{?}$$

Then do the multiplication.

$$= \frac{5{,}280 \cdot \ ? \ \cdot 2.54}{? \ \cdot \ ?}$$

$$= \underline{\ ?\ }$$

b. Which method do you prefer? Why?

17. The speed limit on a highway is 55 miles per hour. If Ned drives at this speed limit for $5\frac{1}{2}$ hours, about how many *kilometers* will he have driven?

18. When Yasmin went to Europe, she found that 1 Euro was worth 1.33 U.S. dollars. She also found that 1 Euro was worth 0.67 British pound. How many British pounds could she get for $100 U.S.?

REVIEW

19. A regular pentagon has sides of length $8.1r$. Write two different expressions for its perimeter. **(Lesson 8-1)**

20. Ace bought 3 containers of tennis balls on Monday, 2 on Tuesday, and 8 on Thursday. If there are b balls in a container, how many tennis balls did Ace buy? **(Lesson 8-1)**

21. A trapezoid has bases of length x and $2x$ and height of length h. What is its area? **(Lesson 7-5)**

22. Mark is making a school pennant in the shape of a triangle. The pennant will be 36 cm from the vertex to the base and the base will be 18 cm long. How much material will Mark use for the pennant? **(Lesson 7-4)**

23. **a.** Draw a rectangular model to show the result of multiplying $\frac{3}{4}$ by $\frac{3}{8}$.
    b. Write a problem for which this multiplication would yield the answer. **(Lesson 7-2)**

24. **a.** Draw an example of a pair of vertical angles that are also supplementary.
    b. Can two angles in a linear pair both be acute? Explain why or why not. **(Lesson 6-5)**

25. Show an instance of the Property of Opposites. **(Lesson 4-2)**

26. The formula $6t + 1p + 2c + 3f + 2s$ gives the number of points a football team earns when they make t touchdowns, p single points after touchdown, c 2-point conversions after touchdowns, f field goals, and s safeties. Find two different ways that a team can earn 34 points. **(Lesson 2-4)**

27. **a.** Place parentheses in the following expression in two different ways. Evaluate your expression in each case.

$$8 + 4 \cdot 3 \div 6 - 4$$

b. What is the smallest value you can make? **(Lessons 1-7, 1-6)**

EXPLORATION

28. How many words are in a newspaper? Obviously, you do not have time to count them all. However, you can show how to estimate the number of words by using rate factors such as the number of lines per column. Come up with an estimate for a recent day's newspaper.

29. **a.** Some units of measurement are not common. One example is $\frac{\text{furlongs}}{\text{fortnight}}$. The speed of light is $186{,}000 \frac{\text{miles}}{\text{second}}$. Find the speed of light in $\frac{\text{furlongs}}{\text{fortnight}}$. (*Hint:* 1 furlong is $\frac{1}{8}$ mile and 1 fortnight = 14 days.)

b. Find at least two other unusual units of measurement, and convert some common measurement to these strange units.

QY ANSWER

about 15.15 mi

Lesson 8-3

Multiplication with Negative Numbers

> **BIG IDEA** Rates that indicate downward or backward change are negative quantities that can be multiplied just like other quantities.

A Situation Involving Multiplication by a Negative Number

Any loss can lead to a negative rate. Suppose a person loses 2.4 pounds per month on a medically supervised diet. The rate of change in weight is then

$$-2.4 \frac{\text{pounds}}{\text{month}}.$$

If the person continues to lose weight at this rate for 5 months, multiplying gives the total loss.

$$5 \text{ months} \cdot -2.4 \frac{\text{pounds}}{\text{month}} = -12 \text{ pounds}$$

We can see that if someone loses weight (a negative value) over a number of months (a positive value) the result should be a loss in weight (a negative value). A positive number and a negative number are being multiplied. The product is negative. The same equation is shown below without units.

$$5 \cdot -2.4 = -12$$

Mental Math

Calculate.
a. $8 \cdot 3 \cdot -1$
b. $-1 \cdot 6 \cdot 7$
c. $15 \cdot -1 \cdot 4$
d. $12 \cdot 11 \cdot -1 \cdot -1$

Example 1

The temperature decreased by 1.3° every hour from noon until 7:00 P.M. What was the net change in temperature?

Solution Use the Rate-Factor Model for Multiplication. The rate is $1.3 \frac{\text{degrees}}{\text{hour}}$. From noon to 7:00 is 7 hours.

$$-1.3 \frac{\text{degrees}}{\text{hour}} \cdot 7 \text{ hours} = -9.1 \text{ degrees}$$

The net change is a decrease in temperature of 9.1°.

 QY1

> ▶ **QY1**
>
> Suppose the value of a particular kind of luxury car goes down at a rate of $2,450 every year. Identify the negative rate for this situation and find the value the car will have lost after $2\frac{1}{2}$ years.

Multiplication with Two Negative Numbers

What happens if both factors are negative? Again think of a weight-loss situation. Suppose a person lost 2.4 pounds a month. At this rate, 5 months *before* this time, the person weighed 12 pounds more. Going back is the negative direction for time, so here is the multiplication for this situation.

$$5 \text{ months } ago \cdot loss \text{ of } 2.4 \frac{\text{pounds}}{\text{month}} = 12 \text{ pounds } more$$

$$-5 \text{ months} \cdot -2.4 \frac{\text{pounds}}{\text{month}} = 12 \text{ pounds}$$

Ignoring the units, $-5 \cdot -2.4 = 12$.

 QY2

You have now seen that the product of a positive number and a negative number is negative. You have also seen that the product of two negative numbers is positive. Of course, you already know that the product of two positive numbers is positive. These facts are summarized below.

> ### Multiplication of Positive and Negative Numbers
>
> The product of two numbers with the same sign is positive. The product of two numbers having opposite signs is negative.

Example 2

Is $-5.4 \cdot -7\frac{3}{5} \cdot 10 \cdot 2 \cdot -\frac{9}{100} \cdot -4 \cdot -15 \cdot 6.03 \cdot -9.\overline{3}$ positive or negative? Justify your answer without using a calculator.

Solution Each multiplication by a negative number changes the product's sign. Every two changes keeps it positive. Because there are six negative numbers, the product is positive.

Caution: The kind of thinking in the solution to Example 2 works because the numbers are all multiplied. It does not work for addition or subtraction.

 QY3

Multiplication Property of −1

Multiplication by −1 follows the above pattern, but it is even more special.

$$-1 \cdot 13 = -13$$
$$-1 \cdot -30.2 = 30.2$$
$$-1 \cdot \frac{8}{19} = -\frac{8}{19}$$

▶ **QY2**

Suppose again that the value of a particular kind of luxury car goes down at a rate of $2,450 every year. How much more value did the car have $1\frac{1}{2}$ years ago?

▶ **QY3**

Is $-2.1 \cdot 41 \cdot -1\frac{4}{7} \cdot -0.15 \cdot -\frac{50}{3} \cdot -1{,}200 \cdot -10.4 \cdot -1{,}000$ positive or negative?

Multiplication by –1 changes a number to its opposite. Here is a description with variables.

Multiplication Property of –1

For any number x, $-1 \cdot x = -x$.

Notice that $-x$ can be negative, positive, or zero, depending on the value of x, as the following example illustrates.

Example 3

When $x = -8$, determine whether x^2, $(-x)^2$, and $-x^2$ are positive or negative.

Solution $x^2 = (-8)^2 = 64$, which is positive.

$(-x)^2 = (- -8)^2 = (8)^2 = 64$, which is positive.

$-x^2 = -(-8)^2 = -64$, which is negative.

In the previous example, some students believe that all of the answers should be positive. However, $-(-8)^2$ must be negative. One way to see this is by the Multiplication Property of –1:

$-(-8)^2 = -1 \cdot (-8)^2 = -1 \cdot 64 = -64.$

Multiplication Property of Zero

Activity 1

Step 1 Multiply the number 4 by positive numbers that get smaller and smaller. Use the numbers 1.2, 0.3, 0.0052, and 0.0000019 and then complete the sentence.
The smaller the positive number, the closer the product is to ____?____.

Step 2 Multiply -3 by the same numbers and then complete the sentence.
The products are all ____?____, but again they get closer and closer to ____?____.

These examples help us see why the following property makes sense.

Multiplication Property of Zero

For any number x, $x \cdot 0 = 0$.

STOP QY4

Picturing Multiplication by a Negative Number

Activity 2

At the right is quadrilateral *ABCD*, with $A = (0, -4)$, $B = (2, -1)$, $C = (-2, 3)$, and $D = (-2, -3)$. We will transform *ABCD* under an expansion of magnitude -2.

Step 1 Multiply each *x*- and *y*-coordinate by -2. Use the rules for multiplication of negative numbers and zero from this lesson.

$A = (0, -4)$, so $A' = (0 \cdot -2, -4 \cdot -2) = (\underline{\ ?\ }, \underline{\ ?\ })$.

$B = (2, -1)$, so $B' = (2 \cdot -2, \underline{\ ?\ } \cdot -2) = (\underline{\ ?\ }, \underline{\ ?\ })$.

$C = (-2, 3)$, so $C' = (\underline{\ ?\ } \cdot \underline{\ ?\ }, \underline{\ ?\ } \cdot \underline{\ ?\ }) = (\underline{\ ?\ }, \underline{\ ?\ })$.

$D = (-2, -3)$, so $D' = (\underline{\ ?\ } \cdot \underline{\ ?\ }, \underline{\ ?\ } \cdot \underline{\ ?\ }) = (\underline{\ ?\ }, \underline{\ ?\ })$.

Step 2 Copy the preimage *ABCD* on graph paper and then draw *A'B'C'D'* on the same set of axes in a different color.

▶ **QY4**

Perform each multiplication.

a. $-1 \cdot \frac{15}{4}$

b. $-1 \cdot -\frac{15}{4}$

c. $0 \cdot -\frac{15}{4}$

Notice how the size change of magnitude -2 compares to a size change of magnitude 2. The images are much the same: the figure has been expanded, the corresponding sides are parallel, and the corresponding angles are equal in measure. But one new thing has happened: *the figure has been rotated 180°*. It has been turned upside down. What was right is now left. What was up is now down.

With some calculators, you can see images under size changes with different negative magnitudes. Use the images to draw some conclusions. The figures show images of *ABCD* above under size changes with four negative values for *k*. The first size change has the same magnitude as in Activity 2.

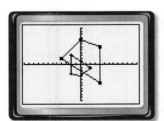

Screen 1

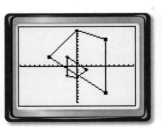

Screen 2

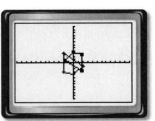

Screen 3

Screen 4

STOP QY5

Multiplying the coordinates of all points on a figure by the number k performs the transformation known as a *size change of magnitude k*. The number k may be positive or negative. But in all cases:

1. The resulting figure (the image) is similar to its preimage.

2. Lengths of sides of the resulting figure are $|k|$ times the lengths of sides of the preimage.

3. Corresponding sides are parallel.

4. Corresponding angles are equal in measure.

5. The line through any preimage point and its image contains $(0, 0)$.

6. The image points are $|k|$ times as far from $(0, 0)$ as preimage points.

7. If k is negative, the figure is rotated $180°$.

> ▶ **QY5**
>
> Estimate the magnitude of the size change shown in Screens 2, 3, and 4 on the previous page.

Questions

COVERING THE IDEAS

1. What is the negative unit rate in each sentence?
   a. While hiking, a group descended 235 feet in elevation each hour.
   b. A stock fell on average 0.75 point every 15 minutes.

In 2 and 3, a situation is given.

a. What multiplication problem involving negative numbers is suggested by the situation?

b. What is the product and what does it mean?

2. A person loses 6 pounds a month for 4 months. How much will the person lose in all?

3. A person has been losing 3 pounds a month. How does the person's weight 5 months ago compare with the weight now?

4. **Fill in the Blank** Multiplication of a number by __?__ results in the opposite of the number.

5. **Fill in the Blank** Multiplication of a number by __?__ results in zero.

In 6–11, compute.

6. $-8 \cdot -13$

7. $26 \cdot -\frac{1}{2}$

8. $-17 \cdot 9 \cdot -9$

9. $-5.3 \cdot -9.24 + -1$

10. a. -5^2
    b. $(-5)^2$

11. a. $50 - (-3)(-2)$
    b. $50 + (-3)(-2)$

12. Tell whether xy is positive or negative.

   a. x is positive and y is positive.

   b. x is positive and y is negative.

   c. x is negative and y is positive.

   d. x is negative and y is negative.

13. Tell whether $-8 \cdot 7 \cdot -2 \cdot -1 \cdot -5 \cdot 1 \cdot 3 \cdot -6$ is positive, negative, or zero. Explain why.

14. Calculate $-3 \cdot -2 \cdot -1 \cdot 0 \cdot 1 \cdot 2$.

15. In a size change of magnitude -3, the image of $(6, -2)$ is __?__.

16. What is the major difference between a size change of magnitude -0.5 and a size change of magnitude 0.5?

17. Let $M = (-6, -6)$, $V = (15, -12)$, and $W = (-6, 0)$. Graph $\triangle MVW$ and its image under a size change of magnitude $-\frac{2}{3}$.

APPLYING THE MATHEMATICS

18. Find the value of $-3n$ for the given value of n.

   a. -4 b. 12 c. 1 d. -1 e. $-2a$

19. Evaluate $-4m + 7n - 8$ when $m = -2$ and $n = 3$.

20. If two negative numbers are multiplied, their product is positive.

   a. Write the converse.

   b. Is the converse true or false? If false, give a counterexample.

In 21 and 22, solve the equation.

21. $17x = -17$

22. $-1 \cdot y = 39.5$

23. A couple currently has credit-card debts of $3,000. They have been running up additional debt at the rate of $250/month.

   a. **Multiple Choice** Assuming the couple has not made any payments toward the debt, what expression indicates their financial situation 4 months ago?

   A $3,000 + 4 \cdot -250$ B $3,000 - 4 \cdot -250$

   C $-3,000 + 4 \cdot -250$ D $-3,000 - 4 \cdot -250$

   b. At this rate, what expression indicates their financial situation m months from now?

24. Evaluate.

   a. $(-8)^2$ b. $(-8)^3$ c. $(-8)^4$

   d. $-(-8)^2$ e. $-(-8)^3$ f. $-(-8)^4$

25. Let $P = (4, -76)$. Suppose that P' is the image of P under a size change of magnitude -4.2. True or false? $\overline{PP'}$ contains $(0, 0)$.

26. Jesse performed a size change on $\triangle JES$ and said that $JE = J'E'$, $ES = E'S'$, and $JS = J'S'$. $\triangle J'E'S'$ is a $180°$ rotation image of $\triangle JES$. What was the magnitude of the size change? Write a short defense of your answer.

27. Recall that the four parts of the coordinate plane can be numbered from I to IV as shown at the right. Consider a size change with negative magnitude. If a preimage is in Quadrant IV, in which quadrant is its image?

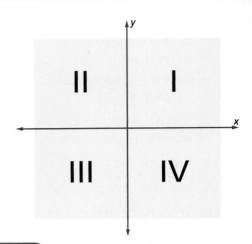

REVIEW

28. A South African cliff swallow was observed in Golden Gate Highland National Park in South Africa on Monday at 8 A.M. It was then observed in Kgalagadi Transfrontier Park, 800 kilometers away, on Tuesday at 3 P.M. What was its average speed? **(Lesson 8-2)**

29. A snail moves at the rate of three centimeters per minute.
    a. What is its speed in millimeters per hour?
    b. How many meters does it go in five hours? **(Lesson 8-2)**

In 30 and 31, consider the polygon below.

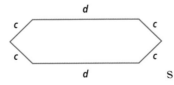

These South African cliff swallows were photographed in Sonop, Northwest Province, South Africa.

30. Write the perimeter of this polygon in simplified form. **(Lesson 8-1)**

31. What kind of polygon is this figure? **(Lesson 4-6)**

EXPLORATION

32. Let $y = x - \dfrac{1 + (-1)^x}{2}$.
    a. Find the values of y when $x = 1, x = 2, x = 3, \ldots$. Calculate enough values to find a pattern.
    b. Find all whole-number solutions to the equation $1,000 = x - \dfrac{1 + (-1)^x}{2}$.

QY ANSWERS

1. $-2,450 \, \frac{\text{dollars}}{\text{year}}$; the car will have lost \$6,125 in value after $2\frac{1}{2}$ years.

2. \$3,675

3. negative

4. a. $-\dfrac{15}{4}$
   b. $\dfrac{15}{4}$
   c. 0

5. Screen 2: $k = -\dfrac{1}{2}$
   Screen 3: $k = -3$
   Screen 4: $k = -1$

Lesson 8-4

Multiplying Probabilities

Vocabulary

independent events

▶ **BIG IDEA** When two events are independent, the probability that both will occur is the product of the probabilities of the events.

A local car dealership is having a promotional event. As one of the first 100 people at the event, Lucky Lucy is given a chance to win a new car. First she draws a keyless-entry remote from a bin of 75 remotes. Then she draws a car key from a bin of 150 keys. If the remote unlocks the car and the key starts it, she wins the car. Only one remote and one key will work. If she does not win, both the remote and the key are put back into the bins. Only one car will be awarded.

Do you think Lucy has a chance of winning? Look at how to calculate her probability of winning. Notice that two events must both happen for her to win the car. She must draw the correct remote *and* the correct key. Also notice that drawing the correct remote and drawing the correct key do not depend on each other. In other words, having the correct key and the correct remote are *independent events*.

To determine Lucy's chance of winning, separate the events. There are 75 remotes to choose from, so you would expect $\frac{1}{75}$ of the people to draw the correct remote. These people now get to sit inside the car and try the key. There are 150 keys to choose from, so you would expect that $\frac{1}{150}$ of the people who sit in the car will be able to start the car. So $\frac{1}{150}$ of $\frac{1}{75}$ of the people would be expected to both open the door and start the car. To calculate $\frac{1}{150}$ of $\frac{1}{75}$, multiply.

$$\frac{1}{150} \cdot \frac{1}{75} = \frac{1}{11,250}$$

You would expect 1 person out of 11,250 to win the car.

Mental Math

A box has four roundies, seven boxies, and eleven longies. A person picks one object.

a. What is the probability of picking a boxie?

b. What is the probability of picking a roundie?

c. What is the probability of picking a longie?

d. What is the probability of not picking a boxie?

e. What is more likely: picking a longie, or not picking a longie?

Be One of the First 100 Visitors, and YOU can WIN THIS CAR!

In the language of probabilities: There are 75 remotes, so the probability of a correct remote is $\frac{1}{75}$, which we abbreviate as $P(\text{correct remote}) = \frac{1}{75}$. There are 150 keys, so the probability of a correct key is $P(\text{correct key}) = \frac{1}{150}$. The probability that both events happen is:

$$P(\text{correct remote and correct key})$$
$$= P(\text{correct remote}) \cdot P(\text{correct key})$$
$$= \frac{1}{75} \cdot \frac{1}{150} = \frac{1}{11,250}$$

 QY1

▶ **QY1**

What is the probability that Lucy will *not* win the car?

When Are Events Independent?

In the car-giveaway situation, picking the correct remote and picking the correct key are independent events. The idea of **independent events** is that the occurrence of one does *not* depend on the occurrence of the other. Picking a remote out of one bin will not affect the chances of picking a key out of the other bin. Whenever two events are independent, you can multiply their probabilities to find the probability that both events will happen.

> **Probability of Independent Events**
>
> Two events A and B are independent events if and only if $P(A \text{ followed by } B) = P(A) \cdot P(B)$.

In the car situation, event A is "choosing the correct remote" and event B is "choosing the correct key."

GUIDED

Example 1

You and a friend are playing a game at the school carnival. You spin a spinner that looks like the one at the right. If the spinner lands on the "You Win!" section, you will win a small prize. The "You Win!" sector is $\frac{1}{3}$ of the circle. You and your friend both decide to play. What is the probability that you lose and your friend wins?

Solution 1 Let Event A = "you lose" and let Event B = "your friend wins." What happens on each spin is not dependent on what happens on the other spin, so the spins are independent. You can multiply the probabilities to find the probability that both will happen.

$$P(A \text{ followed by } B) = P(A) \cdot P(B)$$
$$= \underline{\quad?\quad} \cdot \underline{\quad?\quad}$$
$$= \underline{\quad?\quad}$$

Solution 2 Name the sections of the spinner 1, 2, and 3 with 1 representing the winning sector. The possible outcomes (your spin, your friend's spin) are (1, 1), (1, 2), (1, 3), (2, 1), (2, 2), (2, 3), (3, 1), (3, 2), (3, 3). The outcomes (2, 1) and (3, 1) mean you lost and your friend won. Because each of the 9 outcomes is equally likely,

the probability that you will lose and your friend will win $= \dfrac{?}{?}$.

Notice how easy it is to calculate the probability of A and B when events A and B are independent. In practice, the difficulty is deciding whether A and B are independent events. For example, suppose you and your friend are pulling raffle tickets out of a hat. You go first and pull out one ticket, and your friend pulls out a ticket afterward. When your friend pulls a ticket out of the hat, the hat contains one less ticket because you already pulled one out. So, the probabilities are not the same and the events are *not* independent.

 QY2

It is also possible for more than two events to be independent. In this case, we can extend the idea of multiplying the probabilities to include as many events as necessary.

> ▶ **QY2**
>
> Determine whether events A and B are independent and explain your answer.
> $A =$ a person in your class has brown hair.
> $B =$ a person in your class has blue eyes.

Example 2

Suppose you and three friends decide to play the game in Example 1.
a. What is the probability of the event that all four of you will win?
b. What is the probability of the event that all four of you will lose?

Solution

a. The probability of a person winning is $\frac{1}{3}$ for each spin. As in Example 1, all of the spins are independent, so we can multiply the probabilities.
$\frac{1}{3} \cdot \frac{1}{3} \cdot \frac{1}{3} \cdot \frac{1}{3} = \frac{1}{81}$ is the probability that all four will win.

b. The probability of a person losing on each spin is $\frac{2}{3}$. Because the spins are independent, we multiply.
$\frac{2}{3} \cdot \frac{2}{3} \cdot \frac{2}{3} \cdot \frac{2}{3} = \frac{16}{81}$ is the probability that all four will lose.

A probability can be thought of as a size-change factor. If you and three friends each spin the spinner once and do this 100 times, then it is most likely that:

all four of you in a row would win $100 \cdot \frac{1}{81}$ or about 1 time.

all four of you in a row would lose $100 \cdot \frac{16}{81}$ or about 20 times.

In general, if an event has probability p and the event is independently repeated n times, round the product pn to the nearest integer to find how many times the event is likely to occur.

Questions

COVERING THE IDEAS

1. What is meant by *independent events*?

2. When two events are independent, how is the probability of both occurring calculated?

In 3–7, identify the events as (a) probably independent or (b) probably not independent. Explain your answer.

3. Two people decide to buy concert tickets. They are best friends.

4. Two people decide to buy concert tickets. They are strangers.

5. It rains on Monday and it rains on the next day.

6. You roll a 2 on a fair die. You pick up the die and roll another 2.

7. Jayla's volleyball team wins and her brother's basketball team wins.

8. If the probability of an event happening is $\frac{3}{5}$, what is the probability that it will not happen?

9. Use the spinner at the right to answer the following questions. Assume the spinner is equally likely to land on each of the 5 sections.

    a. What is the probability of getting an even number?

    b. What is the probability of *not* getting an even number?

    c. What is the probability of getting two even numbers in a row?

    d. What is the probability of getting two odd numbers in a row?

    e. What is the probability of getting an odd number and then an even number?

    f. What is the probability of getting four even numbers in a row?

10. Suppose 1 in 100 e-mails to a radio show each day are read on the air. If the e-mails are picked at random,

    a. what is the probability your e-mail will *not* be read on the air?

    b. what is the probability your e-mail will *not* be read on the air all 5 days that you send in e-mails?

APPLYING THE MATHEMATICS

11. Suppose the probability that a basketball player makes a free throw is 60%, and suppose that free throws are independent events.

    a. What is the probability that the player will make two free throws in a row?

    b. What is the probability that the player will miss two free throws in a row?

    c. If the player has 50 opportunities to make two free throws, about how often would you expect both free throws to be made?

12. Alberto figures that the probability of his hockey team winning on Saturday is 65%. Alvin figures that the probability of his basketball team winning on Saturday is 70%. Assume that the events are independent and that the boys' estimates of the probability are accurate.

    a. Find the probability that both teams will win on Saturday.

    b. Find the probability that both teams will lose on Saturday.

    c. Find the probability that Alberto's team will win, but Alvin's team will lose.

    d. Find the probability that Alberto's team will lose, but Alvin's team will win.

The free throw line is 15 feet away from the plane of the backboard.

13. Jennifer is taking a 5-question true-or-false quiz. She has forgotten her glasses and cannot read the questions, so she guesses on each question. Assuming that the questions are equally likely to be true or false, what is the probability that she guesses all five questions correctly?

14. Jennifer goes to her next class and takes a 5-question multiple-choice test. There are four choices for each question. Again, she has to guess answers.

    a. What is the probability that she will get all five questions correct?

    b. What is the probability that she will get all five questions wrong?

15. In 1,000 tosses of a fair quarter, nickel, and dime, what is the most likely number of times the quarter and dime will come up heads and the nickel will come up tails?

REVIEW

16. **a. True or False** If a is a negative number, then $a \cdot a \cdot a$ is negative.

    b. True or False If a is a negative number, then $a \cdot a \cdot a \cdot a$ is positive. **(Lesson 8-3)**

17. A trapezoid has a base of length 10 inches and a height of 7 inches. If the area of the trapezoid is 56 square inches, find the length of the other base of the trapezoid. **(Lesson 7-5)**

18. Determine and describe the rotation symmetry (if any) of each quilt pattern. **(Lesson 6-3)**

a.
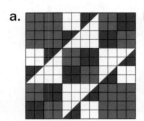
Rocky Road

b.
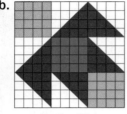
Darting Birds

c.
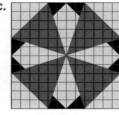
Kaleidoscope

19. **a.** How many lines of symmetry does a regular hexagon have?

    b. How many lines of symmetry does a regular octagon have?

    c. Repeat Parts a and b for other regular polygons with even numbers of sides. **Fill in the blank.** If n is even, then an n-sided polygon has __?__ lines of symmetry. **(Lesson 6-2)**

20. Solve for x. $-4.3 + x = 3.45$ **(Lesson 5-5)**

21. In 1970, the average height of a player in the National Hockey League was 5'11". In 2004, it was 6'1". How much greater was the average height of a hockey player in 2004? **(Lesson 5-3)**

EXPLORATION

22. In the situation described at the beginning of the lesson, the probability of any one person winning the car is $\frac{1}{11,250}$.

    a. What is the probability that, of the 100 people participating, no one will win the car?

    b. What is the probability that *someone* will win the car?

QY ANSWERS

1. $\frac{11,249}{11,250}$

2. They are independent events. Having brown hair or having blue eyes does not affect the chances of having the other.

Lesson

8-5   Combining Percents

▶ **BIG IDEA**   When a percent change of a quantity is followed by a percent change of the result, as in a tax followed by a discount, the final amount can be found by viewing the percent changes as size-change multiplications.

Applying a percent can be thought of as a size change.

Percent Increase as a Size Change

When you buy something in most states, you must pay *sales tax*. Sales taxes are usually from 0% to 8%. A sales tax of 6% is typical on nonfood items.

Example 1

You buy a book for $14.50 in a place where the sales tax is 6%. What will you have to pay, including the tax?

Solution 1 (the longer way) Calculate the 6% tax.

$$6\% \cdot \$14.50 = \$0.87$$

Now add the tax to the price.

$$\$14.50 + 0.87 = \$15.37$$

You will pay $15.37.

Solution 2 (the shorter way) The total with tax is 106% of the original price.

$$106\% \cdot \$14.50 = 1.06 \cdot \$14.50 = \$15.37$$

You will pay $15.37.

We call Solution 1 the longer way because there are two computations. The shorter way has only one computation. Think of the original price as P. Then the amount you pay for the 6% tax is $6\% \cdot P$, or $0.06P$. The total is

$$P + 0.06P.$$

By the Distributive Property,

$$P + 0.06P = 1 \cdot P + 0.06 \cdot P = (1 + 0.06)P = 1.06P.$$

This may seem like a lot of work, but the result shows that the total is 1.06 times, or 106% of, the original price. So all you have to do is one multiplication.

The idea of Example 1 is important. It says that a percent increase can be treated as a single size change. The same is true of a percent decrease.

Percent Decrease as a Size Change

Suppose an item is on sale at 30% off. If the original price of the item was P, then the sale price will be

$$P - 0.30\% \cdot P, \text{ or } P - 0.30P.$$

This expression looks just like sales tax, except that the discount is subtracted. Using the Distributive Property,

$$P - 0.30P = 1 \cdot P - 0.30 \cdot P = (1 - 0.30)P = 0.70P.$$

It may again seem like a lot of work, but the result tells us that when an item is on sale at 30% off, you pay 70% of the original price.

 QY

With this algebra, you can determine what happens when percent discounts are combined.

> ▶ QY
>
> Suppose the sales tax is 5.5% and you buy a book for $14.50. Use one multiplication to determine what you will have to pay, including tax.

GUIDED

Example 2

Michelle had a coupon giving a special 20% birthday discount at her favorite store. She used it to buy an outfit that was already marked down 30%. Michelle said she had saved 50% on the outfit. Was she correct?

Solution If the original price was P, then when the outfit was marked down 30%, the sale price was __?__. Michelle had a 20% coupon, which was applied to the sale price, so she paid __?__% of the sale price. Her total payment was __?__% • (__?__% • P).

$$= \underline{\ ?\ }\% \cdot \underline{\ ?\ }\% \cdot P \quad \text{Associative Property}$$

$$= \underline{\ ?\ } \cdot \underline{\ ?\ } \cdot P \quad \text{Change to decimals.}$$

$$= \underline{\ ?\ } P$$

She paid 56% of the original price. She saved __?__, not 50%.

Check Suppose the outfit sold originally for $200. Then, because 30% of $200 is $60, at 30% off the outfit was on sale for $140. Michelle's coupon gave her 20% off that price, and 20% of $140 is $28. So she saved $60 + $28 = $88, and $\frac{88}{200} = 44\%$.

In Guided Example 2, notice that you can calculate the percentage of saving without knowing the cost of the outfit.

By combining these ideas with what you know about solving equations of the form $ax = b$, you can answer some questions without much difficulty, particularly if you have a calculator to do the arithmetic.

Percent Changes Up and Down

Suppose that there is a combination of a discount and a tax.

Example 3

An item is on sale in a store at 25% off. There is also a 7% tax. What will you pay for the item?

Solution You might think you are getting the item for 18% off its original price, but that is not the case. Suppose the original price is P. Then, using the ideas explained earlier, at 25% off you will pay 75% · P, or 0.75P.

Now you must consider the sales tax. You can calculate the total with a 7% tax by multiplying by 1.07. So you pay

$$1.07 \cdot (0.75P) = 0.8025P.$$

With the tax, you will pay 80.25% of the original price.

Guided Example 4 below illustrates a situation that confuses many people.

GUIDED

Example 4

Suppose the membership of a club increases by 10% and then decreases by 10%. Is the membership back where it started?

Solution If the membership was originally M, then after a 10% increase it is __?__ %M. Now the 10% decrease means that it is 90% of what it was *after* the increase.

So the final membership is __?__ % · __?__ % · M.

$$= \underline{\;?\;} \cdot \underline{\;?\;} M \quad \text{Change to decimals.}$$

$$= \underline{\;?\;} M \quad\quad\quad \text{Arithmetic}$$

It is __?__ % less than it was to begin with. So, the membership is not back where it started.

Questions

COVERING THE IDEAS

1. In Parts a–c, suppose the price of an item is 50 dollars. What is the total amount you will pay in each situation?

   a. There is a 6% tax.

   b. The item is on sale at 35% off and there is no tax.

   c. There is a 6% tax and the item is on sale at 35% off.

   d. Answer Parts a–c if the original price of the item is P dollars.

2. Suppose an item costs C dollars. What will you pay in each circumstance?

   a. There is a 4.5% tax.

   b. The item is on sale at 20% off and there is no tax.

   c. The item is on sale at 20% off and there is a 4.5% tax.

3. Dan gets a senior citizen's discount of 3% at the local auto parts store. He bought an item that was half price. If the item originally cost $43, what did Dan pay?

4. A club had 240 members. The membership then increased by 50%.

   a. What was its new membership?

   b. The membership then decreased by 50%. How did the membership then compare to the original membership?

5. An increase of 20% in price followed an increase of 8% on the new price results in a total increase of __?__%.

6. **Multiple Choice** Catalina used her 15% shopping-day coupon on an item that was already reduced by 40%. What percent of the original price of the item did she pay?

   A 45%　　　B 49%　　　C 51%　　　D 55%

In 7 and 8, consider the following: Children get a **15% discount** on tickets to an amusement park. Jun had a coupon for **5% off** any two tickets. He used the coupon for himself and his 4-year-old son, Jack.

7. If regular admission was $60, what did Jun pay for the two tickets?

8. What was the total discount for Jack's ticket?

APPLYING THE MATHEMATICS

9. In January 2000, the median price of a home in San Diego was $190,000. From January 2000 to January 2003, the median price of a home in San Diego rose 77.6%. From January 2003 to January 2006, the median price rose 46.7%.

   a. What was the median price in 2006?

   b. What was the percent increase from 2000 to 2006?

10. If the membership of a club decreases by 25%, by what percent does it have to increase to return to its original membership?

11. Repeat Question 10 if the membership of the club decreases by 75%.

12. Ms. Ann Thrope went to the outlet mall because there was a 60% off sale on all items. As a senior citizen, she receives an additional 7% discount. Computing $100 - (60 + 7)$, she thought she would pay 33% of the original price. Her nephew computed $0.4 \cdot 0.93$ and said she would pay 37.2% of the original price.

   a. Who was right?

   b. Her niece computed $0.93 \cdot 0.4$ and also said Ms. Thrope would pay 37.2% of the original. Why did Ms. Thrope's niece and nephew get the same answer?

13. Suppose the population of a city is now P, and for each of ten consecutive years, it will increase by 10%. What will its population be at the end of that time?

REVIEW

14. In golf, Paula has a 30% chance of making par on one hole each time she tries it. If Paula plays this hole 3 times, what is the probability that she will make par all three times? (**Lesson 8-4**)

15. If you roll a fair 6-sided die and get a 6 three times in a row during a game show, you win a free cruise to Antarctica. What is the probability that you will win the cruise? (**Lesson 8-4**)

16. The temperature in Mi-Ling's bedroom changed at a rate of 0 degrees per hour. If the temperature was 73°F at 5:00 P.M., what was the temperature when Mi-Ling went to bed at 9:45 P.M.? (**Lesson 8-3**)

17. For homework each night, Rita must read 12 pages of her history book and 8 pages of her Spanish book. Suppose she has this same assignment for 5 days. Write two different expressions to calculate the total number of pages that Rita must read for homework. **(Lesson 7-3)**

18. Write an equation and solve for x in the figure below.
    (Lessons 7-3, 6-5)

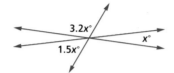

19. If the probability of an event is given by $x - y$, what is the probability, in terms of x and y, that the event will *not* occur? **(Lesson 5-8)**

EXPLORATION

20. Two cities, A and B, have the same population at the beginning of a decade (ten years). Suppose in City A the population grows by 10% in the first year and then in each of the other nine years the population grows by only 1% over the previous year. In City B, the population grows by 1% each year over the previous year for the first nine years and then by 10% in the last year. At the end of the decade, which city, A or B, has the greater population, or are their populations equal?

QY ANSWER

$1.055 \cdot 14.50 = 15.2975 \approx$
$15.30

Lesson

8-6   Solving $ax = b$

> ▶ **BIG IDEA**   An efficient first step in solving an equation of the
> form $ax = b$ for x is to multiply both sides by $\frac{1}{a}$.

How much does a sheet of notebook paper weigh? If you take one
sheet and put it on a scale, the scale register will probably not move.
The sheet may even blow away! One way to answer this question is to
take a large number of sheets of paper and find out what they weigh.

We found that a pad of 500 sheets weighs about 5 pounds 2 ounces,
or about 82 ounces. So, if the weight of one sheet is w ounces, then

$$500 \text{ sheets} \cdot w \, \frac{\text{ounces}}{\text{sheet}} = 82 \text{ ounces.}$$

Without the units, the equation is

$$500w = 82.$$

Because you know 500 times the weight w, you can divide both sides
of this equation by 500 to find $1w$. This is the same as multiplying
both sides of the equation by $\frac{1}{500}$.

$$\frac{1}{500} \cdot 500w = \frac{1}{500} \cdot 82$$

The product of a number and its reciprocal is 1, by the Property
of Reciprocals.

$$1 \cdot w = \frac{82}{500}$$

Now $1 \cdot w = w$, and you can write the right side as a decimal.

$$w = 0.164$$

This process informs us that a sheet of paper weighs about
0.164 ounce, or about $\frac{1}{6}$ of an ounce.

Solving an Equation of the Form $ax = b$

The equation $500w = 82$ is an instance of an equation of the form
$ax = b$, with $a = 500$, w in place of x, and $b = 82$. The strategy
used above relies on multiplying both sides of the equation by the
reciprocal of a, which is the coefficient of x. The strategy will work
for any equation of this form, as long as $a \neq 0$. (When $a = 0$, a has
no reciprocal and the strategy cannot be used.) Multiplying both
sides of an equation by the same number is possible because of the
Multiplication Property of Equality.

Mental Math

Solve for the unknown.

a. $w + 4 = 9$

b. $x - 15 > 4$

c. $y - 8.7 = 0.4$

d. $z + 2.6 < 4.3$

Multiplication Property of Equality

For all real numbers a, x, and y, if $x = y$, then $ax = ay$.

Here is how the Multiplication Property of Equality is used.

$ax = b$ Original equation

$\frac{1}{a}(ax) = \frac{1}{a} \cdot b$ Multiplication Property of Equality ($\text{Multiply both sides by } \frac{1}{a}.$)

$\left(\frac{1}{a} \cdot a\right)x = \frac{1}{a} \cdot b$ Associative Property of Multiplication

$1 \cdot x = \frac{1}{a} \cdot b$ Property of Reciprocals

$x = \frac{1}{a} \cdot b$ Multiplication Property of 1

$x = \frac{b}{a}$ Algebraic definition of division

After a while, you may do all of this in one step. But with more complicated examples, you may wish to include a number of steps.

 QY1

> ▶ QY1
>
> If $120x = 24$, what is the value of x?

Example 1

A pair of boots is marked down 22% to \$58.50. Find the original price.

Solution If the boots are marked down by 22%, they are selling at $100\% - 22\% = 78\%$ of their original price. The price of the boots has been multiplied by a size-change factor of 0.78. Use an equation. Let $p = $ the original price.

78% of the original price = the sale price

$0.78p = 58.50$ Substitute.

$\left(\frac{1}{0.78}\right)0.78p = 58.50\left(\frac{1}{0.78}\right)$ Multiply both sides by $\frac{1}{0.78}$.

$p = 75$ Arithmetic

The original price of the boots was \$75.

 QY2

> ▶ QY2
>
> Check the answer to Example 1.

GUIDED

Example 2

Solve $-\frac{4}{7}m = -\frac{3}{14}$ and check the solution.

Solution This is an equation of the form $ax = b$, with $a = \underline{\quad?\quad}$, $x = m$, and $b = \underline{\quad?\quad}$. We want to multiply both sides by a number that will leave m alone on the left side. That number is $\underline{\quad?\quad}$, the reciprocal of $\underline{\quad?\quad}$.

$$-\frac{4}{7}m = -\frac{3}{14}$$

$$\underline{\ ?\ } \cdot \left(-\frac{4}{7} \cdot m\right) = \underline{\ ?\ } \cdot -\frac{3}{14}$$ Multiply by a reciprocal.

$$\left(\underline{\ ?\ } \cdot -\frac{4}{7}\right) \cdot m = \underline{\ ?\ } \cdot -\frac{3}{14}$$ Associative Property

$$\underline{\ ?\ } \cdot m = \underline{\ ?\ }$$ Multiply.

As a fraction in lowest terms, $m = \underline{\ ?\ }$.

Check Substitute your value for m in the original equation.

Does $-\frac{4}{7} \cdot m = -\frac{3}{14}$?

GUIDED

Example 3

Susannah has 100 shares of a stock that rose by 1.2% over a week's time. At the end of the week, the stock closed at $36.94 a share. What was the opening price at the beginning of the week?

Solution Let $p =$ the opening price of the stock.

The percent increase is 1.2%. So the price of the stock after the increase is $\underline{\ ?\ }\% \cdot p$ or $\underline{\ ?\ }\ p$. Think: $\underline{\ ?\ }\%$ of the original stock price equals 36.94.

$$\underline{\ ?\ }\ p = \underline{\ ?\ }$$

$$(\underline{\ ?\ })\ \underline{\ ?\ }\ p = 36.94\ (\underline{\ ?\ })$$ Multiply both sides by $\frac{1}{\ ?\ }$.

$$p = \underline{\ ?\ }$$ Arithmetic

The opening price of the stock was $\$\underline{\ ?\ }$ a share.

Questions

COVERING THE IDEAS

1. Tamika found that 100 small paper clips together weigh about 50 grams.

   a. Fill in the blanks with numbers, including a w for the unknown quantity.

   $$\underline{\ ?\ }\ \text{paper clips} \cdot \underline{\ ?\ }\ \frac{\text{weight}}{\text{paper clip}} = \underline{\ ?\ }\ \text{total weight}$$

   b. Solve the equation in Part a for w.

On March 26–27, 2004, sixty 9th-grade students at Eisenhower Junior High School in Taylorsville, Utah, constructed the World's Longest Paper Clip Chain. Named "Mega Chain," the continuous paper-clip chain measured an incredible 22.14 miles long and used more than 1,560,000 paper clips.

2. A Cheshire cat slept about 375 hours in a 30-day month.

   a. Write an equation with c as the unknown to determine how many hours, on average, the cat slept per day.

   b. Solve the equation in Part a for c.

In 3–7, a property is named. Give an equation that is an instance of that property in the steps used to solve $ax = b$ for x.

3. Multiplication Property of Equality

4. Multiplicative-Identity Property of 1

5. Associative Property of Multiplication

6. Property of Reciprocals

7. Algebraic definition of division

8. **Fill in the Blank** If $x = y$, then $4.2x = $ __?__ .

9. After a sales tax of 7.5%, a packet of batteries costs $8.60. What is the price of the packet before tax?

10. After a reduction of 30%, the price of a ski jacket was $67.20. What was its original price?

In 11–14, solve and check.

11. $\frac{1}{3}f = 18\%$

12. $\frac{1}{4}r = 2$

13. $3.4w = -5.1$

14. $\frac{3}{7} = \frac{2}{9}x$

In 15 and 16, solve.

15. $3b + 2b = 4{,}500$

16. $9t - 3t + 2t = 2.4$

APPLYING THE MATHEMATICS

17. *Modern School Mathematics Book 2* by Raleigh Schorling was first published in 1935. Solve this problem from that book:

    My father received a tax bill the other day for $78. It was stamped: "Increased 4% because not paid within 60 days of issue." Do you know what the bill was before it was raised?

18. From 2000 to 2004, the Hispanic population in Kendall County, Illinois, grew by 102.7% to 8,284. What was the total Hispanic population in 2000?

19. From 2000 to 2005, the total population in St. Louis County, Missouri, declined by 1.1% to 1,004,666 in 2005. What was the approximate population in 2000?

20. Candace bought two new outfits and paid a total of $226.61. She had a 15% discount coupon for her birthday and the sales tax was 7.5%. What was the total cost of the outfits before the discount was applied and the tax was added?

REVIEW

21. The price of a gallon of gas at one gas station is listed as $3.09 with purchase of a car wash. If that amount is 9% off of the regular price, find the cost per gallon without a car wash. **(Lesson 8-5)**

22. **a.** Graph $\triangle ABC$ with vertices $A = (-2, -1)$, $B = (0, 2)$, and $C = (3, -2)$ and its image $\triangle A'B'C'$ under a size change of magnitude -2.

    b. How do the side lengths of the two triangles compare? **(Lessons 8-3, 7-7)**

23. A size change of magnitude -6 is like a size change of magnitude 6 followed by a rotation of what magnitude? **(Lessons 8-3, 7-7, 6-3)**

24. The lava dome in the crater of Mt. St. Helens was 1,254 feet high in the summer of 2006. It is growing at a rate of 6 feet per day. How many days must pass before the dome is more than $\frac{1}{4}$ mile high? (*Note:* 1 mile = 5,280 feet.) **(Lesson 8-2)**

25. **True or False** A size change of magnitude 1 is an expansion. **(Lesson 7-7)**

The crater and lava dome of Mount Saint Helens is shown above.

EXPLORATION

26. A box holding 100 large paper clips, when empty, weighs about 10 grams. When full, the box weighs about 110 grams.

    a. What is the weight of a single large paper clip?

    b. Suppose the box holding 100 large paper clips weighed e grams when empty and f grams when full. What, then, would be the weight of a single large paper clip?

27. Find an item in your house or elsewhere that weighs so little that it does not register on a scale, but that you may have a lot of (like paper or unpopped popcorn). Weigh a large number of this item and use that weight to determine the weight of one item. Write a few sentences describing what you did.

QY ANSWERS

1. 0.2

2. 22% of $75 is $16.50. $75 − $16.50 = $58.50, so, it checks.

Lesson

8-7

Graphing $y = ax + b$

Match the graph with the equation.

i. $y = 5$

ii. $y = x$

iii. $y = x + 7$

iv. $y = x - 4$

a.

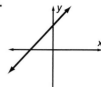

b.

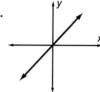

c.

d.

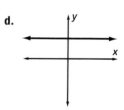

▶ **BIG IDEA**   The graph of all points (x, y) satisfying an equation of the form $y = ax + b$ is a line.

A tortoise is one of the slowest reptiles. In one test, a tortoise walked about 0.11 meter per second. This means that in t seconds, at this rate a tortoise walks about d meters, where $d = 0.11t$.

You can calculate values of d given values of t. If $t = 1$, then $d = 0.11$. That is, in 1 second, a tortoise travels 0.11 meter. If $t = 5$, then $d = 0.55$. That is, in 5 seconds, a tortoise travels 0.55 meter.

STOP QY1

Graphing an Equation of the Form $y = ax$

With a graphing calculator or other graphing utility, you can graph the pairs of values d and t.

Activity 1

Graph the pairs of values that satisfy $d = 0.11t$.

Step 1 *Identify the variables.* Most graphing calculators use only the variables x and y to graph. The variable x is the variable for which we substitute values, and the variable y is the result of calculations using x. In this case, the time t is x and the distance d is y, so you will be graphing $y = 0.11 x$.

Step 2 *Set the window.* Do it the same way as you did in Lesson 1-10. A reasonable domain for x is from 0 to 2 minutes, or 120 seconds, so we set Xmin $= -5$ and Xmax $= 125$. When $x = -5, y = -0.55$. When $x = 120, y = 13.2$. So we set Ymin $= -1$ and Ymax $= 15$.

Step 3 *Enter the equation.* Find the Y= key and enter Y1 $= 0.11*$X . Enter GRAPH and you should see the following graph. The graph is a line.

▶ **QY1**

At this rate, how far does a tortoise travel in 1 minute?

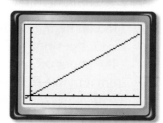

Step 4 *Check your work.* Use the TRACE key to see that points on the graph satisfy the equation $y = 0.11x$.

Notice that the situation described above is in the form $y = ax$, where a is a fixed real number and the points (x, y) are graphed. For instance, in $d = 0.11t$, $a = 0.11$ and d and t take the place of x and y, respectively. Any equation of this form is called a *linear equation* because its graph is a *line*. When x is not restricted to whole numbers, then the graph consists of all points on the line.

Graphing an Equation of the Form $y = k$

Activity 2

Use the graph from Activity 1 to answer this question: About how long does it take the tortoise to travel 3 meters?

To find the number of seconds it will take the tortoise, traveling at 0.11 m/sec, to reach 3 m, you want to solve the equation $0.11x = 3$.

Step 1 Enter a second equation. Use the same variables and the same window and keep the graph that you had for $Y1 = 0.11*X$. Go to the GRAPH menu and enter $Y2 = 3$. Then graph. Your graph should look like the following.

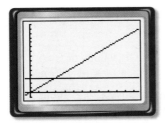

Step 2 *Find the point of intersection of the two graphs.* The graphs of $Y1 = 0.11*X$ and $Y2 = 3$ will intersect at a point. The first coordinate of this point is the solution to the equation $0.11x = 3$. Use the ZOOM and TRACE or INTERSECT keys to approximate the x-coordinate of the intersection point.

Graphs like those in Activity 2 can often only estimate a solution to an equation. Sometimes when you do not know how to solve the equation, graphs can provide a good method. In the case of $3 = 0.11x$, however, you have learned how to solve the equation for an exact value.

 QY2

The equation $Y2 = 3$ is of the form $y = k$, where k is a fixed number. The graph of an equation of this form is a horizontal line.

▶ **QY2**

Solve the equation $3 = 0.11x$ using the Multiplication Property of Equality.

Graphs are often useful for comparing information.

Activity 3

The sloth is a mammal whose average speed is even less than that of the tortoise. It hangs from branches of trees moving at a speed of 0.06 meter per second. Graph the equation $d = 0.06t$ on the same axes as the graph of Activity 1 and use your graph to determine how much farther a tortoise would travel in 1 minute than a sloth does.

Graphing an Equation of the Form $y = ax + b$

The graph of an equation of the form $y = ax$ will always pass through the origin $(0, 0)$ because $0 = a \cdot 0$. If you add b to the right side, the graph will be b units higher (lower, if b is negative). So the graph of an equation of the form $y = ax + b$ is a line that contains the point $(0, b)$. You should be able to graph an equation of this form by hand. The Example shows how to do this.

Example

Graph the line with equation $y = -5x + 3$ and check that the graph is correct.

Solution The graphs on the next page show how to do this using three steps. You should put all your work on one graph.

Step 1 Substitute numbers for x and find the corresponding values of y. For instance, we choose $x = -1$. Then $y = -5 \cdot -1 + 3 = 5 + 3 = 8$. This means that $(-1, 8)$ is on the line. Now we choose $x = 2$. Then $y = -5 \cdot 2 + 3 = -10 + 3 = -7$. So $(2, -7)$ is on the line.

Step 2 Draw a line through the points. Label the line with the equation.

Step 3 Pick a third value for x. We pick $x = 0$ because it simplifies the computation. Then, according to the equation, $y = -5 \cdot 0 + 3 = 3$. This means that $(0, 3)$ should be on the graph. Is it? Yes; so the graph is correct.

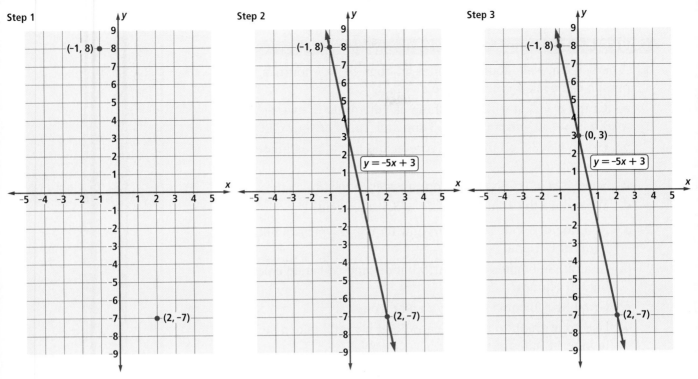

Caution: When graphing lines, it is easy to make errors in calculation. If an error is made, then a point will be incorrect. You must check with a third point. If the three points do not lie on the same line, try a fourth point. Keep trying points until you see the pattern of the graph.

The following activity shows how you can predict what a graph will look like before plotting any points.

Activity 4

Step 1 Clear your calculator of the graphs from Activities 1, 2, and 3.

Step 2 Choose an appropriate window and graph Y1 = −5*X + 3. The graph should match the Example.

Step 3 Graph Y2 = −5*X + 10.

Step 4 At what point does the graph of Y2 = −5*X + 10 intersect the y-axis?

Step 5 Describe how the graphs of Y1 = −5*X + 3 and Y2 = −5*X + 10 compare.

Step 6 Make up an equation of the form Y3 = −5*X + b, where you pick the value of b but b is negative. Predict where its graph will be. Then graph the equation to check your prediction.

Questions

COVERING THE IDEAS

1. A person can walk about 2.5 miles an hour. So in t hours, a person can walk d miles, where $d = 2.5t$.
   a. Graph $d = 2.5t$ with a graphing calculator on the window Xmin = -1, Xmax = 3, and Ymin and Ymax of your choosing.
   b. Graph $y = 3.5$ on the same screen and use it to estimate a solution to $2.5t = 3.5$.
   c. Solve $2.5t = 3.5$ to check your answer to Part b.
   d. What does the solution to $2.5t = 3.5$ represent?

2. a. At a rate of 6 miles per hour, how far could a person bike in 2 hours 15 minutes?
   b. At a rate of 6 miles per hour, what distance d would a person bike in t hours?
   c. Graph the formula relating d and t from Part b.
   d. Use your graph to estimate how long it would take a person to bike 14 miles at this rate.

3. The line $y = -5x + 3$ was graphed in this lesson. Give the coordinates of two points on this line that are not identified on the graph.

4. By hand, graph the line with equation $y = 3x - 7$.

In 5–7, graph the equation.

5. $y = -5x$
6. $6x = y$
7. $y = -2.5x + 3$

8. How do the graphs of $y = \frac{1}{2}x - 4$ and $y = \frac{1}{2}x + 3$ compare? Explain your answer.

9. **Multiple Choice** Which equation has a graph that is a horizontal line?
   A $y = 4$
   B $y = 4x$
   C $x = 4$
   D $x = 4y$

10. Name two points on the graph of $y = -10$.

APPLYING THE MATHEMATICS

11. Water in a swimming pool is currently 3.2 meters deep. The owners will empty the pool for cleaning. After opening a valve, the depth of the water will decrease 2 centimeters, or 0.02 meter, per minute. Then $d = 3.2 - 0.02t$, where d is the depth of the pool when the valve has been open for t minutes.

   a. Graph the equation $d = 3.2 - 0.02t$ on a suitable window.

   b. Use the graph to estimate when the pool will have a depth of 1 meter.

   c. Use the graph to estimate when the pool will be empty, that is, have a depth of 0 meters.

12. **Multiple Choice** Which line could be the graph of $y = 2x - 3$?

   A
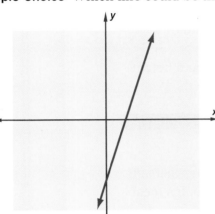

   B
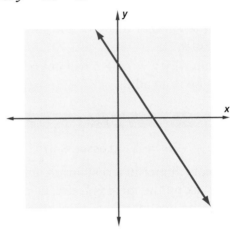

   C
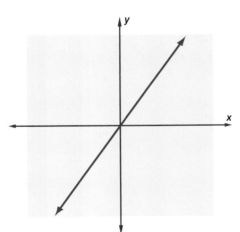

   D
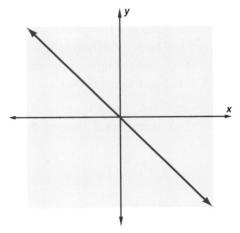

13. Gabriel has a cell phone with a 600-minute-a-month plan for a fixed rate. He figures he can talk 20 minutes a day without having to pay extra. Suppose he talks for 20 minutes a day and after d days he has L minutes left on his plan.

    a. Make a spreadsheet of values of d and L, when $d = 1, 2, 3, 4,$ and 5.

    b. Graph the ordered pairs (d, L) in your table.

    c. Write an equation that gives L in terms of d.

    d. Will he have any minutes left after 3 weeks?

14. Dan Delion is 9 years old. His mother says he is growing "like a weed," 7 centimeters a year. He is now 140 centimeters tall.

    a. Suppose Dan continues to grow at this rate. Make a table with four pairs of numbers for his age x (in years) and his height y (in centimeters).

    b. Graph the four pairs.

    c. An equation that relates x and y is: $y = 7x + b$. Find the value of b.

    d. Explain why $y = 7x + b$ will not relate Dan's age and height when he is an adult.

REVIEW

15. Solve $5w + -2w = 27$. **(Lesson 8-6)**

16. Rodney eats dinner in a restaurant, and his meal costs $38.03. If the sales tax on the meal is 7.25%, calculate the cost of his meal including the tax but without tip. **(Lesson 8-5)**

17. Antoine brings a photo to a photo shop to be enlarged. He first tells the clerk that he wants the photo to be 1.5 times as large. After the clerk enlarges the photo, Antoine realizes that the photo is now too large. He then tells the clerk to shrink the photo by 10%. If the original height of the photo was 6 inches, what is the height of the photo now? **(Lessons 8-5, 7-7)**

18. If the image of $(7, -2)$ is $(3.5, -1)$, is the size change an expansion or a contraction? **(Lesson 7-7)**

19. At the start of Stage 13 of the 2004 Tour de France, Lance Armstrong was in second place with an overall time of 51 hours 56 minutes 31 seconds. Ivan Basso was in sixth place with a time of 51 hours 57 minutes 40 seconds. Both men completed Stage 13 with the same time of 6 hours 4 minutes and 38 seconds. Write an inequality comparing the overall times of the two riders after this stage. **(Lesson 5-6)**

EXPLORATION

20. The formulas for the first-class postal rates for 1990, 2000, and 2006 are listed below. w is the weight (rounded up to the nearest ounce) and c is the cost in cents.

2006: $c = 24w + 15$
2000: $c = 22w + 11$
1990: $c = 20w + 5$

Ann Onimuss
18 Katon Boulevard
Waldonville, GA 12399

Create a scatterplot that displays the cost of mailing a first-class letter in 1990, 2000, and 2006. Use your scatterplot to fill in the blanks. The cost to mail a 6-ounce letter in 1990 would only mail a __?__-ounce letter in 2000 and a __?__-ounce letter in 2006.

Lesson

8-8 Solving *ax* + *b* = *c*

Vocabulary

equation of the form
ax + *b* = *c*

▶ **BIG IDEA** An efficient procedure for solving an equation of the form *ax* + *b* = *c* is to add −*b* to both sides and to then multiply both resulting sides by $\frac{1}{a}$.

In Lesson 8-7, you saw how to solve an equation of the form *ax* + *b* = *c* by graphing. In this lesson, you will solve equations of this form by using the Addition and Multiplication Properties of Equality.

Picturing the Process

Here is a balance-scale picture of the equation $4w + 5 = 17$. On the scale, 4 boxes of equal unknown weight and five 1-kilogram weights balance with seventeen 1-kilogram weights.

$$4w + 5 = 17$$

You can find the weight *w* of one box in two steps. Each step keeps the scale balanced.

Step 1 Remove five 1-kilogram weights from each side.

$$4w = 12$$

Step 2 Distribute the 12 remaining weights equally among the 4 boxes.

$$w = 3$$

So one box weighs 3 kilograms. Example 1 shows the same steps without the balance scale.

Example 1

Solve $4x + 5 = 17$.

Solution

$4x + 5 + \text{-}5 = 17 + \text{-}5$	Addition Property of Equality (Add -5 to each side.)
$4x = 12$	Arithmetic
$\frac{1}{4} \cdot 4x = \frac{1}{4} \cdot 12$	Multiplication Property of Equality (Multiply both sides by $\frac{1}{4}$.)
$x = 3$	Arithmetic

Check Substitute 3 for x in the original equation. Does $4 \cdot 3 + 5 = 17$? Yes. It checks.

In the equation $4x + 5 = 17$, the unknown x is multiplied by a number. Then a second number is added. We call this an **equation of the form $ax + b = c$.** In this case, $a = 4$, $b = 5$, and $c = 17$.

Notice how the solution to Example 1 can be seen on a graph. At the right, the lines with equations $y = 4x + 5$ and $y = 17$ are graphed. They intersect at $(3, 17)$. The point of intersection indicates that when $x = 3$, the value of $4x + 5$ is 17. This shows that 3 is a solution to $4x + 5 = 17$.

Because the graph of $y = ax + b$ is a line, the equation $ax + b = c$ is a *linear equation.* All linear equations in this form can be solved with two major steps. First add $-b$ to both sides. This step leaves the term with the variable alone on one side. Then multiply both sides by $\frac{1}{a}$ (or, equivalently, divide both sides by a).

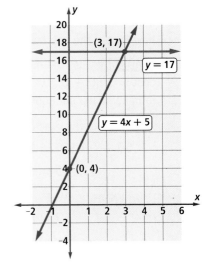

Example 2

Solve the equation $6.4 - 7x = 6.8$.

Solution This equation is of the form $ax + b = c$ with $a = -7$, $b = 6.4$ and $c = 6.8$. Add $-b$ to both sides to isolate the term with the unknown.

$6.4 - 7x = 6.8$	
$\text{-}6.4 + 6.4 - 7x = \text{-}6.4 + 6.8$	Addition Property of Equality
$\text{-}7x = 0.4$	Arithmetic

(continued on next page)

Multiply both sides by the reciprocal of -7.

$$\frac{1}{-7} \cdot -7x = \frac{1}{-7} \cdot 0.4 \qquad \text{Multiplication Property of Equality}$$

$$x = -\frac{0.4}{7}$$

$$= -\frac{4}{70} = -\frac{2}{35} \qquad \text{Arithmetic}$$

Check Substitute.

$$6.4 - 7 \cdot -\frac{2}{35} = 6.4 + \frac{14}{35} = 6.4 + \frac{2}{5} = 6.4 + 0.4 = 6.8.$$

So, it checks.

Here is a problem that leads to an equation of the form $ax + b = c$.

GUIDED

Example 3

Taxicabs in most places in the United States begin each trip by setting the meter at a certain amount. Then they add another amount for every part of a mile that you travel. In Baltimore, Maryland, in 2005, a taxicab meter was set at \$1.80. Then the meter added 20¢ for each $\frac{1}{8}$ mile traveled. If a trip cost \$9.60, how far did the cab travel?

Solution Let n be the number of $\frac{1}{8}$ miles traveled. Then, total cost = $1.80 + 0.20n$ and the equation $9.60 = 1.80 + 0.20n$ represents the situation. Describe what was done in each step.

Baltimore's Inner Harbor

$$9.60 = 1.80 + 0.20n \qquad \text{Original Equation}$$

$$9.60 + (-1.80) = 1.80 + (-1.80) + 0.20n \qquad \underline{\quad ? \quad}$$

$$7.80 = 0.20n \qquad \underline{\quad ? \quad}$$

$$\left(\frac{1}{0.20}\right) 7.80 = \left(\frac{1}{0.20}\right) 0.20n \qquad \underline{\quad ? \quad}$$

$$39 = n \qquad \underline{\quad ? \quad}$$

The taxicab traveled $39 \cdot \frac{1}{8}$ miles, or $4\frac{7}{8}$ miles, in all.

 GAME Now you can play *X-Tac-Toe: ax + b = c*. The directions for this game are on page G13 at the back of your book.

In the following example, the original equation is not in $ax + b = c$ form. Use the Distributive Property, and collect like terms to express the equation in that form.

GUIDED

Example 4

Solve $50 = 3x + 2(x - 2)$.

Solution

Step 1 Use the Distributive Property and combine like terms to put this equation in $ax + b = c$ form.

$$50 = 3x + \underline{\ ?\ } + \underline{\ ?\ }$$

$$50 = \underline{\ ?\ } x + \underline{\ ?\ }$$

Step 2 Apply the Addition Property of Equality.

$$50 + \underline{\ ?\ } = \underline{\ ?\ } x + \underline{\ ?\ } + \underline{\ ?\ }$$

$$\underline{\ ?\ } = \underline{\ ?\ } x$$

Step 3 Apply the Multiplication Property of Equality.

$$\underline{\ ?\ } \cdot \underline{\ ?\ } = \underline{\ ?\ } \cdot \underline{\ ?\ } x$$

$$\underline{\ ?\ } = x$$

Check Use the original equation. Does $50 = 3 \cdot \underline{\ ?\ } + 2(\underline{\ ?\ } - 2)$?

Notice that each step in the examples is written underneath the previous step and the equal signs are lined up. Organization of your work is helpful when solving equations.

Questions

COVERING THE IDEAS

1. **a.** Illustrate how to solve the equation $3w + 7 = 22$ using a balance scale.

   b. Show how the graphs of $y = 3w + 7$ and $y = 22$ picture the solution to the equation $3w + 7 = 22$.

2. **a.** **Fill in the Blank** To solve the equation $8 - 2x = -4$, you can first add $\underline{\ ?\ }$ to both sides.

   b. Solve $8 - 2x = -4$. Show your work.

   c. Show how the graphs of $y = 8 - 2x$ and $y = -4$ picture the solution to the equation $8 - 2x = -4$.

3. **a.** What can be the first step in solving $11 + 12y + 13 = 60$?

   b. Solve this equation. Show your work.

4. At the right, steps are shown to solve the equation $5y - 13 = 32$. Name the property or properties justifying each step.

   a. $5y - 13 + 13 = 32 + 13$

   b. $5y - 0 = 45$

   c. $5y = 45$

   d. $\frac{1}{5} \cdot 5y = \frac{1}{5} \cdot 45$

   e. $1 \cdot y = 9$

   f. $y = 9$

5. a. Solve $14 + 5x = -21$. Show your work.

b. Show how the graphs of $y = 14 + 5x$ and $y = -21$ picture the solution to the equation $14 + 5x = -21$.

6. Use the situation in Example 3.

a. How much would it cost to take a taxicab to go 2 miles?

b. How far did the taxicab travel if a trip cost $10.80?

In 7 and 8, the equation is of the form $ax + b = c$.
a. Identify a, b, and c.
b. Solve the equation.

7. $5y - 13 = 132$

8. $41 = 63 + \frac{3}{2}x$

In 9–12, solve and check.

9. $400 = 6y + 4(y + 5)$

10. $3(2x - 11) = 66$

11. $-3B + 5B + 7 = -9$

12. $0 = 6 + 2v - 0.5v + 3$

APPLYING THE MATHEMATICS

13. Paolo estimates that a trip to Brazil to see relatives will cost $1,500 for air fare and $90 a day for living expenses.

a. What will it cost to stay n days?

b. How long can Paolo stay for $2,500?

14. In 2005, the most expensive U.S. city in which to take a taxicab was Honolulu. In Honolulu, it cost $2.45, plus 35¢ for every $\frac{1}{8}$ mile traveled.

a. How much would it cost for a 2.5-mile taxicab ride?

b. If a taxicab fare in Honolulu was $10.15, how long was the trip?

15. One size of French fries have about 11 calories apiece. So, if you eat F French fries, you take in about $11F$ calories. A plain 4-ounce hamburger with a bun has about 420 calories. So together the hamburger and French fries have about $420 + 11F$ calories.

a. How many calories are in a plain 4-oz hamburger with a bun and 20 French fries?

b. How many French fries can you eat with a plain 4-oz hamburger with a bun for a total of 800 calories?

16. In a *convex* polygon, such as a stop sign, all of the angles point outward. The sum of the measures of the angles of a convex polygon of n sides is $180° (n - 2)$. If the sum of the measures of the angles in a polygon is $2,520°$, you can find the number of sides of the polygon by solving the equation $2,520 = 180(n - 2)$.

   a. Solve this equation by first using the Distributive Property on the right side of the equation and then working from there.

   b. Solve this equation by first dividing both sides by 180 and then working from there.

   c. Which way was easier? Why?

REVIEW

17. Graph the line with equation $y = 4x + 2$. **(Lesson 8-7)**

In **18–21**, simplify. **(Lessons 8-3, 7-2, 3-3)**

18. $-9 \cdot -1 + -9 \cdot -11$

19. $-\frac{4}{5} \cdot -\frac{5}{6}$

20. $\left(\frac{2}{3} + -\frac{1}{2}\right) \cdot (-15)$

21. $18 \cdot 0 \cdot \frac{1}{18} + 3 \cdot -\frac{1}{3}$

22. If a positive and a negative number are multiplied, then their product is negative.

   a. Write the converse.

   b. Is the converse true or false? If false, give a counterexample. **(Lessons 8-3, 4-3)**

23. A copy machine makes copies at the rate of 20 pages per minute. How long will it take to copy 1,200 documents with 4 pages per document? **(Lesson 8-2)**

24. a. Without having her bank statement in front of her, Terri estimates that she has between $32 and $50 in her bank account. Graph this situation on a number line.

   b. Terri then writes a check for $42.12. What could her balance be now? Graph the new result on a number line.

   c. If the probability of any amount within her estimate is equally likely, what is the probability that she will have a negative balance after the check is applied to her account? Round your answer to the nearest percent. **(Lessons 5-8, 2-8)**

EXPLORATION

25. a. Find rates for taxicab rides near where you live.

   b. How far can you travel for $10.00?

Lesson

8-9 Solving $ax + b < c$

> ► **BIG IDEA** An efficient procedure for solving an equation of the form $ax + b < c$ is to add $-b$ to both sides, then multiply both resulting sides by $\frac{1}{a}$.

In Lesson 5-6, you solved inequalities of the form $x + a < b$ by using the Addition Property of Inequality: For any real numbers a, x, and y, if $x < y$, then $x + a < y + a$. This means that you can add any number to both sides of an inequality and a new true inequality is created.

The Multiplication Property of Inequality

When a similar process is used with multiplication, the results are slightly different. Let us begin with five numbers: –5, –2, 0, 1, and 4. Notice they are in order from least to greatest.

| –5 | –2 | 0 | 1 | 4 |

First we multiply each number by 2.

| $2 \cdot -5$ | $2 \cdot -2$ | $2 \cdot 0$ | $2 \cdot 1$ | $2 \cdot 4$ |
| –10 | –4 | 0 | 2 | 8 |

Look at the two number lines below and the order of the products. The order has not changed: $-10 < -4 < 0 < 2 < 8$.

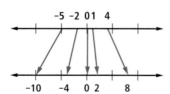

The second number line is an expansion of the first, similar to the expansions of polygons on the coordinate plane in Lesson 7-7.

Next, we multiply by a negative number, say –3.

| $-3 \cdot -5$ | $-3 \cdot -2$ | $-3 \cdot 0$ | $-3 \cdot 1$ | $-3 \cdot 4$ |
| 15 | 6 | 0 | –3 | –12 |

Mental Math

Solve for the unknown.

a. $2m = 8$

b. $n + 5 = 7$

c. $3p + 4 = 13$

d. $9 - 5q = 24$

Look at the order of the products. Now the order is reversed:
15 > 6 > 0 > –3 > –12. When we connect the original numbers to
the products, the segments intersect.

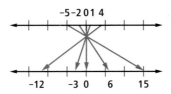

The result is similar to the expansions of polygons on the coordinate
plane in Lesson 8-3, where multiplication by a negative number
rotated them 180°. The points have been rotated 180° and expanded
by a factor of 3.

These examples show that multiplying both sides of an inequality by
a positive number keeps the direction or *sense* of the inequality. But
multiplying both sides by a negative number reverses the direction
or sense. These are the two parts of the *Multiplication Property of
Inequality*.

> ### Multiplication Property of Inequality
>
> For any real numbers x and y:
> If $x < y$ and a is positive, then $ax < ay$.
>
> If $x < y$ and a is negative, then $ax > ay$.

 QY1

A Situation Leading to $ax \geq b$

Before solving more complicated inequalities, we will look at a
simpler situation.

▶ **QY1**

Fill in the blank with the
symbol <, >, or =.
If $x < y$, then
$-2x$ ___?___ $- 2y$.
If $m > n$, then
$\frac{1}{2}m$ ___?___ $\frac{1}{2}n$.

GUIDED

Example 1

Greg said he is planning to trade in his MP3 player for a new model because there is an offer of an 8% discount on the new one. He claims he will save at least $22. How much does the new MP3 player cost?

Solution Let $P =$ the price of the MP3 player before the discount. The amount of the discount is __?__.

Recall that the words "at least" mean "greater than or equal to." So the desired inequality is

$$0.08P \geq 22.$$

This inequality is solved almost exactly as if it were an equation.

$0.08P \geq 22$	Original inequality
__?__ $\cdot\, 0.08P \geq 22 \cdot$ __?__	Multiplication Property of Inequality
__?__ $P \geq 22 \cdot$ __?__	Property of Reciprocals
$P \geq 22 \cdot$ __?__	Multiplicative Identity Property of 1
$P \geq$ __?__	Arithmetic

The new MP3 player costs at least $275.

Check Unlike an equation, there are two parts to the check of any inequality.

Part 1 Does 275 make the *equation* true?
Is $0.08 \cdot 275 = 22$? Yes. This means that the endpoint of the inequality is correct.

Part 2 Does a number greater than 275 make the inequality true?
We choose 280, which is greater than 275. Substitute 280 for p in the original inequality.
Is $0.08 \cdot 280 > 22$? Yes; $22.4 > 22$.

 QY2

Multiplying an Inequality by a Negative Number

Completing both parts of the check for an inequality is particularly important when the inequality must be multiplied by a negative number in order to solve it.

> ▶ **QY2**
>
> Kiyo solved the inequality $24x < -12$ and got the answer $x < -2$. Do one check to show her solution was incorrect.

If you are solving an inequality and multiply by a negative number, you must be careful with the sense of the inequality.

Example 2

Solve and check $-\frac{5}{9} < -\frac{2}{3}m$.

Solution

$$-\frac{5}{9} < -\frac{2}{3}m \qquad \text{Original inequality}$$

$$-\frac{3}{2} \cdot -\frac{5}{9} > -\frac{3}{2} \cdot -\frac{2}{3}m \qquad \text{Multiplication Property of Inequality}$$

$$-\frac{3}{2} \cdot -\frac{5}{9} > 1m \qquad \text{Property of Reciprocals}$$

$$\frac{5}{6} > m \qquad \text{Arithmetic}$$

Many people put m on the left side and write $m < \frac{5}{6}$.

Check

Part 1 Does $\frac{5}{6}$ make the equation true?

$$\text{Is } -\frac{5}{9} = -\frac{2}{3} \cdot \frac{5}{6}?$$

$$\text{Is } -\frac{5}{9} = -\frac{10}{18}?$$

Yes. This means the endpoint of the inequality is correct.

Part 2 Does a number less than $\frac{5}{6}$ make the inequality true? We choose 0, which is less than $\frac{5}{6}$. Substitute 0 for m in the original inequality.

$$\text{Is } -\frac{5}{9} < -\frac{2}{3} \cdot 0?$$

$$\text{Is } -\frac{5}{9} < 0?$$

Yes. This means the direction of the inequality is correct.

 GAME Now you can play *X-Tac-Toe: ax + b < c*. The directions for this game are on page G14 at the back of your book.

A Situation Leading to *ax + b < c*

One size of French fry contains about 11 calories per fry, and a plain 4-ounce hamburger with a bun has about 420 calories. So if you eat a plain hamburger with *F* French fries, you have taken in a total of *y* calories, where

$y = 420 + 11F$ calories.

Of course, if you put ketchup and other things on your hamburger or French fries, you will have more calories. But for Example 3, we assume you have just a hamburger and French fries.

GUIDED

Example 3

In the situation described on page 541, how many French fries can you eat with a plain 4-ounce hamburger and consume fewer than 800 calories?

Solution The question asks how many you can consume and *be under* 800 calories. Consequently, there is an inequality to solve:

$$420 + 11F < 800.$$

Recall that solving $ax < b$ is just like solving $ax = b$ unless a is negative. The same holds for inequalities of the form $ax + b < c$. Add -420 to both sides.

$$\underline{?} + 420 + 11F < \underline{?} + 800$$

$$11F < \underline{?}$$

Now multiply both sides by $\underline{?}$. Because you are multiplying by a $\underline{?}$ number, the sense of the inequality does not change.

$$\underline{?} \cdot 11F < \underline{?} \cdot \underline{?}$$

$$F < \underline{?}$$

You can eat $\underline{?}$ or fewer French fries.

 QY3

> ▶ **QY3**
>
> A turkey burger on a bun has about 340 calories. If you order a plain turkey burger and bun and want to consume fewer than 800 calories, how may French fries can you eat?

Questions

COVERING THE IDEAS

1. Consider the inequality $2 < 7$. Give the true inequality that results from each operation.

   a. 4 is subtracted from both sides.

   b. Each side is multiplied by 1.5.

   c. Each side is multiplied by -2.

2. The Multiplication Property of Inequality has two parts.

   a. How are they different?   b. How are they the same?

In 3 and 4, translate the situation into an inequality of the form $ax > b$, $ax \geq b$, $ax < b$, or $ax \leq b$. Then solve the inequality to answer the question.

3. Cicely bought identical sweaters for her six sisters and paid no more than $180 in all. How much did she pay for each sweater?

4. If an auditorium seats at least 2,000 people and there are 25 rows, then what is the average number of seats in each row?

5. Group these inequalities by those that have the same solutions.
   a. $2x > 4$ b. $-2x > -4$ c. $4 > 2x$ d. $-4 > -2x$
   e. $4 < 2x$ f. $-4 > -2x$ g. $-4 < -2x$ h. $2x < 4$

In 6–8, refer to the situation in Example 3.

6. One restaurant puts about 50 small French fries in its medium-size side order of fries. Each fry has about 9 calories. If you eat a medium-size order of fries with a 4-ounce plain hamburger and a bun, how many calories will you take in?

7. How many 11-calorie French fries can you eat with a plain 4-ounce hamburger and consume *more than* 800 calories?

8. How many 11-calorie French fries can you eat with a plain 4-ounce hamburger and consume *fewer than* 600 calories?

For 9–12, solve each inequality. Check your solution.

9. $3x \geq 276$

10. $\frac{3}{5}z > -\frac{1}{2}$

11. $12 - 4a < 10$

12. $880 \geq 3{,}120 - 100b$

APPLYING THE MATHEMATICS

13. Al budgets $100 for lunches during a month, and he estimates that each lunch costs $5.

    a. After he has purchased x lunches, how much money does he have left?

    b. Let y be the amount of money he has left after he has purchased x lunches. Graph the relationship between y and x.

    c. Use your graph to determine how many lunches he can purchase and have at least $20 left for a nice dinner.

    d. What inequality can be solved to give the answer to Part c?

14. Let m and n be two real numbers such that $m < n$. Name the property justifying each step to show that taking the opposite of each side of an inequality changes the direction of that inequality.

$$m < n$$
   a. $m - n < n - n$
   b. $m - n < 0$
   c. $m - m - n < 0 - m$
   d. $-n < -m$
            or $-m > -n$

In 15 and 16, write an inequality and solve.

15. A couple budgeted $12,000 for the dinner after their wedding. They chose a meal priced at $85 per person. What is the greatest number of people that they could accommodate at the dinner?

16. Use the drawing at the right. m∠*FAC* < 90°. Solve for *x*.

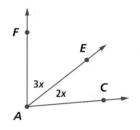

In 17–19, solve the inequality.

17. $5n + 3n \geq -40$

18. $1{,}001 \geq -13(7t - 10)$

19. $(x + 1) + (2x + 2) + (3x + 3) > 4$

20. Three students wanted to solve the problem $-2 > -r$.

Nina's Solution	Booker's Solution	Andrew's Solution
Add 2 to both sides. Add *r* to both sides. The result is the solution.	Multiply both sides by –1 and change the sense of the inequality. The result is the solution.	Graph the inequality. Then think that *r* is the opposite of –*r* and flip the graph.

Which solution gives a correct answer? Show work to prove your claim. Which way do you prefer to solve inequalities of this type? Use your preferred way to solve $-a \geq 121$.

REVIEW

21. Water drains from a pool at a rate of 3 cm per minute. If the original depth of the water in the pool is 150 cm, how long will it take the water in the pool to be only 90 cm deep? **(Lesson 8-6)**

22. In his first season with the New York Knicks, Stephon Marbury scored 931 points, averaging 19.8 points per game. How many games did he play for the Knicks that season? **(Lesson 8-6)**

23. If the area of a rectangular plot of land is $\frac{2}{5}$ square kilometer and one dimension of the plot is $\frac{1}{4}$ kilometer, what is the other dimension? **(Lessons 8-6, 7-2)**

24. In the Northern Hemisphere, tornados and cyclones rotate counterclockwise. In one second, a weak tornado may complete 1.25 full rotations. What is the magnitude of the rotation such a tornado would complete in one minute? **(Lesson 6-3)**

The United States averages over 1,000 tornadoes per year, more than any other country in the world. Canada is in second place with 80–100 per year.

EXPLORATION

25. Use the Internet or another resource to find the numbers of calories for some foods that you like and make up a situation that leads to an inequality like the one in Example 3.

QY ANSWERS

1. > ; >

2. $24(-2) = -48$, not -12

3. 41 or fewer French fries

Chapter 8 Projects

1 Complex Rate Units

Some rate units contain more than one unit in the numerator or denominator. For example, the price of electricity is often measured in $\frac{\text{cents}}{\text{kilowatt-hour}}$, where the kilowatt is a unit of power. If the price is $10 \frac{\text{cents}}{\text{kilowatt-hour}}$, then electricity costs 10 cents for each kilowatt of power used each hour. With additional information, you can convert these rates into simple rates. For instance, a 100-watt (0.1-kilowatt) light bulb would cost

$$0.1 \text{ kilowatt} \cdot 10 \frac{\text{cents}}{\text{kilowatt-hour}} = 1 \frac{\text{cent}}{\text{hour}} \text{ to run.}$$

In other words, you pay 1 cent for every hour the light bulb is on. Running an appliance for 8 hours would cost

$$8 \text{ hours} \cdot \frac{\text{cents}}{\text{kilowatt-hour}} = 8 \frac{\text{cents}}{\text{kilowatt}},$$

that is, 8 cents for every kilowatt of power it uses. Find other rate units that have more than one unit in the numerator or denominator, and explain in words what these units mean. Then give examples to show how these units can be converted into simple rates with additional information.

2 Independent or Dependent?

a. Write the numbers 1 through 6 on small pieces of paper and place them in a hat. Draw three pieces of paper from the hat and record the numbers in order and whether or not all three are even. Put the numbers back into the hat and repeat this process a total of 50 times. What is the ratio of the number of times you drew three even numbers to the total number of times you drew numbers (50 times)?

b. What is the probability that the first number you draw is even? What is the probability that the second number you draw is even? The third?

c. If drawing an even number as the first, second, and third numbers were independent events, what would the probability of drawing three even numbers be? Is this probability consistent with your relative frequencies in Part a? Draw a conclusion about whether these three events are independent, and explain why or why not.

Tennessee Valley Authority dams and the Raccoon Mountain Pumped Storage Plant generated 15.7 billion kilowatt-hours of electricity during fiscal year 2005.

3 Life on the Mississippi River

In his book *Life on the Mississippi,* written in 1883, the famous humorist Mark Twain wrote:

> In the space of 176 years the lower Mississippi has shortened itself 242 miles. That is an average of a trifle over 1.3 miles per year. Therefore, any calm person... can see that in the Old Oolitic Silurian Period, just a million years ago next November, the Lower Mississippi River was upward of 1,300,000 miles long, and stuck out over the Gulf of Mexico like a fishing rod. And by the same token any person can see that 742 years from now the lower Mississippi River will be only 1.75 miles long, and Cairo and New Orleans will have joined their streets together, and be plodding comfortably along under a single mayor and a mutual board of aldermen.
>
> Chapter 17, page 3

a. The first bit of information is true. Look in reference books or on the Internet to find out why the Mississippi became shorter in the 176 years prior to 1883.

b. The Mississippi River is about 4,000 miles long. Is Mark Twain correct that at the rate 1.3 miles per year, it would have been "upward of 1,300,000 miles long" a million years ago?

c. The Lower Mississippi River stretches from Cairo, Illinois, to the mouth of the river in the Gulf of Mexico. If its shortening would cause it to be only 1.75 miles long 742 years from 1883, how long was it in 1883?

d. In this writing, Mark Twain was making fun of something that people often do. What is that?

4 Unequal Reciprocals

In this chapter, you often multiplied both sides of an equation by the reciprocal of a number. As you know, $\frac{1}{2} = 0.5$, $\frac{1}{3} = 0.\overline{3}$, $\frac{1}{4} = 0.25$, $\frac{1}{5} = 0.2$, and $\frac{1}{6} = 0.1\overline{6}$. Whereas consecutive whole numbers differ by 1, the reciprocals of consecutive whole numbers get closer and closer together. For instance, $\frac{1}{5} - \frac{1}{6}$ is less than $\frac{1}{2} - \frac{1}{3}$.

a. How large does n have to be before $\frac{1}{n} - \frac{1}{n+1}$ is less than $\frac{1}{1,000}$?

b. How large does n have to be before $\frac{1}{n} - \frac{1}{n+1}$ is less than 0.000001?

c. How large does n have to be before $\frac{1}{n} - \frac{1}{n+2}$ is less than $\frac{1}{1,000}$?

5 Getting Back to Where You Started

In Lesson 8-5, you saw that a 10% increase followed by a 10% decrease does not get a quantity back to where it started.

a. Suppose an original price is reduced by 20% for a sale. By what percent must the sale price increase in order to get back to the original price?

b. Many people would answer 20% to the question of Part a. Write a short explanation why the answer is not 20%.

c. Create a table that indicates the percent you need to get back to the original price after a decrease of 10%, 20%, ..., 90%. If you can, explain in general how to calculate the percent to get back to the original price if the price of an item is decreased by x percent. Does the same "getting-back" rule work if the price of an in item is increased by x percent?

Chapter 8 Summary and Vocabulary

○ Two major models for multiplication are the subject of this chapter. The rate-factor model indicates what happens when a number or quantity is multiplied by a rate. Units are multiplied just as fractions are. Even the common use of multiplication as repeated addition can be viewed as rate-factor multiplication:

$$\text{number of addends} \cdot \frac{\text{quantity}}{\text{addend}} = \text{total quantity}$$

○ Conversion factors are special types of rate factors that enable you to convert from one unit to another.

○ The size-change model fits those situations when a quantity is scaled up or down. The size-change factor has no unit. Percents are common size-change factors. So are fractions, when dealing with parts of wholes. Probabilities are size-change factors that can tell you how often to expect an event to occur if it is repeated many times. If events are independent, then multiplying their probabilities gives the probability of both events occurring.

○ Size changes can be pictured nicely on a 2-dimensional graph. When the size-change factor is greater than 1, the size change is an expansion. When the size-change factor is between 0 and 1, the size change is a contraction. If the size-change factor is negative, then the taking of the opposite has the effect of rotating a figure 180°. Figures and their size-change images are similar. Corresponding sides are parallel and corresponding angles have the same measure. Multiplying the length of a side on a preimage by the size-change factor will give you the length of the corresponding side on the image.

○ Solving equations and inequalities involving multiplication is very similar to solving equations and inequalities involving addition. You do the same thing to both sides. The important properties to remember are the Multiplication Properties of Equality and Inequality that hold for all real numbers a, x, and y:

> If $x = y$, then $ax = ay$.
> If $x < y$ and a is positive, then $ax < ay$.
> If $x < y$ and a is negative, then $ax > ay$.

So if you are faced with an equation or inequality to solve for x and ax is on one side with no other appearance of x, then you can multiply both sides by $\frac{1}{a}$. The sign will stay the same unless you began with an inequality and $\frac{1}{a}$ is negative.

Vocabulary

8-1
terms
coefficients
like terms
collecting like terms

8-2
rate factors
conversion factor

8-4
independent events

8-8
equation of the form
$ax + b = c$

Theorems and Properties

Repeated-Addition Property of Multiplication (p. 487)
Multiplicative-Identity Property of 1 (p. 487)
Rate-Factor Model for Multiplication (p. 494)
Multiplication Property of −1 (p. 502)
Multiplication Property of Zero (p. 502)
Probability of Independent Events (p. 508)
Multiplication Property of Equality (p. 520)
Multiplication Property of Inequality (p. 539)

Chapter 8 — Self-Test

Take this test as you would take a test in class. You will need a calculator. Then use the Selected Answers section in the back of the book to check your work.

In 1–3, complete the following steps.
a. Write as one multiplication.
b. Simplify your answer from Part a.

1. $13.8 + 13.8 + 13.8 + 13.8 + 13.8 + 13.8 + 13.8 + 13.8 + 13.8 + 13.8$

2. $-2.5 + -2.5 + -2.5 + -2.5$

3. $-6 \cdot (-4) + 11 \cdot (-4) + 17 \cdot (-4)$

4. The largest carpet at a carpet store is 12 meters by 13.5 meters. The dimensions of a second carpet are 60% of the dimensions of the largest. The dimensions of the smallest carpet are only 10% of the dimensions of the second carpet. What are the dimensions of the carpet store's smallest carpet?

5. Molly is 156 centimeters tall. Molly's brother Tim is 112% of her height. How tall is Tim?

6. How many hours are there in a year that is not a leap year?

In 7 and 8, evaluate when $a = -1$ and $b = -9$.

7. $-1 \cdot 20 \cdot ab$

8. $(a + b)^2 + (a - b)^2$

In 9–13, solve.

9. $1{,}121 = 19r$

10. $2\frac{3}{4} = \frac{11}{12}b + 1\frac{3}{4}$

11. $8v + v + v = 921$

12. $42.7 \geq 6.1w$

13. $-7p + 5 < 54$

14. a. If $\frac{9}{4}k = y$, what does $9k$ equal?
    b. Write the name of the property of equality you used to get your answer to Part a.

In 15 and 16, use this information: Ines runs d miles each weekday and e miles each weekend.

15. Write an expression for the number of miles Ines runs in four weeks.

16. Evaluate your expression in Question 15 if $d = 3$ and $e = 5$.

17. Brian usually brushes his teeth in the morning, but 10% of the time he forgets. What is the probability that he will forget to brush his teeth three days in a row? (Assume that forgetting one day does not influence any other day.)

18. Colin tosses a fair coin while Jun and Luanda roll fair dice. What is the probability that all of the following occur: the coin lands heads, Jun's die lands on an even number, and Luanda's die lands on an odd number?

In 19 and 20, first write an equation or inequality to represent the situation and then answer the question.

19. A school recently bought calculators for its students. The school spent $914.06 on fourteen calculators. What is the cost of one calculator?

20. John makes $8.50 an hour. He needs to make at least $114 this week to buy a new bicycle. How many hours should he work this week?

21. Solve for x: $0.44x + 10 < 405$.

22. Graph the equation $y = 7 - 3x$.

23. Parallelogram *FLIP* has coordinates $F = (1, 4)$, $L = (-5, 7)$, $I = (-4, -3)$, and $P = (6, -8)$. Draw the image of *FLIP* under a size change of -2.9.

Chapter 8 Chapter Review

SKILLS Concepts used to solve problems

OBJECTIVE A Multiply positive and negative numbers. (Lesson 8-3)

In 1–4, perform the indicated operations.

1. $-9 \cdot -11$

2. $6.5 \cdot -4 \cdot -1$

3. $(-12)^2$

4. $\frac{1}{4} \cdot -\frac{1}{4}$

5. Find the value of $-8x$ when:

   a. $x = -2$ b. $x = \frac{2}{9}$

6. Find the value of $ab - cd$ when $a = -1$, $b = -2$, $c = -3$, and $d = 4$.

7. Find the value of $30 - 12t$ when $t = 15$.

8. Find the value of $-0.6x + 0.4y$ when $x = 15$ and $y = -20$.

OBJECTIVE B Solve and check equations of the form $ax = b$ and $ax + b = c$. (Lessons 8-6, 8-8)

In 9–22, solve and check by substitution.

9. $20A = 5$

10. $-6B = -420$

11. $11 = 13c$

12. $0.8d = -0.488$

13. $\frac{4}{5} = \frac{7}{9}m$

14. $-\frac{7}{3}h = 0.35$

15. $j + j + j = 39$

16. $2k + 3k = 120$

17. $75g - 675 = 42{,}000$

18. $-0.0912 + 0.96v = -0.168$

19. $15 = 3H + 6$

20. $-\frac{3}{7}p = 36$

21. $459 = 16x + 7$

22. $-\frac{x}{5} - 1.2 = 6.6$

OBJECTIVE C Solve and check inequalities of the form $ax + b < c$. (Lesson 8-9)

In 23–30, solve and give the 2-part check.

23. $5r \le 40$

24. $-3.2u \ge 0.64$

25. $-81 > 9v$

26. $6 < -w + -w$

27. $4r + 9 > 5.5$

28. $1.2u - 18 < 0$

29. $-\frac{k}{21} + 27 > -\frac{3}{7}$

30. $-6t - 5 \le 25$

PROPERTIES Principles behind the mathematics

OBJECTIVE D Recognize and use the Repeated-Addition Property of Multiplication and the Multiplication Properties of 1, 0, −1, and positive and negative numbers. (Lessons 8-1, 8-3)

In 31–34, simplify.

31. $-56(3 + -3)$

32. $6a + a + b + 4b$

33. $0 \cdot y + 1 \cdot y + -1 \cdot y + 0 \cdot 1 \cdot -1$

34. $8x - x - x$

In 35–38, finish the statement and name the property.

35. For any number x, $-x = \underline{\ ?\ } \cdot x$.

36. $n + n + n + n + n + n + n = \underline{\ ?\ } \cdot n$.

37. For any number q, $-q \cdot 0 = \underline{\ ?\ }$.

38. The product of $\underline{\ ?\ }$ and a number is the number itself.

39. **Multiple Choice** Suppose x is positive and y is negative. Then $-xy$ is:

   A always positive.

   B zero.

   C always negative.

   D sometimes positive, sometimes negative.

40. a and b are numbers between 0 and −1. $5ab$ will be between what two numbers?

OBJECTIVE E Recognize and use the Multiplication Properties of Equality and Inequality. (Lessons 8-6, 8-9)

41. In solving $\frac{4}{5}p = 0.6$, Ted's next step was $4p = 3$. What had Ted done?

42. To get y alone on the left side, what should be done with the equation $1.25y = 50$?

43. In solving the inequality $-54q > -540$, Federico multiplied both sides by -1. What inequality should Federico get?

44. Which two of the following inequalities are equivalent?

   A $3n < -3$ **B** $-3 < 3n$

   C $-3n < 3$ **D** $-3n > 3$

USES Applications of mathematics in real-world situations

OBJECTIVE F Apply the Rate-Factor Model for Multiplication. (Lesson 8-2)

In 45 and 46, a multiplication problem is given.
a. Do the multiplication.
b. Make up a question that leads to the multiplication.

45. $26 \frac{\text{mi}}{\text{gal}} \cdot 17.5 \text{ gal}$ 46. $2.89 \frac{\text{dollars}}{\text{lb}} \cdot 2.2 \frac{\text{lb}}{\text{kg}}$

47. Sareeta has a summer job at which she will earn $9 an hour working for 7 hours a day, 5 days a week, for 8 weeks. Show how multiplication of rates indicates how much she will earn.

48. Due to a drought, the depth of water in a reservoir has been decreasing 1.5 inches a week for 8 weeks. How did the depth 5 weeks ago compare with today's depth?

49. The average speed of cyclists in the 2005 Tour de France was a record, 41.654 kilometers per hour. What was the average speed in miles per hour? (1 km ≈ 0.62 mi)

50. In October 2005, 1 euro, the currency in much of Europe, had a value of about 1.20 U.S. dollars. The soccer player David Beckham's team, Real Madrid, was paying him $4.4 \cdot 10^6$ euros for the season. How many dollars is this?

In 51 and 52, use rate-factor multiplication to find each answer.

51. How many seconds are in a day?

52. How many inches are in a mile?

OBJECTIVE G Find unknowns in real situations involving multiplication. (Lesson 8-6)

In 53–56, write an equation of the form $ax = b$ that will answer the question and then answer the question.

53. The area of an acre is exactly 43,560 square feet. One dimension of a rectangular 1,200-acre farm is a half-mile. What is the other dimension, in feet? (1 mile = 5,280 feet)

54. If 100 paper clips weigh 3.6 ounces, what is the weight of a single paper clip?

55. Joey weighs 100 pounds and is 5 feet tall. On average, how much does an inch of Joey's height weigh?

56. A picture of an insect says "$\frac{3}{5}$ actual size." If the insect in the picture is $1\frac{1}{4}$ inches long, how long is the actual insect?

OBJECTIVE H Solve inequalities arising from real situations. (Lessons 8-9)

57. The Fine family car is driven about 15,000 miles a year. The car should last up to 110,000 miles before the upkeep is too great to keep it. How many years should the car last?

58. The population of a town increased 30% in the last ten years, but there are still fewer than 10,000 people in the town. What might have been the population of the town ten years ago?

59. Wilma has saved $1,500 for a vacation. If she budgets $200 per day, how long can her vacation last?

OBJECTIVE I Answer questions involving percents and combined percents. (Lesson 8-5)

60. After a discount of 40%, a rug cost $485. What was the original price of the rug?

61. Bill ordered a meal for $12.95. A 5% sales tax was added. If Bill tips 20%, how much will his meal have cost in all?

62. A charity met 35% of its goal when it had raised $50,000. What was its goal?

63. Harry ate 30% of a pie. Ted ate 60% of what was left. How much of the whole pie did Ted eat?

OBJECTIVE J Calculate probabilities of independent events. (Lesson 8-4)

64. Suppose you toss two fair 6-sided dice. What is the probability that both numbers on the dice are greater than 4?

65. What is the probability that you will land in the largest region of this spinner three times in a row?

66. About once every 20 days, the school bus is late. What is the probability that the bus will be late on both of the two days that you have important math tests?

In 67–69, consider the following: The weatherman has declared that there is a **35% chance of snow today** and an **8% chance of snow tomorrow**. Assume the events are independent.

67. What is the probability that it will snow both days?

68. What is the probability that it will snow neither day?

69. What is the probability that it will snow today but not tomorrow?

REPRESENTATIONS Pictures, graphs, or objects that illustrate concepts

OBJECTIVE K Perform expansions or contractions with negative magnitudes on a coordinate graph. (Lesson 8-3)

70. What is the image of $(50, -100)$ under a size change of magnitude -0.4?

In 71 and 72, use the diagram below.

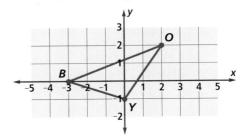

71. Graph the image of $\triangle BOY$ under a size change of magnitude -3.

72. Is the transformation described in Question 71 an expansion or contraction?

73. Let $K = (0, -6)$, $I = (-2, 0)$, $T = (0, 4)$, and $E = (2, 0)$. Graph $KITE$ and its image under a size change of magnitude $-\frac{3}{4}$.

OBJECTIVE L Graph equations of the form $y = ax + b$. (Lesson 8-7)

In 74–77, graph the equation.

74. $y = -6x$

75. $y = -\frac{2x}{3} + 0.5$

76. $y = 10 - 2x$

77. $y = \frac{1}{5}x - 2.8$

Chapter 9

Patterns Leading to Division

Contents

Many kinds of questions can be answered by using division. Here are six questions that can be answered by dividing 17 by 5.

1. A builder has purchased a 17-acre parcel of land, on which 5 houses will be built. If each house is allotted an equal amount of land, what will the area of each lot be?

2. Two sound systems are listed for sale in a local newspaper. One is on sale for $170. The other is being sold for $50. The first sound system costs how many times as much as the second?

3. If one dimension of the rectangle *DIVS* is 5 in. and its area is 17 in², what is the other dimension?

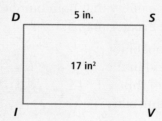

4. Seventeen friends go to a restaurant to eat. The tables at the restaurant each seat five people. How many tables will the friends need?

5. If a cornstalk grows 5 centimeters in a week, how long will it take to grow 17 centimeters?

Mature corn plants can grow to more than 7 feet tall. Because corn is planted new every year, plants have only one growing season to reach that height.

6. Suppose you want to expand the smaller penguin below into the larger figure. What is the magnitude of the size change needed?

Can you think of two more situations that lead to 17 divided by 5?

This chapter is concerned with these and other situations that lead to division.

Lesson 9-1

Integer Division

Vocabulary

real-number division

integer division

quotient-remainder form

▶ **BIG IDEA** The integer division of one number by another results in an integer quotient and a positive integer remainder less than the divisor.

What Is Real-Number Division?

To answer the questions on pages 552–553, you need to divide 17 by 5. But what answer do you get? So far in this book, you have seen that 17 divided by 5 equals the quotient $\frac{17}{5}$, which equals $3\frac{2}{5}$, or 3.4.

This is the answer to Questions 1, 2, 3, 5, and 6. We call this *real-number division*. In **real-number division,** the result of dividing a by b is the single number $\frac{a}{b}$. The numbers a and b can be any number, except that b cannot be zero.

However, the answer to Question 4 should not be 3.4 because in most restaurants you cannot use a fraction of a table. The answer to this question can be represented by *integer division*.

What Is Integer Division?

For some situations, such as that in Question 4, a correct answer to 17 divided by 5 is a quotient of 3 with remainder 2.

In **integer division** of a by b, the number a must be an integer and b must be a positive integer. The result of dividing a by b is given by an integer quotient and a positive integer remainder that is less than b.

An array shows the integer division of 17 by 5. Draw dots in columns, 5 per column, until you reach 17.

Mental Math

Baseball cards are sold in packs of 15.

a. How many cards are in 3 packs?

b. How many cards are in 6 packs?

c. How many cards are in 12 packs?

d. How many cards are in 8 packs?

The array illustrates that there are 3 groups of 5 in 17, with 2 left over. The two remaining dots do not fit in a group of 5. Notice that the remainder, 2, is less than the divisor, 5.

 QY1

Here are other examples of the two types of division.

▶ QY1

Use dots to show the integer division of 14 by 3.

Division	Real-Number Division Answer	Integer Division Answer
214 divided by 4	quotient $53.5 = 53\frac{1}{2}$	quotient 53, remainder 2
15 divided by 5	quotient 3	quotient 3, remainder 0
9 divided by 14	quotient $\frac{9}{14} = 0.6\overline{428571}$	quotient 0, remainder 9
$\frac{7}{3}$ divided by $\frac{5}{9}$	quotient $\frac{21}{5} = 4.2$	does not apply

Finding Answers in Integer Division

Because some situations call for integer division, it is useful to be able to convert real-number division answers to integer division answers, sometimes called **quotient-remainder form.** The first example shows how to do this using arithmetic.

Example 1

An auditorium seats 26 people in every row. If 245 people will be present at an assembly, how many rows will be filled? How many people will be in an unfilled row?

Solution $\frac{245}{26} = 9.42307\ldots$

This indicates that 9 rows will be completely filled. Because 26 does not divide 245 exactly, some individuals will be seated in a row that is not completely filled. The number of people who will be in a complete row is

$$26 \cdot 9 = 234.$$

The number of people left over is

$$245 - 234 = 11.$$

So the answer to the integer division is quotient 9, remainder 11.

9 rows of 26 will be filled and 11 people will be in an unfilled row.

In 2000, almost 46% of newly constructed middle schools had auditoriums or theaters.

The Quotient-Remainder Formula

Some people prefer using formulas to understand integer division. Notice how the divisor, dividend, quotient, and remainder are related in Example 1.

$$
\begin{aligned}
26 &= \text{divisor} &&= d \\
245 &= \text{dividend} &&= n \\
9 &= \text{integer quotient} &&= q \\
11 &= \text{remainder} &&= r
\end{aligned}
$$

In the solution, 245 was the sum of 234, the number of people in the filled rows, and the remainder, 11. Also, $234 = 26 \cdot 9$. This tells us that $245 = 26 \cdot 9 + 11$.

Dividend = divisor · integer quotient + remainder

$$
\text{or} \qquad \overset{\textit{quotient}}{\textit{divisor}\,)\overline{\textit{dividend}}}
$$
$$
\overline{\textit{remainder}}
$$

The more general formula is known as the Quotient-Remainder Formula. It relates the dividend n, divisor d, integer quotient q and remainder r, where r is less than d:

$$
n = d \cdot q + r
$$

 QY2

The power of the Quotient-Remainder Formula is that given any three of the divisor, dividend, quotient, and remainder, the fourth can be found by solving an equation.

> ▶ **QY2**
>
> In the integer-division problem 736 divided by 12, identify n, d, q, and r. Show that these four numbers satisfy the Quotient-Remainder Formula.

Example 2

A flight from Newark, New Jersey, to Las Vegas, Nevada, has a cruising altitude of 36,000 feet. How many miles and feet is this?

Solution Here $n = 36{,}000$ and $d = 5{,}280$, the number of feet in a mile. The question requires finding the quotient and remainder when 36,000 is divided by 5,280.

With a calculator, the real-number quotient is 6.8181.... This means that the quotient $q = 6$. That is, the airplane is between 6 and 7 miles above the ground.

Now substitute the known values into the Quotient-Remainder Formula to find r.

$$n = d \cdot q + r$$
$$36{,}000 = 5{,}280 \cdot 6 + r$$

Solve the equation for r.

$$36{,}000 = 31{,}680 + r$$
$$4{,}320 = r$$

The airplane cruises at an altitude of 6 miles 4,320 feet.

The Quotient-Remainder Formula can help you understand integer division. But in some situations, the wording of the question may lead to different interpretations of the answer.

Example 3

Create a question for $37 \div 5$ in which
a. the answer is 7.
b. the answer is 7, remainder 2.
c. the answer is 8.

Solution

a. The Smythes picked 37 apples from the orchard. They decided to make apple pies. The apple pie recipe calls for 5 apples. How many apple pies can the Smythes make?

In this situation, five apples are needed to make one pie. Because the Smythes have 37 apples and each pie needs 5 apples, they can make only 7 pies. The question does not ask whether any apples are left over.

b. For her party favors, Diem wanted to put 5 candles in a small gift box. If she had 37 candles, how many boxes would she have to buy? Would she have any candles left over?

In this situation, each gift box holds 5 candles, so Diem can fill 7 boxes and will have 2 candles left over.

c. Mr. Kent wanted to reward the 37 students on the student newspaper staff with a framed certificate of achievement. Five certificates come in one packet. How many packets should he order so that each student receives a certificate?

In this situation, the certificates are packed in groups of five. If he ordered 7 packets, he would have only 35 certificates, and 2 students would not receive one. In order to have a certificate for each student, he will need to order 8 packets.

The apple tree originated from an area between the Caspian and Black Seas. There are 7,500 varieties of apples in the world.

Source: University of Illinois Extension

Integer Division **557**

Notice that it is important to pay attention to what the remainder means in the context of the problem. Each situation may lead to a different answer based on the remainder. In certain situations, you may need to round up to the nearest whole number, round down to the nearest whole number, use the exact answer, or use the remainder.

Questions

COVERING THE IDEAS

1. Compute the answer to 105 divided by 8
   a. using real-number division.
   b. using integer division.

Multiple Choice In 2–4, choose from the answers below.
A integer division only
B real-number division only
C both integer and real-number division
D neither integer nor real-number division

2. has a quotient and a remainder

3. has an answer that is a single number

4. can be used with fractions

5. A company with 345 employees is having a picnic. The company is renting buses to take the employees to the picnic. Each bus seats 48 people.
   a. If you were ordering buses to take people to the picnic, how many buses should you order?
   b. How many buses can be completely filled?
   c. What is the least number of people on an unfilled bus?

6. Why is the remainder in whole-number division always less than the divisor? Explain in words or pictures.

7. The number A is divided by B, giving an integer quotient of C and a remainder of D. From the Quotient-Remainder Formula, how are these four numbers related?

8. The highest mountain in Africa is Mt. Kilimanjaro in Tanzania. Its highest peak is 19,340 feet above sea level. How many miles and feet is this?

The peaks of Mt. Kilimanjaro, the highest mountain in Africa, are snow covered year-round.

9. Create a problem for $50 \div 7$ when
   a. the answer is 7.
   b. the answer is 7, remainder 1.
   c. the answer is 8.

APPLYING THE MATHEMATICS

10. When 365 is divided by 7, the quotient is 52 and the remainder is 1.
    a. Show how these numbers are related using the Quotient-Remainder Formula.
    b. What is the everyday significance of these numbers?

11. a. How many years and days old is a person who is 10,000 days old, ignoring leap years?
    b. How many days old is a person who retires at an age of 60 years 3 weeks, ignoring leap years?

12. A teacher has 5 reams of paper at the beginning of the year, each with 500 sheets. The teacher decides to keep 750 sheets and distribute the rest equally to the class of 23 students. How many sheets will each student get? How many sheets will be left over?

13. Lydia cashed a check for $268.00.
    a. Lydia decided that she would like as many $50 bills as possible. So before stepping to the teller, she divided 268 by 50 and got 5.36. Lydia expected to receive five $50 bills and 36 cents. Was she correct to think this? Why?
    b. Suppose the teller exchanges the check with the fewest bills possible with no bill larger than $50. How should Lydia expect to receive her money?

14. What is the quotient and remainder when 4,172 is divided by 4,178?

15. 2,000 is divided by an unknown number x, leaving a quotient of 37 and a remainder of 2. Is this possible? If so, what is x? If not, why not?

16. a. Complete the following table.

Dividend	Divisor	Real Quotient	Integer Quotient	Integer Remainder
65	11	?	?	?
66	11	?	?	?
67	11	?	?	?
68	11	?	?	?
69	11	?	?	?
70	11	?	?	?
71	11	?	?	?
72	11	?	?	?
73	11	?	?	?
74	11	?	?	?
75	11	?	?	?
76	11	?	?	?
77	11	?	?	?

b. Describe any patterns you see in the table.

REVIEW

17. Solve for x. $-3.5x > \frac{7}{3}$ **(Lesson 8-9)**

18. On Friday, Pam's Books will begin a going-out-of-business sale. On the first day, all books will be 20% off the regular price. Each day after that, the price will be 20% off the previous day's price. One book had an original price of $30.98. How much will it cost on Sunday? **(Lesson 8-5)**

19. A "500-year storm" is a storm of such a ferocity that its probability of occurring in any given year is $\frac{1}{500}$.

   a. What is the probability that a 500-year storm will *not* occur next year?

   b. What is the probability that a 500-year storm would occur three years in a row? **(Lesson 8-4)**

20. $\triangle QET$ has coordinates $Q = (-3, 5.7)$, $E = (0, 1.2)$, $T = (-9, -6.6)$. Its expansion image $\triangle Q'E'T'$ has coordinates $Q' = (4, -7.6)$, $E' = (0, -1.6)$, $T' = (12, 8.8)$. What is the magnitude of this size change? **(Lesson 8-3)**

21. Of the choices below, which two size changes produce the same result?

    A   a size change of magnitude 80%

    B   a size change of magnitude $\frac{5}{4}$

    C   a size change of magnitude $-\frac{4}{5}$

    D   a size change of magnitude -1.25

    E   a size change of magnitude -0.8 (**Lessons 8-3, 7-7, 3-5**)

22. A racetrack is shaped like an oval. It is two semicircles connected by 0.75-mile-long straight edges, as shown below. If the perimeter of the oval is 3 miles, what is the radius r of the semicircles to the nearest hundredth of a mile? (**Lesson 7-6**)

    0.75 mile

    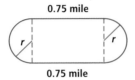

    0.75 mile

23. Draw a fact triangle for the statement $x + -3y = 12$ and write the related facts. (**Lesson 5-4**)

24. In the following statement, identify the rate and the rate unit. In New Jersey in 2000, the population density was about 438 people per square kilometer. (**Lesson 1-3**)

EXPLORATION

25. Consider the positive integers n with the following properties:
    (1) The remainder is 1 when n is divided by 2.
    (2) The remainder is 2 when n is divided by 3.
    (3) The remainder is 3 when n is divided by 4.
    (4) The remainder is 4 when n is divided by 5.
    (5) The remainder is 5 when n is divided by 6.
    (6) The remainder is 6 when n is divided by 7.

    a. Find the smallest positive integer n with property (1).

    b. Find the smallest positive integer n with properties (1) and (2).

    c. Find the smallest positive integer n with properties (1)–(3).

    d. Find the smallest positive integer n with properties (1)–(4).

    e. Find the smallest positive integer n with properties (1)–(5).

    f. Find the smallest positive integer n with properties (1)–(6).

    g. Generalize the answers to Parts a–f.

QY ANSWERS

1. $14 \div 3$ is 4 R2

2. $n = 736, d = 12,$
   $q = 61, r = 4$
   $n = d \cdot q + r$
   $736 = 12 \cdot 61 + 4$
   $736 = 732 + 4$
   $736 = 736$

Lesson 9-2

The Rate Model for Division

▶ **BIG IDEA** Rates such as 40 miles per hour, $2.99 per pound, and $1\frac{1}{2}$ minutes per page are calculated by dividing one quantity by another of a different unit.

Recall from Lesson 8-2 that rate units can be written as fractions.

$$250 \frac{\text{words}}{\text{minute}} \qquad 65 \frac{\text{miles}}{\text{hour}} \qquad 2.3 \frac{\text{children}}{\text{family}}$$

Knowing the rate unit that you want for your answer can help you decide what values to divide.

Activity

Can you write as well with your right hand as with your left, much like Albert Einstein and Leonardo da Vinci did? If you can, then you are *ambidextrous.* To help answer the question, see how well you write your name with each hand in a certain amount of time. Be sure that your handwriting is clear!

Step 1 Use a timer to find out how long it takes you to write your *last* name with your right hand.

Step 2 Time how long it takes you to write your *first* name with your left hand. Fill in the table below.

Rate	First name	Last name
Number of letters	?	?
Number of seconds	?	?

1. What is your right-hand rate? That is, how many letters per second did you write?

2. What is your left-hand rate?

3. Based on just your rates, can you say that you are ambidextrous? Explain.

Mental Math

One school bus holds 54 students.

a. How many buses will 200 students fill? How many will be on the unfilled bus?

b. A group of 300 students has 6 buses. Will all the students fit onto these buses?

c. How many buses will 700 students need if all but one bus is filled?

Example 1

A car went 243.4 miles between fill-ups of the gas tank. Then the driver filled the tank with 12.1 gallons of gas. How many miles per gallon did the car get?

Solution The key to the division is "miles per gallon." This indicates to divide miles by gallons.

$$\frac{243.4 \text{ miles}}{12.1 \text{ gallons}} \approx 20.1 \frac{miles}{gallon}$$

Do not let the numbers in rate problems scare you. If you get confused, try simpler numbers and examine how you get the answer.

The Activity and Example 1 are instances of the Rate Model for Division.

Rate Model for Division

If a and b are quantities with different units, then $\frac{a}{b}$ is the amount of quantity a per amount of quantity b.

One of the most common examples of rate is unit cost.

GUIDED

Example 2

A 5-pound bag of dog food costs $4.89. A 12-pound bag costs $9.59. Which is the better buy?

Solution Calculate the cost per pound. That is, divide the total cost by the number of pounds.

Cost per pound for 5-pound bag:

$$\frac{\$ \underline{\ ?\ }}{\underline{\ ?\ } \text{ lb}} \approx \underline{\ ?\ } \text{ dollar per pound}$$

Cost per pound for 12-pound bag:

$$\frac{\$ \underline{\ ?\ }}{\underline{\ ?\ } \text{ lb}} \approx \underline{\ ?\ } \text{ dollar per pound}$$

The __?__-pound bag is the better value.

Example 3

Six library aides must sort and shelve 218 books. If the job is shared equally, how many books will each aide shelve? How many books will be left over?

Solution Think of the rate "books per aide." This means to divide the number of books by the number of aides.

$$\frac{218 \text{ books}}{6 \text{ aides}} = 36.333\ldots \frac{\text{books}}{\text{aide}}$$

Each aide will have to shelve 36 books. To find the remainder, use integer division and the Quotient-Remainder Formula.

$$n = dq + r$$

$$218 = 6 \cdot 36 + r \qquad \text{Here } n = 218, d = 6, \text{ and } q = 36.$$

$$218 = 216 + r$$

So $r = 2$, meaning that 2 books would still not be shelved.

 QY1

Of course, rates can involve variables.

Example 4

A basketball player scored P points in G games last season. What was her scoring average?

Solution The usual unit of scoring rate is points per game. So divide the total number of points scored by the number of games. She scored P points per G games, which is $\frac{P \text{ points}}{G \text{ games}} = \frac{P}{G}$ points per game.

 QY2

Questions

COVERING THE IDEAS

1. State the Rate Model for Division.

In 2–6, calculate a rate suggested by each situation. Round if appropriate.

2. A package of 16 rolls of paper towels costs $11.99.

3. Esteban entered 523 scores into a spreadsheet in 13 minutes.

4. Eggs were priced at $0.69 a dozen.

5. On a test, there are p pages with a total of 50 questions.

6. A taxi takes you m miles at a cost of D dollars.

In 2005, about 115,770 people worked as library technicians and about 146,740 people worked as librarians.

Source: U.S. Department of Labor

▸ **QY1**

A florist made 26 bouquets from 80 roses. How many roses were in each bouquet? How many roses were left to sell as single stems?

▸ **QY2**

A batting average is the rate "hits per times at bat." If Rolando has B times at bat and H hits, what is his batting average?

7. Answer the questions of Example 3 if another library aide comes in and is able to help shelve the books.

8. Which of the fabric softeners at the right is the better buy?

9. Georgia is making peach cobblers from baskets of peaches bought at the farmer's market. There are 30 peaches in a basket and Georgia's cobbler recipe calls for 7 peaches.

   a. How many cobblers can Georgia make if she bought 2 baskets of peaches?

   b. How many peaches will be left over?

APPLYING THE MATHEMATICS

10. Mr. Burns is planning a cookout for a family reunion. He can purchase a package of 18 one-third-pound gourmet hamburgers for $29.95.

    a. What is the price per hamburger?

    b. What is the price per pound of hamburger?

    c. Mr. Burns bought 9 of the packages to serve the 75 people expected at the reunion. How many hamburgers per person did he plan for? What was the cost of hamburgers per person?

11. If a cyclist rides $1\frac{1}{2}$ miles in 12 minutes, find the cyclist's rate

    a. in miles per minute.

    b. in miles per hour.

12. Researchers at the University of Wisconsin have found that, on average, 1.3 acres of pasture land are needed for each cow in a dairy herd. A farmer owns 480 acres of land and has a herd of 225 cows. He needs 150 acres to grow enough feed for the winter. Four acres are used for his home and a garden.

    a. Explain why he has enough land to graze his current dairy herd.

    b. Could he increase the herd size to 275?

13. a. If you measure your pulse by counting h heartbeats in m minutes, what is your heart rate?

    b. If you count h heartbeats in s seconds, what is your heart rate in beats per *minute*?

A person over the age of 10 typically has a resting heart rate between 60 and 100 beats per minute.

The Rate Model for Division **565**

14. At a school dance, there were G girls and B boys.

    a. How many girls per boy were there?

    b. How many boys per girl were there?

    c. How are the answers to Parts a and b related?

15. Use examples of rates to explain why the following statement is true:

    If a, b, and c are positive numbers and $b > c$, then $\frac{a}{b} < \frac{a}{c}$.

REVIEW

16. From 1912 until 1959 when Alaska and Hawaii became states, the United States consisted of 48 states and its flag displayed 48 stars. What are the possible ways to arrange 48 stars in rows with the same number of stars in each row and no remainder? **(Lesson 9-1)**

17. A number is divided by 18, resulting in an integer quotient of 37 and a remainder of 14. Find the number. **(Lesson 9-1)**

18. On Sunday, it began raining early in the day. Cassie looked at her previously empty rain gauge at 2:00 P.M. and it had 7 mm of water in it. At 4:00 P.M., she measured again and the gauge had 10 mm of water in it. Assuming that the rain fell at the same rate the whole day, between what hours did it start raining? **(Lesson 8-5)**

19. A triangle has angles measuring $87°$, $x°$, and $2x°$. Solve for x. **(Lessons 8-4, 6-7)**

20. If you roll two fair dice, what is the probability that both dice will show odd numbers or that the sum will be greater than 8? **(Lesson 5-10)**

21. Is $\frac{17.8}{0}$ a rational number? Explain your reasoning. **(Lesson 4-9)**

22. Find at least 3 fractions equal to $\frac{4}{166}$ whose numerators end with the digit 6. **(Lesson 2-3)**

EXPLORATION

23. Some of the best-known world records are rates. Look up the following world records and identify the rate:

    a. fastest-swimming bird

    b. most densely populated country

    c. most expensive metal commodity traded

QY ANSWERS

1. 3 roses per bouquet with 2 left over

2. $\frac{H}{B}$

Lesson
9-3 Division of Fractions

▶ **BIG IDEA** The Algebraic Definition of Division $a \div b = a \cdot \frac{1}{b}$ justifies the fact that division by the fraction $\frac{c}{d}$ produces the same result as multiplication by its reciprocal $\frac{d}{c}$.

April went with her friends Mae, June, Julius, and Augie to a restaurant. The bill totaled $27.30. Each person owed $\frac{1}{5}$ of the bill. Everyone knew that to find $\frac{1}{5}$ of $27.30 they could divide $27.30 by 5. That is, $27.30 \cdot \frac{1}{5} = \$27.30 \div 5$.

In general, instead of dividing by b you can multiply by $\frac{1}{b}$. We call this the Algebraic Definition of Division. You used this definition in Chapter 2 to rewrite fractions as decimals.

Algebraic Definition of Division

For any numbers a and b, $b \neq 0$, $a \div b = a \cdot \frac{1}{b}$.

Why is this true? Just think of multiplying fractions. For any fraction $\frac{a}{b}$,

$$a \div b = \frac{a}{b}$$
$$= \frac{a}{1} \cdot \frac{1}{b}$$
$$= a \cdot \frac{1}{b}.$$

Using the Algebraic Definition of Division to Divide Fractions

Since the Algebraic Definition of Division holds for *any* numbers, it is true when a and b are themselves fractions. Then it is critical to remember that the reciprocal of the fraction $\frac{x}{y}$ is the fraction $\frac{y}{x}$.

Example 1

What is $\frac{9}{4}$ divided by $\frac{3}{5}$?

Solution By the Algebraic Definition of Division,

$\frac{9}{4}$ divided by $\frac{3}{5}$ equals $\frac{9}{4}$ times the reciprocal of $\frac{3}{5}$.

You can think of the division in either of two ways.

$$\frac{\frac{9}{4}}{\frac{3}{5}} = \frac{9}{4} \cdot \frac{5}{3} \qquad \text{or} \qquad \frac{9}{4} \div \frac{3}{5} = \frac{9}{4} \cdot \frac{5}{3}$$

$$= \frac{45}{12} \qquad\qquad\qquad\qquad = \frac{45}{12}$$

$$= \frac{15}{4} \qquad\qquad\qquad\qquad = \frac{15}{4}$$

Check

Check 1 Draw (or imagine) a fact triangle with $\frac{9}{4} \div \frac{3}{5} = \frac{15}{4}$, as shown at the right. The fact triangle will be correct if $\frac{3}{5} \cdot \frac{15}{4} = \frac{9}{4}$ is also true. $\frac{3}{5} \cdot \frac{15}{4} = \frac{45}{20} = \frac{9}{4}$, so the answer is correct.

Check 2 To check that $\frac{15}{4}$ is the answer, you can change the given fractions to decimals. $\frac{9}{4} = 2.25$ and $\frac{3}{5} = 0.6$, so $\frac{\frac{9}{4}}{\frac{3}{5}} = \frac{2.25}{0.6} = 3.75$.

Because $\frac{15}{4} = 3.75$, the answer checks.

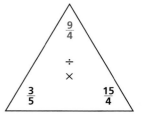

GUIDED

Example 2

Simplify $\frac{\frac{2}{7}}{3}$.

Step 1 Rewrite the expression as division. __?__ ÷ __?__

Step 2 Rewrite the division as multiplication by the reciprocal. __?__ · __?__

Step 3 Simplify the result. __?__

 QY

Rate situations can lead to division of fractions.

▶ **QY**

Simplify $\frac{\frac{a}{b}}{x}$.

Example 3

Suppose you earn $10 for babysitting 1 hour 40 minutes. How much are you earning per hour?

Solution *Earnings per hour* is a rate, so divide the total earned by the number of hours. First, change the hours and minutes to just hours.

$$40 \text{ minutes} = \frac{40}{60} \text{ hour}$$
$$= \frac{2}{3} \text{ hour,}$$
$$\text{so } 1 \text{ hour } 40 \text{ minutes} = 1\frac{2}{3} \text{ hours}$$
$$= \frac{5}{3} \text{ hours}$$
$$\text{Earnings per hour} = r = \frac{10 \text{ dollars}}{1 \text{ hour } 40 \text{ min}} = \frac{10 \text{ dollars}}{\frac{5}{3} \text{ hours}}$$

To divide 10 by $\frac{5}{3}$, use the Algebraic Definition of Division.

$$\frac{10 \text{ dollars}}{\frac{5}{3} \text{ hours}} = 10 \cdot \frac{3}{5} \frac{\text{dollars}}{\text{hour}}$$
$$= \frac{30}{5} \frac{\text{dollars}}{\text{hour}}$$
$$= 6 \frac{\text{dollars}}{\text{hour}}$$

You are earning $6.00 per hour.

The next example shows another application of dividing fractions to find a rate.

Example 4

Two-thirds of the way through the 2006 baseball season, the Atlanta Braves had won 50 games. At this rate, how many games would they have won in the entire season?

Solution Games won per entire season $= \dfrac{50 \text{ games}}{\frac{2}{3} \text{ season}}$

$$= 50 \cdot \frac{3}{2} \frac{\text{games}}{\text{season}}$$
$$= \frac{150}{2} \frac{\text{games}}{\text{season}}$$
$$= 75 \frac{\text{games}}{\text{season}}$$

At this rate, the Braves would have won 75 games in the entire season. (They actually won 79 games.)

At the end of the 2006 season, Kyle Davies had a career earned run average of 6.38 and a career batting average of .105.

GAME Now you can play *Match-It: Fraction Division*. The directions for this game are on page G17 at the back of your book.

Questions

COVERING THE IDEAS

1. **Fill in the Blank** Instead of multiplying a number by $\frac{1}{4}$, you can divide the number by __?__ .

2. State the Algebraic Definition of Division.

3. Suppose a person earns $17 for working two and a half hours. What is the person's wage per hour?

In 4–7, simplify.

4. $\dfrac{\frac{8}{9}}{\frac{4}{3}}$ 5. $\dfrac{\frac{2}{5}}{7}$ 6. $\dfrac{\frac{17}{6}}{\frac{2}{3}}$ 7. $\dfrac{\frac{10}{3}}{\frac{6}{5}}$

8. Three-fourths of the way into the 2006 soccer season, D.C. United had won 13 games. At this rate, how many games would they win in the entire season?

APPLYING THE MATHEMATICS

9. **a.** Divide $4\frac{1}{4}$ by $3\frac{2}{5}$.
   b. The answer you get to Part a should be greater than 1. How could you tell this before you did any division?

10. **a.** Divide $1\frac{2}{3}$ by $5\frac{4}{7}$.
    b. Your answer to Part a should be less than 1. How could you tell this before you divided?
    c. Check the answer you get to Part a by changing each fraction to a decimal, dividing the decimals, and comparing the answers.
    d. In this question, what advantage do the fractions have over the decimals?

11. Vijay walked $\frac{1}{3}$ of a mile in $\frac{1}{6}$ of an hour.
    a. At this rate, how far would Vijay have walked in one hour?
    b. Explain how you obtained your answer to Part a.

12. Elizabeth is cutting wire for earrings from a wire $26\frac{1}{2}$ inches long. Each earring requires $\frac{3}{4}$ of an inch of wire. How many earrings can she make? How much wire will she not use?

In **13** and **14**, simplify.

13. $\dfrac{\frac{2}{x}}{\frac{1}{y}}$

14. $\dfrac{\frac{a}{b}}{\frac{c}{d}}$

15. Seven and one-half times a number is 375. What is the number?

REVIEW

16. According to the 2000 census, the population of Wyoming was 493,782. The state's land area is approximately 62.6 million acres. Find the following rates. **(Lesson 9-2)**

    a. people per acre   **b.** acres per person

    c. What is the relationship between the answers to Parts a and b?

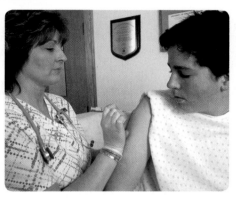

17. A health clinic is offering flu shots. Between noon and 1:30 P.M., the clinic administered 153 shots. How many shots per minute did it give? **(Lesson 9-2)**

Flu shots are recommended for children aged 6 months to 5 years and for adults aged 50 years or older.

18. **Multiple Choice** Which of the following are solutions to $\frac{1}{4}c < \frac{15}{8}$? There may be more than one correct answer. **(Lesson 8-9)**

    A 0   **B** $\frac{15}{4}$ **C** -2 **D** -15 **E** $\frac{-15}{2}$

19. Solve for n. $16.5n = -23.3$ **(Lesson 8-6)**

In **20–23**, calculate. Express your answers as fractions in lowest terms.

20. (area of an isosceles right triangle with leg d) $\div$ (area of the figure at the right) **(Lesson 7-4)**

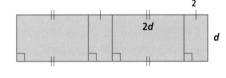

21. $\frac{1}{12} \cdot 13 + \frac{1}{12} \cdot -45 + \frac{1}{12} \cdot 191 + \frac{1}{12} \cdot -78$ **(Lesson 7-3)**

22. (number of degrees in a full revolution) $\div$ (number of regular polygon types that tessellate) **(Lessons 6-4, 6-3)**

23. $|3 + -7| - |-7 + -3| \div 2$ **(Lessons 5-2, 1-7, 1-6)**

EXPLORATION

24. Explain why the following statement is true:
The quotient of two fractions is the fraction whose numerator is the quotient of the numerators of the fractions, and whose denominator is the quotient of the denominators of the fractions.

Lesson
9-4 — Division with Negative Numbers

> **BIG IDEA** Division involving positive and negative numbers follows the same rules for signs as does multiplication.

Dividing a Negative Number by a Positive Number

Rates can be calculated with negative numbers.

Mental Math

Calculate.

a. $15 \cdot -5$

b. $-14 \cdot -3 + 15 \cdot -3$

c. $-7 \cdot 5 \cdot 2 \cdot -4$

d. $-2 \cdot 3 \cdot -4 \cdot 5 \cdot -5$

Example 1

Snow melts in some mountainous areas at a constant rate once the temperature is above freezing. Suppose that in a certain mountain pass, the snow melts 31 inches in 25 days. What is the rate of snow melt?

Solution The answer is found by division.

$$\frac{31 \text{ inches of snow melt}}{25 \text{ days}} = 1.24 \text{ inches of snow melt per day}$$

You can translate the melting snow into a negative number.

$$\frac{-31 \text{ inches}}{25 \text{ days}} = -1.24 \frac{\text{inches}}{\text{day}}$$

Check Draw (or imagine) a fact triangle as shown at the right. If $25 \cdot -1.24 = -31$, then $-31 \div 25 = -1.24$ is correct. The product of a positive number and a negative number is negative. So, $25 \cdot -1.24 = -31$ is correct, and the answer is correct.

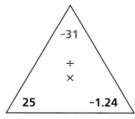

This situation is an instance of the division $\frac{-31}{25} = -1.24$. Remember that dividing by 25 is the same as multiplying by its reciprocal, $\frac{1}{25}$.

$$\frac{-31}{25} = -31 \cdot \frac{1}{25}$$
$$= -1.24$$

In general, if a negative number is divided by a positive number, the quotient is negative.

 QY1

> **QY1**
>
> Calculate $\frac{-10}{5} + \frac{-1}{1}$.

GUIDED

Example 2

On five consecutive days, the low temperatures in Versoix, Switzerland, were −1°, 5°, 1°, −2°, and −6°C. What was the mean low temperature for the five days?

Solution Recall that the mean, or average, of a set of numbers is found by adding the numbers and dividing by the total number of numbers.

$$\frac{\underline{} + \underline{} + \underline{} + \underline{} + \underline{}}{5} = \frac{\underline{}}{5} = \underline{}$$

The mean low temperature was __?__, or about −1°C.

On the Celsius scale, that is just below freezing.

In January 2005, strong winds forced water from Lake Geneva to splash over the shoreline in Versoix, causing the ice shown in the photo above.

Dividing a Positive Number by a Negative Number

In Example 3, a positive number is divided by a negative number. The quotient is again negative.

Example 3

What is 31 divided by −25?

Solution Dividing by −25 is the same as multiplying by $-\frac{1}{25}$, the reciprocal of −25.

$$\frac{31}{-25} = 31 \cdot -\frac{1}{25}$$ Because a positive times a negative
is negative, you know that the
$$= -1.24$$ quotient is negative.

Check Think of the snow melting in Example 1, but go back in time for the 25 days. The snow cover was 31 inches deeper 25 days ago. How has the depth of the snow changed?

$$\frac{31 \text{ inches more}}{25 \text{ days ago}} = \frac{31 \text{ inches}}{-25 \text{ days}}$$

$$= -1.24 \frac{\text{inches}}{\text{day}}$$

That is, $\frac{31}{-25} = \frac{-31}{25}$.

 QY2

▶ **QY2**

Find $\frac{-12}{12} + \frac{12}{-6} + \frac{-6}{12}$.

Dividing a Negative Number by a Negative Number

Example 4 is a division question in which both numbers are negative. Is the sign of the quotient obvious?

Example 4

What is −422 divided by −15?

Solution

$$\frac{-422}{-15} = -422 \cdot -\frac{1}{15}$$ Because a negative times a negative is positive, you know the quotient is positive.

$$= \frac{422}{15}$$

$$\approx 28.13$$

 QY3

Division with two negative numbers can also be thought of using the Rate Model for Division. A young killer whale grows approximately 9.5 centimeters in length every 3 months for the first 16 years of its life. The numerator and denominator are positive quantities.

$$\frac{9.5 \text{ cm more}}{3 \text{ months later}} = 3\frac{1}{6} \frac{\text{cm}}{\text{month}} \text{ gain}$$

Another way of looking at the situation is that 3 months ago the killer whale measured 9.5 centimeters less. The numerator and denominator are negative quantities.

$$\frac{9.5 \text{ cm less}}{3 \text{ months ago}} = \frac{-9.5 \text{ cm}}{-3 \text{ months}}$$

$$= 3.1\overline{6} \frac{\text{cm}}{\text{month}} \text{ gain}$$

Notice the equal rates. $\dfrac{9.5 \text{ cm less}}{3 \text{ months ago}} = \dfrac{9.5 \text{ cm more}}{3 \text{ months later}}$

Ignoring the units but using negative numbers when appropriate:

$$\frac{-9.5}{-3} = \frac{9.5}{3}$$

That is, $\dfrac{-9.5}{-3} = 3.1\overline{6}$.

The rules for dividing with negative numbers are just like those for multiplying. If both divisor and dividend are negative, the quotient is positive. If one is positive and the other is negative, the quotient will be negative. These properties can be stated with variables.

> ▶ **QY3**
>
> Find these quotients: $\dfrac{-15}{-3}$, $\dfrac{-15}{3}$, $\dfrac{15}{-3}$.

The largest killer whale on record was 32 feet long and weighed 22,000 pounds.

Source: SeaWorld

> **For all numbers a and b, $b \neq 0$:**
>
> $$\frac{a}{b} = \frac{-a}{-b}, \text{ and}$$
>
> $$\frac{-a}{b} = \frac{a}{-b} = -\frac{a}{b}.$$

If you forget how to perform operations with negative numbers, there are two things you can do. (1) Rewrite subtractions as additions; rewrite divisions as multiplications. (2) Think of a real situation using negative numbers. Use the situation to help you find the answer.

Questions

COVERING THE IDEAS

In 1–3, find the mean of each set of numbers.

1. –20, –50, –80, –90

2. –11, 14, –17, –20, 6, –30

3. 12.2, –11.4, 1.3, 2.6, –4.7

In 4–7, tell whether the number is positive or negative. Give a reason for your answer.

4. $\frac{-4.1}{3} \cdot 7$

5. $\frac{-200}{700}$

6. $\frac{-96}{-12}$

7. $\frac{-48}{-3}$

8. Separate these numbers into two collections of equal numbers.

$$-\frac{3}{5} \qquad \frac{-3}{5} \qquad \frac{-3}{-5} \qquad \frac{3}{-5} \qquad -\frac{-3}{-5} \qquad \frac{3}{5} \qquad -\frac{-3}{5}$$

9. Maxine spent $7.50 for lunch over 2 days.

    a. Calculate a rate from this information.

    b. What division problem with negative numbers gives this rate?

    c. **Fill in the Blanks** __?__ days ago, Maxine had __?__ dollars __?__ than she has now.

    d. What division problem is suggested by Part c?

10. A puppy gains about 6 ounces every 5 weeks for the first months of its life.

    a. Express a growth rate in terms of ounces per 5 weeks using positive numbers.

    b. Express a growth rate in terms of ounces per week using negative numbers.

    c. Explain how the two growth rates are the same.

11. What two things can you do if you forget how to calculate with negative numbers? Which one is easier for you to do? Why?

Division with Negative Numbers **575**

APPLYING THE MATHEMATICS

12. In the twenty years from 1980 to 2000, the population of Yuba City, California, increased by about 18,000 people.

    a. Calculate a rate from this information.

    b. **Fill in the Blanks** __?__ years before 2000, Yuba City's population was 18,000 ___?___ than it was in 2000.

    c. What division problem is suggested by Part b? What is the quotient?

You can use a balance board to strengthen your ankles. Balancing your weight over the center of such a board is similar in concept to Question 20.

In 13–16, calculate $x + y$, $x - y$, xy, and $\frac{x}{y}$ for the given values of x and y.

13. $x = 2$ and $y = 8$

14. $x = -26$ and $y = -26$

15. $x = -\frac{17}{6}$ and $y = -\frac{1}{6}$

16. $x = -\frac{1}{2}$ and $y = \frac{1}{3}$

17. Use $C = \frac{5(F - 32)}{9}$ to convert $-40°$ Fahrenheit to degrees Celsius.

18. Round $\frac{370}{-8}$ to the nearest integer.

19. Evaluate $\frac{-5u}{6w}$ when $u = -30$ and $w = -2$.

20. The center of gravity of a polygonal region of given points is the point on which the region would balance if cut out and placed horizontally. The first coordinate of the center of gravity is the mean of the first coordinates of the polygon's vertices; the second coordinate of the center of gravity is the mean of the second coordinates of the vertices.

    a. Find the coordinates of the center of gravity of the region graphed at the right.

    b. Copy the drawing and plot the center of gravity on your copy.

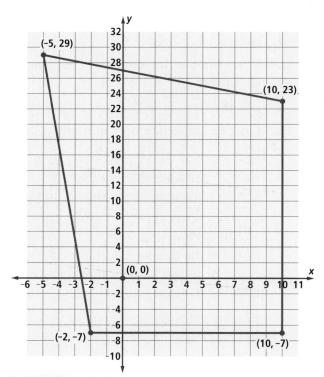

REVIEW

21. Evaluate $\frac{x}{2pq} \div \frac{16xp}{q}$ when $x = 4$, $p = 3$, and $q = 2$. **(Lesson 9-3)**

22. Planks of wood from an old boardwalk are being recycled to make furniture. The planks are $5\frac{1}{3}$ feet long, and the carpenter needs pieces $\frac{2}{3}$ foot long. How many can he cut from the plank, assuming nothing is lost in the cutting? **(Lesson 9-3)**

23. A 16-ounce jar of salsa costs $3.29. A 12-ounce jar costs $2.79. Which is the better deal? (**Lesson 9-2**)

24. On the day before Thanksgiving 2005, about 217,000 passengers traveled through O'Hare Airport in Chicago. The Aviation Department states that this was about 5.3% more passengers than on an average day. How many passengers travel through O'Hare on an average day? (**Lesson 8-5**)

O'Hare International Airport

25. Solve for g. $12 + 0.25g = 104$ (**Lesson 8-8**)

26. Solve for b in terms of x in the figure below. (**Lessons 6-6, 6-5**)

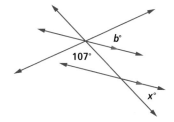

In 27–29, identify the ratio in the statement and state what is being compared.

27. The store brand costs half the price of the name brand.

28. Only 0.4% of the population of Canada live in the province of Prince Edward Island.

29. The women's volleyball team had a winning percentage of .672 this season. (**Lesson 1-3**)

EXPLORATION

30. In integer division of a dividend n by a positive divisor d, the remainder r must be a whole number that is less than d. But if the divisor is a negative number, this requirement must be replaced with the requirement $0 \leq r < |d|$. Under this new condition, for any integers n and d, $d \neq 0$, the Quotient-Remainder Formula holds with integer quotient q and remainder r: $n = d \cdot q + r$. In Parts a–d, fill in the blanks to determine the quotient and remainder.

   a. $17 = 3 \cdot \underline{\ ?\ } + \underline{\ ?\ }$

   b. $17 = -3 \cdot \underline{\ ?\ } + \underline{\ ?\ }$

   c. $-17 = 3 \cdot \underline{\ ?\ } + \underline{\ ?\ }$

   d. $-17 = -3 \cdot \underline{\ ?\ } + \underline{\ ?\ }$

   e. Use real-number division to compute $17 \div 3$, $17 \div -3$, $-17 \div 3$, and $-17 \div -3$. How do these quotients relate to the corresponding integer quotients in Parts a–d? Make a generalization of this result.

QY ANSWERS

1. -3

2. $-3\frac{1}{2}$

3. $5, -5, -5$

Lesson

9-5 Division in Equations and Inequalities

> ▶ **BIG IDEA** A possible first step in solving sentences of the form $ax = b$ or $ax < b$ for x is to divide both sides by a.

The Division Property of Equality

Consider an equation of the form $ax = b$, such as $45x = 20$. In Chapter 8, you saw how to solve an equation of this form by multiplying both sides by $\frac{1}{a}$. Here is how the equation $45x = 20$ might be solved.

Step 1	$45x = 20$
Step 2	$\frac{1}{45} \cdot 45x = \frac{1}{45} \cdot 20$
Step 3	$1 \cdot x = \frac{20}{45}$
	$x = \frac{4}{9}$

Step 2 shows that multiplying a number by $\frac{1}{45}$ is, from the Algebraic Definition of Division, the same as dividing by 45. Notice that when you divide both sides of the original equation by 45, then the result would be the equation in Step 3. So you can get the solution to this equation by dividing both sides of the equation by 45.

The general property, the Division Property of Equality, states that if you divide both sides of an equation by the same number, the results will be equal. Of course, you cannot divide by zero.

Division Property of Equality

If $a = b$ and $c \neq 0$, then $\frac{a}{c} = \frac{b}{c}$.

Mental Math

Solve for the variable.

a. $3m + 5 < 17$

b. $2.5 - n = 4.8$

c. $8 - 4w = -16$

d. $z + 7 + z > 15$

So you have two ways to solve an equation of the form $ax = b$. You can either multiply both sides by the reciprocal of a or you can divide both sides by a. Many people find multiplication easier when a is a fraction, and division easier when a is a decimal or percent. Both ways work.

 QY1

▶ **QY1**

Solve $24x = 15$ in the two ways mentioned in the preceding paragraph.

GUIDED

Example 1

High Mountain breakfast-blend coffee beans are selling at $6.78 a pound. If you bought some coffee beans and paid $16.95, how many pounds did you buy?

Solution The cost of w pounds of coffee beans is $6.78w$. So you would want to know when

$$6.78w = 16.95.$$

Divide both sides by 6.78.

$$\frac{6.78w}{6.78} = \frac{?}{?}$$
$$1 \cdot w = \underline{\ ?\ }$$

I bought about __?__ pounds of coffee beans.

Brazil is the largest producer of coffee in the world.

Source: International Coffee Organization

The Division Property of Inequality

Just as there is a Division Property of Equality, there is also a Division Property of Inequality. Consider how $-2n < 40$ might be solved.

Step 1	$-2n < 40$
Step 2	$\left(-\frac{1}{2}\right)(-2n) > \left(-\frac{1}{2}\right)(40)$
Step 3	$1 \cdot n > -\frac{40}{2}$
	$n > -20$

Steps 2 and 3 show that multiplying a number by $-\frac{1}{2}$ is the same as dividing by -2. So, you could have divided both sides of the original inequality by -2. Notice that the sense of the inequality changed.

The general property, the Division Property of Inequality, states that if you divide both sides of an inequality by a positive number, the inequality sign will be preserved. However, if you divide both sides of the inequality by a negative number, the inequality sign will be reversed. This covers all possibilities because you cannot divide by zero.

Division Property of Inequality

For any real numbers x and y: If $x < y$ and a is positive, then $\frac{x}{a} < \frac{y}{a}$.

For any real numbers x and y: If $x < y$ and a is negative, then $\frac{x}{a} > \frac{y}{a}$.

So just as there are two ways to solve an equation of the form $ax = b$, there are two ways to solve $ax < b$. You can either multiply both sides by $\frac{1}{a}$ or divide each side by a. Be careful to remember to reverse the inequality sign if you multiply or divide both sides of an inequality by a negative number.

 QY2

▶ **QY2**

If you divide both sides of $-3x > 24$ by -3, what is the resulting inequality?

Example 2

The weight of a sheet of paper is about 0.17 ounce. A book cover weighs about 8 ounces. If a book can weigh no more than 6 pounds, how many pages can the book have?

Solution If the book has p pages, then the weight of the book is $8 + 0.17p$ ounces. Because 6 pounds = 96 ounces, p must satisfy:

$$8 + 0.17p \le 96$$
$$0.17p \le 88 \qquad \text{Add } -8 \text{ to both sides.}$$
$$\frac{0.17p}{0.17} \le \frac{88}{0.17} \qquad \text{Divide both sides by 0.17.}$$
$$p \le 517.6$$

So the book can have as many as 517 pages.

Check

Step 1 Is $8 + 0.17 \cdot 517 \approx 96$? Yes; $8 + 0.17 \cdot 517 = 95.89$.

Step 2 Pick some value for w that is less than 517. Suppose you pick 100. Is $8 + 0.17 \cdot 100 \le 96$? Yes; $8 + 17 = 25$, which is less than or equal to 96.

Questions

COVERING THE IDEAS

In **1–4**, solve the equation using the Division Property of Equality.

1. $3n = 20$

2. $-46 = 0.46t$

3. $\frac{5}{9}F = -40$

4. $1{,}500p = -250{,}000$

5. In which of Questions 1–4 would you have preferred to solve the equation using the Multiplication Property of Equality rather than the Division Property of Equality?

6. A salad bar sells salad by weight, charging $4.99 per pound. If you paid $6.25 for your salad, how much did your salad weigh?

In **7–10**, solve each inequality using the Division Property of Inequality.

7. $4m \leq 30$

8. $-1.5x \geq 2.25$

9. $-2 < -6y + 4$

10. $16c + 8 > 264$

11. Suppose the cover of a book weighs 600 grams and each page weighs 5 grams. How many pages does the book have if its total weight is over 2 kilograms?

12. The length of a rectangle is 15 centimeters. Its area is less than 183 square centimeters. Find the width of the rectangle.

APPLYING THE MATHEMATICS

13. Find the value of $b - 3$ if $4(b - 3) = 76$.

14. In a settlement of a class-action lawsuit, $1,000,000 was divided among people so that each person received $83.47.
   a. What equation can you solve to determine how many people received money?
   b. Solve your equation from Part a.

15. An average-size person will burn about 660 calories per hour riding a bicycle at a moderate speed. How many hours would an average-size person need to ride a bike in order to burn about 3,500 calories?

In **16** and **17**, solve each equation.

16. $\frac{5x}{3} = -120$

17. $3.7 = -3x + x - 30x$

18. The building code in a certain village will not allow the ground floor of a building to be more than 2,800 square feet. If the width of the foundation is to be 125 feet, then how long can the foundation f be?

In 19 and 20, solve each inequality.

19. $\frac{2}{3}p \le \frac{1}{8}$

20. $-d < -15 + d$

REVIEW

In 21–23, rewrite each division as a multiplication and find the quotient. (Lessons 9-4, 9-2)

21. $-9.6 \div 3$

22. 16 miles $\div$ 25 minutes

23. $-\$15 \div 3$

24. **Multiple Choice** Suppose a is positive, b is negative, c is negative, and $a + bx = c$. Which is true? (Lesson 9-4)

A x is positive

B x is negative

C $x = 0$

D x may be positive, negative, or 0

25. Pat has an 8-foot board that he needs to saw into 9-inch pieces. How many pieces can he cut from the board? How long will the remaining piece of wood be? (Lesson 9-1)

26. The probability that luggage checked on airlines worldwide will reach the correct destination is about 99.5% per flight. Given this, what is the probability that a person could fly 20 times and always have his or her luggage arrive? (Lesson 8-4)

27. The chinstrap penguin's face contains two pairs of lines that are approximately parallel as shown at the right. The length of its chin $\overline{AD}$ is $\frac{11}{16}$ inch and the length of the white portion $\overline{CD}$ is $1\frac{3}{4}$ inches. (Lesson 6-7)

a. Find the perimeter of the parallelogram $ABCD$ drawn on the penguin's face.

b. If the measure of one of the angles of $ABCD$ is 28°, find the measures of the other three angles.

Chinstrap penguins live in the Antarctic and can often be seen on the South Sandwich Islands.

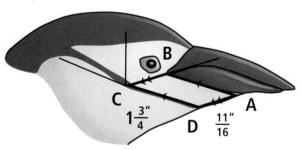

EXPLORATION

28. Find a number $x < 0$ such that $0.10 < x^2 < 0.20$.

QY ANSWERS

1. Multiply both sides by $\frac{1}{24}$ or divide both sides by 24. Both ways result in $x = \frac{5}{8}$.

2. $x < -8$

Lesson 9-6

The Ratio-Comparison Model for Division

Vocabulary

ratio comparison

▶ **BIG IDEA** Ratios are formed by dividing one quantity by another with the same type of unit.

At Abigail's school, students are required to take a foreign language. There are 24 students in her class. Nine choose to take French, and 15 choose to take Spanish. In Chapter 5, you learned how to compare the numbers 9, 15, and 24 by subtraction.

These numbers can also be compared with ratios. For example, you can say that the ratio of the number of students taking French to the total number of students is 9 students to 24 students. One way we write this is $\frac{9 \text{ students}}{24 \text{ students}}$ or, in lowest terms, $\frac{3}{8}$.

You can also say that the ratio of French students to all students is 3 to 8, or that 37.5% of the students are taking French.

Notice that because the units in the numerator and the denominator are the same, they cancel each other out in the division, so the answer has no unit. This is an important difference between rates and ratios. Because 9 students are being compared to 24 students, this use of division is called **ratio comparison.**

Mental Math

Decide whether the number is a prime number.

a. 6

b. 93

c. 79

d. 143

Ratio-Comparison Model for Division

If a and b are quantities with the same units, then $\frac{a}{b}$ compares a to b.

In the above situation, you could compare any of the numbers 9, 15, and 24 to each other. For example:

$$\frac{\text{number of students taking Spanish}}{\text{total number of students}} = \frac{15 \text{ students}}{24 \text{ students}} = \frac{5}{8}$$

So $\frac{5}{8}$ or 62.5% of the students are taking Spanish.

$$\frac{\text{total number of students}}{\text{number of students taking Spanish}} = \frac{24 \text{ students}}{15 \text{ students}} = \frac{8}{5}, \text{ or } 1\frac{3}{5}$$

The number of students in the class is $1\frac{3}{5}$ times, or 160%, of the number of students taking Spanish.

$$\frac{\text{number of students taking Spanish}}{\text{number of students taking French}} = \frac{15 \text{ students}}{9 \text{ students}} = \frac{5}{3}$$

You can say that $\frac{5}{3}$ as many students are taking Spanish as are taking French.

 QY1

Percents as Ratios

A percent can always be considered the result of a division. Because percents have no units, they are ratios.

> **QY1**
>
> Suppose three more students were added to Abigail's class and all of them took Spanish.
>
> a. What is the ratio of the total number of students to the number taking Spanish?
>
> b. What is ratio of the number of students taking Spanish to the number of students taking French?

GUIDED

Example 1

Suppose the tax on a purchase of $6.00 is $0.54. What is the tax rate? It's called a tax rate even though technically it is a ratio.

Solution Divide the tax by the amount being taxed. That is, compare $0.54 to $6.00 by division.

$$\frac{\$0.54}{\$6.00} = \underline{\quad?\quad} = \underline{\quad?\quad}\%.$$

The tax rate is __?__ %.

Check With a __?__ % tax rate, you pay __?__ ¢ on each purchase dollar. So you would pay 54¢ on a $6 purchase.

Example 2

The drive from Los Angeles to Chicago is approximately 2,000 miles. The drive from Los Angeles to Washington, D.C., is approximately 2,700 miles. Compare the distances using two different ratios, writing the ratios as percents.

Solution Compare the drive from Los Angeles to Chicago to the drive from Los Angeles to Washington, D.C.:

$$\frac{2,000 \text{ miles}}{2,700 \text{ miles}} \approx 0.74$$

This means **the driving distance from Los Angeles to Chicago is about 74% of the driving distance from Los Angeles to Washington, D.C.**

Dividing in the other order gives the reciprocal.

$$\frac{2,700 \text{ miles}}{2,000 \text{ miles}} = 1.35,$$ so the distance from Los Angeles to Washington, D.C., is about 1.35 times, or 135% of, the distance from Los Angeles to Chicago.

> **QY2**
>
> The cheetah has a top speed of 70 miles per hour and the lion has a top speed of 50 miles per hour over short distances. Compare the speeds in both orders, writing the ratios as percents.

 QY2

Questions

COVERING THE IDEAS

In 1–4 , consider a class in which 16 of the 28 students are boys. Write each number as a fraction in lowest terms or to the nearest tenth of a percent.

1. the ratio of boys to girls

2. the ratio of boys to all the students

3. the percent of students in the class who are boys

4. the percent of students in the class who are girls

5. In Michigan, a tax of $2.10 was charged on a purchase of $34.95. What was the tax rate?

6. The road distance from Reno, Nevada, to Denver, Colorado, is about 1,100 miles and the road distance from Boston, Massachusetts, to Miami, Florida, is about 1,500 miles. Compare the distances in both orders, writing the ratios as percents.

Fill in the Blank In 7–12, use the table of average daily sleep times of animals below.

Animal	Daily Sleep Time	Animal	Daily Sleep Time
Python	18 hours	Human	8 hours
Tiger	16 hours	Pig	8 hours
Gerbil	13 hours	Cow	4 hours
Cheetah	12 hours	Horse	3 hours
Baboon	10 hours	Giraffe	2 hours

Reticulated pythons can grow to over 34 feet in length. This one is over 22 feet long and weighs 310 pounds.

7. A python sleeps about __?__ times as long as a horse per day.

8. A pig sleeps about __?__ times as long as a cheetah per day.

9. A horse sleeps about __?__ hours less than a gerbil each day.

10. A tiger sleeps about __?__ percent of the time that a baboon sleeps each day.

11. In lowest terms, the ratio of the time a cow sleeps per day to the time a human sleeps is __?__.

12. In lowest terms, the ratio of the time a cow is awake during the day to the time a human is awake is __?__.

13. Australia and the Republic of South Africa are the world leaders in the production of gold. Gold is measured in troy ounces, which are about 1.1 times as heavy as the Avoirdupois ounces used to measure everyday items such as food.

a. In 2003, South Africa produced 12,100,000 troy ounces of gold and Australia produced 9,070,000 troy ounces of gold. Compare the amount of gold produced in both orders, writing the ratios as percents. Round to the nearest hundredth.

b. The total production of gold worldwide in 2003 was 83,300,000 troy ounces. Find the percent of the total amount of gold that is produced by Australia and South Africa together.

In 14 and 15, use this information. Every two years, there is an election for the House of Representatives in the U.S. Congress. The 57th Congress held office during the years 1901–1903. The 106th Congress held office during the years 1999–2001. The majority of representatives were Democrats in 32 of the Congresses in the 20th century. These are called Democratic Congresses. The majority were Republicans in the other 18 Congresses. These are called Republican Congresses.

14. a. Write the ratio of Republican Congresses to Democratic Congresses in lowest terms.

b. Write the ratio of Democratic Congresses to Republican Congresses in lowest terms.

15. a. What percent of Congresses in the 20th century had Republican majorities?

b. What percent of Congresses in the 20th century had Democratic majorities?

The U.S. Capitol Building houses the meeting chambers of the U.S. Senate in the north wing and the U.S. House of Representatives in the south wing.

APPLYING THE MATHEMATICS

16. The population of the United States in 2006 was about 300 million. At this time, the population of Canada was about 33 million. Perform the indicated operation and use the answer to write a sentence comparing the populations of the two countries.

a. 300 million − 33 million

b. 33 million − 300 million

c. $\dfrac{300\text{ million}}{33\text{ million}}$

d. $\dfrac{33\text{ million}}{300\text{ million}}$

17. Here are the populations of some cities in North America in the year 2000 and the cities in England for which they were named.

North American City	Population	British City	Population
Birmingham, Alabama	233,000	Birmingham, England	977,000
London, Ontario	432,000	London, England	7,172,000
Manchester, New Hampshire	109,000	Manchester, England	393,000
New York, New York	8,104,000	York, England	138,000

a. The ratio of the populations of which British city to its North American namesake is the greatest?

b. The ratio of the populations of which British city to its North American namesake is the least?

In 18–21, use this table of information about the planets. The volume, mass, and gravity are given as ratios to those of Earth. The distance from the Sun is in millions of miles and is the average of the maximum and minimum distances from the Sun.

Planet	Volume	Mass	Gravity at Surface	Distance from Sun
Mercury	0.0562	0.0553	0.38	36.0
Venus	0.857	0.815	0.91	67.2
Earth	1.000	1.000	1.00	93.0
Mars	0.151	0.107	0.38	141.6
Jupiter	1,321	317.8	2.53	483.8
Saturn	764	95.16	1.06	890.8
Uranus	63.1	14.54	0.90	1,784
Neptune	57.7	17.15	1.14	2,793

18. The greater the gravity at the surface, the more you would weigh. On which planets would you weigh more than on Earth? On which planets would you weigh the least?

19. The ratio of mass to volume is a measure of the *density* of a planet. Which planet is the least dense?

20. **Fill in the Blank** Answer to the nearest integer. Earth's volume is about __?__ times the volume of Mars.

21. **Multiple Choice** The ratio of the distance from Earth to the Sun to the distance from Mars to the Sun is closest to which ratio?

A $\frac{3}{2}$ B $\frac{2}{3}$ C $\frac{3}{4}$ D $\frac{4}{3}$

In this image of Earth, the Western Hemisphere is in daylight while the Eastern Hemisphere is not.

REVIEW

22. A car travels 300 miles using 17 gallons of gas. At the same rate of fuel efficiency, how far can it go on 10 gallons? (**Lessons 9-5, 9-2**)

23. Write the related facts for this fact triangle and solve for x. (**Lesson 9-4**)

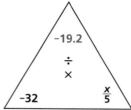

24. The town of St. Trout, Minnesota, placed an 8-foot-tall ice sculpture in the center of the town's skating rink. On Sunday at 8 A.M., the temperature increased and the sculpture began to melt. By noon, the sculpture was 6 feet 8 inches tall. What was the change per hour in the height of the sculpture? (**Lesson 9-4**)

25. **Multiple Choice** Which of the following is true? (**Lesson 9-3**)

    A $\frac{a}{b} \div \frac{c}{d} = \frac{ab}{cd}$

    B $\frac{a}{b} \div \frac{c}{d} = \frac{b}{a} \cdot \frac{c}{d}$

    C $\frac{a}{b} \div \frac{c}{d} = \frac{a}{b} \cdot \frac{d}{c}$

    D $\frac{a}{b} \div \frac{c}{d} = \frac{ac}{(b+d)}$

26. Suppose a car-rental agency charges $35 per day or any part of a day to rent an economy car, and there is a 7% sales tax. How much does it cost to rent a car for 100 hours? (**Lessons 9-2, 9-1, 3-7**)

27. Many stars are now known to have planets orbiting them. Suppose $\frac{1}{L}$ of the planets have life on them. And suppose $\frac{1}{H}$ of the planets with life on them have intelligent life. What fraction of the planets have intelligent life? (**Lesson 8-4**)

28. Rewrite the expression without using parentheses.
    $\frac{3}{5}(2x + 3y) - \frac{2}{5}(3x - 2y)$ (**Lesson 7-3**)

EXPLORATION

29. In aerospace travel, the Mach number is the ratio of the speed of an object to the speed of sound in a gas. Do research to find the four types of flight conditions based on the value of the Mach number.

QY ANSWERS

1. $\frac{3}{2}$; $\frac{2}{1}$

2. $\frac{\text{lion}}{\text{cheetah}} = \frac{50}{70} \approx 71.4\%$;

   $\frac{\text{cheetah}}{\text{lion}} = \frac{70}{50} = 140\%$

Lesson

9-7 Proportions

▶ **BIG IDEA** A proportion is an equation of the form $\frac{a}{b} = \frac{c}{d}$. If one of the four terms of a proportion is not known, the proportion can be solved as you solve other equations.

What Is a Proportion?

Applying the Ratio-Comparison Model for Division, when 18 out of 24 students in a class ride a bus to school, then $\frac{18}{24}$ of the class ride the bus. Because $\frac{18}{24} = \frac{3}{4}$, you could say that 3 out of 4 students ride a bus to school. Equal ratios give rise to equal fractions.

Suppose your heart beats 20 times in 15 seconds. Using the Rate Model for Division, your heart rate is $\frac{20 \text{ beats}}{15 \text{ seconds}}$.

Usually you want to know how many beats there are in a minute. 20 beats in 15 seconds is the same rate as 80 beats in 60 seconds. Equal rates give rise to equal fractions.

$$\frac{20 \text{ beats}}{15 \text{ seconds}} = \frac{80 \text{ beats}}{60 \text{ seconds}}$$

A **proportion** is an equation stating that two fractions are equal. $\frac{18}{24} = \frac{3}{4}$ and $\frac{20 \text{ beats}}{15 \text{ seconds}} = \frac{80 \text{ beats}}{60 \text{ seconds}}$ are proportions. Here are three more examples:

$$\frac{68}{170} = \frac{2}{5} \qquad \frac{9xy}{3x} = \frac{36y}{12} \qquad \frac{400 \text{ mi}}{15 \text{ gal}} = \frac{200 \text{ mi}}{7.5 \text{ gal}}$$

Some equations with fractions are *not* proportions. Examine these two equations.

$$\frac{y + 3}{4} = \frac{y}{2} \qquad\qquad \frac{y}{4} + \frac{3}{4} = \frac{y}{2}$$

a proportion   not a proportion

The equation above at the left is a proportion because on each side there is only one fraction. The equation above at the right is equivalent to the equation at the left. However, it is not a proportion because its left side is not a single fraction.

Solving Proportions

Like other equations, proportions can be true or false.

$$\frac{30}{100} = \frac{1}{3} \qquad\qquad \frac{30}{100} = \frac{3}{10}$$

false   true

When a proportion contains variables, the task is often to solve the proportion. That means to find the values that make the proportion true. For example,

$\frac{30}{100} = \frac{3}{x}$ has the solution $x = 10$, because $\frac{30}{100} = \frac{3}{10}$.

Sometimes proportions can be solved in your head.

GUIDED

Example 1

Solve for x. $\frac{3}{2} = \frac{12}{x}$

Solution Because true proportions are equal fractions, we know that 3 can be multiplied by __?__ to produce 12, so 2 must be multiplied by the *same* factor to produce x. So x = __?__.

Some proportions may require more work to solve.

Example 2

Cesar went to a store where 5 bags of peanuts cost $12. How much should he pay for 8 bags?

Solution 1 Find the price per bag. If 5 bags cost $12, then the unit price is $\frac{\$12}{5 \text{ bags}}$, or $2.40 per bag.

The cost of 8 bags would be $2.40 • 8, or $19.20.

Solution 2 The problem suggests equal rates.

$$\frac{5 \text{ bags}}{\$12} = \frac{8 \text{ bags}}{\$x} \text{ or } \frac{5}{12} = \frac{8}{x}$$

Now solve for x in the proportion. Use the Multiplication Property of Equality to multiply both sides by 12x, the product of the denominators.

$$12x • \frac{5}{12} = \frac{8}{x} • 12x$$

$$\frac{12x • 5}{12} = \frac{8 • 12x}{x}$$

Now simplify the fractions and apply the Division Property of Equality to solve.

$$x • 5 = 8 • 12$$
$$5x = 96$$
$$x = 19\frac{1}{5}, \text{ or } 19.2, \text{ or } \$19.20$$

Check Write each fraction in lowest terms or as equivalent decimals. In this case, equivalent decimals is probably easier:

$$\frac{5}{12} = 0.41\overline{6} \text{ and } \frac{8}{19.2} = 0.41\overline{6}$$

Because the decimals are equivalent, $19.20 is the correct value for x.

The Means-Extremes Property

Consider the true proportion $\frac{4}{18} = \frac{6}{27}$.

This proportion can also be written as $4:18 = 6:27$.

In the United States, the colon is used to indicate a ratio. You can say, "The ratio of 4 to 18 equals the ratio of 6 to 27" or you can say, "4 is to 18 as 6 is to 27."

Look again at the way $4:18 = 6:27$ is written. The numbers 4 and 27 are on the ends of the equation and are called the **extremes** of the proportion. The numbers 18 and 6 are on the inside and are called the **means.** Notice that 4 times 27 equals 18 times 6. The product of the means equals the product of the extremes.

 QY

The general pattern can be shown to be true by using the Multiplication Property of Equality. Suppose $\frac{a}{b} = \frac{c}{d}$.

Now multiply both sides of the proportion by bd, the product of the denominators.

$$bd \cdot \frac{a}{b} = bd \cdot \frac{c}{d}$$
$$da = bc$$
$$\text{or} \quad ad = bc$$

The left side of $ad = bc$ is the product of the extremes; the right side, bc, is the product of the means. This is an important property.

> **QY**
>
> Consider the proportion $\frac{42}{17.5} = \frac{12}{5}$. Verify that the product of the means equals the product of the extremes.

Means-Extremes Property

In any true proportion, the product of the means equals the product of the extremes.

GUIDED

Example 3

Use the Means-Extremes Property to solve $\frac{5}{7} = \frac{8}{x}$.

Step 1 Write an equation using the products of the means and extremes.

$5 \cdot \underline{\ ?\ } = 7 \cdot \underline{\ ?\ }$

Step 2 Simplify.

$5\underline{\ ?\ } = \underline{\ ?\ }$

Step 3 Use the Division Property of Equality to solve for x.

$x = \underline{\ ?\ }$

Check Substitute your answer from Step 3 for x in the proportion, and use the Means-Extremes Property to check that the products are equal.

You have now seen three ways to solve a proportion. You will need to decide which way works best for you in each situation. One common application of proportions is estimating distances on a map.

GUIDED

Example 4

Julie knows that the distance from San Antonio, Texas, to Houston, Texas, is 200 miles. On a map of the state, this distance is $6\frac{3}{4}$ inches. On the same map, the distance from Orange, Texas, to El Paso, Texas, is $28\frac{3}{4}$ inches. How far is it from Orange to El Paso?

Solution Set up the proportion as equal rates.

$$\frac{?}{?} = \frac{28\frac{3}{4}}{x \text{ miles}}. \text{ Then use the Means-Extremes Property to solve.}$$

$$\underline{\quad?\quad}\, x = \underline{\quad?\quad} \cdot \underline{\quad?\quad}$$

$$\underline{\quad?\quad}\, x = \underline{\quad?\quad}$$

Divide both sides of the equation by __?__.

$$x = \underline{\quad?\quad}$$

El Paso, Texas, is about __?__ miles from Orange, Texas.

Questions

COVERING THE IDEAS

1. Define *proportion*.

2. a. **Fill in the Blanks** 24 out of 60 students in a class are boys. In lowest terms, __?__ out of __?__ students are boys.
   b. Write a proportion using the numbers of Part a.

3. a. **Fill in the Blank** You stuff 300 envelopes in 10 minutes. At this rate, you would stuff __?__ envelopes in an hour.
   b. Write a proportion using the numbers of Part a.

4. **Multiple Choice** Which proportion is *not* true?
   A $\frac{2}{3} = \frac{66}{100}$ B $\frac{5}{13} = \frac{25}{65}$ C $\frac{40}{12} = \frac{2}{0.6}$ D $\frac{7}{9} = \frac{21}{27}$

5. **Multiple Choice** Which equation is *not* a proportion?
   A $\frac{x}{11} = \frac{1}{5}$ B $\frac{\frac{3}{4}}{\frac{1}{2}} = \frac{3}{2}$ C $\frac{1}{3} + \frac{2}{3} = \frac{3}{3}$ D $\frac{6.1x}{4} = \frac{61}{10}$

6. Write how the proportion $2:3 = 6:9$ is read.

7. Describe a situation in which the proportion in Question 6 would arise.

8. Consider the equation $\frac{144}{27} = \frac{432}{x}$.

   a. Solve by finding the factor by which the numerator on the left has been multiplied to produce the numerator on the right.

   b. Solve using the Multiplication Property of Equality.

   c. Solve using the Means-Extremes Property.

   d. Check by writing both fractions in lowest terms or as equal decimals.

In 9–12, solve.

9. $\frac{A}{6} = \frac{7}{12}$

10. $\frac{30}{B} = \frac{2}{5}$

11. $\frac{2.4}{12} = \frac{1.6}{C}$

12. $\frac{88}{121} = \frac{33}{D}$

13. A 15-ounce box of cereal costs $3.25. At this rate, what should you expect to pay for a 21-ounce box of the same cereal?

14. A basketball player scored 7 points in the first 10 minutes of the game. At this rate, how many points would the player score in the full 48-minute game?

15. The distance from Pensacola, Florida, to Tallahassee, Florida, on a map is 8 inches, which represents 200 miles. How many miles is it from Pensacola to Miami if the distance on the map measures 27 inches?

APPLYING THE MATHEMATICS

16. Luther tried to solve the proportion of Question 9 by multiplying both sides by 12. Will this work?

17. A volleyball team plays 30 matches in a season. The team has won 4 of their first 5 matches. At this rate, how many matches will they win in the season?

18. If you want to walk the 7 blocks to a friend's house in 20 minutes, how long should it take you to walk the first two blocks?

19. If $\frac{w}{z} = \frac{x}{y}$ with $z \neq 0$ and $y \neq 0$, is each statement *always, sometimes but not always,* or *never* true?

   a. $wz = xy$

   b. $wx = yz$

   c. $wy = xz$

   d. $zw = yx$

20. Why won't the Means-Extremes Property work on the equation $x + \frac{2}{3} = \frac{4}{5}$?

21. A recipe says to use $\frac{3}{4}$ of a teaspoon of salt for 6 people. How many teaspoons of salt should be used to serve 24 people?

Sand volleyball has been an Olympic event since 1996.

22. In his first 100 games, basketball player LeBron James of the Cleveland Cavaliers scored 2,181 points.

    a. At this rate, how many games would it take for him to surpass Kareem Abdul-Jabbar's National Basketball Association record of 38,387 career points?

    b. If there are 82 games in a regular season, how many full seasons would it take?

23. Stephen volunteers at the local animal shelter on Saturday mornings. He can clean and disinfect 3 cages in ten minutes. His friend Carlos cleans 4 cages in fifteen minutes. If both work one and one-half hours, how many more cages will Stephen clean than Carlos?

REVIEW

24. a. What percent of 15 is 30?

    b. What percent of 30 is 15?

    c. What is the relationship between the answers to Parts a and b? (**Lesson 9-6**)

25. In the Sierra Nevada mountain range in California, Mount Lamarck is 4,090 meters above sea level and Mount Goethe is 4,043 meters above sea level. What percent higher is Mount Lamarck? (**Lesson 9-6**)

Overlooking Mt. Darwin and Mt. Mendel from the summit plateau of Mt. Lamark

26. a. Copy the triangle below and draw the image of the triangle under a size change of $-\frac{3}{5}$.

    b. Compare the areas of the two triangles. (**Lessons 9-6, 7-7, 7-4**)

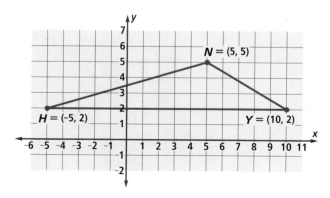

27. If Miles bikes 5.2 kilometers each way to and from work 5 days per week, how far will he bike in 6 weeks? **(Lesson 9-2)**

28. Suppose Jamie reads 38 pages of a novel every night.
    a. How many days will it take her to finish a novel that is 231 pages long?
    b. How many pages will she read on the last night? **(Lesson 9-1)**

29. In 1995, physicist Lene Hau passed a beam of light through an extremely cold form of matter called a *Bose-Einstein condensate*. Light traveled through the material at only 38 miles per hour. How long in seconds would it take a beam of light to travel 3 inches through this material? **(Lesson 8-2)**

Lene Hau in her laboratory

EXPLORATION

30. Suppose a 10-inch pizza costs $7.
    a. Use a proportion based on the diameters of the pizzas to find the cost of a 12-inch pizza.
    b. Many pizza restaurants charge more for a large pizza than what would be calculated by proportions using the diameter. Why must they charge more?
    c. Find a menu from a restaurant that sells pizza. Do the larger pizzas cost more or less per inch of diameter?

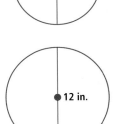

10 in.

12 in.

QY ANSWER

$42 \cdot 5 = 12 \cdot 17.5 = 210$

Lesson 9-8
Proportional Thinking

Vocabulary

proportional thinking

▶ **BIG IDEA** Proportional thinking can help you to estimate answers to proportions.

What Is Proportional Thinking?

In the last lesson, you learned about proportions and how to solve them using the Means-Extremes Property. You also saw how to solve proportions in your head without using an equation, pencil and paper, or a calculator. Here is a situation involving proportional thinking that you should be able to solve in your head.

Mental Math

A store advertises that shirts are being sold at "2 for the price of 1." Fill in the blank to make the equivalent proportion.

a. "_____ for the price of 4"

b. "10 for the price of _____"

c. "_____ for the price of 13"

d. "190 for the price of _____"

Example 1

Suppose you are planning a party for a school club that has 24 members. You decide to order one bag of peanuts for each person at the party. You go to the store and find that you can get 3 small bags of peanuts for $2.50. What will it cost you for 24 bags?

Solution

Notice that 24 is 8 times 3. So the cost should be 8 times $2.50. To calculate the cost without pencil and paper you could think this way:

Twice $2.50 is $5, so 4 times $2.50 is $10 and 8 times $2.50 is $20.

It will cost $20 for 24 bags.

The kind of thinking used to figure out that 24 bags would cost $20 is called *proportional thinking*. There are two parts to **proportional thinking:** (1) the sense to recognize situations in which setting up a proportion is a way to find an answer and (2) the ability to get or estimate an answer to a proportion without solving an equation. Some people believe that proportional thinking is one of the most important kinds of thinking you can have in mathematics.

 QY1

▶ **QY1**

In Example 1, what would 36 bags cost?

GUIDED

Example 2

One portable audio player with 4 GB (gigabytes) of memory can store about 1,150 songs. How many songs could a similar player with 20 GB of memory store?

Solution 1 Use proportional thinking. Since 20 GB is 5 times 4 GB, a similar player could store __?__ times __?__ songs. This is __?__ songs.

Solution 2 Set up a proportion and solve it using the Means-Extremes Property.

$$\frac{\underline{\;?\;}\ GB}{\underline{\;?\;}\ songs} = \frac{\underline{\;?\;}\ GB}{S\ songs}$$

$$\underline{\;?\;} \cdot S = \underline{\;?\;} \cdot \underline{\;?\;}$$

$$\underline{\;?\;}\ S = \underline{\;?\;}$$

$$S = \underline{\;?\;}$$

So a player with 20 GB of memory can store __?__ songs.

 QY2

> ▶ QY2
>
> In Example 2, how many songs could a similar player with 80 GB of memory store?

Activity

Here are four situations from the real world, some of which involve proportional thinking and some of which do not. Sort the situations into two groups. If the situation calls for proportional thinking, give the answer without using pencil and paper or a calculator. If the situation does not call for proportional thinking, explain why it does not.

Situation A A car can travel 80,000 miles on 4 tires without changing them how far can it travel on 3 tires without changing them?

Situation B If a person can run a mile in 7 minutes 30 seconds, how long would it take the person to run 6 miles?

Situation C A punch recipe calls for $\frac{1}{2}$ cup of sugar for every 2 cups of water. How much sugar is needed if you use 24 cups of water?

Situation D A bronze statue that is two feet tall weighs 125 pounds. How much will a similar statue that is 5 feet tall weigh?

Using Proportional Thinking to Estimate an Answer

In Examples 1 and 2, you could find an exact answer with proportional thinking. You can also use proportional thinking to estimate answers even when the problem does not seem to involve a proportion.

Example 3

A bowl of cereal has about 280 calories. Omar ate about $\frac{2}{3}$ of a bowl. How many calories did he consume?

Solution Use proportional thinking and estimate. 280 calories is a little less than 300 calories. If he ate $\frac{1}{3}$ of a bowl with 300 calories, he would have consumed $\frac{1}{3}$ of 300 calories, or 100 calories. So $\frac{2}{3}$ of a bowl with 300 calories has 200 calories. **He consumed a little less than 200 calories.**

Check 1 Multiply.

$$\frac{2}{3} \text{ bowl} \cdot 280 \frac{\text{calories}}{\text{bowl}} = \frac{560 \text{ calories}}{3} \approx 187 \text{ calories}$$

Check 2 Set up a proportion.

$$\frac{1 \text{ bowl}}{280 \text{ calories}} = \frac{\frac{2}{3} \text{ bowl}}{x \text{ calories}}$$

$$1 \cdot x = \frac{2}{3} \cdot 280$$

$$x = \frac{560}{3}$$

$$x \approx 187.$$

You may be able to solve a proportion in your head or with pencil and paper. You should have at least two ways of solving these sorts of problems. Use one way to check the other. However, be sure that the situation is one that calls for proportional thinking before you use proportions to answer the question.

Questions

COVERING THE IDEAS

1. What two things does proportional thinking involve?

In 2–4, use proportional thinking to answer the question. Explain how you got an answer without using pencil and paper or a calculator.

2. If 3 cans of orange juice cost $2.25, what will 9 cans cost?

3. If 10% of a number is 4.3, what is 20% of the number?

4. A recipe for making rice in a pressure cooker calls for 6 ounces of water for every 4 ounces of rice. How much water would you need for 10 ounces of rice?

In 5–8, tell why you cannot use proportional thinking in the situation.

5. It takes 20 minutes for a restaurant to bake a pizza. How long will it take the restaurant to bake 4 pizzas?

6. Jessicah Schipper of Australia set a world-record time of 2.09 minutes for the women's 200-meter butterfly on August 17, 2006. At this rate, how long would it take her to swim the 600-meter butterfly?

7. If it takes you 45 minutes to walk to a friend's house, then how long will it take you if you walk twice as fast?

8. The area of a square with a side of 10 inches is 100 square inches. What is the area of a square with a side of 20 inches?

In 9 and 10, estimate by using proportional thinking. Then find the exact answer.

9. If your heart beats 19 times in 10 seconds, how many times will it beat in a minute?

10. Graciana biked 125 miles in the first 3 days of a trip from Denver to Minneapolis. At this rate, how many days will it take her to bike the entire 920-mile trip?

11. **a. Fill in the Blanks** Traveling at 45 kilometers per hour, it takes between __?__ and __?__ hours to go 200 kilometers.

    b. At 45 km/h, exactly how long does it take to go 200 km?

APPLYING THE MATHEMATICS

12. Katisha kept careful records of her gas mileage. She found that in her normal driving she could get 20.5 miles per gallon of gas.

    a. Make a chart for gas consumption and distance driven, with 5 gallons to 40 gallons of gas using 5-gallon increments.

    b. Use your chart to graph the gallons of gas used and the distance driven. What characteristic does the graph have that is shared by other proportional situations?

    c. How many miles can Katisha drive on 18 gallons of gas?

13. There are 640 acres in a square mile. On August 20 and 21, 1910, what may have been the largest forest fire in American history burned three million acres of timberland in northern Idaho and western Montana. About how many square miles is this?

Drought and hurricane-force winds contributed to the 1910 Fire. Some areas destroyed by the fire are still recovering.

Source: Idaho Forest Products Commission

14. Alisha wondered how many words were defined in her dictionary. She picked 3 pages at random and counted a total of 251 words. Her dictionary has 1,375 pages. Estimate the number of words defined in the dictionary, to the nearest 10,000.

15. On a map, the scale is given as 1 inch to 50 miles. If two points are $2\frac{3}{8}$ inches apart on the map, what is the actual distance?

16. Tissue is on sale at 3 boxes for $4. At this rate, what will it cost for 5 boxes? (Round up to the nearest penny.)

17. Chef Luis and Chef Moiya can each bake and decorate 2 cakes in 3 hours. If the chefs work together, how many cakes can they bake and decorate in 9 hours?

REVIEW

In 18–20, use the Means-Extremes Property to determine whether the proportions are true. **(Lesson 9-7)**

18. $\frac{3.4}{17} = \frac{4}{20}$

19. $\frac{4x}{3.2h} = \frac{10h}{8x}$

20. $\frac{14.5b}{p\ell} = \frac{58b}{4p\ell}$

21. From January 1 to March 15, Roberto earned $14,000 in salary. At this rate, how much would he earn in a 365-day year? **(Lesson 9-7)**

22. Solve for r in two different ways. $\frac{19}{2r} = \frac{190}{8}$ **(Lesson 9-7)**

23. What is the ratio of vowels to consonants in the quotation below, including the name? **(Lesson 9-6)**

> If we knew what we were doing, it would not be called research, would it? —Albert Einstein

In 24 and 25, use the figure at the right.

24. a. Copy the figure and draw its image under a size change of magnitude 3. **(Lesson 7-7)**

b. What is the ratio of the area of the image to the area of the preimage? **(Lesson 8-3)**

25. a. Draw the image of the figure under the translation in which the image of (x, y) is $(x + -3, y + 1)$.

b. Find the ratio of the area of the image to the area of the preimage. **(Lessons 9-6, 6-1)**

Albert Einstein received the Nobel Prize in 1921 for developing the theory of relativity.

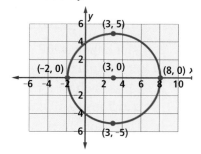

EXPLORATION

26. The U.S. government calculates the "consumer price index" (CPI) to measure the cost of living. When the CPI doubles, it means that prices have doubled. Here we consider the CPI for the year 1967 to be 100. In 1970, the CPI was 116.3. In 2000, the CPI was 515.8.

a. If a new car cost $2,500 in 1970, what would you expect a corresponding new car price to have been in 2000?

b. If a job paid $20/hour in 2000, what pay/hour in 1950, when the CPI was 72.1, would have the same purchasing value?

c. Find out a recent value of the CPI and make up and solve a problem that compares costs now with costs many years ago.

QY ANSWERS

1. $30

2. 23,000 songs

Lesson
9-9
Proportions in Similar Figures

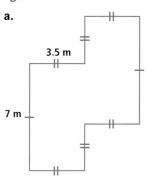
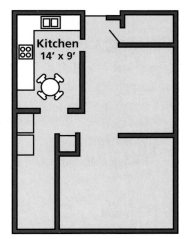
> **BIG IDEA** In similar figures, ratios of corresponding sides form true proportions that can be solved to find unknown lengths.

In Chapters 7 and 8, you saw and created some size-change images of figures. Many professions use size-change images in their work. For example, architects draw scale models of floor plans like the one shown below at the right. The Activity shows how to determine the size-change factor when given two similar figures.

Activity

Work with a partner. You will need a sheet of cm grid paper. Polygons *ABCDE* and *A'B'C'D'E'* at the right are similar.

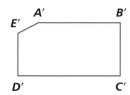

Step 1 Measure the lengths of all ten sides.

$AB = \underline{\ ?\ }$ $BC = \underline{\ ?\ }$ $CD = \underline{\ ?\ }$
$DE = \underline{\ ?\ }$ $EA = \underline{\ ?\ }$

$A'B' = \underline{\ ?\ }$ $B'C' = \underline{\ ?\ }$ $C'D' = \underline{\ ?\ }$
$D'E' = \underline{\ ?\ }$ $E'A' = \underline{\ ?\ }$

Step 2 Compute the ratios of lengths of corresponding sides.

$\dfrac{A'B'}{AB} = \underline{\ ?\ }$ $\dfrac{B'C'}{BC} = \underline{\ ?\ }$ $\dfrac{C'D'}{CD} = \underline{\ ?\ }$

$\dfrac{D'E'}{DE} = \underline{\ ?\ }$ $\dfrac{E'A'}{EA} = \underline{\ ?\ }$

Step 3 *A'B'C'D'E'* is the image of *ABCDE* under a size change. From the ratios of lengths of corresponding sides that you found, what do you think is the magnitude of that size change? $\underline{\ ?\ }$

Step 4 Pick a size-change magnitude to use to draw a triangle and its image. Do not tell your partner the size-change magnitude you picked. After you and your partner have completed your drawings, give them to each other. Measure lengths of segments and compute ratios to determine what size-change magnitude your partner used.

 QY

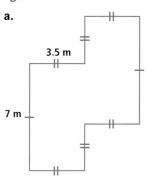

Kitchen
14' x 9'

> **QY**

What is the approximate magnitude of the size change from the scale drawing above to the actual floor plan? Measure the scale drawing inner wall to inner wall.

From the Activity, you have seen the following property:

> **Fundamental Property of Similar Figures**
>
> If two figures are similar, then ratios of corresponding lengths are equal.

Example 1

The two triangles shown here are similar. Name the corresponding sides.

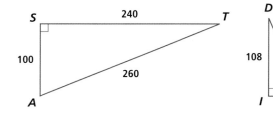

Solution The sides correspond in order of their lengths. The shortest sides $\overline{SA}$ and $\overline{IH}$ correspond. The middle-length sides $\overline{ST}$ and $\overline{ID}$ are corresponding sides. So are $\overline{TA}$ and $\overline{DH}$, the longest sides.

Notice that the ratios of these sides are equal: $\frac{100}{45} = \frac{240}{108} = \frac{260}{117} = \frac{20}{9}$.

Finding Lengths in Similar Figures

If you know which sides of similar figures correspond, you can find unknown lengths by solving proportions.

Example 2

Triangles *ABC* and *ADE* are similar. Find *DE*.

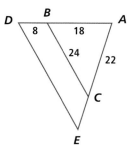

Solution $\overline{DE}$ corresponds to $\overline{BC}$. The only corresponding sides with both lengths given are $\overline{AD}$ and $\overline{AB}$. Use them in the proportion.

$$\frac{DE}{BC} = \frac{AD}{AB}$$

Now substitute what is known. $\frac{DE}{24} = \frac{18 + 8}{18}$

Solve as you would any other proportion. Use the Means-Extremes Property.

$$18 \cdot DE = 24 \cdot (18 + 8)$$

$$18DE = 624$$

Divide both sides by 18. $\qquad DE = \frac{624}{18}$

$$= 34\frac{2}{3}$$

Check For a rough check, look at the figure. Does a length of about 34 for $\overline{DE}$ seem reasonable? It seems so. For an exact check, substitute in the proportion.

$$\frac{34\frac{2}{3}}{24} = \frac{26}{18}$$

Division shows each side to equal $1.\overline{4}$.

When Do Similar Figures Occur?

Real objects do not always come in a size you can manipulate. If an object is very big, you may construct a scale model. If an object is very small, you might magnify it. You might take a photograph of it or draw a picture of it. Any of these activities lead to similar figures for which you might want to find lengths of sides. For these reasons, you often encounter proportions involving similar figures.

GUIDED

Example 3

In this scaled picture, the bus is 60 millimeters long and its top is 17 millimeters above the ground. If the actual bus being pictured is 9 feet high, how long is the bus?

Solution Here you should imagine the actual bus or draw a picture. Its height of 9 feet corresponds to 17 millimeters, while the unknown length L of the bus corresponds to 60 millimeters. Because the picture and the actual bus are similar,

$$\frac{\text{actual height of bus}}{\text{height of bus in picture}} = \frac{\text{actual length of bus, } L}{\text{length of bus in picture}}$$

(continued on next page)

Substitute.
$$\frac{?}{?} = \frac{L}{?}$$

Use the Means-Extremes Property to solve for L.

$$\frac{?}{?} \cdot ? = ? \cdot L$$

Solve for L.
$$L = \frac{540}{17}$$
$$\approx 31.76$$

The bus is about __?__ feet __?__ inches long.

Questions

COVERING THE IDEAS

1. If two figures are similar, what is true about their corresponding lengths?

2. Polygon *HUGE* is an expansion image of polygon *TINY,* as shown at the right.
   a. Name the ratios equal to $\frac{IN}{UG}$.
   b. If $YN = 20$, $EG = 30$, and $TY = 26$, what is HE?

3. Refer to Example 2. Find AE.

4. Draw an example of similar pentagons whose corresponding sides are not parallel.

5. *ABCD* and *EFGH* are similar. What is the value of x?

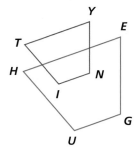

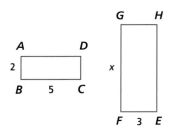

6. Name three places where similar figures can be found.

7. Are the figures below similar? Explain why or why not.

8. A front view of a picture of the bus in Example 3 is 15 millimeters wide. How wide is the actual bus?

APPLYING THE MATHEMATICS

In 9 and 10, a right triangle has sides with lengths 3, 4, and 5 centimeters.

9. If the longest side of a similar right triangle has length 15 centimeters, find the lengths of the other two sides of this similar right triangle.

10. Suppose the shortest side of a similar right triangle has length 15 millimeters.
    a. Draw an accurate picture of the similar right triangle.
    b. Find the lengths of the other two sides of the similar right triangle.
    c. Draw an accurate picture of a similar right triangle if the longest side's length is 15 mm.

11. A drawing 20 centimeters by 15 centimeters is put into a copy machine at a setting to be shrunk to 75% of its original size.
    a. What will the dimensions of the copy be?
    b. Are the ratios of corresponding sides of the drawing and its copy equal?
    c. Are the drawing and its copy similar?

12. A boat is 40 feet long. A scale model of the boat is 18 inches long. If the scale model is 5 inches wide, how wide is the actual boat?

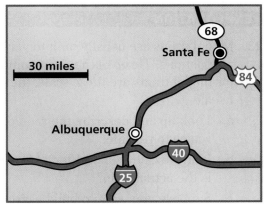

13. At the right is a map of the region around Santa Fe, New Mexico. A distance of 14 millimeters on the map means an actual distance of about 30 miles. The distance from Albuquerque to Santa Fe on the map is about 22 millimeters. How far is this in actual miles?

REVIEW

14. Explain whether you should use proportional thinking to answer the question. (Lesson 9-8)
    a. 4 gallons of gasoline cost $8.76. How much do 17 gallons cost?
    b. Jameel rode his bicycle 2.3 miles in 12 minutes. How far can he ride in an hour?
    c. The first novel in a series is 309 pages long. How many pages will the fifth book in the series be?

In 15 and 16, solve. (Lesson 9-7)

15. $\dfrac{j}{25} = \dfrac{7}{20}$

16. $\dfrac{6.5}{90} = \dfrac{200}{x}$

17. Multiple Choice Which value of p makes the proportion $\dfrac{p^2}{3.9} = \dfrac{-p}{15.6}$ true? (Lesson 9-7)

A $\dfrac{1}{4}$ B -4 C $-\dfrac{1}{4}$ D 4

18. If $x = 45$ and $y = -60$, tell whether the expression is positive or negative. (Lessons 9-4, 8-3, 5-2)

a. $x - y$ b. $y - x$ c. $\dfrac{x}{y}$

d. $\dfrac{y}{x}$ e. xy f. $-xy$

19. A boy walked $3\dfrac{2}{3}$ miles in $1\dfrac{1}{2}$ hours. What rate is this? (Lessons 9-3, 9-2)

20. A number was divided by 17, giving a quotient of 4 and a remainder of 13. What was the number? (Lesson 9-1)

In 21 and 22, solve. (Lesson 8-6)

21. $\dfrac{4}{5}x = 91.3$

22. $\$3.80 = 70\%B$

EXPLORATION

23. Model trains are usually built to very specific proportions. Three of the most common scale factors for model trains are the Z scale, the N scale, and the I scale.

a. Look up and describe the ratio of each of the three scales to real life.

b. If an N-scale train is 1 foot 4 inches long, how long is the actual train?

c. Suppose you want to build a circular Z-scale model track similar to a track that is 3 miles long. How long would the model track be?

The image above shows an N scale model of the SD 75M locomotive. This type of locomotive is still used on major U.S. railroads.

QY ANSWER

about 170

Chapter 9 Projects

Mona Lisa by Da Vinci

Portrait of Anna Zborowska by Modigliani

1 Cats and Dogs

Survey your class to find out how many students consider themselves to be a "dog person," how many a "cat person," how many like both, and how many like neither. Then find the total number of students in your class.

1. What is the ratio of the number of students who stated "cat person" to the total number of students? Write your answer as a fraction in lowest terms and to the nearest tenth of a percent.

2. What is the ratio of the number of students who said "dog person" to the total number of students? Write your answer as a fraction in lowest terms and to the nearest tenth of a percent.

3. Create a circle graph of your results, with one sector each representing students who are cat people, dog people, like both, and like neither.

4. From your survey, find out how many "like" cats, "love" cats, "love" dogs, or "like" dogs. Find the ratio of people who like dogs to people who like cats, and the ratio of people who love dogs to people who love cats. Are the ratios different? Why do you think this is so?

5. Create a circle graph with one sector each representing students who like cats, love cats, like dogs, love dogs, like neither, like both, and love both.

L' Arlesienne (Madame Ginoux) by van Gogh

2 The Face

Observe the three paintings above by Leonardo da Vinci, Amedeo Modigliani, and Vincent van Gogh.

1. In each case, find the ratio of
   a. the distance from the top of the head to the bottom of the chin, l, to the width of the head, w.
   b. the distance from the tip of the nose to the bottom of the chin, n, to the distance from the lips to the bottom of the chin, p.

2. How are the ratios similar? How are they different?

3. Compare these ratios to the ratios of distances on your own face. To which painting are you most similar?

3 Best Buys

Go to a grocery store and find examples of at least five foods that are packaged in different sizes. Calculate the unit cost for each size to determine best buys. Is it true that bigger packages are more economical? The size of a food item can be measured by its volume, weight, quantity, or some other attribute. Does this result vary with the choice of attribute?

4 How Fast Do You Type?

In Lesson 9-2, you calculated how long it took you to write with your left and right hands. When you type, you can use both hands. At home or at school, use a computer to calculate how long it takes you to type your name. What is your rate in letters per second? Usually, typing speed is measured in words per minute, not letters per second. There are 10 words in the following sentence:

The quick brown fox jumped over the lazy sleeping dog.

Type the paragraph above (beginning with "In Lesson 9-2") as fast as you can without any mistakes. How long did it take? How many words per minute do you type? Find information on the Dvorak keyboard shown below, which is designed to help people type faster.

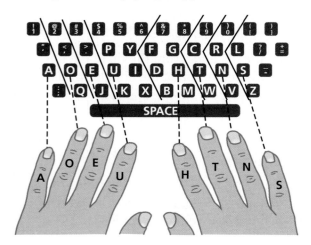

5 Proportional Measurement

Depending on where the Sun is in the sky, your shadow can be much shorter than you or it can be very long. But at a given time, the length of any object's shadow will be proportional to its height. Find a flagpole or other tall object that casts a shadow whose length you can measure. Measure this length. Then find an object whose height you know (a meterstick works well, or a friend), and measure the length of its shadow at the same time of day that you measured the tall object's shadow. Set up and solve a proportion that gives you the height of the tall object.

6 Mapping Your Home

Draw a to-scale map of your home by measuring walls, doors, and windows with a tape measure and use these measurements to draw the rooms proportionally on a large sheet of paper.

Chapter 9 Summary and Vocabulary

- There are two types of division. For **integer division** $x \div y$, x must be an integer and y must be a whole number. The answer is a quotient with a remainder. For **real-number division** $x \div y$, x and y can be any numbers, $y \neq 0$, and the answer is the single-number quotient $\frac{x}{y}$.

- Division is related to multiplication in two ways. The first way is through related facts: If $\frac{x}{y} = z$, then $yz = x$ and also $\frac{x}{z} = y$. The second is through the **Algebraic Definition of Division**: $\frac{x}{y} = x \cdot \frac{1}{y}$. To solve the equation $ax = b$, you can use related facts to conclude that $x = \frac{b}{a}$. Or you can divide both sides by a or multiply both sides by $\frac{1}{a}$ and reach the same conclusion. If a is positive, then $\frac{1}{a}$ is positive. If a is negative, then $\frac{1}{a}$ is negative. Dividing both sides of an inequality by the same number follows the same rules as multiplying both sides of an inequality by a number: if the number is negative, you must change the direction of the inequality; otherwise, its direction remains unchanged.

- One basic use of division is to calculate rates. In a rate, the dividend and the divisor have different units. The unit of the rate is written as a fraction. For example, if x words are divided by y minutes, the quotient is $\frac{x}{y}$ words per minute, which can be written as $\frac{x}{y} \frac{\text{words}}{\text{minute}}$. The numbers involved in rates can be fractions, decimals, or negative numbers. Rates can help you learn how to divide these kinds of numbers. To divide fractions, you can use the Algebraic Definition of Division: Take the reciprocal of the divisor and multiply. To divide with negative numbers, follow the same rules for signs as you follow for multiplication.

- Another basic use of division is to calculate ratios. Ratios are numbers that compare two quantities having the same units. Because both the dividend and the divisor in a ratio have the same units, the quotient has no unit. Ratios may be decimals, fractions, or integers. Percents are ratios.

- A **proportion** is a statement of the form $\frac{a}{b} = \frac{c}{d}$. Proportions occur daily and in all areas of mathematics. Simple proportions can be solved in your head. For other proportions, use the Means-Extremes Property or the Multiplication Property of Equality. In all cases, if $\frac{a}{b} = \frac{c}{d}$, then $ad = bc$.

Vocabulary

9-1
real-number division
integer division
quotient-remainder form

9-6
ratio comparison

9-7
proportion
extremes
means

9-8
proportional thinking

Theorems and Properties

Quotient-Remainder Formula (p. 556)
Rate Model for Division (p. 563)
Algebraic Definition of Division (p. 567)
Division Property of Equality (p. 578)
Division Property of Inequality (p. 580)
Ratio-Comparison Model for Division (p. 583)
Means-Extremes Property (p. 591)
Fundamental Property of Similar Figures (p. 602)

Chapter

9 Self-Test

Take this test as you would take a test in class. You will need a calculator. Then use the Selected Answers section in the back of the book to check your work.

In 1–3, simplify and express your answer as a fraction in lowest terms.

1. 13 divided by $\frac{2}{3}$

2. $-\dfrac{-\frac{6}{5}}{\frac{9}{15}}$

3. $\dfrac{5\frac{4}{9}}{12\frac{1}{3}}$

4. According to one source, the fastest speed ever attained by a bicycle on a flat surface was 81 miles per hour. If you traveled at this speed for one minute, how far would you travel?

5. 35 oranges can fit into a crate.

   a. How many crates will be filled with 390 oranges?

   b. How many oranges remain when those crates are filled?

6. Marla is 4 feet 2 inches. Geoff is 6 feet 3 inches. Geoff is how many times as tall as Marla?

In 7–10, solve.

7. $12p = 96$

8. $18 < -12d + 7$

9. $1.05 = 21k - 4.3$

10. $-900p \le 360$

In 11 and 12, use the fact triangle below.

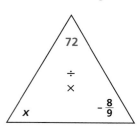

11. Write the related facts.

12. What is the missing value in the fact triangle?

In 13 and 14, solve the proportion.

13. $\dfrac{9}{10} = \dfrac{w}{15}$

14. $\dfrac{7}{r} = \dfrac{245}{350}$

15. **True or False** If a and b are negative numbers, then their quotient is also a negative number.

In 16 and 17, write a rate from the situation.

16. Raheem correctly solved 32 math problems in 20 minutes.

17. Tonya ran a 26.2-mile marathon in 6 hours 23 minutes.

18. Write the related facts for the given sentence.
$$\frac{7p}{34} = 129$$

In 19–21, solve.

19. Jamila makes $8.50 an hour. She needs to make at least $114 this week to buy a new bicycle. How many hours must she work this week?

20. 44% of the students at Hollings High School watched their school's tennis team play in the state championship. There were 405 Hollings students at the match. What is the total number of students in the school?

21. A 5″ × 7″ photograph is enlarged so that the shorter dimension is 9 inches. What is the other dimension of the new print?

22. Consider the similar figures. Find t.

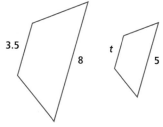

Chapter 9 Chapter Review

SKILLS Procedures used to get answers

OBJECTIVE A Divide fractions with numbers or variables. (Lesson 9-3)

In 1–6, simplify and express your answer as a fraction in lowest terms.

1. $15 \div \frac{5}{7}$

2. $13p$ divided by $\frac{6}{p}$

3. $\dfrac{\frac{42}{5}}{\frac{8}{35}}$

4. $\dfrac{3\frac{3}{8}}{2\frac{1}{4}}$

5. $\dfrac{\frac{2w}{q}}{\frac{4j}{s}}$

6. Divide $\frac{z}{5}$ by $\frac{1}{2}$.

OBJECTIVE B Divide positive and negative numbers. (Lesson 9-4)

In 7–10, simplify.

7. $\frac{-6}{3}$

8. $\frac{-415}{-5}$

9. $\frac{19.8}{-1.32}$

10. $\frac{-6.2 \times 10^2}{-3.6}$

11. What is the value of $\frac{3a}{-2b}$ when $a = -6.6$ and $b = -4.2$?

12. What is the value of $\dfrac{\frac{7q}{-p}}{\frac{p}{-4m}}$ when $q = -10$,

$p = 0.7$, and $m = -1$?

OBJECTIVE C Solve equations and inequalities using the Division Property of Equality and the Division Property of Inequality. (Lesson 9-5)

In 13–20, solve.

13. $-9t = 3$

14. $\frac{4}{9}g = 0.18$

15. $36.8 = 7.1p + 2.3$

16. 92% of $z = 580$

17. $-3p < 30$

18. $-19u \geq 4\frac{3}{4}$

19. $241 < 120j - 52$

20. $\frac{82}{11} \leq -h + 0.25$

PROPERTIES Principles behind the mathematics

OBJECTIVE D Know related facts of multiplication and division. (Lesson 9-4)

21. **Multiple Choice** If $5v \div 16 = -2.5$, what other fact is true?

A $\frac{-2.5}{5v} = 16$

B $16 \div 2.5 = 5v$

C $\frac{5v}{-2.5} = 16$

D $5v \cdot -2.5 = 16$

22. Write the related facts for the following sentence: $\$3.40 \cdot 5 = \$17$.

23. Write the related facts and solve for k in the sentence $k \cdot 0.9 = 36$.

OBJECTIVE E Recognize the Means-Extremes Property and know why it works. (Lesson 9-7)

24. According to the Means-Extremes Property, if $\frac{b}{a} = \frac{f}{e}$, what products are equal?

25. To get rid of fractions in the equation $\frac{6}{7} = \frac{5}{x}$, by what value can you multiply both sides?

26. Why won't the Means-Extremes Property work on the equation $y + \frac{5}{3} = \frac{12}{78}$?

OBJECTIVE F Know the general properties for dividing positive and negative numbers. (Lesson 9-4)

27. **Multiple Choice** Which does *not* equal $\frac{b}{-f}$, where $f \neq 0$?

A $-\frac{b}{f}$

B $\frac{-b}{-f}$

C $\frac{-b}{f}$

D $-b \cdot \frac{1}{f}$

28. If $\frac{x}{y} = z$, x is positive, and z is negative, then is y positive or negative?

29. **Fill in the Blank** If either the divisor or the dividend is negative and the other is positive, the quotient will be ___?___.

USES Applications of mathematics in real-world situations

OBJECTIVE G Use integer division in real-world situations. (Lesson 9-1)

In 30–33, a question is asked.
a. Write an equation to answer the question using division.
b. Solve your equation from Part a.

30. How many weeks and days are in 1,000 days?

31. A certain laundry machine costs a dollar in quarters to use. If Drew has 35 quarters, how many times can he use the machine, and how many quarters will he have left over?

32. Eighteen *Transition Mathematics* books can fit in a certain type of box. If a school orders 95 books, how many boxes can be filled and how many books will be left in the unfilled box?

33. The 223 students at a basketball camp were split into teams of 15. How many full teams were formed and how many students were left over?

OBJECTIVE H Use the Rate Model for Division. (Lesson 9-2)

34. The earth travels about 1.6 million miles in its orbit around the Sun in an average day. What is its average speed in miles per hour?

35. A restaurant makes twelve salads from 50 ounces of lettuce. How much lettuce is this per salad?

36. Mrs. Annora spent $145.98 in 11 days. At what rate is she spending her money?

37. In 2000, Oklahoma City had a population of about 506,132 people and an area of about 607 square miles. About how many people is this per square mile?

38. Two-thirds of the way through the summer, 67,904 people had visited Waterland Amusement Park. At this rate, how many visitors will visit during the entire summer?

39. Blanca spent $325 to rent a car for six days. Use this information to make up a question involving division and negative numbers and then answer your question.

OBJECTIVE I Use the Ratio-Comparison Model for Division. (Lesson 9-6)

40. Celeste went to three concerts last year. This year she went to 11. This year's number of concerts is how many times last year's number?

41. If Elise answered 38 questions correctly on a 45-question test, what percent did she miss?

42. In Memphis, Tennessee, the weather is clear or partly cloudy 214 days per year, on average. What percent of days is this? Round your answer to the nearest percent.

43. **Fill in the Blank** In 2003, 47,525 hybrid cars were sold in the United States. In 2004, 88,000 hybrid cars were sold. So, in 2004, __?__ times as many customers bought hybrid cars as in the previous year. (Round your answer to the nearest tenth.)

OBJECTIVE J Recognize and solve problems involving proportions in real-world situations. (Lessons 9-7, 9-8)

44. During National Novel Writing Month (abbreviated as NaNoWriMo), Dyami wrote 12,983 words in the first seven days. At this rate, how many words will he write in his novel by the end of the thirty days of NaNoWriMo?

45. A recipe for 6 people calls for $3\frac{3}{4}$ cups of flour. How much flour is needed for a similar recipe for 10 people?

46. A 6-pack of mountain spring water costs $2.39. How much is this per bottle?

REPRESENTATIONS Pictures, graphs, or objects that illustrate concepts

OBJECTIVE K Represent multiplication and division related facts with a fact triangle. (Lesson 9-4)

47. Fill in the missing element in the fact triangle below.

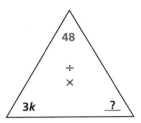

In 48 and 49, consider the given equation.
a. Draw a fact triangle.
b. Solve.

48. $\frac{6.2}{p} = 23$ 49. $\frac{-15}{8} \cdot n = 7$

OBJECTIVE L Find missing lengths in similar figures. (Lesson 9-9)

50. A bonsai tree is a miniature tree similar to a normal-size tree of the same species. The leaf of the normal-size tree is 5 inches long. On the bonsai, the length of the leaf is 0.2 inch. If the bonsai is 16 inches tall, how tall is a normal-size tree?

In 51 and 52, the figures below are similar.

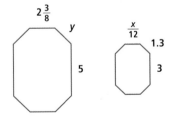

51. Find the value of x.

52. Find the value of y.

Linear Equations and Inequalities

Contents

Imagine a friend who is walking on a sidewalk 100 feet in front of you. You want to catch up to your friend, so you try to walk faster than your friend does. If your friend is walking at a rate of 3.5 feet per second and you walk at a rate of 4 feet per second, how long will it take for you to catch up?

Here are three approaches to the problem.

An Arithmetic Approach

Make a table like the one at the right.

You can continue the table to see how long it will take until the distances in a row are equal.

Seconds	Distance (in ft) You Have Gone	Distance (in ft) Your Friend Has Gone
0	0	100
10	40	135
20	80	170
30	120	205
40	160	240
50	200	275
60	240	310
70	280	345
80	320	380
90	360	415
100	400	450

An Algebraic Approach

In t seconds, you will have walked $4t$ feet. In the same amount of time, your friend will have walked $100 + 3.5t$ feet because your friend had a 100-foot head start. The distances are the same when $4t = 100 + 3.5t$.

In this chapter, you will learn how to solve equations of this type.

A Geometric Approach

At the right are graphs of the two equations $d = 4t$ and $d = 100 + 3.5t$. These graphs show the distance you and your friend have traveled in t seconds. The point of intersection of the lines indicates when you will catch up with your friend.

Because it can be pictured by a graph that is a line, the equation $d = 100 + 3.5t$ is

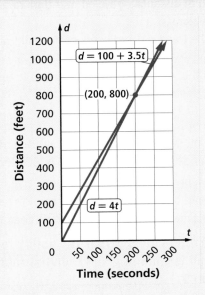

called a *linear equation.* In this chapter, you will encounter a wide variety of situations that lead to linear equations and inequalities. You will see how algebra and geometry can help answer questions about them.

Lesson 10-1

Finding Solutions Using Graphs

▶ **BIG IDEA** The common solution to two linear equations can be found on a coordinate grid from the coordinates of the point of intersection of the two lines.

Mental Math

Use each equation's solution to get the next solution.

a. $x + 5 = 19$

b. $2y + 5 = 19$

c. $2(z - 3) + 5 = 19$

d. $2(w - 3) + 5 > 19$

On the previous page, the distance traveled over time by you and a friend is approached in three different ways: arithmetically, algebraically, and geometrically. In this lesson, we examine a geometric approach to this kind of problem.

Finding Solutions Graphically

Consider the graph from the Chapter Opener, reproduced at the right.

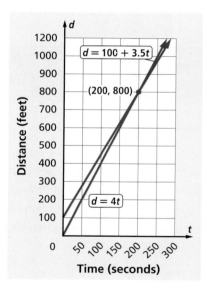

Example 1

Use the graph of distances traveled over time to answer the following questions.

a. What are the *t* and *d* coordinates of the point of intersection of the lines?

b. What does that point of intersection mean in terms of the distance traveled by you and your friend?

Solution

a. The lines intersect at the point (200, 800). The t-coordinate is 200 seconds. The d-coordinate is 800 feet.

b. The point represents the moment in time when you and your friend have traveled the same distance. After 200 seconds both you and your friend have traveled 800 feet.

An important mathematical skill is the ability to write an expression for a quantity that is changing and then to graph it and gather information from the graph.

Example 2

Spencer is spending money, while his sister Sabina is saving it. At present, Spencer has $100, but he spends about $2 more than his allowance each week. Sabina has $50, but she is saving about $3 of her allowance each week. Use graphs to estimate when they will have the same amount of money.

Solution First, identify the variables you will use. Here we let A be the amount of money that each will have after w weeks. Then we need to think about the equations.

Spencer begins with $100 and spends $2 per week. So the amount he has at the start (week 0) is $100; at the end of week 6, he has $100 − 2(6)$. At week w, Spencer has $100 − 2w$ dollars. For Spencer,

$$A = 100 - 2w.$$

Sabina begins with $50 and adds $3 each week. So, at week 6 she has $50 + 3(6)$. At week w, Sabina has $50 + 3w$ dollars. For Sabina,

$$A = 50 + 3w.$$

Now graph these two equations on the same axes so that they can be compared easily. The graph of each equation is a line. Look at the graph at the right. Where do the lines seem to intersect?

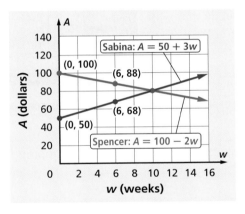

The lines seem to intersect at (10, 80). This means that after 10 weeks, Spencer and Sabina will both have $80.

 QY1

> ▶ **QY1**
>
> Spencer and Sabina's cousin Sebastian has $60 in the bank and is saving $1 every week from his allowance. Write an equation for the amount A he has in terms of the number of weeks w.

Checking with a Graphing Utility

A hand-drawn graph pictures the situation nicely, but often it is not particularly accurate and may not give an exact answer to any of the questions asked. However, a graphing utility can give you enough accuracy for an exact or nearly exact solution.

Activity

Check the solution given in Example 2 using a graphing utility.

Step 1 Enter the expression $100 - 2x$ into Y1. Enter the expression $50 + 3x$ into Y2. Set your window to $0 \leq x \leq 15$ and $0 \leq y \leq 100$.

Step 2 Use the INTERSECT command to obtain the coordinates of the intersection point of the two graphs. The graphs intersect at what point?

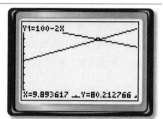

Step 3 Check with a table. Set the TableStart to 0 and ΔTable to 5. When $x = 10$, what do you notice about Y1 and Y2? What does that mean?

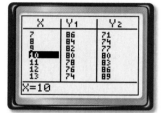

Step 4 Write a short sentence explaining the meaning of what is seen on each calculator screen.

Graphs of equations can help you compare costs when shopping for the best value.

Example 3

The Nomad family is moving again. They want to rent a 26-foot truck for a day. Here are two plans that existed in 2006.
Plan I: $50 plus 99¢ per mile   Plan II: $80 plus 59¢ per mile
At how many miles will the two plans cost the same?

Solution Let C be the cost (in dollars) for driving m miles. Here are equations relating m and C for each plan. Each is based on the fixed cost plus a certain number of cents for every mile driven.

Plan I: $C = 50 + 0.99m$ Plan II: $C = 80 + 0.59m$

Graph the two equations on the same set of axes.

The lines seem to intersect when m is about 75.

Check Check this on your graphing utility. The graph shows that the lines intersect near the point (75, 125). The table shows that the exact point of intersection is (75, 124.25). That means that the plans cost the same, $124.25, when the truck is driven 75 miles.

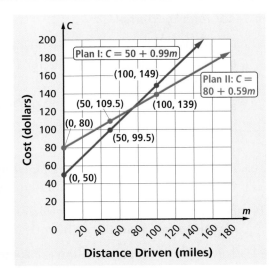

Distance Driven (miles)

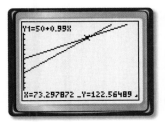
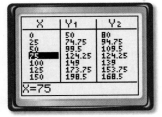

 QY2

Questions

▶ **QY2**

Write an equation for the cost C of renting a 26-foot truck for a day if the charge is a fee of $75 plus 69 cents per mile.

COVERING THE IDEAS

1. In Example 1, suppose that another friend walks at 3 feet per second and has a 150-foot head start, making her equation $d = 150 + 3t$. Use a graph to estimate the time at which you will catch up with her. How far will you have walked?

In 2–6, refer to Example 2 and QY1.

2. After 4 weeks, how much will Spencer have?

3. After 4 weeks, how much will Sabina have?

4. What would Sabina's equation be if she started with $25 and saved $3 every week?

5. What would Sabina's equation be if she saved $3.50 each week and started with $50?

6. Make a graph for the amount of money A that Sabina and her cousin Sebastian have after w weeks. After how many weeks will they have the same amount of money? How much money will that be?

In 7–11, refer to Example 3.

7. **a.** What will it cost to drive 5 miles using Plan I?

   b. Name the point on the line for Plan I that shows the answer to Part a.

8. **a.** What will it cost to drive 10 miles using Plan II?

   b. Name the point on the line for Plan II that shows the answer to Part a.

9. How can you tell from the *graph* which plan is more expensive when you drive the truck for 120 miles?

10. How can you tell from the *equations* which plan is more expensive when you drive 30 miles?

11. Solving what single equation tells when the plans cost the same?

APPLYING THE MATHEMATICS

12. Camelback Mountain in Phoenix, Arizona, is 2,704 feet high. A hiking trail to its summit climbs 1,200 feet. Xavier hikes down from the top of the trail, losing 7 feet in elevation each minute. Ilia hikes up from the bottom of the trail at the same time, gaining 5 feet in elevation each minute. The graph below shows their heights over time.

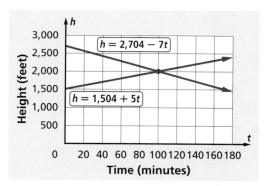

$h = 2,704 - 7t$

$h = 1,504 + 5t$

   a. At what point do the two lines intersect?

   b. If Ilia and Xavier both started at noon, at what time did they meet on the trail?

   c. At what elevation were they when they met?

   d. If Ilia gained 7 feet of elevation each minute and Xavier lost 5 feet of elevation each minute, would they meet at the same time and elevation as in Parts b and c? Use a graph to justify your answer.

13. At the beginning of the 2006 basketball season, Vince Carter had scored 12,900 points in his professional career and was averaging 24.1 points per game. LeBron James had 6,307 points so far in his career but was averaging 31.4 points per game. Let P be the number of points in a career after g more games at these averages.

    a. For Vince, what equation relates P and g?

    b. Graph the equation you found in Part a.

    c. For LeBron, what equation relates P and g?

    d. Graph the equation from Part c on the axes you used for Part b.

    e. From your graph, estimate the number of games it will take LeBron to catch up to Vince in the number of points scored.

    f. Solving what equation will show when the two players will have scored the same number of points?

14. Long Distance Phone Company I charges 20¢ for the first minute plus 15¢ for each additional minute for a call to a foreign country. Company II charges 26¢ for the first minute plus 13¢ for each additional minute. Let C be the cost of an m-minute call.

    a. Write an equation relating m and C for Company I.

    b. Write an equation relating m and C for Company II.

    c. Solving what equation will show when the plans cost the same?

    d. Sunil decided to use his graphing utility to find when the costs were the same. He displayed the graph and the table below. What is the solution to the equation? Explain how each display shows you the solution.

New Jersey Nets' Vince Carter goes up for a shot.

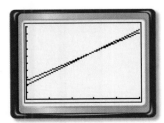

$0 \le x \le 5, 0 \le y \le 1$

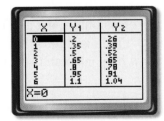

REVIEW

15. Jennifer has a summer job cleaning swimming pools. After 30 minutes, a 5-foot-deep pool is filled to the 2-foot level. At the same rate, how long will it take to fill the pool entirely? (**Lesson 9-8**)

16. Suppose $a \neq b$. Is there any case in which the equation $\frac{a}{b} = \frac{b}{a}$ is true? If so, give an example. (**Lessons 9-7, 8-3**)

17. **Multiple Choice** Which of the following inequalities has −6 as a solution? (**Lesson 8-9**)

    A $4x + 1.5 > 2$ B $-\frac{5}{2}x + 9 < -12$

    C $-2x - 6 \geq 18$ D $3x + 18 \geq 0$

18. Grover spent $19.50 at the nursery buying one dozen tulip bulbs and a watering can. If the watering can cost $4.50, what was the price of each tulip bulb? (**Lesson 8-8**)

19. On the average day in 2005, the U.S. government took in x dollars in revenue and spent y dollars on expenses. According to some estimates, this situation could be described by the equation $x - y = -\$2.83$ billion. Graph this equation showing three possible pairs of values for x and y. (**Lessons 8-7, 5-7**)

The pH (a measure of acidity) level of a pool should be checked regularly. A pH less than 7.0 can corrode pipes, and a pH greater than 8.0 can prevent chlorine from killing germs effectively.

In 20 and 21, simplify. (**Lesson 7-3**)

20. $42t + 3p - -y + 16t - \frac{3p}{8} + y^2 + 45$

21. $\frac{-1}{2}x + x - x + \frac{x}{2} - (-x) - \frac{-x}{2}$

EXPLORATION

22. Design a spreadsheet with the following columns.

m	$50 + 0.99m$	$80 + 0.59m$

Show how the spreadsheet can answer Example 3.

23. Look up your favorite players in a professional sport and make up a question similar to Question 13. Find equations that can help you answer your question. Show how you can use a graph or table to estimate the solution.

QY ANSWERS

1. $A = 60 + 1w$

2. $C = 75 + 0.69m$

Lesson

10-2

Solving
$ax + b = cx + d$

▶ **BIG IDEA** An efficient procedure for solving an equation of the form $ax + b = cx + d$ is to add $-cx$ to both sides to create a new equation with the variable on only one side.

Recall the equations for the amounts of money Spencer and Sabina had in Example 2 of Lesson 10-1.

Spencer: $A = 100 - 2w$ Sabina: $A = 50 + 3w$

To find the point in time that they had the same amount of money, you graphed the equations and found the point of intersection of the lines. You can always estimate the point of intersection with a table or a graph, but using algebra is a way to ensure that you will find the exact value.

At the point of intersection, the values of A and w are the same for both equations. Because $A = 100 - 2w$ and $A = 50 + 3w$, by substitution,

$$100 - 2w = 50 + 3w.$$

This is called *equating* the values of A. Because the variable x is on both sides of the equal sign, this equation is of the form

$$ax + b = cx + d,$$

with $x = w$, $a = -2$, $b = 100$, $c = 3$, and $d = 50$.

Example 1 shows how to solve this type of equation to answer the question about Spencer and Sabina.

Example 1

Solve $100 - 2w = 50 + 3w$.

Solution 1 One way to start is to add $-3w$ to both sides. This results in an equation with w on only the left side.

$100 - 2w = 50 + 3w$	original equation
$100 - 2w + -3w = 50 + 3w + -3w$	Add $-3w$ to both sides.
$100 - 5w = 50$	Collect like terms.

Now proceed as you previously have with equations of this type.

(continued on next page)

(continued on next page)

Mental Math

Match each equation to its graph.

i.
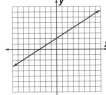

ii.
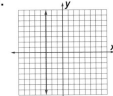

iii.
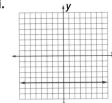

iv.
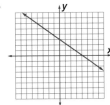

a. $y = \frac{2}{3}x + 2$

b. $x = -3$

c. $y = -\frac{3}{4}x + 3$

d. $y = -5$

$$-100 + 100 - 5w = -100 + 50 \qquad \text{Add } -100 \text{ to both sides.}$$
$$-5w = -50 \qquad \text{Simplify.}$$
$$-\frac{1}{5} \cdot -5w = -\frac{1}{5} \cdot -50 \qquad \text{Multiply both sides by } -\frac{1}{5}.$$
$$w = 10 \qquad \text{Simplify.}$$

Solution 2 Another way is to add $2w$ to both sides. This results in an equation with w on only the right side.

$$100 - 2w = 50 + 3w \qquad \text{original equation}$$
$$100 - 2w + 2w = 50 + 3w + 2w \qquad \text{Add } 2w \text{ to both sides.}$$
$$100 = 50 + 5w \qquad \text{Collect like terms.}$$

Solve this equation as you have done in earlier lessons.

$$-50 + 100 = -50 + 50 + 5w \qquad \text{Add } -50 \text{ to both sides.}$$
$$50 = 5w \qquad \text{Simplify.}$$
$$10 = w \qquad \text{Multiply both sides by } \frac{1}{5}.$$

Both solutions to Example 1 confirm that Spencer and Sabina will have the same amount of money in 10 weeks.

 QY

> **QY**
>
> In the last step of Solution 2, what could you have done instead of multiplying by $\frac{1}{5}$ that would have had the same result?

GUIDED

Example 2

Patrizia and Duncan are skating the same direction along the shore of a frozen lake. Duncan is skating at a speed of 4 feet per second and is 12 feet beyond the warming house. Patrizia is skating at 13 feet per second and is 30 feet beyond the warming house. At what time were the two in the same location?

Solution

Step 1 Write an equation. $\quad 4x + 12 = 13x + 30$

Step 2 Add $-4x$ to both sides to get the variable terms on one side of the equation. $\quad \underline{\ ?\ } + 4x + 12 = \underline{\ ?\ } + 13x + 30$

Step 3 Simplify. $\qquad\qquad 12 = \underline{\ ?\ } + 30$

Step 4 Add -30 to both sides.
$$12 + \underline{\ ?\ } = 9x + 30 + \underline{\ ?\ }$$

Step 5 Simplify. $\qquad\qquad \underline{\ ?\ } = \underline{\ ?\ }$

Step 6 Use the Division Property of Equality to solve for x.
$$x = \underline{\ ?\ }$$

Patrizia and Duncan were in the same place $\underline{\ ?\ }$ seconds ago.

Frog Pond is located in Boston Common, America's oldest park. It was founded in 1634.

Source: City of Boston

Check Substitute the value for *x* every place it occurs in the original equation. Does 4 · __?__ + 12 = 13 · __?__ + 30?

Notice that it takes only one more step to solve an equation of the form $ax + b = cx + d$ than to solve one of the form $ax + b = c$. In the next example, the equation may look as if it is solved for *y,* but there is a *y* on the right side.

GUIDED

Example 3

Solve $y = 391 - 16y$.

Solution

Step 1 Add 16*y* to both sides.
The result after simplifying is __?__ $y = 391$.

Step 2 Use the Division Property of Equality. $y =$ __?__

Check Does __?__ $= 391 - 16 \cdot$ __?__ ?

The next example combines a number of ideas from this and the preceding chapters.

Example 4

Solve $\dfrac{2x - 5}{3} = \dfrac{x + 1}{6}$.

Solution This is a proportion, so you can use the Means-Extremes Property.

$$6(2x - 5) = 3(x + 1)$$

The Distributive Property gives

$$6 \cdot 2x - 6 \cdot 5 = 3x + 3 \cdot 1.$$

$$12x - 30 = 3x + 3$$

In this form, the equation is like those of Examples 1 through 3.

$-3x + 12x - 30 = -3x + 3x + 3$	Add $-3x$ to both sides.
$9x - 30 = 3$	Collect like terms.
$9x = 33$	Add 30 to both sides.
$x = \dfrac{33}{9}$	Divide both sides by 9.
$= \dfrac{11}{3}$	Simplify.

(continued on next page)

Solving $ax + b = cx + d$ **625**

Check Does $\dfrac{2 \cdot \frac{11}{3} - 5}{3} = \dfrac{\frac{11}{3} + 1}{6}$?

Does $\dfrac{\frac{22}{3} - \frac{15}{3}}{3} = \dfrac{\frac{11}{3} + \frac{3}{3}}{6}$?

Does $\dfrac{\frac{7}{3}}{3} = \dfrac{\frac{14}{3}}{6}$?

Does $\dfrac{7}{9} = \dfrac{14}{18}$? Yes, it checks.

In Example 4, the check by substitution takes many steps. In some ways, it is as complex as solving the equation. Another way to check the solution is to graph $y = \dfrac{2x - 5}{3}$ and $y = \dfrac{x + 1}{6}$ with a graphing utility. Each equation can be put into the form $y = ax + b$, so the graphs are lines, as shown here. The lines intersect at the point where $\dfrac{2x - 5}{3} = \dfrac{x + 1}{6}$. So look at the x-coordinate of the point of intersection. The intersect command shows that the x-coordinate of the point of intersection is about 3.67. So the solution $x = \dfrac{11}{3}$ checks.

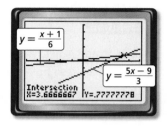

 GAME Now you can play *X-Tac-Toe: ax + b = cx + d*. The directions for this game are on pages G12 and G15 at the back of your book.

Questions

COVERING THE IDEAS

1. In solving $8x + 46 = 13 - 4x$, name two different things you could do to both sides to obtain an equation with the variable on one side.

2. **a.** Solve $6n + 18 = 42 - 10n$ by first adding $10n$ to both sides.
   b. Solve $6n + 18 = 42 - 10n$ by first adding $-6n$ to both sides.
   c. Check the solution to Parts a and b by graphing.

3. **a. Fill in the Blank** To solve $t = 180 - 5t$, first add __?__ to both sides.
   b. Solve the equation in Part a.

4. Solve the equation in Example 1 by adding -100 to each side as the first step.

In 5–10, solve and check either by substitution or by graphing.

5. $p + 3p - 5 = -2p - 4$

6. $8 + 3v = 32 - 5v$

7. $99 + 19m = 99m + 19$

8. $-2(w - 6) = 8w$

9. $36 - 42x = 6(7x + 8)$

10. $\dfrac{5}{1 - y} = \dfrac{15}{1 + y}$

APPLYING THE MATHEMATICS

11. The numbers in the equation below were generated by picking integers randomly from –99 to 99. Solve the equation.
$$88(-22x - 23) = 25(-55x + 11)$$

In 12–15, solve the equation and check your result.

12. $\frac{r}{r + 1} = 6$

13. $48 + d + 2(30 - 4d) = d$

14. $7x = 16x$

15. $\frac{7}{12}y + \frac{3}{4} = 2y + \frac{y}{4}$

16. Under Plan 1, a new car costs $2,000 down plus $400 per month. Under Plan 2, the same car costs $2,800 down and $325 per month.
    a. Write an expression for the total amount paid after n months under Plan 1.
    b. Write an expression for the total amount paid after n months under Plan 2.
    c. In how many months will the amount paid be the same for both plans?

The total amount paid for a car often depends on its rate plan. For the same car, a small down payment with a 60-month loan usually results in a greater total cost than a large down payment and a 36-month loan.

17. Quick Quincy tried to solve $6x - 2 = 4x + 5$. He wrote what is shown here. When he checked his answer, it didn't work.

	$6x - 2 = 4x + 5$
Step 1	$-4x + 6x - 2 = -4x + 4x + 5$
Step 2	$2x - 2 = 0 + 5$
Step 3	$2x = 5 - 2$
Step 4	$2x = 3$
Step 5	$x = 1.5$

   a. In which step did Quincy make a mistake?
   b. What is the correct solution?

REVIEW

18. Find the area of the shaded region in the graph at the right.
    (Lessons 10-1, 7-5)

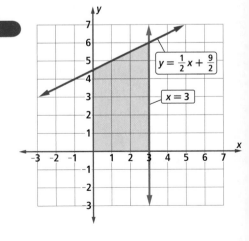

$$y = \frac{1}{2}x + \frac{9}{2}$$

$$x = 3$$

19. Juan earns $12.75 per hour and worked 38 hours last week. After taxes, he received a paycheck for $398.87 for last week's work.
    a. What percent of his paycheck was deducted for taxes? (Round your answer to the nearest hundredth of a percent.)
    b. If he works 27.5 hours next week, how much should he expect his paycheck to be after taxes? (**Lessons 9-7, 9-6**)

20. Use a graphing utility to graph the equation $y = -(x - 4.5)^2 + 20$. Use the Trace function to determine whether the graph contains any points in Quadrant II. (If necessary, use the zoom feature of your graphing utility to enlarge the image.) If it does, give a point that is a solution to this equation located in that quadrant. (**Lesson 8-7**)

21. Write an equation relating y and x, and graph the possible solutions. (**Lessons 6-8, 6-6**)

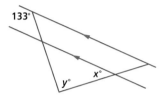

22. A circle is inscribed in a square as shown at the right. If the area of the square is 9 square meters, what is the area of the circle? (**Lesson 7-6**)

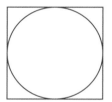

23. Refer to the diagram below.

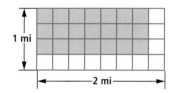

    a. What multiplication is pictured by the shaded area?
    b. What is the product? (**Lesson 7-1**)

24. In $\triangle ABC$, angles A and B have the same measure. If the measure of angle A is 4 times the measure of angle C, find the measure of each angle of the triangle. (**Lesson 6-8**)

EXPLORATION

25. The equation $x^3 = 4x - 2$ has three solutions. Estimate each solution to the nearest tenth by graphing $y = x^3$ and $y = 4x - 2$ on the same axes and examining the points of intersection.

QY ANSWER

Use the Division Property of Equality and divide both sides by 5.

Lesson

10-3 Graphing y < ax + b

Vocabulary

half-plane

boundary, edge

oblique line

▶ **BIG IDEA** The graph of an inequality of the form $y < ax + b$ consists of all the points on one side of a line.

Consider the two fractions $\frac{70}{29}$ and $\frac{99}{41}$. Which is greater? It is hard to tell by just looking at the fractions. But, if you rewrite the fractions as decimals, $\frac{70}{29} = 2.41379\ldots$ and $\frac{99}{41} = 2.41463\ldots$, you can see that $\frac{70}{29} < \frac{99}{41}$.

A fundamental property of real numbers is the following: *Given two numbers: the numbers are equal, the first is greater than the second, or the second is greater than the first. No two of these statements can be true at the same time.* In the language of variables, if a and b are real numbers, then $a = b$, $a > b$, or $a < b$, and no two of these can happen at the same time.

This property is called the *Trichotomy Property* because any number b splits all real numbers into three sets: those numbers less than b, the number b itself, and those numbers greater than b. You can see the Trichotomy Property on a number line. If b is a number on a number line, then any other number a is equal to b itself, is graphed on one side of b, or is graphed on the other side of b; a cannot be in two of these places.

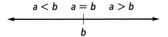

Suppose $b = 2$. Then any number x is less than, equal to, or greater than 2. The graphs of $x < 2$, $x = 2$, and $x > 2$ are shown here. The point that is the graph of 2 partitions the line into two other parts.

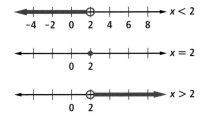

Mental Math

a. What is the area of a square with perimeter 60 cm?

b. Will a circle of perimeter 60 cm have an area greater or less than your answer to Part a?

Inequalities Involving Horizontal or Vertical Lines

Just as points partition lines, lines partition planes. The horizontal line graphed here is described by the equation $y = 4$, because it contains all the points that have a y-coordinate equal to 4. Above the line are points that have a y-coordinate greater than 4. Below the line are all points that have a y-coordinate less than 4.

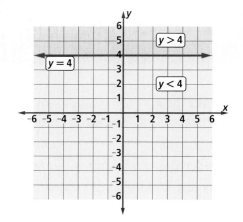

The regions on either side of a line in a plane are called **half-planes.** The line is the **boundary,** or **edge,** of the half-plane. In the graph at the right, the line $y = 4$ is the edge of the half-planes $y < 4$ and $y > 4$.

Example 1

Graph the solutions to each sentence in the coordinate plane.

a. $x = -5$ b. $x > -5$ c. $x \le -5$

Solution

a. Every point on the line $x = -5$ has first coordinate -5. So the solution set is the set of points that make up the vertical line $x = -5$.

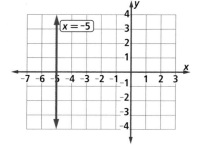

b. Every point whose coordinates satisfy $x > -5$ has a first coordinate greater than -5. These points make up the half-plane to the right of $x = -5$. So shade the region to the right of the line and use dashes for the boundary line to show that it is *not* included. The solution set consists of all the points in the shaded area.

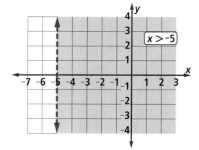

c. Every point whose coordinates satisfy $x \le -5$ has a first coordinate less than or equal to -5. These points are on the half-plane to the left of $x = -5$ or on the line $x = -5$ itself because $x \le -5$ is a combination of the equation $x = -5$ and the inequality $x < -5$. So shade the region to the left of the line and draw a solid line to show that it is included. The solution set consists of all the points in the shaded area *and* the points on the vertical line.

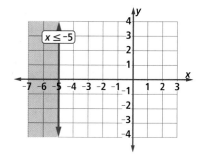

Inequalities Involving Oblique Lines

In Lesson 8-7 you saw that the graph of $y = ax + b$ is a line. If $a \neq 0$, the line is not horizontal or vertical; it is *oblique*. An **oblique line** is a line which is neither horizontal nor vertical. As you might expect, the graph of $y < ax + b$ is the half-plane below $y = ax + b$, while the graph of $y > ax + b$ is the half-plane above it.

Example 2

Graph the solutions to each sentence in the coordinate plane.

a. $y = 7 - 2x$ b. $y > 7 - 2x$ c. $y < 7 - 2x$

Solution

a. Graph $y = 7 - 2x$ by finding two points on the line. We find $(0, 7)$ and $(3, 1)$ and draw the line through them.

b. The $>$ sign in $y > 7 - 2x$ indicates that the y-coordinate is greater than the y-values that satisfy $y = 7 - 2x$. Because y-values increase as you move up the coordinate grid, this half-plane is *above* the line.

c. The graph of $y < 7 - 2x$ is the half-plane *below* $y = 7 - 2x$.

a.
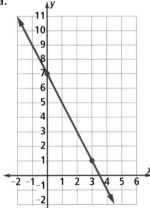

b.
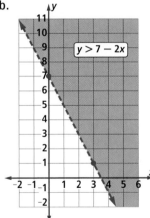

c.
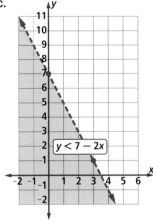

Check

a. Choose a point on the line and substitute the coordinates into the equation to verify that the point yields a true statement. For example, if we choose $(2, 3)$, substitute 2 for x and 3 for y. We get $3 = 7 - 2(2)$.

b. Choose a point in the shaded area, for example, $(5, 1)$. Do these coordinates make this inequality true?

c. Choose a point in the shaded area, for example, $(0, 0)$. Do these coordinates make the inequality true?

(continued on next page)

Graphing $y < ax + b$ **631**

GUIDED

Example 3

Graph the solution set of $y \geq \frac{2}{3}x - 2$.

Solution

Step 1 Find two points that lie on the line $y = \frac{2}{3}x - 2$ by choosing two values for x and determining the corresponding values for y. (*Hint:* Choose values for x that are multiples of 3. Why?)

Step 2 Determine whether the line will be dashed or solid and draw the line.

Step 3 Shade the half-plane that represents the solutions for the inequality.

Step 4 Choose a point in the shaded area to check that the correct half-plane has been shaded.

Questions

COVERING THE IDEAS

In 1–4, tell whether $a > b$, $a = b$, or $a < b$.

1. $a = 33\frac{1}{3}\%$, $b = \frac{1}{3}$

2. $a = 0.5$, $b = 0.23$

3. $a = -\frac{1}{\pi}$, $b = \frac{-113}{355}$

4. $a = \sqrt{9} - 2 + \sqrt{2}$, $b = 1 + \sqrt{2}$

5. **Fill in the Blanks** According to the Trichotomy Property, since no simple fraction is equal to π, every simple fraction must be either ___?___ or ___?___.

In 6 and 7, a sentence is given.
a. Graph the set of points satisfying the sentence on a number line.
b. Graph the points satisfying the sentence on a coordinate plane.

6. $x \geq 7$

7. $y < 1.5$

In 8 and 9, write an inequality describing each graph.

8.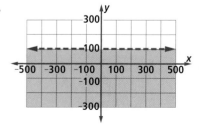

9.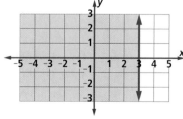

10. Graph the line with equation $y = x + 4$. Then identify on your graph the region whose graph is described by $y < x + 4$ and the region whose graph is described by $y > x + 4$.

11. Graph all points (x, y) that satisfy $y \leq \frac{2}{3}x + 6$.

APPLYING THE MATHEMATICS

12. Find a solution (x, y) to the inequality $y \leq 5x - 7$ that is *not* a solution to the inequality $y < 5x - 7$.

In 13–17, match each inequality with the graph of its solution set. Justify your answers.

13. $y \geq \frac{1}{2}x + 3$ 14. $y < x - \frac{3}{4}$ 15. $y \geq x - \frac{3}{4}$

16. $y < 2$ 17. $y \geq -4$

i.

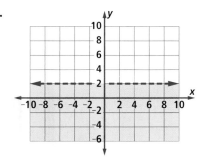

ii.

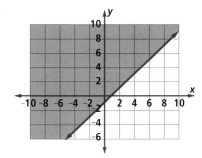

iii.

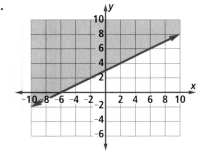

iv.

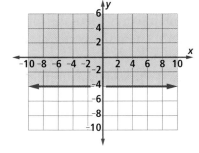

v.

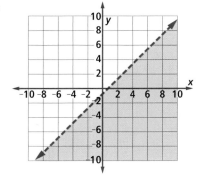

18. If a, b, and c are the lengths of sides of a triangle, then $a + b > c$. Suppose that a, b, and c are *integer* lengths of sides of a triangle, and the longest side $c = 12$. Then $a < 12$, $b < 12$, and $a + b > 12$. Graph all possible pairs of numbers a and b that satisfy all three inequalities.

REVIEW

19. Recall the story of Achilles and the tortoise from the beginning of Chapter 3. Suppose Achilles runs 5 meters per second, and the tortoise runs 5 centimeters per second. The tortoise begins at the 10-meter marker, and Achilles begins at the 0-meter marker. Determine the precise time and distance when Achilles will overtake the tortoise. **(Lesson 10-2)**

20. **a.** Graph the three lines with equations $y = 4x + 6$, $y = -6x - 16$, and $y = -x - 5$ on the same coordinate grid.
    b. Do the lines all intersect at the same point? If so, estimate the coordinates of the point from your graph. **(Lesson 10-1)**

21. Suppose the circle at the right has an area of 45,000 square units. To the nearest square unit, find the area of
    a. the purple region.
    b. the pink region. **(Lessons 9-8, 7-6)**

22. Determine the union of the solutions to the two sentences $4n - 3 \geq 75$ and $-4n + 3 \geq -75$. **(Lessons 8-9, 4-4)**

23. Suppose a home builder offers the following chart estimating the time it will take to build houses, given the square feet of space contained in each.
    a. Graph these values in a scatterplot. **(Lesson 1-10)**
    b. The points on the scatterplot all lie on a single line. Determine an equation for that line. **(Lessons 8-7, 2-1)**

EXPLORATION

24. The robot at right is described by the following inequalities:
    Chest: $2 \leq x \leq 6, 4 \leq y \leq 8$
    Middle: $3 \leq x \leq 5, 2 \leq y \leq 4$
    Legs: $3 \leq x \leq 3.5, 0 \leq y \leq 2$
             $4.5 \leq x \leq 5, 0 \leq y \leq 2$
    Copy the diagram and put a head on the robot. Describe the head with inequalities.

Achilles is a hero in Greek mythology. His mother tried to make him immortal by bathing him in the river Styx, but his heel, where she held onto him, remained mortal.

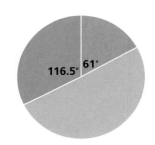

116.5° 61°

Square Feet	Days to Complete
1,200	30
3,000	48
4,000	58
5,000	68
7,000	88

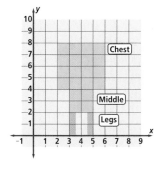

Lesson 10-4

Solving $ax + b < cx + d$

An efficient procedure to solve an inequality of the form $ax + b < cx + d$ is to add $-cx$ to both sides to create a new inequality with the variable on only one side.

In Lesson 10-2, you solved equations of the form $ax + b = cx + d$. The same steps can be used to solve inequalities of the form

$$ax + b < cx + d.$$

Example 1 below uses the same expressions as Example 1 of Lesson 10-2 to demonstrate how to solve inequalities of the form $ax + b < cx + d$. The situation involves Spencer and Sabina. Compare Solutions 1 and 2 line by line with the solutions given there.

Mental Math

Write in scientific notation.

a. 750

b. 750 million

c. 750 millionths

Example 1

Spencer has $100 - 2w$ dollars in his account after w weeks. Sabina has $50 + 3w$ dollars after w weeks. When will Spencer have less than Sabina? To answer this question, solve $100 - 2w < 50 + 3w$.

Solution 1 One way to start is to add $-3w$ to both sides. This results in an inequality with w on only one side.

$100 - 2w < 50 + 3w$	original inequality
$100 - 2w + -3w < 50 + 3w + -3w$	Add $-3w$ to both sides.
$100 - 5w < 50$	Collect like terms.

Now proceed as you previously have with inequalities of this type.

$-100 + 100 - 5w < -100 + 50$	Add -100 to both sides.
$-5w < -50$	Simplify.

Recall that the direction of the inequality changes when you multiply both sides by a negative number. *You must change the sense of the inequality.*

$-\frac{1}{5} \cdot -5w > -\frac{1}{5} \cdot -50$	Multiply both sides by $-\frac{1}{5}$.
$w > 10$	Simplify.

(continued on next page)

Solution 2 Another way is to add $2w$ to both sides. This results in an inequality with w on only the right side.

$100 - 2w < 50 + 3w$	original inequality
$100 - 2w + 2w < 50 + 3w + 2w$	Add $2w$ to both sides.
$100 < 50 + 5w$	Collect like terms.

Solve this inequality as you have done in earlier lessons.

$-50 + 100 < -50 + 50 + 5w$	Add -50 to both sides.
$50 < 5w$	Simplify.
$10 < w$	Multiply both sides by $\frac{1}{5}$.

The sense of the inequality does not change because $\frac{1}{5}$ is a positive number.

Solutions 1 and 2 are equivalent, because $w > 10$ and $10 < w$ mean the same thing. After more than 10 weeks, Spencer will have less money than Sabina.

Graphs of the two equations $y = 100 - 2x$ and $y = 50 + 3x$ show the solutions. The line with equation $y = 100 - 2x$ is below the line $y = 50 + 3x$ when $x > 10$.

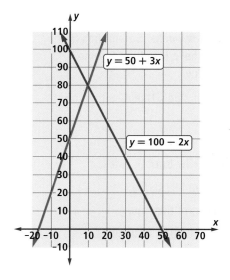

STOP **QY**

> **QY**
>
> What operation on both sides of an inequality should cause you to change the sense of the inequality?

Example 2

One machine can sort 500 cards per minute. A second machine can sort 700 cards per minute but takes 2 minutes longer to warm up. In *m* minutes of use,

a. how many cards can be sorted by the first machine?

b. how many cards can be sorted by the second machine?

c. for how many cards would it take less time to use the first machine than the second?

Solution

a. The first machine sorts

$$500 \frac{cards}{minute} \cdot m \text{ minutes} = 500m \text{ cards}.$$

b. Because the second machine sorts cards for 2 minutes less time than the first machine, it is in use for $m - 2$ minutes.

So the second machine sorts

$$700 \frac{cards}{minute} \cdot (m - 2) \text{ minutes} = 700(m - 2) \text{ cards}.$$

c. The first machine takes less time when the number of cards it sorts is greater than the number of cards the second machine sorts. So solve

$$500m > 700(m - 2).$$

$500m > 700m - 1{,}400$	Use the Distributive Property.
$-200m > -1{,}400$	Add $-700m$ to each side.
$m < 7$	Divide both sides by -200. This changes the sense of the inequality.

So it would take less time to use the first machine when the machine is run for less than 7 minutes. In this time, the machine can sort 3,500 cards. Therefore, it would take less time to use the first machine if you needed to sort fewer than 3,500 cards.

Check In 7 minutes for the first machine, the second machine has been going for 5 minutes. It has sorted 5 · 700 or 3,500 cards. So at 7 minutes the two machines have sorted the same number of cards. After that point in time, the second machine is faster, so it will sort more cards.

GUIDED

Example 3

Recall Example 3 from Lesson 10-1 about the Nomad family. They want to rent a moving truck for a day. If the Nomad family chooses Plan I, then after how many miles would it be more expensive than Plan II?

Plan I: $50 plus 99¢ per mile   **Plan II: $80 plus 59¢ per mile**

Solution The Nomad family is interested in knowing when Plan I will be more expensive than Plan II. So write the sentence that represents the situation.

$$\$50 + 0.99m \underline{\ ?\ } \$80 + 0.59m$$

Add $-0.59m$ to both sides. $\$50 + \underline{\ ?\ }m \underline{\ ?\ } \$80$

Subtract $50 from both sides. $\underline{\ ?\ }m \underline{\ ?\ } \underline{\ ?\ }$

Solve for m by dividing. $m \underline{\ ?\ } \underline{\ ?\ }$

So, Plan I will be more expensive when the Nomads travel more than $\underline{\ ?\ }$ miles.

Americans move, on average, 11 times during their lifetimes.

Source: Population Reference Bureau

 GAME Now you can play *X-Tac-Toe: ax + b < cx + d*. The directions for this game are on pages G12 and G16 at the back of your book.

Questions

COVERING THE IDEAS

In 1 and 2, use this information: Bill and his sister Belle each have jars in which they save their change. At the beginning of the year, Bill had $37.14 in his jar while Belle had $46.35. Bill is putting about $2.30 a week into his jar while Belle is putting in about $1.95.

1. a. In w weeks, about how much money will be in Bill's jar?
   b. In w weeks, about how much money will be in Belle's jar?
   c. In about how many weeks will Bill have more money than Belle has?

2. Bill and Belle's parents decide they will start saving their change, too. They are able to put in about $3.50 a week.
   a. In w weeks, how much money will be in their jar?
   b. What sentence can be solved to estimate when they will have more money in their jar than Bill has in his?
   c. Solve the sentence from Part b.
   d. What sentence can be solved to estimate when they will have more money in their jar than Belle has in hers?
   e. Solve the sentence from Part d.

3. **a.** Solve $4z - 5 > 7z + 11$ by first adding $-7z$ to both sides.

   b. Solve $4z - 5 > 7z + 11$ by first adding $-4z$ to both sides.

   c. Which method, that of Part a or Part b, do you prefer? Why?

   d. Check the solution to Parts a and b by graphing.

4. One English translation of the novel *Les Miserables,* by Victor Hugo, has 1,231 pages. Phillipe and Monique were determined to read the entire book. Phillipe decided to read 20 pages per day. Monique started 4 days later and decided to read 22 pages per day in order to catch up to Phillipe.

   a. When Monique has been reading for d days, how many pages will Phillipe have read?

   b. How many pages will Monique read in d days?

   c. Will Monique ever catch up to Phillipe?

In 5–8, solve the inequality.

5. $-8q + 24 < 4q + 6$

6. $77T > 27T + 5$

7. $\frac{x}{7} + 5 \geq \frac{x}{3} + 1$

8. $1.06w - 3.87 \leq 1.03w + 2.58$

9. Solve the inequality in Guided Example 3 by adding $-0.99m$ to each side at the beginning.

<hr>

APPLYING THE MATHEMATICS

10. Explain what was done for each step and find the mistake.

$$20 + 2.8v > 16 + 3.2v$$

Step 1	$20 - 0.4v > 16$
Step 2	$-0.4v > -4$
Step 3	$v > 10$

11. A telephone company offers two international telephone-saver plans. The first plan costs $3.95 per month plus a per-minute charge and the second plan costs $4.95 per month plus a per-minute charge. Phone calls to the Philippines cost 19¢ per minute under the first plan and 16¢ per minute under the second plan. Suppose you are going to make one call per month to the Philippines and no other international calls.

    a. What sentence can you solve to determine when the second plan is cheaper?

    b. Solve that sentence.

12. For a checking account, one bank charges $2.50 per month and 5¢ per check. A second bank charges $1.00 per month and 10¢ per check. A third bank charges $2.00 per month and 8¢ per check. For what number of checks per month is each bank the cheapest?

13. According to the U.S. Census Bureau, the population of Philadelphia in 2004 was 1,470,151 and had been decreasing at a rate of 11,800 people per year. The population of San Diego in 2004 was 1,263,756 and had been increasing at a rate of 10,082 people per year. If these rates continue, during what year will the population of San Diego overtake the population of Philadelphia?

The Schuylkill River, shown above, runs through Philadelphia and joins the Delaware River just south of the city.

14. Luanda is thinking of a number. She says that when she multiplies her number by 5, she gets a greater answer than when she multiplies her number by 10 and adds 6 to the product. For what numbers is this possible?

REVIEW

15. Graph $y > -\frac{2}{3}x + -2$. **(Lesson 10-3)**

16. Graph the inequalities $y < 0.6x + 7$, $y > -0.5x + 10$, and $x < 5$ on the same axes. What shape is their intersection? **(Lessons 10-3, 4-4)**

17. Use the graph at the right.
    a. Find the value of y on the line when $x = 7$.
       (Lessons 10-1, 9-8)
    b. Find the value of x when $y = 20,000$.
       (Lessons 10-1, 9-8)
    c. What is the area of the region under the line and in the first quadrant?
       (Lessons 10-1, 9-8, 7-4)

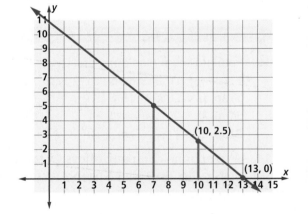

18. A line has equation $y = -20x + 5$. It is translated 4 units up. What is an equation for the translation image? **(Lessons 8-7, 6-1)**

EXPLORATION

19. In 2005, India's population was estimated at 1,080,000,000 and China's population was estimated at 1,306,000,000. In 2000, their respective populations were about 1,014,000,000 and 1,262,000,000. From this information, make some assumptions about how fast the populations of these countries are growing. Use graphs, tables, equations, and/or inequalities to estimate when India will have more people than China.

QY ANSWER

When you multiply or divide each side by a negative number

Lesson

10-5 Linear Combinations

Vocabulary

linear combination

▶ **BIG IDEA** In many situations, a multiple of one variable is added to a multiple of another variable, creating a linear combination of variables.

In many high schools and colleges, grades in courses are summarized by a *grade point average,* or *GPA*. To calculate a GPA, you give each letter grade a value. Often an A is 4 points, a B is 3 points, a C is 2 points, a D is 1 point, and a failing grade of F receives 0 points.

Suppose a student took 20 semester courses over 2 high school years and received 5 A's, 11 B's, 4 C's, and no D's or F's. The following table summarizes this information.

Letter Grade	Value	Frequency of Grade	Points
A	4	5	$5 \cdot 4 = 20$
B	3	11	$11 \cdot 3 = 33$
C	2	4	$4 \cdot 2 = 8$
D	1	0	$0 \cdot 1 = 0$
F	0	0	$0 \cdot 0 = 0$
Totals		20	61

The student has a total of 61 points from 20 courses. The grade point average is found by dividing the total number of points by the number of courses. Here the GPA is $\frac{61}{20}$, or 3.05. Normally the GPA is written as a decimal, often with two places.

A school has to calculate GPAs for all the students. No one wants to do this by hand, so it is often done with a spreadsheet. Some parts of the spreadsheet are the same for all students, but some parts vary. Below we let a = the number of courses with A's, b = the number of courses with B's, and so on. Here is the general form.

Letter Grade	Value	Frequency of Grade	Points
A	4	a	$4a$
B	3	b	$3b$
C	2	c	$2c$
D	1	d	$1d$
F	0	f	$0f$
Totals		$a + b + c + d + f$	$4a + 3b + 2c + d$

Mental Math

Determine whether you can make the given amount with exactly three U.S. coins. If so, identify the coins.

a. 75 cents

b. 28 cents

c. 7 cents

d. 50 cents

QY1

The expression $4a + 3b + 2c + d$ is called a linear combination of a, b, c, and d. A **linear combination** is the sum or difference of multiples of variables to the first power that are not multiplied or divided by each other. Recall from Lesson 8-1 that the numbers by which the variables are multiplied are the coefficients of the variables. For example, 4 is the coefficient of a and 1 is the coefficient of d because $d = 1 \cdot d$.

The sum $a + b + c + d + f$ is a linear combination of these five variables in which all the coefficients are 1. The GPA is
$$\frac{4a + 3b + 2c + d}{a + b + c + d + f}.$$

 QY2

Linear combinations occur in a wide variety of real-world situations. The simplest linear combinations are those with two variables.

> ▸ **QY1**
>
> Why is the total number of points written as
> $4a + 3b + 2c + d$
> and not as
> $4a + 3b + 2c + 1d + 0f$?

> ▸ **QY2**
>
> Calculate the GPA to two decimal places for a student who has 17 B's, 13 C's, 5 D's, and 1 F.

GUIDED

Example 1

A school organized a fund-raiser to raise money for the school library. Each class sold boxes of mixed nuts for $3.00 each and rolls of wrapping paper for $4.00 each. One class collected $127 but forgot to record how many of each item they sold. Write an equation the class could use to determine how many boxes of nuts and how many rolls of wrapping paper they sold.

Solution Let n = the number of boxes of nuts the class sold and let w = the number of rolls of wrapping paper the class sold.

Each box of nuts costs $3.00, so n boxes of nuts cost __?__ dollars.

A roll of wrapping paper costs $4.00, so w rolls of wrapping paper cost __?__ dollars.

The total is $127.00, so __?__ + __?__ = 127.

Activity

What combinations of boxes of nuts and number of rolls of wrapping paper could the class have sold?

Step 1 Find some pairs of values of n and w that satisfy the equation. You might proceed in a systematic way. Could the class have sold 0 boxes of nuts?

Try $n = 0$.

$$3 \cdot 0 + 4w = 127 \qquad \text{Substitution}$$
$$4w = 127 \qquad \text{Zero Product Property}$$
$$\frac{4w}{4} = \frac{127}{4} \qquad \text{Divide both sides by 4.}$$
$$w = 31.75 \qquad \text{Arithmetic}$$

The pair $(0, 31.75)$ is a solution to the equation $3n + 4w = 127$. But it is *not* a solution to the problem because w must be a whole number. You can't sell 0.75 of a roll of wrapping paper. Could the class have sold just 1 box of nuts?

Try $n = 1$.

$$3 \cdot 1 + 4w = 127 \qquad \text{Substitution}$$
$$3 + 4w = 127 \qquad \text{Zero Product Property}$$
$$-3 + 3 + 4w = 127 + -3 \qquad \text{Add } -3 \text{ to both sides.}$$
$$\frac{4w}{4} = \frac{124}{4} \qquad \text{Divide both sides by 4.}$$
$$w = 31 \qquad \text{Arithmetic}$$

The class could have sold 1 box of nuts and 31 rolls of wrapping paper. Solve an equation to continue this process.

a. Could the class have sold exactly 2 boxes of nuts?

b. Could the class have sold exactly 3 boxes of nuts?

c. Could the class have sold exactly 4 boxes of nuts?

Step 2 To solve an equation for every possible number of boxes of nuts is tedious. You may want to solve the general equation $3n + 4w = 127$ for w to find a formula for w in terms of n. Fill in the steps.

$$3n + 4w = 127$$
$$\underline{\quad ? \quad} = \underline{\quad ? \quad} \qquad \text{Add } -3n \text{ to both sides.}$$
$$4w = \underline{\quad ? \quad} \qquad \text{Collect like terms.}$$
$$\frac{4w}{4} = \frac{127 - 3n}{4} \qquad \text{Divide both sides by 4.}$$
$$w = \frac{127 - 3n}{4} \qquad \text{Multiplication Identity Property}$$

Step 3 Substitute various whole numbers for n to find at least three other combinations of boxes of nuts and rolls of wrapping paper the class could have sold.

Linear Combinations of Coins and Bills

The value of the money you have in your pocket is a linear combination of the number of pennies, nickels, dimes, quarters, dollar bills, five-dollar bills, and so on, that you have. This is because: p pennies are worth $0.01p$ dollars, n nickels are worth $0.05n$ dollars, f five-dollar bills are worth $5f$ dollars, and so on. So p pennies, n nickels, and f five-dollar bills are worth a total of $0.01p + 0.05n + 5f$ dollars.

 QY3

Thomas Jefferson has not always been the face you see on a nickel. The first nickels in 1866 showed a shield on the front. Lady Liberty appeared from 1883 to 1913 and a buffalo from 1914 to 1937. Jefferson first appeared on nickels in 1938.

Example 2

Suppose you have less than $5.00 in quarters and dimes. Find an inequality to describe how many of each coin you might have.

Solution Let d = the number of dimes you have and q = the number of quarters you have. Because each quarter is worth 0.25 and each dime is worth 0.10,

$$0.25q + 0.10d < 5.00.$$

Multiply both sides by 100 to clear the decimals.

$$25q + 10d < 500$$

 QY4

▶ **QY3**

If you had $5.07 and at least one $5 bill, what are the values of p, n, and f?

▶ **QY4**

In the situation described in Example 2, what is the most quarters you can have if you have 20 dimes?

Questions

COVERING THE IDEAS

1. **Fill in the Blanks** If A and B are numbers and x and y are variables, then $Ax + By$ is a linear combination of ___?___ and ___?___.

In 2–4, refer to the GPA calculation in this lesson.

2. If a student has 2 A's and 3 B's, what is the student's GPA?

3. If a student has 3 C's and 1 A, what is the student's GPA?

4. If a student has 2 A's, 5 B's, 1 C, 2 D's, and 1 F for a year, what is the student's GPA?

In 5 and 6, refer to the Activity in this lesson.

5. If a class earned $206, could it have sold exactly 10 boxes of mixed nuts? Explain how you can solve an equation to find out.

6. If a class earned $206, could the class have sold exactly 25 rolls of wrapping paper? Why or why not?

7. Suppose you have n nickels, d dimes, and q quarters.

   a. What is the total value of this money?

   b. Give three different possible ordered triples (n, d, q) if the total value is $1.00.

8. If you have no nickels, 20 coins that are dimes or quarters, and the total value is $3.05, how many dimes do you have?

9. In a cash register are n one-dollar bills, f five-dollar bills, t ten-dollar bills, and w twenty-dollar bills.

   a. What is the total value of this money?

   b. Suppose the total value is $326, and there are 31 one-dollar bills and 21 ten-dollar bills. What equation must f and w satisfy?

10. At the botanical gardens, Latayna bought a annuals at $2.49 each and p perennials at $5.99 each. Write an expression that represents how much Latanya spent.

APPLYING THE MATHEMATICS

11. At a garage sale, magazines sold for $0.10 and books sold for $0.25. Kareem spent $2.35 on magazines and books.

    a. Write an equation relating the number of magazines m, the number of books b, and the total amount spent by Kareem.

    b. Find a solution for this situation.

12. Ida saved $30.00 of her allowance to buy calendars as gifts and figurines for her collection. The calendars sold for $2.95 each and the figurines sold for $5.99.

    a. Find an inequality to describe how many calendars and figurines Ida might have purchased.

    b. If Ida bought 4 calendars, how many figurines could she buy?

13. Currently, Irene has a GPA of 3.37 after having taken 30 classes in high school. She has 10 classes left. If she gets all A's in these 10 classes, can she raise her GPA to the 3.50 she needs for an academic award?

14. Miguel has $80 to spend on CDs and DVDs. Suppose CDs cost $12 each and DVDs cost $15 each. Let x = the number of CDs and y = the number of DVDs Miguel buys.

    a. Write an inequality to describe the numbers of CDs and DVDs Miguel can buy.

    b. Find two solutions to the inequality.

    c. In what ways can Miguel buy only CDs and still have money left?

About 1,200 species of plants as well as some birds live in the Climatron® conservatory at the Missouri Botanical Garden.

15. A number written in base 10 is a linear combination of its digits. For instance, $3,572 = 3 \cdot 1,000 + 5 \cdot 100 + 7 \cdot 10 + 2 \cdot 1$. Suppose the thousands digit of a number is T, the hundreds digit is h, the tens digit is t, and the ones digit is u. What is the value of the number?

REVIEW

16. Car-Go Rentals charges $30 per day plus 28¢ per mile to rent an economy car. Rapid Rent charges $50 for one day and 15¢ per mile. The Winderwere family is going to rent a car for two days while on vacation. For how many miles will Car-Go be the better value? **(Lesson 10-4)**

In 17 and 18, Jamie and Amy were hired by different companies. Jamie was offered a $30,000 salary with a $3,000 raise every year, and Amy was offered a $45,000 salary with a $1,500 raise every year.

17. Write an equation describing the time in years, t, until they earn the same salary.

18. **a.** After how many years will Jamie and Amy earn the same salary?
    b. What will their salaries be at that time? **(Lessons 10-5, 10-2)**

19. Solve $-5x + 14 \geq 8x - 25$. Show each step. **(Lesson 10-4)**

20. A pillar candle is 8" tall when Cody first lights it. After 3 hours, it is $2\frac{1}{4}$" tall. What is the rate at which it has burned? **(Lesson 9-3)**

21. Find the x-coordinate of the point where $Y_1 = 1.20389X + 2.1048$ intersects the y-axis. **(Lesson 8-7)**

22. **a.** Write an expression for the inequality graphed below.

    b. Which of the following are solutions to the inequality? There may be more than one. **(Lesson 2-8)**
    i. -4.3 ii. 4.3 iii. 0 iv. 5 v. -5

EXPLORATION

23. Hinda likes to do things in hundreds. She spent $100 on 100 items. Some items cost $10.00 each, some cost $3 each, and some cost $0.50 each. How many of each item did Hinda buy?

Lesson
10-6

Graphing $Ax + By = C$ and $Ax + By < C$

> ▶ **BIG IDEA** When a linear combination of two variables equals a constant, the graph of the equation is a line.

Graphing a Line by Plotting Points

In Lesson 10-5, the equation $3n + 4w = 127$ arose when a class sold n boxes of mixed nuts at \$3 each and w rolls of wrapping paper at \$4 each. The class took in \$127, but did not remember how much of each item was sold. There are many possible pairs of positive integer values (n, w) that satisfy this equation. But, as the table below shows, some integer values of n do not correspond to integer values of w. For example, the class could not have sold 2 or 3 boxes of nuts.

n	w
0	$31\frac{3}{4}$
1	31
2	$30\frac{1}{4}$
3	$29\frac{1}{2}$
4	$28\frac{3}{4}$
5	28
6	$27\frac{1}{4}$
7	$26\frac{1}{2}$
8	$25\frac{3}{4}$
9	25
10	$24\frac{1}{4}$

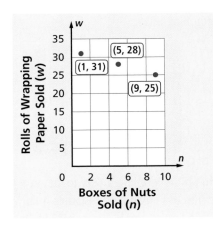

Mental Math

Use the data set {2, 3, 6, 6, 7, 7, 7, 9, x}.

a. Find the mode if $x = 6$.

b. Find the mode if $x \neq 6$.

c. Find the median if $x = 6$.

d. Find the median if $x > 7$.

e. Find the mean if $x = 6$.

f. Find the mean if $x = 15$.

Notice that the points that satisfy the equation all lie on the same line. Even the points without integer coordinates lie on this line. If you were to continue in the same direction of the line, all possible solutions to the situation would be represented. The graph of the set of ordered pairs satisfying the equation $3n + 4w = 127$ is a line. That is why we call $3n + 4w$ a *linear* combination of n and w.

Lines are basic figures in mathematics because so many other figures are made up of parts of lines or bounded by lines. In your future mathematics courses, you will study lines in great detail. In this lesson, you will see how to quickly graph lines when their equations are given in the form $Ax + By = C$.

Using a Calculator to Graph Equations

One way to graph equations of the form $Ax + By = C$ is to rewrite the equation so that it is in the form of $y = ax + b$ and then use a graphing calculator. To do so, you need to solve equations of the form $Ax + By = C$ for y.

Example 1

Graph the equation $3x + 2y = 18$ with a graphing utility.

Solution

$3x + 2y = 18$	Start with the original equation.
$3x + 2y - 3x = 18 - 3x$	Subtract $3x$ in order to isolate the y term.
$2y = 18 - 3x$	
$\dfrac{2y}{2} = \dfrac{18 - 3x}{2}$	Divide each term by 2.
$y = \dfrac{18 - 3x}{2}$	Simplify.

Enter the equation into your graphing utility.

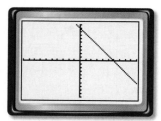

Check Use the trace feature on the graphing utility to locate a point on the line. Substitute the values into the original equation. Is it correct? The screen below shows that $(0, 9)$ is on the graph.

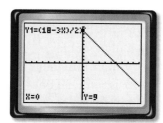

$$3x + 2y = 18$$

Does $3(0) + 2(9) = 18$?

$$0 + 18 = 18?$$

Yes, it checks.

In the wrapping-paper and mixed-nuts situation, $3n + 4w = 127$ was solved for w. In that case, $w = \frac{127 - 3n}{4}$. By changing n to x, and changing w to y, you can graph this equation on a calculator.

 QY

> ▶ QY
>
> Graph $y = \frac{127 - 3x}{4}$ with a graphing calculator. Use the trace feature to show that the line goes through the points in the table on page 647.

Graphing Linear Inequalities

Many calculators can graph inequalities.

Activity

Graph the inequality $y \geq 0.5x + 3$.

Step 1 Make the window the standard window.

Step 2 Enter the inequality $y \geq 0.5x + 3$ into the graphing utility. Adjust your calculator so that it will graph the inequality. The procedure for your calculator may be to first enter $Y1 = 0.5 \cdot X + 3$. With your calculator still in Y= mode, press ◀ until the cursor is left of Y1, then press ENTER 2 times until it looks like the screen below. Notice the change in the icon to the left of the Y1.

Step 3 Press **GRAPH**. You should see something similar to what is shown below.

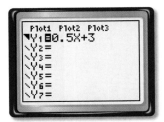
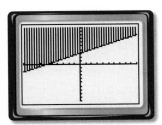

In Lesson 10-5, the following situation was given.

Example 2

Suppose you have less than $5.00 in quarters and dimes. Sketch a graph to describe how many of each coin you might have.

Solution Let d = the number of dimes you have. Let q = the number of quarters you have.

Because each quarter is worth 25¢, each dime is worth 10¢, and $5.00 is 500¢, you saw that

$$25q + 10d < 500.$$

To graph this inequality, first graph the line $25q + 10d = 500$. This equation describes the situation in which you have exactly $5.00. On this line, if $q = 0$, then $d = 50$. That is, if you have no quarters, then you have 50 dimes. If $d = 0$, then $q = 20$. Because q and d cannot be negative, only the points in the first quadrant or on the axes are shaded.

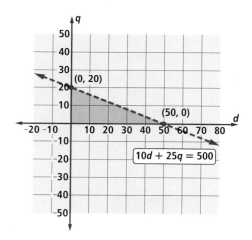

The graph is actually made up of only the points with integer coordinates because q and d must be integers. But there are so many points that shading is easier. The shading thus shows that there are many solutions.

Questions

COVERING THE IDEAS

In 1–4, consider the mixed-nuts and wrapping-paper situation that led
to $3n + 4w = 127$.

1. a. When $n = 9$, what is w?
   b. What do the values of n and w from Part a mean in
      the situation?

2. a. When $w = 30$, what is n?
   b. What do the values of n and w from Part a mean
      in the situation?

3. **Multiple Choice** What is the graph of all the values of x and y that
   satisfy $3x + 4y = 127$?

   A   a line   B   a line segment

   C   a ray   D   a certain number of points

4. **Multiple Choice** What is the graph of all the values of n and w
   that have meaning in the situation?

   A   a line   B   a line segment

   C   a ray   D   a certain number of points

5. **Multiple Choice** To graph an equation of the form $Ax + By = C$
   with a calculator, you may need to solve the equation for which
   variable?

   A A B B C C D x E y

In 6 and 7, refer to the graph of $y = \dfrac{18 - 3x}{2}$ in Example 1.

6. What is the point of intersection of this graph and the y-axis?

7. Explain why $(-4, 15)$ is on the graph.

8. **Multiple Choice** To use a graphing utility to graph $17x + 12y = 35$,
   which key sequence should you use?

   A   Y1 $= 35 \boxed{-} 17x \boxed{\div} 12$ B   Y1 $= 35 + 12y \boxed{\div} 17$

   C   Y1 $= \boxed{(} 35 \boxed{-} 17x \boxed{)} \boxed{\div} 12$ D   Y1 $= 35 \boxed{-} 17x + 12y$

In 9 and 10, an equation is given.
a. Solve the equation for y.
b. Sketch its graph.

9. $3x - 2y = 6$ 10. $x + 5y = -20$

In 11–13, match the sentence with one of the four graphs shown here. All four graphs are in the same window.

11. $7x + 5y = 12$ **12.** $7x + 5y < 12$ **13.** $7x + 5y > 12$

A
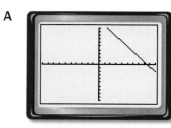

B
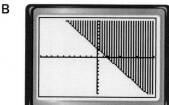

C
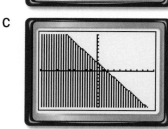

D
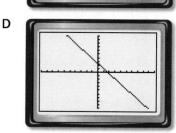

In 14 and 15, refer to Example 2.

14. Why does the graph of solutions to $25q + 10d < 500$ have no points in the 2nd, 3rd, or 4th quadrants?

15. What change in the situation would cause the oblique line to be solid rather than dotted in the graph?

16. Suppose you have no more than $1.00 in quarters and dimes. Graph all possible pairs (d, q) of numbers of quarters and dimes you could have.

APPLYING THE MATHEMATICS

17. Carmen and Dylan were tossing beanbags. They decided to make up a game. If a beanbag landed in a bucket, 5 points would be awarded. If it landed on the rim or against the bucket, then 3 points would be awarded. No points would be awarded for any toss that did not rest in contact with the bucket. Dylan scored 62 points.
   a. Write an equation that represents the situation.
   b. Graph the equation.
   c. Find three possible solutions.

18. a. Sketch the graph of all pairs of numbers x and y whose difference $x - y$ is greater than 4.
   b. On the same axes, use a different color to sketch the graph of all pairs of numbers x and y whose difference $x - y$ is less than 8.
   c. Describe the intersection of the graphs of Parts a and b.

19. Graph all pairs of numbers x and y that satisfy all three of these conditions.

    1. x is positive.   2. y is negative.   3. $x + y < 10$

20. In one soccer league, a team gets 2 points for a win and 1 point for a tie. The teams play 10 games in the season and 15 points are needed to make the playoffs. Graph the pairs of wins w and ties t that will enable a team to make the playoffs.

The American Youth Soccer Organization has more than 600,000 members nationwide who range from ages $4\frac{1}{2}$ to 19.

REVIEW

21. Harry took 6 classes in the first semester. He earned 3 A's, a D, and two C's. **(Lesson 10-5)**

    a. At 4 points for an A, 3 points for a B, and so on, calculate the total number of grade points Harry received.

    b. Suppose one of the C grades had been a B. What would be the change in Harry's GPA?

22. In how many quadrants are there solutions to the inequality $y \geq 2.1x + 1.6$? **(Lesson 10-3)**

In 23 and 24, a sprinter runs 100 meters in 10.3 seconds.

23. a. Rounded to the nearest hundredth, what was his speed in meters per second? **(Lesson 9-2)**

    b. If he continues at this speed, how long would it take to run 1,609 meters (about 1 mile)? **(Lesson 9-7)**

24. Is the calculation of how long it would take a sprinter to run a mile an example of a good use of proportional thinking? Explain your reasoning. **(Lesson 9-8)**

25. Two sides of a triangle are $3x + y$ and $5x - 2y$. What expressions describe the greatest and least possible values of the third side? **(Lesson 5-10)**

26. A formula for the volume of a cone with radius r and height h is $\frac{1}{3}\pi r^2 h$. An ice cream cone has a height of 4.5 inches and a diameter of 1.5 inches. How many cubic inches of ice cream can fit inside? **(Lessons 2-4, 1-6)**

QY ANSWER

EXPLORATION

27. A man goes to the bank and asks for x dollars and y cents. The banker by mistake gives him y dollars and x cents. After a nickel drops on the floor, the man looks at his money and realizes that he now has twice the amount he asked for. What was the amount he asked for?

Lesson

10-7   Time-Distance Graphs

Vocabulary

time-distance graph

▶ **BIG IDEA**   It is possible to graph the distance a person is from a fixed point over a period of time, and the graph can reveal other information about the situation.

Some graphs on a coordinate grid are unions of line segments.

Activity

Consider the graph at the right.

Note the general situation. The *y*-axis represents distance from home and the *x*-axis represents time in minutes. As you move from left to right on the *x*-axis, time is increasing and distance from home is increasing, decreasing, or staying the same.

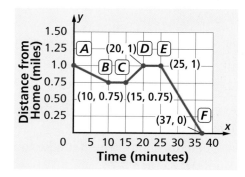

Mental Math

A world-class time for the mile run is four minutes. If a person could run at this rate without slowing, how long would it take the person to run:

a. 6 miles?

b. 0.75 mile?

c. 26.2 miles (length of a marathon)?

Step 1 Fill in the blanks.

Point *A* represents __?__ miles from home at __?__ minutes.
Point *B* represents __?__ miles from home at __?__ minutes.
Point *C* represents __?__ miles from home at __?__ minutes.
Point *D* represents __?__ miles from home at __?__ minutes.
Point *E* represents __?__ miles from home at __?__ minutes.
Point *F* represents __?__ miles from home at __?__ minutes.

Step 2 Use the information in Step 1 to write a story based on the graph.

In the Activity, you wrote a story from a graph. In Example 1, a graph is created from a story.

Example 1

It took Bick 10 minutes to bike at a constant rate from home to a store that was 1.4 miles away. He stayed in the store for 15 minutes. Then he biked 2 minutes at a constant rate to the library that was 0.2 mile father away. He stayed there for 13 minutes and then biked home at a quicker constant rate, taking 10 minutes to get back. Show this information in a graph.

Solution

Step 1 Let the horizontal axis stand for Bick's time in minutes
from when he started. The vertical axis stands for Bick's
distance away from home.

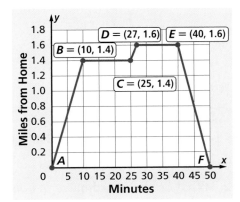

Step 2 Call his starting point $A = (0, 0)$. At 10 minutes, Bick
was 1.4 miles away from home. Let $B = (10, 1.4)$.
Draw $\overline{AB}$. When Bick is traveling at a constant speed, the
graph of his distance away from home is a line segment.
The segment $\overline{AB}$ shows that he was going from his home
at A to the store at B at a constant speed. The steeper
the line segment, the greater the speed.

Step 3 Bick stays at the store for 15 minutes, so
$C = (10 + 15, 1.4) = (25, 1.4)$. Draw and label $\overline{BC}$. When Bick is
not moving, the graph of his distance away from home is a *horizontal*
segment. $\overline{BC}$ stands for the part of the trip that Bick was in the store.
While he is at the store, his distance from home *does not change*.

Step 4 Because Bick biked for 2 minutes and went 0.2 mile farther,
$D = (25 + 2, 1.4 + 0.2) = (27, 1.6)$. Draw and label $\overline{CD}$.

Step 5 Because Bick stayed at the library for 13 minutes,
$E = (27 + 13, 1.6 + 0) = (40, 1.6)$. Draw $\overline{DE}$.

Step 6 The last segment of his trip only took 10 minutes.
So $F = (40 + 10, 1.6 - 1.6) = (50, 0)$. Draw $\overline{EF}$.

 QY1

▶ **QY1**

What happened between
points C and D in the
graph of Example 1?

The graph in Example 1 is called a **time-distance graph**. A part
of a time-distance graph will be a line segment when the object is
traveling in a straight line and its speed does not change.

Example 2

A train will be passing through a station S, going from east to west. It is
now 35 miles east of the station, traveling at 70 mph. If it is going at a
constant rate, then $\frac{1}{2}$ hour from now it will be at S. 1.5 hours from now it
will be 70 miles west of S. Draw a graph of this situation.

Solution We will call east *positive* and west *negative*. The train is 35
miles east of the station now, so its position now is $(0, 35)$. It is traveling
at 70 mph, so in a half hour it will be at the station S. This means that
it will be at 0 distance from the station S, so its position is indicated by
$(0.5, 0)$. It will keep going, and an hour later it will be 70 miles west of
the station S. Its position will be $(1.5, -70)$. The graph at the right shows this.

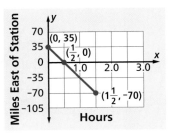

An equation for the graph of Example 2 is $y = 35 - 70x$. You can check that the three points identified on the graph satisfy this equation.

STOP **QY2**

> ▶ **QY2**
>
> Show that $(1.5, -70)$ satisfies the equation $y = 35 - 70x$.

Questions

COVERING THE IDEAS

In 1–7, consider the graph of Bick's bike ride in Example 1.

1. What do the coordinates of point E mean?

2. What do the coordinates of point F mean?

3. What does $\overline{DE}$ represent, and what does its length mean?

4. What does $\overline{EF}$ represent?

5. **Multiple Choice** Which is an equation of $\overleftrightarrow{AB}$?

   A $y = 1.4$ B $x = 10$ C $y = 0.14x$ D $y = 10 - 1.4x$

6. **Multiple Choice** Which is an equation of $\overleftrightarrow{BC}$?

   A $x = 25 - 10$ B $y = 1.4$ C $y = 0.14x$ D $y = 0.056x$

7. What property of the graph indicates that Bick biked faster on his way home than on his way to the store?

In 8 and 9, refer to Example 2.

8. Which point on the graph indicates the moment when the train passed the station?

9. The point $(1, -35)$ is on the graph. What does that point mean?

APPLYING THE MATHEMATICS

10. **Multiple Choice** Margo sets off on her bike from tae kwan do practice, which is 3 miles from her house. After going about a mile she gets a flat tire and has to walk the rest of the way home. Which graph best represents the situation? Justify your answer.

U.S. commuter trains traveled a total of 294,659,000 miles in 2004.

Source: American Public Transportation Association

A
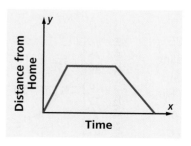

B
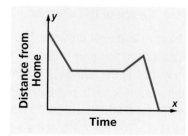

C
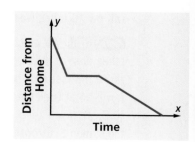

11. Jamila lives 2 miles from school. Suppose she walks home from school at a constant rate and it takes her 70 minutes. Graph her distance from home over time, beginning with the time she leaves school.

12. a. Draw a time-distance graph for this story. The Gurney family drove at a constant rate for 2.5 hours to reach a cousin's house 125 miles away. After an hour at the cousin's house, they drove 15 minutes to a restaurant 5 miles closer to their home. They ate at the restaurant for 75 minutes, and then they drove back home, taking 2 hours to get home.

    b. How fast were they traveling to get to their cousin's house?

    c. How fast did they travel, on average, to get back home?

13. Make up your own story that leads to a time-distance graph.

14. A trucker picked up his freight and averaged 25 mph for an hour in the city. The trucker then drove for another hour at 55 mph on some state highways. Then the trucker drove for three hours on an interstate at 65 mph.

    a. At the end of this time, how far had the trucker driven?

    b. From this information, create a time-distance graph of how far the trucker had driven over time.

Many truckers own their own cabs and customize them with paint, lights, and accessories.

REVIEW

15. In one game of darts, the inner circle I is worth 8 points, and the outer circle O is worth 5 points. Megan scores 52 points.

    a. If her darts landed x times in the inner ring and y times in the outer ring, write an equation representing this situation.

    b. Graph the equation of Part a. Do values of the variables in Part a make sense if they are not integers? Why or why not? (Lessons 10-6, 10-5)

16. Tell whether the equation is a linear equation. Justify your answer. (Lesson 10-1)

    a. $y = 3x + 67$ b. $x = \frac{9}{y} + -8$ c. $x = \frac{y}{9} + -8$

    d. $x + y = 73$ e. $y = \frac{x + 9}{3} + 4.2$

17. It costs $3.43 to buy seven Flurbs. Eight Flurbs cost $3.92. Thirteen Flurbs cost $6.37. Write an equation describing the total cost C of n Flurbs. (**Lesson 10-1**)

18. a. Graph $y = -2x + -2$.
    b. Which quadrant does not contain the graph from Part a? (**Lessons 10-1, 8-7, 1-9**)

19. On average, a telemarketer can call 5 people in a half hour. At this rate, how many people can the telemarketer call in
    a. 2 hours?   b. 12 minutes?
    c. an 8-hour workday? (**Lesson 9-8**)

20. Fill in the table below to compare the weight of the following dinosaurs to the weight of a farm horse (450 kg). Round to the nearest hundredth. (**Lesson 9-6**)

Dinosaur	Weight (kg)	Times as Heavy as a Farm Horse
Apatosaurus	3.0×10^5	?
Triceratops	5,440	?
Compsognathus	5.5	?
Iguanodon	4,540	?
Tyrannosaurus	6,350	?

Paleontologist Jack McIntosh with an Apatosaurus at the Carnegie Museum of Natural History. This 40-ton vegetarian is more than 77 feet long and is the longest mounted dinosaur in the world.

21. **Multiple Choice** If $y = x + 5$, which is also true? (**Lesson 9-5**)
    A $y + 5 = x$ B $\frac{y}{5} = x - 1$ C $\frac{y}{5} = \frac{x + 5}{5}$ D $5y = 5x + 5$

22. Graph the line with equation $y - x = 3$. (**Lesson 8-7**)

EXPLORATION

23. Some time-distance graphs are not made up of lines or parts of lines. If you are in a Ferris wheel and going around at a constant speed without stopping, your distance above ground will alternately increase (as you go up) and decrease (as you go down). The curve that describes your distance is a *sine curve*. A graphing utility can display sine curves. Graph $y = \sin x$ using a graphing utility. Then copy the graph onto a piece of paper, identifying some of the points on the curve.

QY ANSWERS

1. Bick biked at a constant rate to the library.

2. Does $-70 = 35 - 70 \cdot 1.5$?
   Does $-70 = 35 - 105$?
   Yes

Lesson

10-8 Graphs of Formulas

Vocabulary

parabola

▶ **BIG IDEA**   Formulas in which one variable is given in terms of another variable can be graphed on a coordinate grid.

Some formulas, like the area formula $A = \ell w$ for a rectangle, state one variable (A) in terms of two others (ℓ and w). To graph them requires graphs in three dimensions. But other formulas, like the formula $C = \pi d$ for the circumference of a circle, present one variable (C) in terms of one other (d). These formulas can be graphed just as you have done with other equations in previous lessons.

Example 1

Graph $C = \pi d$, where C is the circumference of a circle with diameter d.

Solution Think of d as x and C as y. To plot points, use an approximation to π, such as 3.14.

When $d = 1$, $C = \pi \cdot 1 \approx 3.14 \cdot 1 = 3.14$.

When $d = 2$, $C = \pi \cdot 2 \approx 3.14 \cdot 2 = 6.28$.

When $d = 5$, $C = \pi \cdot 5 \approx 3.14 \cdot 5 = 15.7$.

Plot as many points as you think you need to get a good graph. A graph is shown here. Notice that the scales on the axes are different.

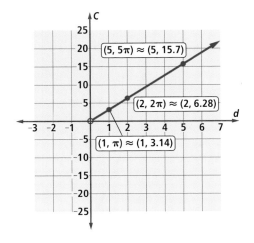

Because d and C stand for lengths, the graph contains only positive values of d and C. The graph is a ray without its endpoint.

Mental Math

Match each inequality to its graph.

i.

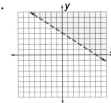

ii.

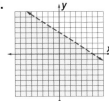

iii.

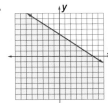

iv.

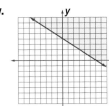

a. $2x + 3y < 12$

b. $2x + 3y > 12$

c. $2x + 3y \leq 12$

d. $2x + 3y \geq 12$

Another formula that involves only two variables is the formula $A = s^2$ for the area of a square. The graph of this formula is *not* linear, as Example 2 shows.

Example 2

Let A be the area of a square with side s. Graph all possible pairs of values (s, A).

Solution Since $A = s^2$, the values (s, A) are the same as the values (s, s^2) by substitution. So the graph contains all ordered pairs in which the first coordinate is a nonnegative number, since it is a length, and the second coordinate is the square of that number.

Below is a table of some values. At the right is the graph.

s	A
2	4
1	1
3	9
4	16
$\frac{1}{2}$	$\frac{1}{4}$

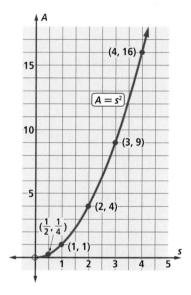

The arc in Example 2 is part of the curve known as a *parabola*. The **parabola** is the shape of all graphs of equations of the form $y = ax^2$.

To graph all the possible pairs of numbers satisfying $y = x^2$, including negative coordinates, remember that a number and its opposite have the same square. Thus $(-x)^2 = x^2$. For this reason, the graph is symmetric to the y-axis. The full graph cannot be shown because it extends forever. Its shape is the entire parabola.

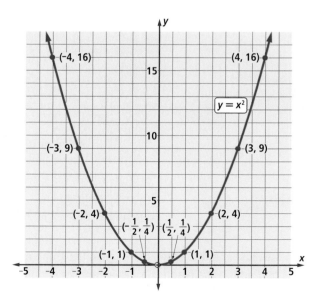

The parabola has important properties. These properties cause it to be a shape used in the manufacture of automobile headlights, satellite dishes, and telescopes.

As *x* increases, the curve of the parabola goes up more quickly than any line. This illustrates the fact that the area of a square grows more quickly than the length of a side. For instance, if the length of a side of a square is multiplied by 10, its area is multiplied by 100.

This is just one of the communication antennas at the Canberra Deep Space Communication Complex in Australia.

Activity

Recall that a *diagonal* of a polygon is a line segment connecting two nonadjacent vertices of the polygon. The interior segments in the polygons below show the diagonals for a triangle, a quadrilateral, and a pentagon.

0 diagonals   2 diagonals   5 diagonals

Step 1 Copy the table below and complete the rows for the number of diagonals in a hexagon and heptagon.

Number of Sides			Total Number of Diagonals
3			0
4			2
5			5
6			?
7			?
20			?
n			?

This string-art was created from many diagonals of a 28-sided polygon.

Step 2 Do you notice a relationship between the number of sides and the number of diagonals?

(continued on next page)

Step 3 Label the blank columns as shown below. Complete the rows for the hexagon and heptagon. What do you notice?

Number of Sides	Number of Vertices	Number of Diagonals Drawn from Each Vertex	Total Number of Diagonals
3	3	0	0
4	4	1	2
5	5	2	5
6	?	?	?
7	?	?	?
20	?	?	?
n	?	?	?

Step 4 You may have noticed that the number of vertices is the same as the number of sides. You may have also noticed that the number of diagonals drawn from each vertex is 3 fewer than the number of sides. Finally, you might have seen that the number of diagonals is half the product of Column 2 and Column 3. You can now complete the rows for the 20-gon and n-gon.

Number of Sides	Number of Vertices	Number of Diagonals Drawn from Each Vertex	Total Number of Diagonals
3	3	$3 - 3 = 0$	$\frac{3(0)}{2} = 0$
4	4	$4 - 3 = 1$	$\frac{4(1)}{2} = 2$
5	5	$5 - 3 = 2$	$\frac{5(2)}{2} = 5$
6	?	?	?
7	?	?	?
20	?	?	?
n	?	?	?

Diagonals of an *n*-gon

The number d, of diagonals of a polygon with n sides is given by $d = \frac{n(n-3)}{2}$.

Example 3

Use a graphing utility to graph the formula for the diagonals of an *n*-gon.

Solution Change the variables in the formula to reflect the variables used in graphing utilities: $y = \dfrac{x(x-3)}{2}$, where y represents the number of diagonals and x represents the number of sides. Set the minimum value for x in the window to be 3. (Why?) Choose a reasonable value for the maximum of x, say 30. The minimum value for y should be 0 (Why?) and the maximum should be something reasonable as well. We'll choose 500. Your graph should look something like the graph at the right above.

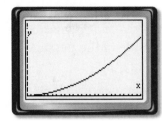

If you had included values for x less than 3 in your window range you would notice that, like $y = x^2$, this graph is also a parabola. Only certain points on this parabola have meaning in this problem.

As Examples 2 and 3 show, graphs of formulas and other equations may have shapes quite different from lines. As you study more mathematics, you will become familiar with many of these shapes.

Questions

COVERING THE IDEAS

In 1–3, consider the graph of $C = \pi d$ in this lesson.

1. a. Which variable is the first coordinate of points on the graph?
   b. Which variable is the second coordinate of points on the graph?

2. **Multiple Choice** Which is the best description of the graph?

   A a line   **B** a line segment   **C** a ray

3. Name a point on the graph other than those given in Example 1.

In 4–7, consider the graph of $A = s^2$.

4. a. Which variable is the first coordinate of points on the graph?
   b. Which variable is the second coordinate of points on the graph?

5. **Fill in the Blank** The graph is part of the curve known as a __?__.

6. Suppose the point $(5, t)$ is on this graph. What is t?

7. a. How does this graph differ from the graph of $y = x^2$?
   b. How is this graph the same as the graph of $y = x^2$?

8. Explain the formula for finding the diagonals of an n-gon in your own words.

APPLYING THE MATHEMATICS

9. A formula for the perimeter p of a regular pentagon is $p = 5s$, where s is the length of a side of the pentagon.
    a. Graph 6 pairs of values (s, p).
    b. Sketch a graph of all pairs (s, p) that satisfy $p = 5s$.
    c. Describe the graph.

10. To find the measure of one angle a of a regular n-gon you can divide the sum of the measures of the interior angles, $(n - 2)180°$, by the number of sides. So, $a = \dfrac{(n - 2)180°}{n}$.
    a. Find 6 pairs of values (n, a).
    b. Use a graphing calculator to sketch a graph of all pairs that satisfy the formula.
    c. Describe the graph.

11. Refer to Example 3. Use a graphing utility to graph $y = x^2$ on the same axes as $y = \dfrac{x(x - 3)}{2}$. Compare the graphs.

12. Recall that the formula $F = \dfrac{9}{5}C + 32$ converts temperatures in degrees Celsius to temperatures in degrees Fahrenheit. Draw a graph of this formula.

13. a. Find at least 6 ordered pairs that satisfy $y = |x|$.
    b. Draw the graph of $y = |x|$.

14. $F = ma$ is a formula that relates the force F of an object in newtons to its mass m in kg and acceleration a in m/sec². If an object weighs 30 kg, graph its force as it changes acceleration.

15. The amount of work required to move an object is determined by the equation $W = F \cdot d$, where W is work, F is force in newtons, and d is distance in meters. Draw a graph showing how much work is required to move an object 100 meters.

REVIEW

16. Juana leaves school, 3 miles away from her house, at 2 P.M. to go to drum and bugle corps practice. She arrives at practice at 2:15, 2 miles away from her house. Halfway through the 2-hour-long practice, she gets sick and goes home for some medicine. She gets home at 3:45. Draw a time-distance graph representing this situation. **(Lesson 10-7)**

17. Paul is taking the bus to see a basketball game. On the bus, he is eating 17 ounces of French onion soup. He is 10 miles away from the game. The bus ride takes 20 minutes, and he must eat all of the soup before he arrives at the game.
    a. Draw a time-distance graph representing his distance from the game.
    b. What is the minimum rate at which Paul must eat his soup so that he can be sure to finish it before he gets to the game? (**Lessons 10-7, 9-2**)

18. To get from school to home, Roshanda walked $\frac{1}{2}$ mile north and $\frac{3}{8}$ mile west. She walks at a rate of 2 miles per hour. If she had been able to walk in a straight line home (ignoring all the buildings in the way!), how much time would she have saved? (**Lessons 8-2, 6-9**)

19. From the view of a helicopter, it is apparent that the streets of Chicago primarily follow a grid system. As you head toward Lake Michigan, the irregular shoreline is outlined by Lake Shore Drive and, as a result, the roads form various shapes. As shown at the right, these streets of Chicago form a trapezoid. Find the area. (**Lesson 7-5**)

Oak Street
0.22 mi

Michigan Ave.
0.27 mi

Lake Shore Drive
0.31 mi

Chicago Ave.
0.35 mi

20. A right triangle has an area of 45 square inches. One of its legs measures 15 inches. Find the lengths of the other two sides. (**Lessons 7-4, 7-1**)

21. Slice of Pi, a new pizzeria, hired 22 people as cooks or waiters when it first opened. 14 people work as cooks, and 15 people work as waiters. How many people were hired to do both jobs? (**Lesson 4-4**)

EXPLORATION

22. The graph of $y = x^2$ contains the points (–1, 1), (0, 0), and (1, 1).
    a. Draw an accurate picture of the part of the curve from (–1, 1) to (1, 1) on the window $-1 \leq x \leq 1$, $-1 \leq y \leq 1$.
    b. Graph the equation $y = x^3$ on the same window as Part a. Describe one similarity and one difference in the graphs of $y = x^2$ and $y = x^3$.
    c. Graph the equation $y = x^4$ on the same window as Part a. Explore these graphs with different windows. Describe what happens.

Chapter 10 Projects

1 Creating Graphic Art Using Inequalities

When you graph an inequality of the form $y < ax + b$, the result is a shaded region above or below a line. Many graphing utilities will let you graph the *intersection* of several of these inequalities. What would this look like? Experiment with your graphing utility, or create the graphs of intersections of inequalities by hand. Can you write a formula for a shaded octagon? A pentagonal house?

2 How Frequently Is a Solution an Integer?

When real situations lead to equations, sometimes the only solutions that make sense are those that are integers. But do all equations have integer solutions? Use a 6-sided die and roll it three times to determine values a, b, and c. Then determine whether $ax + b = c$ has an integer solution for x. Repeat this 25 times. What is the relative frequency of rolling an equation with an integer solution? Try using four rolls of a die to determine values of a, b, c, and d in $ax + b = cx + d$. Repeat this many times. What is the relative frequency of integer solutions to the equations you roll? Do you think the probability of rolling an equation $ax + b = c$ with an integer solution is more than, less than, or the same as the probability of rolling an equation $ax + b = cx + d$ with an integer solution?

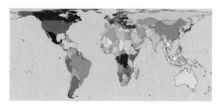

The world according to area

3 Graphing Your Movements

For a week, keep track of the distances you travel from home and the time these trips take. Create a time-distance graph of your location. Mark events on your graph. Are there patterns to your movement? Does it take you the same amount of time to go to school every day? Do you go anywhere after school on certain days? Do you take any special trips?

4 Ax + By = C in the Newspaper

Look through a newspaper for examples of situations that lead to equations of the form $Ax + By = C$. Explain why the situations you found can be described using equations of this type and describe some of the information you can conclude from solutions to these equations.

5 Linear Increase and Decrease

Predicting the populations of countries in the future is very important for predicting the use of resources. Research several countries, and compare their current populations and the rate of population change, assuming it is linear. For example, the United States has the third largest population of any nation in the world; but Indonesia, the country with the fourth largest population, is growing at a faster rate. Compare their populations as an equation of the form $ax + b = cx + d$. When do you estimate the population of Indonesia will be larger than the population of the United States?

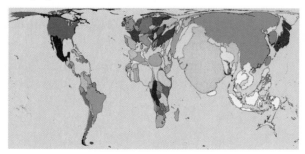

The world according to population

Chapter 10 Summary and Vocabulary

○ It is natural to compare two quantities that are changing to determine when one is greater or less than the other. If the first quantity is described by $y = ax + b$ and the second quantity is described by $y = cx + d$, then the quantities will be equal when $ax + b = cx + d$. This equation, which has an unknown on both sides, can be solved by adding either $-ax$ or $-cx$ to both sides. The resulting equation has an unknown on only one side and can be solved like $ax + b = c$. The corresponding inequality $ax + b < cx + d$ can be solved in much the same way.

○ The solutions to any algebraic sentence (equation or inequality) can be graphed. If the sentence has two variables, then the graph is a set of ordered pairs that can be plotted on a coordinate grid. If an equation is equivalent to one of the form $y = ax + b$, then its graph is a line. The graph of the corresponding inequalities $y < ax + b$ and $y > ax + b$ consists of all the points on one of the two sides of that line.

The graph of all the pairs (x, y) of numbers satisfying the equation $Ax + By = C$ is also a line. The graph of all pairs (x, y) of numbers satisfying $x = h$ make up a vertical line. The graph of all the pairs (x, y) of numbers satisfying the equation $y = k$ make up a horizontal line. Again, the graphs of the corresponding inequalities consist of the points on either side of the line. The graphs of $y \leq ax + b$ and $y \geq ax + b$ consist of points on the line $y = ax + b$ and one side of that line.

○ Graphs of segments can be pieced together to form a time-distance graph. Formulas can also be graphed on a coordinate plane. Doing so can illustrate the relationship that the formula describes. The graphs of formulas may be lines, parabolas, or other curves.

Theorems and Properties

Trichotomy Property (p. 629)
Diagonals of an n-gon (p. 662)

Vocabulary

10-3
half-plane
boundary, edge
oblique line

10-5
linear combination

10-7
time-distance graph

10-8
parabola

Chapter 10 Self-Test

Take this test as you would take a test in class. You will need a calculator. Then use the Selected Answers section in the back of the book to check your work.

In 1–3, solve the equation or inequality.

1. $3y - 12 = 4y + 88$

2. $8a - 1.5 = 3a - 7$

3. $\frac{3}{2}x + 2 \le -\frac{1}{2}x - 2$

4. An online nut store sells walnuts for $2 per pound, with a flat shipping rate of $10.95. Francisca can buy walnuts at her local grocery store for $3 per pound.

   a. Write a sentence of the form $ax + b < cx + d$ to describe how many pounds of walnuts Francisca would have to order online to save money over buying them at the store.

   b. Solve your inequality from Part a.

In 5–7, graph the equation or inequality.

5. $3x - 8y = -40$

6. $4 - 4x \ge y$

7. $y - 2x > 7$

In 8 and 9, translate the situation into a sentence of the form $Ax + By = C$ or $Ax + By < C$.

8. The Outdoors Club had a bake sale to raise money for a backpacking trip. They sold cakes for $12 and pies for $10. They raised a total of $480 by selling m cakes and n pies.

9. A freight elevator can carry up to 4,000 kilograms. A chair weighs 4 kilograms, and a desk weighs 22 kilograms. Mario loads c chairs and d desks onto the elevator without exceeding the weight limit.

10. a. Make a table of values for the formula for the volume V of a cone with height 5 and radius r: $V = \frac{5}{3}\pi r^2$.

    b. Draw a graph of this formula.

In 11–13, solve the equation or inequality.

11. $5.5 - 0.5r > \frac{2}{5} + 2r$

12. $0.08d + 0.09 = 0.09d + 0.08$

13. $\frac{2h}{7} - \frac{3}{14} < -\frac{4h}{7} - 66$

In 14–16, Lorraine and Nell are having a race. Lorraine gives Nell a head start of 100 feet. Lorraine runs at 20 feet per second, while Nell runs at 18 feet per second.

14. Draw time-distance graphs for Lorraine and Nell on the same set of axes. Make sure to include the intersection of the two lines on your graph.

15. Write an equation of the form $ax + b = cx + d$ that describes the time at which Nell catches up to Lorraine.

16. Use your graph from Question 14 to solve your equation from Question 15.

17. Graph the formula $h = -4.9t^2$, for the height h (in meters) of a ball, after t seconds, that has been dropped into a canyon.

Chapter 10 Chapter Review

SKILLS Procedures used to get answers

OBJECTIVE A Solve equations of the form $ax + b = cx + d$. (Lesson 10-2)

In 1–6, solve.

1. $5x + 7 = 14x - 200$

2. $-2.1f - 25 = 2.1f + 17$

3. $18g + 7 = 14g - 9$

4. $(0.03)d + 3{,}000 = 10{,}000 + -(0.25)d$

5. $560\ell - 34 = 310\ell + 941$

6. $-\frac{6x}{25} - -95 = 2x - 30$

OBJECTIVE B Solve inequalities of the form $ax + b < cx + d$. (Lesson 10-4)

In 7–12, solve.

7. $121q + 132 > 22 + 77q$

8. $-f - 400 \le -85f - 15$

9. $-8s + 410 \ge 6s - 500$

10. $15p + 5 > -35(p - 9)$

11. $-\frac{n}{3} + 5 \le \frac{2n}{27} - 16$

12. $5(7 + w) < \frac{w}{35} + 11$

PROPERTIES Principles behind the mathematics

There are no objectives in Properties for this chapter.

USES Applications of mathematics in real-world situations

OBJECTIVE C Translate situations of constant increase or decrease that lead to sentences of the form $ax + b = cx + d$ or $ax + b < cx + d$. (Lessons 10-1, 10-2, 10-4)

In 13–16, a situation is given.
a. Translate the given information into a sentence of the form $ax + b = cx + d$ or $ax + b < cx + d$ that will answer the question.
b. Solve the equation or inequality.

13. Clara's new car cost $25,000 and uses 5¢ of gasoline per mile. Sue's car cost $20,000 and uses 16¢ of gasoline per mile. After how many miles will the cost of purchasing and driving both cars be the same?

14. A professional note-taking service pays people to take notes for medical-school lectures. For one class, the pay is $50 + $18 per hour. For another class, the pay is $100 + $15 per hour. How many hours would you have to work for the first job to pay more?

15. A soccer player has scored 30 goals so far in his career and is scoring 0.4 goal per game this season. Another has already scored 55 career goals and scores 0.2 goal per game this season. If these rates continue, when will the first player have more career goals than the second?

16. Sending a package by Speed Demon Delivery costs $4.85 plus 25 cents per ounce. Extra Express Shipping charges $6.15 plus 15 cents per ounce. What weight packages are cheaper at Extra Express?

In 17 and 18, a situation is given.

a. Translate the given information into a sentence of the form $ax + b = cx + d$ or $ax + b < cx + d$.

b. Graph the situation, and use your graph to estimate the solutions to the sentence from Part a.

17. Lev's Lumberyard sells a certain type of lumber for $3.00 per board foot. Sal's Sawmill sells the same lumber for $2.95 per board foot. Rachel would need to use $2 of gas to get to Lev's and back, but $20 of gas to get to Sal's and back. How much lumber would Rachel have to buy to make it cheaper for her to go to Sal's?

18. In a baseball game, Pop Fly hits a ball straight toward the center field fence with a forward speed of $100 \frac{\text{ft}}{\text{sec}}$. The center fielder, Tex Wonder, who is 300 feet closer to the fence, immediately begins sprinting back toward the fence at $30 \frac{\text{ft}}{\text{sec}}$. Tex leaps and makes a spectacular catch just as the ball is going over the fence. How far away is the fence from home plate, where Pop hit the ball?

OBJECTIVE D Translate situations of linear combinations that lead to sentences of the form $Ax + By = C$ and $Ax + By < C$. (Lesson 10-5)

In 19–24, a situation is given. Translate the given information into a sentence of the form $Ax + By = C$ or $Ax + By < C$ that describes the situation.

19. Admission to a theater is $15 for adults and $10 for children. A group of people went to the theater and spent $265 on tickets. They bought a adult tickets and c children's tickets.

20. A truck is hauling 2,000 lb. Smaller packing crates weigh 75 lb and larger packing crates weigh 200 lb. It has s smaller crates and ℓ larger crates.

21. Chocolate drops contain 15 calories apiece and mints contain 5 calories apiece. Jack does not want to consume more than 150 calories. He is eating d drops and m mints.

22. Lanie scored more than 32 points in a basketball game, making w 2-point and h 3-point baskets.

23. The Raiders football team scored 43 points, on t 7-point touchdowns and f 3-point field goals.

24. Marcy spent less than $13 on berries, buying b boxes of blueberries at $4.49 each and s boxes of strawberries at $2.89 each.

REPRESENTATIONS Pictures, graphs, or objects that illustrate concepts

OBJECTIVE E Graph inequalities of the form $y < ax + b$. (Lesson 10-3)

In 25–32, graph.

25. $y > \frac{x}{3} + 1$

26. $y > 3$

27. $10 + 2x \le y$

28. $y \le -7x + 5$

29. $b > 2a$

30. $d \ge 7e + 1$

31. $g < \frac{f}{2} - 8$

32. $q \ge \frac{-p}{4} + q$

OBJECTIVE F Graph sentences of the form $ax + by = c$ and $ax + by < c$. (Lesson 10-6)

In 33–40, graph the equation or inequality using a graphing utility.

33. $4x + 16y = -4$

34. $2x - 3y = 12$

35. $-6.3x + 5y > 4.1$

36. $\frac{1}{2}x + \frac{2}{3}y \le \frac{13}{18}$

37. $\frac{x}{4} - 2y = 13$

38. $-3x + 6y = 0$

39. $x - y = -1$

40. $\frac{2}{5}x + \frac{3}{2}y = 7$

OBJECTIVE G Graph situations involving time and distance. (Lesson 10-7)

In 41–44, draw a time-distance graph based upon the situation given.

41. During a trip across the country, the Speedy family drove 800 miles to Cincinnati, taking 12 hours to get there. They arrived at 8 P.M. and left at 7 A.M. the next morning. By noon, they were 350 miles past Cincinnati.

42. The Slowdown family took 11 hours to drive 450 miles from Grinnell, Iowa, to Richmond, Indiana. They then immediately drove for 17 hours from Richmond to Omaha, Nebraska, a distance of 650 miles.

43. In Pennsylvania, the maximum speed limit is 65 miles per hour. In West Virginia, it is 70 miles per hour. Alyssa drove at exactly the speed limit for 75 minutes in Pennsylvania, and half an hour in West Virginia.

44. Nehra is training for a marathon, and it takes her 4 hours and 12 minutes to run the 26.2-mile course. Assume she runs at the same pace throughout the race.

OBJECTIVE H Graph a formula. (Lesson 10-8)

In 45–50,
a. make a table of values, and
b. draw a graph of the given formula.

45. the surface area A of a sphere with radius r: $A = 4\pi r^2$

46. the 6% sales tax T on a item with price P: $T = 0.06P$

47. the cost C of a rental car based on m miles driven: $C = 75 + 0.4m$

48. the height h of an object some amount of time t seconds after it is dropped from a height of 10 meters: $h = 10 - 4.9t^2$

49. the area A of a square with side length ℓ: $A = \ell^2$

50. the distance in miles traveled d of a car going 50 miles per hour after h hours: $d = 50h$

Chapter

11 Geometry in Space

▶ Contents

In this book, you have studied a great deal of geometry. All of this geometry has been *2-dimensional geometry,* often called *plane geometry*—the study of figures that lie in the same plane. In this chapter, you will study how 2-dimensional figures relate in 3-dimensional space.

Every object in the physical world takes up space. The sizes of these objects range from quarks and atoms to galaxies and clusters of galaxies. The natural objects of everyday life, such as rocks, oceans, plants, and animals, are between these sizes. So are man-made objects, such as cars, paper, and buildings.

There are two basic questions that we ask regarding all objects. In turn, each of these questions has related questions.

1. What is the shape of the object?
   How do I describe the shape?
   Does it look different from different angles?
   How can I draw or create something like it?

2. What is the size of the object?
   How much space does it take up? This is a question of *volume*.
   How much material does it use? This is a question of *surface area*.

You will study questions like these in this chapter. By examining these questions, you will see how the shapes and sizes of different objects are related to each other. You will also see that what you have learned about 2-dimensional objects is used to describe the shapes and sizes of 3-dimensional objects.

Lesson

11-1

Lines and Planes in Space

▶ **BIG IDEA** The basic properties of planes in three dimensions are similar to the basic properties of lines in two dimensions.

Models and Pictures of Planes

Just as we think of a line as a set of points, we think of a *plane* as a set of points. We describe a plane by its characteristics. Your desktop, the ceiling of your classroom, and the wall of your classroom are all models of parts of planes. You can think of planes as flat and having no thickness; but unlike these models, a plane goes on forever.

It is common to picture a plane with a parallelogram outline to give the idea that the plane is floating in space. The result is to view the plane as if it were horizontal and being viewed from above (plane *X* below), as if it were vertical and being viewed from slightly in front (plane *Y*), or as if it were slanted (plane *Z*). Planes are often named with a single capital letter.

Many of the properties of points and lines that you saw in Lesson 4-5 have counterparts when it comes to planes. In this lesson, we discuss some of these corresponding properties.

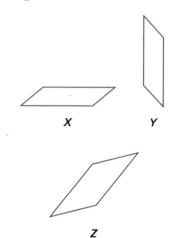

Mental Math

Calculate.

a. 1% of 100

b. 1% of 1,000

c. 1% of 300 million

d. 1% of 6.5 billion

old milking stool

What Determines a Plane?

As you know, through two different points, there is exactly one line. We say that two points determine a line. The counterpart for planes is that through three noncollinear points, there is exactly one plane. We say that *three noncollinear points determine a plane.*

This first property of planes has been used for centuries. It was common for farmers to use 3-legged milking stools to sit on as they milked their cows. Why? Even if a floor was not flat, the three legs of the stool would determine a plane and be a steady seat on which to complete the chore by hand. Even today, 3-legged stools or tables are sold for their stability on any floor.

modern stool

Straightness and Flatness

You have seen the Betweenness Property: If point B is between points A and C, then $AB + BC = AC$. This property ensures that the shortest distance between two points is along the segment connecting them. This property is what causes lines to be straight. The counterpart for planes is a property that ensures a plane is a flat surface. *If two points lie in a plane, the line containing them lies in the plane.*

This second property of planes ensures that a plane is a flat surface. Think of connecting two points on a wall by a string. If the wall has a dent, then the string will be above the dent. If the wall has a bump, then the string will have to ride the bump and not be a model of a line. But if the wall is flat, as shown at right, then the entire string will be straight and hug the wall. All points of $\overleftrightarrow{PQ}$ are in plane S.

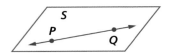

How Many Points Are on a Plane?

A line contains infinitely many points. These points can be identified by real numbers and pictured on a number line. Similarly, a plane contains infinitely many points. These points can be identified by ordered pairs of real numbers and graphed on a coordinate grid. This is what you do when you graph pairs of numbers such as (2, 3) and (–0.5, –7). You are graphing on a *coordinate plane.*

How Planes and Lines Intersect

Two different *lines* either do not intersect or intersect in exactly one *point*. What about a line and a plane? How can they intersect?

Think of an infinitely long needle and a piece of fabric that is stretched tight as a model of a line and a plane. The needle can intersect the fabric at one point, it can lie on the fabric, or it can be parallel to the fabric.

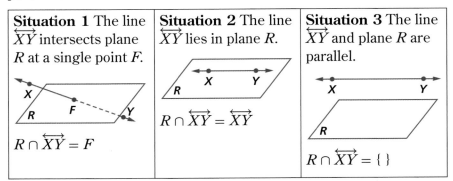

Situation 1 The line $\overleftrightarrow{XY}$ intersects plane R at a single point F.	**Situation 2** The line $\overleftrightarrow{XY}$ lies in plane R.	**Situation 3** The line $\overleftrightarrow{XY}$ and plane R are parallel.
$R \cap \overleftrightarrow{XY} = F$	$R \cap \overleftrightarrow{XY} = \overleftrightarrow{XY}$	$R \cap \overleftrightarrow{XY} = \{\ \}$

The three ways in which lines and planes can intersect lead to a third property of planes.

A line that is not entirely in a plane can intersect the plane in at most one point.

How does one plane intersect another plane? You can see the answers in the ways in which the walls, ceiling, and floor of almost any classroom intersect. Think of the front wall and one side wall of your classroom. Imagine that they are planes stretching on beyond the classroom space. You can see that they intersect at the corner of your classroom.

If two different planes intersect, then their intersection is a line.

Must planes always intersect? The answer to this question is also modeled in any room. Consider the floor and the ceiling of the room. Clearly, they do not intersect even if they are extended forever. Planes that do not intersect are **parallel planes.** They can be drawn as a parallelogram and its translation image.

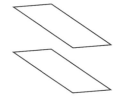

Activity 1

Many people store things in desk drawers. It is often useful to partition the drawer into compartments.

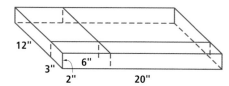

Suppose you want to partition a desk drawer as shown above. You can do this by cutting sheets of cardboard:

Step 1 Cut a sheet of cardboard 2 inches high and 20 inches long.

Step 2 Make a slit halfway *up* the cardboard, 6 inches from one end.

Step 3 Cut a sheet of cardboard 2 inches by 12 inches.

Step 4 Make a slit in this cardboard 3 inches form the end, halfway *down* the cardboard.

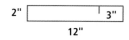

Step 5 Use the slits to fit the two pieces together.

Step 6 What property of planes is pictured by the result of Step 5?

Lines That Are Not Parallel and Do Not Intersect

Two different lines in a plane must either intersect at exactly one point or be parallel and intersect at no points. In space, there is a third possibility. They may be nonintersecting and not parallel.

Look in your classroom for the intersections of walls, ceilings, and floors. Let line m be the intersection of a wall and a ceiling. Let line n be the intersection of two different walls.

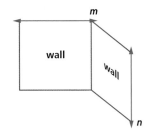

Then lines m and n are called *skew lines*. **Skew lines** are lines that are not in the same plane and do not intersect.

 QY

> ▶ **QY**
>
> Find another line in your classroom such that this line and line m are skew lines.

Activity 2

Complete this activity with a partner. Use pencils and pieces of paper to model lines and planes. Figures are identified below.
a. Show your partner the figure using the models.
b. Draw the figure on a piece of paper.

1. two parallel lines   **2.** a line intersecting a plane

3. two intersecting planes   **4.** two skew lines

The following table lists some of the basic properties of lines and planes.

Basic Properties of Lines and Planes	
Lines	**Planes**
1. Through 2 points, there is exactly one line.	**1.** Through 3 noncollinear points, there is exactly one plane.
2. If B is between points A and C, then $AB + BC = AC$.	**2.** If two points lie in a plane, the line containing them lies in the plane.
3. Two different *lines* either do not intersect or they intersect in exactly one *point*.	**3.** Two different *planes* either do not intersect or they intersect in exactly one *line*.
4. There is a 1-to-1 correspondence between the set of points on a line and the set of real numbers.	**4.** There is a 1-to-1 correspondence between the set of points in a plane and the set of ordered pairs of real numbers.

Questions

COVERING THE IDEAS

1. Identify a real-world model for a plane.

In 2 and 3, fill in the blanks.

2. Through ___?___ noncollinear points there is exactly one ___?___.

3. If two points lie in a ___?___, the line containing them lies in the ___?___.

4. Name the three ways in which a line and a plane can intersect.

In 5–11, refer to the diagram at the right. Plane *A* and plane *B* are intersecting planes.

5. Name the line of intersection of the two planes.

6. Name 5 points in plane *A*.

7. Name 3 points in plane *B*.

8. Name three lines that lie in plane *A*.

9. Name a line that intersects plane *B* in a point.

10. Describe $\overleftrightarrow{HR} \cap$ plane *A*.

11. What is the relationship between $\overleftrightarrow{PQ}$ and $\overleftrightarrow{HR}$?

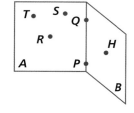

In 12–14, tell whether the statement is *always* true, *sometimes but not always* true, or *never* true.

12. There is exactly one plane through two points.

13. If two different planes intersect, they intersect in a line.

14. Two planes do not intersect.

15. Draw two planes *C* and *D* that intersect in line $\overleftrightarrow{MN}$.

16. **Fill in the Blank** Two lines that do not intersect and are not in the same plane are ___?___ lines.

In 17–21 name the planes by the rectangular faces of the box shown at the right. Name an example of each situation.

17. two planes intersecting in a line

18. two parallel planes

19. a line that intersects a plane in exactly one point

20. a line that is parallel to a plane

21. two skew lines

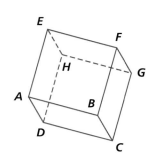

APPLYING THE MATHEMATICS

22. What property of planes does a camera tripod rely on?

23. A slanted roof and a wall of a house can be used to model what property of planes?

24. A property of points and lines not mentioned in this lesson is that through a point not on a line ℓ, there is exactly one line parallel to ℓ. What property of points and planes, not mentioned in this lesson, is similar to this property?

25. a. Is it possible to have three lines ℓ, m, and n, so that all three are skew to each other?
    b. If not, why not? If so, can four lines be skew to each other?

26. The surface of a ball is not a plane. What property of a plane does the surface not have?

27. Points are called **coplanar** if they lie in the same plane. Use the figure of Questions 17–21. Name a point that is coplanar with the three given points
    a. A, D, E b. A, D, G c. C, E, F

REVIEW

28. Draw a graph of $6x + 2y = 12$. (**Lesson 10-6**)

29. A decagon (10-sided polygon) has side lengths 13.1, 9, 8.6, 3.5, 2.9, 11, 4, 6.8, 11, and 7.6. Two similar decagons have side lengths given below that correspond to the 13.1 length of the first decagon. Calculate the side lengths for each of the similar decagons. You may find it useful to use a spreadsheet. (**Lesson 9-9**)
    a. 18.34   b. 7.86

30. A trapezoid has a base length of 10 inches and a height of 7 inches. If the area of the trapezoid is 56 square inches, find the length of the other base of the trapezoid. (**Lesson 7-5**)

31. A4 paper is the most common size of duplicating paper in Europe. It measures 210 mm by 297 mm. Is it possible to draw a straight line 14" long on this paper? Justify your answer. (**Lesson 2-5**)

EXPLORATION

32. All of the major planets, including Earth, orbit our Sun in a plane called the *ecliptic*. In August 2006, Pluto was classified as a dwarf planet. One of the reasons for this is that Pluto orbits the Sun in a different plane. Find out the differences between the ecliptic and Pluto's plane and make a drawing of them.

QY ANSWER

Answers vary. Sample: the intersection of an adjacent wall and the floor

Depicting 3-Dimensional Figures on a Plane

Vocabulary

face
box
edge
vertex of a prism
prism
base of a prism
right prism
rectangular prism
triangular prism
pentagonal prism
hexagonal prism
dimension
length
width
height
depth
isometric dot paper

▶ **BIG IDEA**   There are many ways to picture 3-dimensional objects on a flat sheet of paper.

3-Dimensional (3-D) Figures

There are many 3-dimensional objects that you may want to picture on a flat surface. While some objects, such as apples, are rounded, others, like books, have distinct sides. These sides are called **faces**.

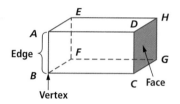

In Lesson 11-1, you saw that a classroom can be thought of as a box. A **box** is a 3-dimensional figure with six faces that are rectangles. Each face of a box is a part of a plane. You can identify each face by its location: top (*EADH*), bottom (*BFGC*), right (*DCGH*), left (*ABFE*), front (*ABCD*), and back (*EFGH*). The sides of the faces are called the **edges** of the box. The edges are parts of the lines of intersections of the planes of the faces. For instance, edge $\overline{AB}$ is part of the intersection of planes *ABFE* and *ABCD*. A point where three faces intersect is called a **vertex**. The eight vertices of this box are *A*, *B*, *C*, *D*, *E*, *F*, *G*, and *H*.

 QY1

Introduction to Prisms

Boxes are special types of *prisms*. **Prisms** are 3-dimensional figures with the following characteristics:

1. Prisms have two **bases** (shaded in the pictures on the next page) that are polygons.

2. The bases are translation images of each other in space. So, the bases are congruent and lie in parallel planes.

Mental Math

Calculate.

a. $53 \cdot 10^{-5}$

b. $14 \cdot 1{,}000 \cdot 2 \cdot 100$

c. $10^7 \cdot 10^{-4} \cdot 10^{11} \cdot 10^{-6} \cdot 10^{-8}$

d. $1{,}500 \cdot 30 \cdot 0.04$

▶ **QY1**

Which edge is the intersection of the back face and the right face of the box pictured above?

3. The prism contains all the points of the bases and the points on the line segments connecting corresponding points of the bases.

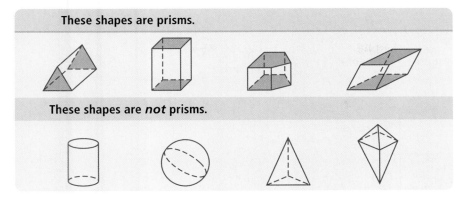

These shapes are prisms.

These shapes are *not* prisms.

In prisms, as in boxes, the faces are polygons, the edges are line segments, and the intersections of three edges are vertices. Examine the vertices of the four prisms above. In the first three, the edges of the bases form right angles with the edges of the other faces. They are **right prisms**. The last prism is not a right prism because it is on a slant. The prisms that we will work with are right prisms.

The shape of the bases is often used to name a prism. The shape of the bases of both a box and a cube is a rectangle, so cubes and boxes are often called **rectangular prisms**. The left-most prism pictured above is a **triangular prism**. It has triangles as its bases. Similarly, prisms with pentagons for bases are called **pentagonal prisms**; those with hexagons for bases are called **hexagonal prisms**, and so on.

 QY2

Drawing 2-Dimensional Representations of Prisms

Examine the drawing of the box on page 680. Notice that three edges intersect at each vertex. Their lengths are the **dimensions** of the box. The dimensions are called its **length**, **width**, and **height**. Sometimes one dimension (either front to back, or top to bottom) is called the **depth**. All of the figures above are called 3-dimensional because they have 3 dimensions. There are several methods to draw 3-dimensional figures on 2-dimensional paper. One of the most common ways to draw prisms is shown in Activity 1 on the next page.

▶ **QY2**

Why is the figure shown below not a prism?

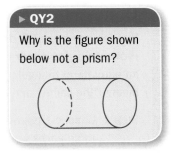

Activity 1

Follow these steps and draw these three figures in your notebook.

Steps to Draw a Prism			
Name of 3-Dimensional Figure	Cube	Box	Triangular Prism
Step 1 Draw a figure to represent the lower base.	?	?	?
Step 2 Draw parallel and congruent line segments from each vertex. These represent the nonbase edges of the prism. Use dashed lines for the edges at the lower left. Using congruent segments ensures that the bases are in parallel planes.	?	?	?
Step 3 Connect the vertices of the rear base in clockwise or counterclockwise order. Use dashed lines to indicate the edges of the prism that are not visible from the front.	?	?	?

You can also use a special kind of paper to draw the figures.

Activity 2

Using Isometric Dot Paper

You can use *isometric dot paper* to draw prisms. Unlike grid paper, **isometric dot paper** is not a pattern of squares, but a pattern of dots in an equilateral triangular pattern. The word *isometric* comes from Greek: *iso* means "the same," and *metric* means "measure."

Step 1 Choose a point and label it *A*. Draw three edges with certain lengths in different directions from *A*. We use height 3, width 4, and depth 5. Label the three endpoints.

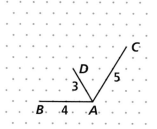

Step 2 Draw edges at *B* and *C* that are each 3 units high and parallel to $\overline{DA}$.

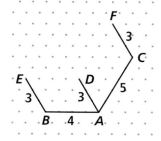

Step 3 With dashes, create the missing edges at vertices *B* and *C* that are parallel to the respective edges $\overline{BA}$ and $\overline{CA}$. Draw dashed height $\overline{GH}$.

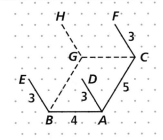

Step 4 Connect in order *E*, *D*, *F*, *H*, and *E* to complete the box.

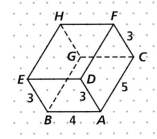

Activity 3

Creating Prisms with DGS 3-D

A third way to draw 3-dimensional figures is with a dynamic geometry system (DGS) that has 3-D ability. A DGS uses a *vector* to draw a prism. A vector is an arrow with a fixed length and a fixed direction.

1. Create a rectangular base for a prism. Use a vector to represent the height. Use the prism tool to create a rectangular prism.

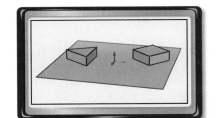

2. Follow the procedure above to create a triangular prism with an equilateral triangle as its base. Use the same vector for the height.

3. Choose another regular polygon and create a prism with that as its base. Use the same vector for its height. We choose a regular octagon.

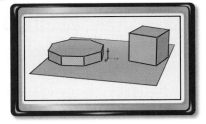

4. Find the cube tool and use it to create a cube.

Questions

COVERING THE IDEAS

1. **True or False** The bases of any prism lie in planes that are parallel.

In 2 and 3, use the triangular prism at the right.

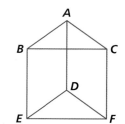

2. a. What do dashed lines represent?

   b. If △ABC is the top face of the figure at the right, and if $\overline{BC}$ is closer to you than point A, which edge or edges should be drawn as dashed lines?

3. a. Name the faces. b. Name the vertices. c. Name the edges.

4. Copy the 3-dimensional figure at the right and label the parts.

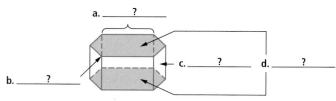

In 5–8, examine the shapes below. Identify each as a prism or not a prism. If not a prism, explain why.

5.   6.   7.   8.

In 9–12, the bases of the prisms are shaded. Name the prism.

9.   10.   11.   12.

13. Fill in the Blanks ___?___, ___?___, and ___?___ are the dimensions of a rectangular prism.

In 14–16, sketch each figure.

14. box   15. cube   16. triangular prism

17. A particular 3-dimensional figure has 8 faces. Its bases are shaped like hexagons. An example of it can often be found as the writing tool of choice in many classes. What is it?

APPLYING THE MATHEMATICS

18. a. List the steps to draw a cube with side length of 3 units on isometric dot paper.

    b. Follow your steps to draw the cube.

19. Three students were asked to shade the bases of a box. Their answers are shown below. Which answers are correct and why? Explain.

                    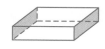

I   II   III

In 20 and 21, use isometric dot paper.

20. **a.** Draw a box that is 6 units long, 2 units wide, and 1 unit high.

    b. Reflect the box over a horizontal line.

21. Draw a triangular prism with nonbase edges 4 units long.

22. Create a riddle for a triangular prism similar to Question 17.

23. Mara bought a dresser that was $4\frac{1}{2}$ feet tall, 5 feet wide, and $1\frac{1}{2}$ feet deep. Draw Mara's dresser on isometric dot paper. Make each unit on the paper equal to 6 inches.

In 24–26, tell whether the statement is *always, sometimes but not always,* or *never* true.

24. The bases of prisms are perpendicular.

25. If the nonbase edges of a prism form a right angle with the base edges, then the prism is considered a right prism.

26. Prisms with rectangular faces and octagonal bases are called rectangular prisms.

This chest of drawers is 38 feet tall. It was built in the 1920s by the High Point, North Carolina, Chamber of Commerce.

REVIEW

27. Identify the possible intersections of a line and a plane. **(Lesson 11-1)**

28. Recall that in an isosceles triangle, the two base angles are congruent. The vertex angle of such a triangle measures $102°$. Find the measure of each base angle. **(Lesson 6-8)**

29. **a.** Draw a parallelogram *FROG*.

    b. List two properties of the sides of this parallelogram.

    c. List two properties of its angles. **(Lesson 6-7)**

30. Simplify $|-2 - 4| + |-15| - 8$ **(Lessons 5-2, 5-1)**

31. Find an example in the real world of the following conditions: **(Lesson 4-9)**

    a. a real number that is not rational

    b. a number that is rational but not an integer

    c. a number that is an integer but not a positive number

    d. a number that is prime and odd

EXPLORATION

32. The methods of drawing figures in this lesson lack perspective because the back of a figure is the same size as the front. Consult a reference and show how to draw a box in perspective.

QY ANSWERS

1. $\overline{HG}$

2. The base is a circle, which is not a polygon.

Lesson
11-3

2-Dimensional Nets for 3-Dimensional Shapes

▶ **BIG IDEA** By folding a 2-dimensional pattern called a *net,* you can create a 3-dimensional surface.

The shapes of the faces of prisms are always polygons. The faces that are not bases are called **lateral faces** from the Latin word *latus,* meaning "side." The numbers of edges, vertices, and faces of prisms are related.

Mental Math

Name the 3-dimensional figure shown.

a.

Activity 1

Consider the prisms drawn below. Copy and complete the table.

	Cube	Rectangular Prism	Triangular Prism
Number of Edges	?	?	?
Number of Vertices	?	?	?
Number of Faces	?	?	?
Shape of Bases	?	?	?
Shape of Lateral Faces	?	?	?

b.
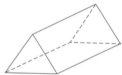

As Activity 1 shows, some prisms, like a triangular prism, involve more than one type of polygon. The steps in Activity 2 show how to create prisms from their faces. It may help to work with a partner.

c.
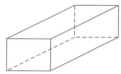

d.

Activity 2

Step 1 Copy the shapes below onto a piece of card stock.

 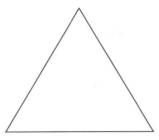

Step 2 Cut out as many as you need to build a triangular prism. How many of each shape do you need?

Step 3 Tape the shapes together to form a prism.

Step 4 Examine the prism you have made. Does it fit the definition of a prism? Check that the number of edges, vertices, and faces agree with those in the table on the previous page.

Step 5 Cut along some edges of your prism so that you can unfold the prism without completely separating any of the faces from each other. When you are done unfolding, all of your faces should still be taped together, but your pieces should be able to lie flat. Check that you are still able to fold the connected flattened pieces to restore your triangular prism.

Step 6 Draw a picture of your flattened figure. Your flat pattern is a *net* of a triangular prism. A connected pattern of polygons that folds to form a 3-dimensional object is called a **net** of that object. Compare the net you have made with those of others in your class. Are all the nets congruent? How many different nets did your class make?

Activity 3

Examine the net at the right. The dashed segments show where folds are made. The folds become the edges of a 3-dimensional figure. What figure is formed from this net? Draw a picture of the figure.

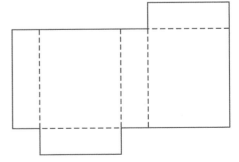

Some computer drawing tools can create 2-dimensional nets from 3-dimensional figures. A closed 3-dimensional figure whose faces are all polygons is called a **polyhedron**. The plural of polyhedron is **polyhedra.** All prisms are polyhedra.

Activity 4

Step 1 Create a cube using the cube tool on a DGS 3-D.

Step 2 Determine how to make a net from a cube on your DGS 3-D. On some DGS, you may need to choose the command **OPEN POLYHEDRON**. Then with the **SELECT** tool, open the net until it is flat.

Step 3 Create a net for the cube on another page of your document. On some DGS you will need to select the net and choose the command **ADD NET PAGE**.

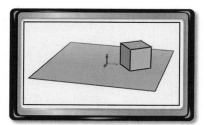

Step 4 Print your net and fold it into a cube.

Step 5 Create another type of prism and its net in the same way you created the net for the cube. Print it out and fold it into the prism. How many bases does it have? What is their shape? How many lateral faces does it have? What shape are they? Give a precise name for your prism.

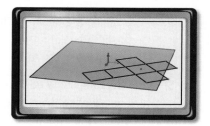

Step 6 Create a pyramid with a square base and then have the DGS 3-D create a net for the pyramid. Describe the shape of the base and the lateral faces.

 GAME Now you can play *Shape Capture: 3-D.* The directions for this game are on page G18 at the back of your book.

Questions

COVERING THE IDEAS

In 1–8, consider the prism at the right.

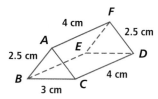

1. What shape are the bases of the prism?

2. What shape are the lateral faces of the prism?

3. How many edges does the prism have?

4. How many faces (including bases) does the prism have?

5. How many vertices does the prism have?

6. Draw and label the two bases.

7. Draw and label the lateral faces.

8. Are all the rectangular faces congruent?

In 9–11, use the prism that is drawn.

9. 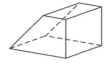   10.   11.

    a. Trace the prism and shade its bases.

    b. Draw a net for the prism.

    c. What type of prism is it?

    d. Make a table listing the number of faces, edges, and vertices.

APPLYING THE MATHEMATICS

12. Consider the terms *box, cube, prism,* and *triangular prism.* Draw the hierarchy that relates these terms.

13. Draw three different nets for a rectangular prism measuring 3 cm × 5.1 cm × 4.8 cm. Label the lengths of the sides.

In 14–17, determine whether the statement is *true* or *false.*

14. The bases of a prism are always parallel.

15. All the edges of a box are the same length.

16. All boxes are cubes.

17. Some, but not all, cubes are boxes.

In 18–20, name the figure the net will make.

18. 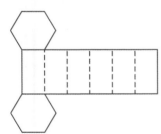   19.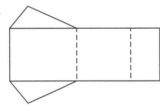

20.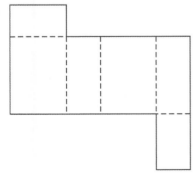

In 21–24, tell whether the figure is a net for a cube. If it is a net for a cube, tell which faces would be opposite each other on the cube.

21.

1	2
3	4
5	6

22.

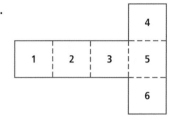

23.

24.

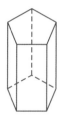

REVIEW

25. Is the polyhedron shown at the right a prism? Explain your answer. **(Lesson 11-2)**

26. Draw a prism with 9 edges, 5 faces, and 6 vertices. **(Lesson 11-2)**

27. Malcolm McLean (1913–2001) is credited with the widespread use of shipping containers used in freight trains and tractor-trailers. The standard shipping container measures 40 feet long, 8 feet wide, and 8 feet 6 inches high. Draw and label this shape, making it appear 3-dimensional. **(Lesson 11-2)**

28. **True or False** If two lines do not intersect, then they are parallel. Explain your answer. **(Lesson 11-1)**

29. Solve for j. $\frac{15}{j} = \frac{12}{23}$ **(Lesson 7-2)**

30. State the Property of Reciprocals. **(Lesson 7-2)**

EXPLORATION

31. In the mid-1700s the Swiss mathematician Leonhard Euler (OY ler) discovered that the numbers of vertices, edges, and faces of many 3-dimensional figures satisfy the formula $V - E + F = 2$, where V stands for the number of vertices, E for the number of edges, and F for the number of faces.

    a. Show that the formula works for all boxes.

    b. Do you think this formula applies to all prisms? Why or why not?

Leonhard Euler

Lesson 11-4

2-Dimensional Views of 3-Dimensional Figures

Vocabulary

views, elevations

pyramid

apex

square pyramid

> ▶ **BIG IDEA** A 3-dimensional shape may look quite different when viewed from different angles, but from these views you may be able to determine the shape.

Mental Math

a. Find the exact area of a circle with radius b cm.

b. Find the exact area of a circle with circumference 8π meters.

When architects and engineers design buildings and other structures, they create 2-dimensional drawings for building 3-dimensional structures. This drawing represents the left, right, and back **views**, or **elevations**, of a home that will be remodeled.

Recognizing characteristics of 3-dimensional figures from 2-dimensional views is an important skill in geometry. We use the abbreviations L (left), R (right), F (front), and B (back) to distinguish the views.

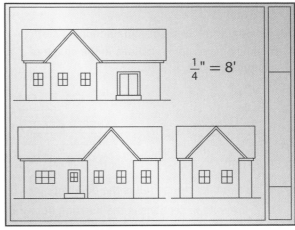

left

$\frac{1}{4}{}'' = 8'$

right   back

Views of Prisms

Example 1

Many new pencils without erasers are hexagonal prisms. Suppose a pencil is put on a table facing you, as shown here. Draw its front, right, and top views.

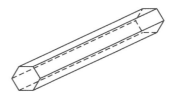

Solution When you look at the pencil head on, you will only see a hexagon, so the front view is a hexagon. From the top, you will see one long face head on and two other faces at an angle. From the right, you will see two long faces at an angle. Here are the three views:

front view

top view

right view

Views of Pyramids

A **pyramid** is a 3-dimensional shape formed by connecting a polygonal base with a point not on the base, called the **apex**. The lateral faces of pyramids are triangles.

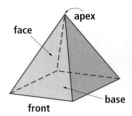

The figure at the right is a **square pyramid**, so named because its base is a square. It is the shape of the famous pyramids of Giza near Cairo, Egypt.

Activity

Draw views of the square pyramid from the front, right side, top, and bottom. The apex of the pyramid is above the center of the base

Example 2

Here are three views of a prefabricated storage building made up of sections in the shape of congruent boxes.

front

right side

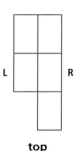

top

a. How many stories tall is the building?

b. How long in sections is the building from front to back?

c. Where is the tallest part of the building located?

Solution

a. The top view tells you nothing about the height of the building. The front view tells you that it is three stories high on the left. The right-side view confirms that the height, in the back, is 3 stories.

b. The top view tells you that it is 3 sections long from back to front. The right-side view confirms this.

c. The front view tells you that the tallest point is somewhere on the left side. The right-side view tells you that the highest point is at the back. Combining these observations, you can conclude that the tallest point of the building is at the back left corner.

Questions

COVERING THE IDEAS

1. What are elevations in structure designs?

In 2–6, sketch the top, front, and right-side views of each shape. You do not have to include designs on the shape.

2. a cube

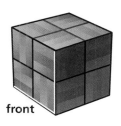

front

3. a sphere

4. a triangular prism

5.

front   right

6.

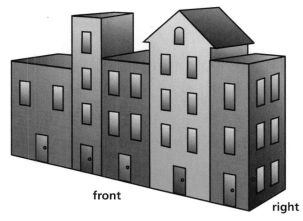

front

right

7. The outline of a building is pictured at the right.
   a. Draw a top view.
   b. Draw a view from the left side.
   c. Draw a front view.

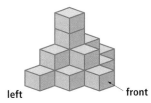

left   front

8. A building has the views shown at the right.

front view

right-side view

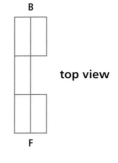

top view

   a. How tall in stories is the building?
   b. How many sections is the building from front to back?
   c. Where is the tallest part of the building located?

9. **Multiple Choice** The top, right, and front views of a 3-dimensional figure are given. Which one of the figures below does it represent?

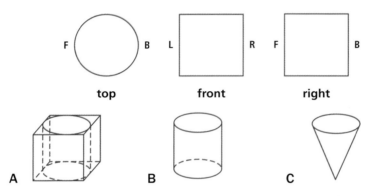

top   front   right

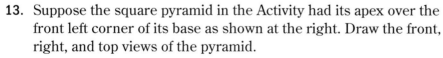

A   B   C

APPLYING THE MATHEMATICS

In 10 and 11, refer to the elevations at the beginning of this lesson.

10. At its widest point, how wide (in feet) is the house from front to back?

11. How high is it (in feet) from the ground to the highest point on the roof?

12. A pyramid has a base that is a regular hexagon and its apex is directly above the center of its base. Draw front, right-side, and top views of the pyramid.

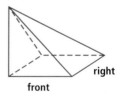

right

front

13. Suppose the square pyramid in the Activity had its apex over the front left corner of its base as shown at the right. Draw the front, right, and top views of the pyramid.

14. Here is a top view of a building, like the one in Example 2, made up of sections in the shape of congruent cubes. The number in each square tells how many are stacked in that space. Draw the building as seen from the front and from the right side.

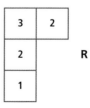

15. Draw the teacup and saucer as seen from the top.

REVIEW

16. Draw a net for the new pencil without an eraser from Example 1. (**Lesson 11-3**)

17. Consider the following statement: A prism is a 3-dimensional object with two congruent faces. Is the statement an accurate definition of *prism*? Provide instances or counterexamples to support your claim. (**Lessons 11-2, 4-7**)

18 a. In Quadrant I, graph the function comparing the radius to the area of a circle, $y = \pi x^2$, where y is the area and x is the radius.

   b. Why is the graph only in Quadrant I? (Lesson 10-8)

19. Suppose the distance between the towns of Wedge and Antilles is actually 19 miles, and it is represented on a map by 1.5 in. Find the scale of the drawing to the nearest ten thousand. (**Lesson 9-9**)

20. What inequality results if both sides of $-x \le 10$ are multiplied by -1? (**Lesson 8-9**)

21. Santiago opens a bottle of water and drinks $\frac{1}{5}$ of it. If 16 fl oz of water now remain in the bottle, how much water was in the bottle before Santiago drank from it? (**Lesson 8-6**)

22. In the year 1420, the Chinese built a temple in Beijing, China, known as the Temple of Heaven. Within this temple, they built the Altar of Prayer for Good Harvests, which is a 3-story circular hall under a cone-shaped roof. This circular hall has an outside diameter of approximately 98.2 feet. To the nearest foot, how far is it to walk around the Altar? (**Lesson 7-6**)

EXPLORATION

23. Draw a front, side, and top view of the building in which you live.

Lesson
11-5

The Surface Area and Volume of a Box

Vocabulary

surface area

volume, capacity

cubic units

cube

cubic centimeter

▶ **BIG IDEA**   The surface area of a box can be found by adding the areas of its rectangular faces; the volume is found by multiplying the lengths of its dimensions.

Many closed shipping cartons are boxes. Bricks are often box-shaped, rectangular solids. Furniture drawers, cabinets, boxcars on freight trains, paperback books, and many other objects are box-shaped. The raisin box below is an example of a box or a rectangular right prism. This raisin box can be constructed by drawing its net on a flat piece of cardboard, cutting it out, and folding. For a real box, some overlap is needed, but the same idea is used.

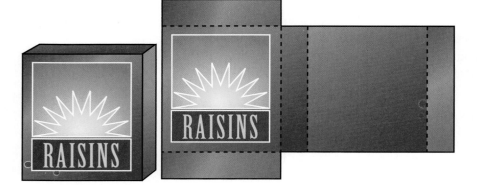

Calculating the Surface Area of a Box

The **surface area** of a box tells you how much material is used to make the box. It is an area, so it is measured in square units. The surface area does *not* tell you how much the box will hold. The *total surface area* of a rectangular prism is the sum of the areas of its six faces.

Mental Math

Find the area of the figure shown.

a.
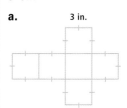
3 in.

b.
Area of small triangle: 3 cm²
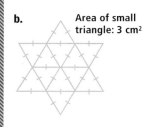

c.
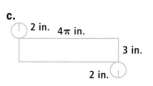
2 in.   4π in.
3 in.
2 in.

d.
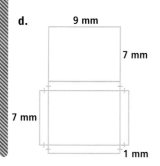
9 mm
7 mm
7 mm
1 mm

Activity

Follow the steps to calculate the total surface area of a box.

Step 1 Find an empty box.

Step 2 Flatten the box into its net by cutting along its edges.

Step 3 Copy and complete the chart below. Use a ruler to measure the edges of the box to the nearest millimeter.

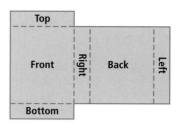

Face	Length	Width	Area (mm²)
Top	?	?	?
Front	?	?	?
Bottom	?	?	?
Right	?	?	?
Back	?	?	?
Left	?	?	?

Step 4 Add the six areas to find the total surface area.

Total surface area of box ___?___

 QY1

When you examine the faces of a box, you notice that the front and the back of a box are congruent rectangles. However, the right and left faces of the box are not necessarily congruent to the front and back, but they are congruent to each other. The same is true for the top and bottom faces.

> ▶ **QY1**
>
> Which faces of the box have equal areas?

GUIDED

Example

Ashanti wanted to use bricks to create a border for her garden. The bricks she used were 4 inches by $2\frac{2}{3}$ inches by 8 inches. After she laid the bricks along the edges, Ashanti decided to paint the bricks white to add to the look of her garden. To save paint, she realized that she needed to paint only the surfaces that were exposed. For one of the corner bricks, the exposed faces were the top, front, and right faces. What area needs to be painted on this corner brick?

(continued on next page)

Solution

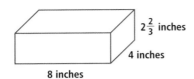

$2\frac{2}{3}$ inches

4 inches

8 inches

Step 1 Begin by drawing and labeling an informal drawing of the exposed faces of the brick.

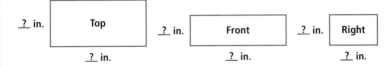

? in.   Top

? in.

? in.   Front

? in.

? in.   Right

? in.

Step 2 Find the area of each of the surfaces.

Area of top: __?__ in. • 8 in. = __?__ in²

Area of front: $2\frac{2}{3}$ in. • __?__ in. = __?__ in²

Area of right: $2\frac{2}{3}$ in. • __?__ in. = __?__ in²

Step 3 Because these three faces are the only faces that will be painted, add the areas to find the total surface area of the three faces.

area of top + area of front + area of right = total surface area of the 3 faces

__?__ in² + __?__ in² + __?__ in² = __?__ in²

What Is Volume?

Volume is a measure of the space inside a 3-dimensional or solid figure. Think of volume as measuring the amount a box, jar, or other container can hold. This is also called the container's **capacity**. That is, volume is how much material is in something that is solid. Whatever the shape of a figure, its volume is usually measured in **cubic units**. A **cube** is a box in which each face is a square. Sugar cubes, number cubes, and dice are examples. The most common units for measuring volume are cubes with edges of unit length.

In a **cubic centimeter**, each edge has a length of 1 centimeter. Each face is a square with an area of 1 square centimeter. A cubic centimeter can also be expressed as cm³, which is read *cubic centimeters*. The same relationship holds true for any other unit of measure. For example, if the sides are measured in inches, the volume is measured in in³, which is read *cubic inches*.

1 cm

1 cm

1 cm

1 cubic centimeter, or 1 cm³

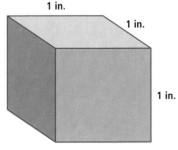

1 in.

1 in.

1 in.

1 cubic inch, or 1 in³

Volume of a Box

Volume can be calculated by counting cubes, by cutting and pasting cubic units together, or by using a formula. Below is a box that is 2 units high, 8 units wide, and 5 units deep.

There are two layers. Each layer has 8 · 5, or 40, cubes. In all, there are 2 · 8 · 5, or 80, cubes.

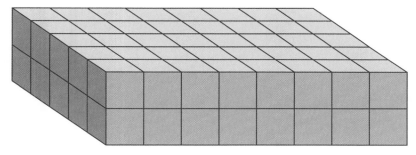

Volume = 80 cubic units = 80 units³

Notice that volume is quite different from area. Area is 2-dimensional. The amount of paper it would take to cover the outside surface of a box is an area—the surface area of the box. The volume of a box indicates how much sand could be poured into the box.

Notice that the volume of this box is the product of its three dimensions.

$$\text{Volume} = 2 \text{ cm} \cdot 8 \text{ cm} \cdot 5 \text{ cm} = 80 \text{ cm}^3$$

The volume of any box or rectangular solid is the product of its three dimensions, even when the dimensions are not whole numbers. You can multiply the dimensions in any order because multiplication is commutative and associative.

Box Volume Formula

Let V be the volume of a box or a rectangular solid with dimensions a, b, and c. Then

$$V = abc.$$

For example, the volume of a room whose floor measures 9 feet by 12 feet and whose ceilings are 8 feet high:

$$9 \text{ ft} \cdot 12 \text{ ft} \cdot 8 \text{ ft} = 864 \text{ ft}^3$$

 QY2

> ▶ **QY2**
>
> Find the volume of a box whose dimensions are 0.7 m · 0.9 m · 0.6 m.

Questions

COVERING THE IDEAS

1. What does volume measure in a solid figure?

2. Suppose length is measured in millimeters.
   a. Surface area will most likely be measured in what unit?
   b. Volume will most likely be measured in what unit?

Multiple Choice In 3–7, choose from these:

    A volume   **B** surface area   **C** perimeter

3. how much a container holds

4. the length around a face of a container

5. how much material it takes to cover a container

6. measured in cubic units

7. measured in square units

In 8 and 9, refer to the box drawn here. A box of its size and shape was used to ship books.

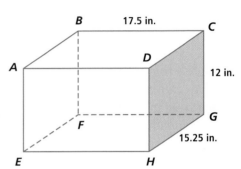

8. a. Name its faces.
   b. Name its edges.
   c. Name its vertices.

9. a. What are its dimensions?
   b. What is its surface area?
   c. What is its volume?

In 10 and 11, sketches are given for boxes.
a. Draw and label a net for the box;
b. Find the volume of the box;
c. Find the total surface area of the box.

10.

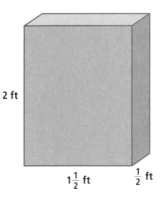

11.

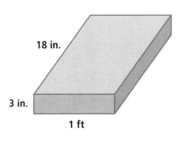

APPLYING THE MATHEMATICS

12. A box measures 6 inches high, 2 feet long, and 15 inches wide.
   a. Find the total surface area in square inches.
   b. Find the total surface area in square feet.

13. A box is 2 feet long, 15 inches wide, and 6 inches high.
    a. What is its volume in cubic inches?
    b. What is its volume in cubic feet?

14. Without cutting, tell which of the nets below fold into a box and which do not. If a net does not work, redraw it so that it will work.

    a.

    b.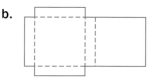

    c.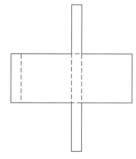

    d.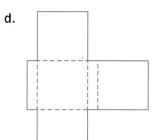

15. A file cabinet measure 66 inches high, 30 inches wide, and 18 inches deep. You want to paint the top, the front, the left, and right sides.
    a. How many square inches will you be painting?
    b. A spray paint can uses square feet as a measure of coverage. Calculate how many square feet you must paint.

16. One refrigerated boxcar has an outside length of 50 feet, a width of 9 feet 1 inch, and a height of 9 feet 6 inches. Determine exact values and values rounded to the nearest hundred cubic feet.
    a. What is the volume of the boxcar?
    b. If the walls, top, and bottom of the boxcar are 4 inches thick, how much can the boxcar hold inside?

17. A paper lunch bag measures approximately 32 cm in height, 15.3 cm in width, and 10.2 cm in depth. Ignoring overlap, how many square centimeters of paper are needed to make the bag? (Remember, a paper bag has a bottom, but not a top.)

REVIEW

18. Draw a picture of a triangular pyramid. (**Lesson 11-4**)

19. Draw the building at the right as seen from the front, top, and left. (**Lesson 11-4**)

front

20. Tell whether the figure can be the net for a cube. (Lesson 11-3)

a.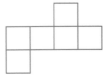

b.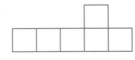

c.

d.

21. Solve for x. (Lesson 9-7)

a. $\frac{9}{15} = \frac{x}{30}$

b. $\frac{x}{18} = \frac{10}{36}$

c. $\frac{x}{46} = \frac{12}{23}$

d. $\frac{x}{a} = \frac{28}{2a}$

22. When a baseball player gets a hit several games in a row, it is called a *hitting streak*. If the probability that a player will get a hit in a game is .290, what is the probability she will have a 10-game hitting streak over the next 10 games? (Lesson 8-4)

23. Consider the circles drawn at the right. (Lesson 7-6)

a. What is the area of the larger circle?

b. What is the area of the smaller circle?

c. What is the area of the shaded region?

d. Find the circumference of the larger circle.

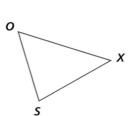

24. a. Without performing any calculations, explain why the areas of the figures below are be the same.

b. Find the areas to validate your argument. (Lesson 7-5)

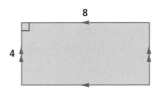

25. Name the triangle at the right in three different ways. (Lesson 4-6)

26. Write each number as a decimal. (Lesson 1-3)

a. fifty-eight thousandths

b. 7.9 million

EXPLORATION

27. Many different dimensions of boxes can have the same volume. Find the dimensions of 10 different boxes with volume 1 ft³, where all side lengths are a whole number of inches.

11-6

Surface Areas of Prisms and Cylinders

Vocabulary

lateral area

cylinder

▶ **BIG IDEA**   The surface areas of prisms and cylinders can be found by examining their 2-dimensional nets.

Surface Area of Prisms

Imagine that you are working for a company that decides to create a distinctive triangular-shaped box for its products. A designer cut out a cardboard net to use as a pattern. The net is pictured below. (For a real box, some overlap is needed, but the same idea is used.)

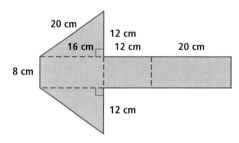

The total surface area tells you how much cardboard is needed. This surface area consists of the area of the lateral faces, called the **lateral area,** and the area of the two triangular bases.

Example 1

Use the net of the box shown above.
a. What is the lateral area (*L.A.*)?
b. What is the area of the bases?
c. What is the total surface area (*S.A.*)?

Solution

a.   In the net, the three lateral faces of the triangular prism form one long rectangle. The length of the rectangle formed by the three lateral faces is the same as the perimeter of the triangular base. The lateral area (*L.A.*) is the perimeter of the base multiplied by the height of the prism. So:

$$L.A. = (16 + 12 + 20) \cdot 8 = 48 \cdot 8 = 384 \text{ cm}^2.$$

(continued on next page)

Mental Math

8 brown cows, 3 red robins, and 4 green geese went to the market to buy some fruit.

a. If they each bought 3 bananas, how many bananas did they buy in all?

b. If each cow bought 5 pears, each robin bought 12 apples, and each goose bought 9 kiwi fruits, which type of animal bought the most pieces of fruit?

c. In Part b, how many pieces of fruit did they buy in all?

d. If each type of animal buys the same number of pieces of fruit, how many pieces should each animal buy in each group?

e. Give another possible answer to the previous question.

b. The bases are triangles. Recall that the formula for the area of a triangle is $A = \frac{1}{2}bh$. So, each base of the triangular prism has area $\frac{1}{2} \cdot 12 \cdot 16$, or 96, cm². Because the bases are congruent, the total area of the bases is $2 \cdot 96 = 192$ cm².

c. The total surface area (S.A.) is the sum of the areas of the bases of the prism (the triangles) and the lateral area (L.A.). So

total surface area $= 384 + 192 = 576$ cm².

576 cm² of cardboard is needed to construct the box.

 QY1

Surface Area of a Cylinder

Many cans are shaped like *circular cylinders,* or **cylinders** for short. Cylinders are like prisms except their bases are circles rather than polygons. Some cans have paper labels that can be peeled off. If you peel off the label, you will see that the label is a rectangular piece of paper. The image of a can of soup may help you to understand what the net of a cylinder looks like.

> **QY1**
>
> Find the lateral area of the prism below.
>
>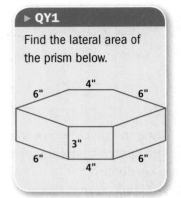

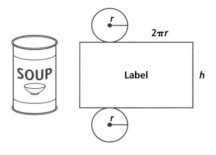

Circumference of base $= 2\pi r$.
Length of rectangle $= 2\pi r$.
Width of rectangle $= h$.

The area of the label is the lateral area of the can. The height of the label is the height h of the cylinder. If you ignore any overlap, the other dimension of the label is the circumference ($C = \pi d$ or $C = 2\pi r$) of a base, because the length of the label wraps around the edge of the bases.

> **GUIDED**

Example 2

A typical soup can is a cylinder with height of about $3\frac{3}{4}$ inches and a diameter of about $2\frac{1}{2}$ inches.

a. How much paper is needed to create a label?

b. How much metal is needed to create the can?

(continued on next page)

a. First create an informal sketch of a cylinder to help you visualize the can. For convenience, we have changed the dimensions to decimals.

Remember that the lateral area of a prism is the perimeter of the base multiplied by the height of the prism. Similarly, the lateral area of a cylinder is the circumference C of the base (perimeter of the circle) multiplied by the height of the cylinder.

3.75 in.

2.5 in.

Circumference = π • diameter

Lateral area = Ch = πdh

= π___?___ • ___?___

≈ ___?___ in²

About ___?___ of paper will be needed to create the label.

b. The amount of metal needed for the can is the total surface area. You have already calculated the amount of metal needed for the curved side of the can. It is the same as the amount of paper needed for the label, which is the lateral area.

Now you need to add the lateral area and the areas of the bases to find the total surface area. Because the diameter of the base is 2.5 inches, the radius r is ___?___. To find the area of the bases, use the area formula for a circle, $A = \pi r^2$. So the area of one of the bases is
$A = \pi$___?___$^2 \approx$ ___?___ in². Together, the bases have an area of about 2 • ___?___ ≈ ___?___

Total surface area = L.A. + area of bases

S.A. ≈ ___?___ + ___?___ ≈ ___?___

The total surface area of a typical soup can is about ___?___, which is the amount of metal needed.

You may have noticed that the same pattern works in calculating the total surface area of prisms and cylinders.

Total Surface Area of a Prism or Cylinder

The total surface area S.A. of any prism or cylinder is the sum of its lateral area L.A. and twice the area B of a base.

$$S.A. = L.A. + 2B$$

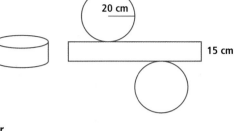

GUIDED

Example 3

Calculate the surface area of the hat box at the right from its net.

Solution

Step 1 Find the lateral area of the hat box.

> Lateral area = L.A. = length • width =
> = circumference of circle • height of cylinder
> = 2π___?___ • ___?___ ≈ ___?___ cm²

Step 2 Find the area of the bases. The bases are circles. Find the area of one circle and multiply it by 2 because there are two circular bases.

> Area of bases = πr² • 2
> = π • ___?___² • 2 ≈ ___?___ cm²

Step 3 Add the lateral and base areas to find the total surface area.

> ___?___ cm² + ___?___ cm² = ___?___ cm²

 QY2

Questions

COVERING THE IDEAS

1. **Fill in the Blank** The three lateral faces of a ___?___ meet the triangular bases at right angles.

2. **a.** The net of a cylinder consists of what figures?

   b. Draw a net of a cylinder with a height of 4 cm and base radius of 1 cm.

3. Make an informal sketch of a cylinder.

4. What is wrong with this calculation of the total surface area of a cylinder with height 9 m and a base radius 6 m?

> L.A. = hπd   A = π • r²
>   = 9π(12)   = π • 6²
>   ≈ 339.12 m²   = π • 36
>   ≈ 3.14(36) = 113.04 m²
> S.A. = 339.12 + 113.04 = 452.16

> ▶ **QY2**
>
> If the diameter of a cylindrical-shaped, unsharpened color pencil is 0.5 cm and its length is 19 cm, what is its surface area?

5. Shown at the right is a wedge.
   a. Draw a net for the wedge.   b. What is its lateral area?
   c. Find the area of one base.   d. Find its total surface area.

6. **Fill in the Blanks** In a prism or cylinder, $S.A. = $ _____?_____ + _____?_____.

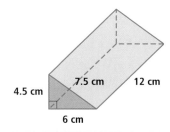

4.5 cm 7.5 cm 12 cm 6 cm

APPLYING THE MATHEMATICS

7. Bales of hay are often wrapped in plastic coverings in order to prevent damage. If a rectangular bale of hay is 7.5 feet long, 1.5 feet high, and 2 feet wide, how much plastic is needed to wrap 30 bales of hay? (Do not consider overlap.)

8. **Multiple Choice** Suppose each dimension of the can in Example 2 were doubled. What happens to the total surface area?

   A   It is doubled.   B   It is multiplied by 4.

   C   It is multiplied by 6.   D   It is multiplied by 8.

9. Sabrina decorated a pillar candle by rolling it in a plate of glitter. She did not put any glitter on the top or bottom of the candle.
   a. If the candle is 5 inches high and has a diameter of 3 inches, how much of the surface of the candle is covered by glitter?
   b. How much of the candle's surface is *not* covered in glitter?

10. Use the water trough pictured at the right.
    a. What is the shape of the base of the prism?
    b. If you were to paint the outside of the trough, how many faces would you paint?
    c. Calculate how many square centimeters you would paint.

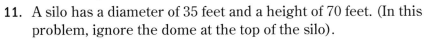

100 cm 52 cm 500 cm 60 cm 60 cm 40 cm

11. A silo has a diameter of 35 feet and a height of 70 feet. (In this problem, ignore the dome at the top of the silo).
    a. What is the shape of the base?
    b. Make a net of the silo and mark an X on the surfaces that will be painted.
    c. Calculate how many square feet you would need to cover the surface with one coat of paint.
    d. If a gallon of paint covers 300 ft^2, how many gallons are needed for two coats of paint?

REVIEW

12. A box has dimensions 20 cm, 18 cm, and 9 cm. (**Lesson 11-5**)
    a. What is the area of the largest face of the box?
    b. What is the total surface area of the box?
    c. What is the volume of the box?

13. Use a graphing utility to graph the inequality $y < \frac{2}{3}x - 4$. (**Lesson 10-3**)

14. If the probability that a baseball player will get a hit is 32%, what is the probability he will get three hits in a row? (**Lesson 8-4**)

15. In the 17th century, the Dutch built a circular fort at the southernmost point of New Amsterdam, which is now Manhattan Island in New York City. The fort was also used to protect the city during the War of 1812. Today it is known as Castle Clinton National Monument. Castle Clinton is about 236 feet across at its widest. What is the length of its outside wall to the nearest foot? (**Lesson 7-6**)

Castle Clinton National Monument

16. Explain how the Distributive Property can help to calculate $\$9.95 \cdot 5$ in your head. (**Lesson 7-3**)

17. Central Park in New York City is shaped like a rectangle, about 2.5 miles long and $\frac{1}{2}$ mile wide. What is its area? (**Lessons 7-2, 7-1, 3-5**)

18. Find the value of x in parallelogram $BAKE$ at the right. (**Lesson 6-7**)

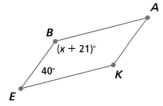

19. How many lines of symmetry does the figure at the right have? (**Lesson 6-2**)

20. Let $T =$ the set of multiples of 3 and $N =$ the set of multiples of 9.
    a. Describe $T \cup N$.
    b. Describe $T \cap N$. (**Lesson 4-4**)

21. The solution set to what sentence is graphed below? (**Lesson 2-8**)

EXPLORATION

22. Locate containers in the shape of a cylinder and a prism. Calculate the total surface area of each object.

QY ANSWERS

1. 96 in²

2. 9.625π, or about 30.24 cm²

Lesson 11-7

Volume of Prisms and Cylinders

> ▶ **BIG IDEA** The volumes of both prisms and cylinders are found by multiplying the area of their base by their height.

We find the volume of a prism by thinking of it as a stack of thin sheets. The area of each sheet is B, the area of the base. The height of the stack is h. To find the volume, multiply the area of the base by the height. This idea applies to all prisms.

Mental Math

Solve for the variable.

a. $1{,}000{,}001 = 999{,}998 + A$

b. $3B = 36{,}120{,}459$

c. $83C = 82C + 7.126$

d. $5D - 4D = -1$

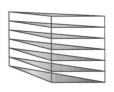  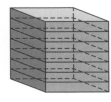

Volume Formula for a Prism

The volume V of a prism with height h and a base with area B is given by

$$V = Bh.$$

Example 1

Find the volume of a swimming pool that is 22 feet long, 18 feet wide, 12 feet at the deep end and 4 feet deep in the shallow end. Assume that the walls of the pool are perpendicular to the opening and that the opening is a rectangle.

Solution

To find the volume of the prism, first identify the bases. The trapezoids are the only congruent parallel faces, so the bases of this prism are trapezoids.

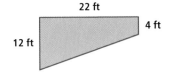

(continued on next page)

To find the area of a trapezoid, use the formula $A = \frac{1}{2}h(b_1 + b_2)$. The height of the trapezoid is 22 feet and b_1 and b_2 are 12 feet and 4 feet.

$$A = \frac{1}{2}h(b_1 + b_2) = \frac{1}{2} \cdot 22(12 + 4) = 11(16) = 176$$

The area of the base is 176 ft².

The volume is equal to the area of the base of the prism multiplied by the height of the prism. The height of the prism is the perpendicular distance between the bases of the prism, 18 feet.

$$V = Bh = 176 \text{ ft}^2 \cdot 18 \text{ ft} = 3{,}168 \text{ ft}^3$$

 QY

> ▶ **QY**
>
> Find the volume of a triangular prism if the base of the triangular face is 24 inches, the height of the triangular face is 8 inches, and the height of the prism is 12 inches.

Volume of a Cylinder

You can find the volume of a cylinder using the same idea you used to find the volume of a prism. Think of stacked circular sheets when considering the volume of a cylinder. The area of each sheet in the stack, *B*, can be found using the area formula for a circle. The height of the stack is *h*. To find the volume of the cylinder, multiply the area of the base by the height.

Area ***B*** square units

height *h*

Because the base is a circle, if it has radius *r*, its area is πr^2.

Volume Formula for a Cylinder

The volume *V* of a cylinder with height *h* and base with radius *r* is given by

$$V = Bh = \pi r^2 h.$$

GUIDED

Example 2

A 12-ounce aluminum soft drink can is about 12 centimeters high. It has a radius of about 3.2 centimeters. What is its volume?

Solution

Step 1 Draw a picture, as shown at the right.

Step 2 Find the area of the base of the cylinder.

It is a circle, so the area is __?__.

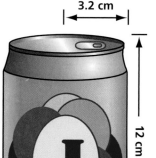

3.2 cm

12 cm

Step 3 Find the volume by multiplying the area of the base, which is a circle, by the height.

The volume is ___?___.

Step 4 Make sure you express the volume with the correct units.

Questions

In 1 and 2, find the volume of the figure.

1.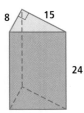

triangular prism

2.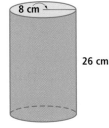

cylinder

3. Find the volume to the nearest tenth of a cubic inch of a soup can with height 5 inches and diameter of base 4 inches.

4. Find the volume to the nearest 0.1 mm^3 of a prism whose base is a heptagon with area 45 square millimeters and whose height is 15 millimeters.

5. **a.** This book is a prism. Its base is a ___?___.
   b. Approximate the volume of this book to the nearest cubic inch.

6. A skyscraper is a prism 350 feet high. A view from the top is shown at the right. Its base is a reflection-symmetric pentagon.

   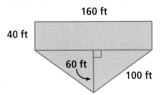

   a. Find the area of the base.
   b. Find the volume of the skyscraper.

7. Elena and Erica bought two types of gourmet cheese for their party. Elena bought a piece of cheese shaped like a triangular prism for $8.25. Erica bought a piece of cheese shaped like a cylinder for $10.25. The dimensions are shown below. Who got a greater volume of cheese for her money? Justify your answer.

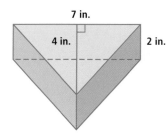

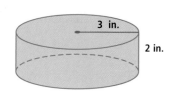

8. Here is a net for a circular cylinder with *one* base—an open can. Find its volume to the nearest tenth of a cubic inch.

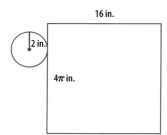

9. A trapezoidal prism can be used as a drinking trough for farm animals. The dimensions are given below. How many cubic centimeters of water can it hold?

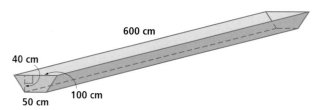

10. Consider an 7-inch-long straw with a $\frac{1}{4}$-inch inside radius.

   a. What is its capacity?
   b. If the straw is $\frac{1}{32}$-inch thick, what is the volume of the material that went into making the straw?
   c. What is the outside surface area of the straw?
   d. Does a straw have a great deal of surface area for its volume or not much surface area for its volume?

REVIEW

11. Find the surface area of the square pyramid at the right. The apex of the pyramid is above the center of the base. (**Lesson 11-6**)

12. A cylinder has a base with radius 3 meters and height of 8 meters. Find its surface area. (**Lesson 11-6**)

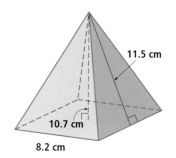

13. Find the height of the box at the right if its volume is 1,500 cubic inches. (**Lesson 11-5**)

14. $\triangle ABC$ and $\triangle A'B'C'$ are similar. Find $A'B'$ and $B'C'$.
(**Lesson 9-9**)

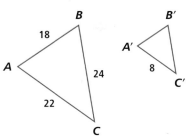

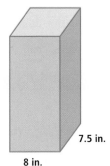

In 15 and 16, U.S. golden dollars minted since 2000 have a diameter of 26.5 millimeters, and U.S. dimes minted since 1946 have a diameter of 17.91 millimeters.

15. Explain why a golden dollar covers more than twice the area of a dime. (**Lesson 7-6**)

16. Explain why a golden dollar has less than twice the circumference of a dime. (**Lesson 7-6**)

17. Solve for w. $-62 + w = 222$ (**Lesson 8-8**)

18. Evaluate the expression $g^4 + \dfrac{9}{k+3}$ to the nearest hundredth when $g = -1.7$ and $k = \dfrac{5}{8}$. (**Lesson 2-3**)

In 19–21, consider the decimal.
a. Rewrite the decimal as a percent. (Lesson 3-6)
b. Rewrite the decimal as a fraction in lowest terms. (Lesson 3-5)

19. 0.001 20. 0.875 21. $1.1\overline{6}$

22. Identify the coordinate of each named point on the number line below. (**Lesson 1-2**)

EXPLORATION

23. A company is considering packaging a new product in either a cylinder or a rectangular prism container. For packaging purposes, the height of the container must be 12 centimeters. The cylinder being considered has a base with diameter 10 centimeters. The rectangular prism being considered has a square base. Find the length of the side of the base of the rectangular prism that will hold approximately the same amount as the cylinder container. Round your answer to the nearest hundredth.

QY ANSWER

1,152 in³

Lesson

11-8 Spheres

Vocabulary

sphere

radius of a sphere

center of a sphere

ball

diameter of a sphere

▶ **BIG IDEA** You can determine the surface area and volume of a sphere if you know its radius.

A **sphere** is the set of points *in space* at a given distance—its **radius**—from a given point—its **center**. Shown below is a sphere with radius *r*. Planets and moons in space, baseballs, marbles, and many other objects are nearly the shape of spheres. In mathematics, a sphere is like a soap bubble. It does not include any points inside. Even the center *C* of a sphere is not a point on the sphere. The union of a sphere and the set of all points inside it is called a **ball.**

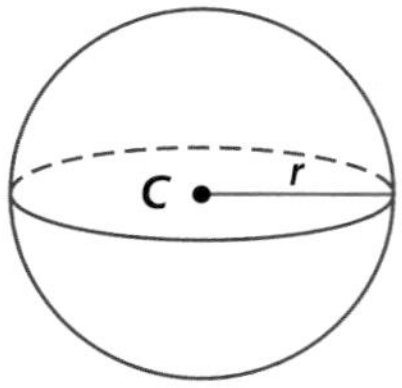

Mental Math

a. Which holds more, a cylinder with height 10 cm and surface area 600 cm², or a cube of the same surface area?

b. Which has greater surface area, a cube with volume 1,000 cm³, or a cylinder with the same volume and height of 10 cm?

A **diameter of a sphere** is a segment from one point on the sphere to another point on the sphere that goes through the center of the sphere. So, just as with circles, the diameter is twice the radius.

The formulas for the surface area and volume of a sphere were first discovered by the mathematician Archimedes, who lived from 284 to 212 BCE. You will learn how these formulas were found when you study geometry in more detail in a later course. Like the formulas for the area and circumference of a circle, they involve the number π.

Surface-Area and Volume Formulas for a Sphere

In a sphere with radius *r*, total surface area S.A., and volume *V*:

$$S.A. = 4\pi r^2$$
$$V = \frac{4}{3}\pi r^3$$

The exponents in these formulas signal the units in which surface area and volume are measured. The surface area of a sphere is measured in square units just like any other area, even though the surface of a sphere is curved.

Earth is not exactly a sphere because its rotation has flattened it slightly at the poles. The length of the equator is about 24,902 miles, while its circumference north to south is about 24,860 miles. Dividing these circumferences by π, we find diameters of about 7,927 and 7,913 miles. These lengths are double the radii, so Earth is nearly a sphere with radius about 3,960 miles.

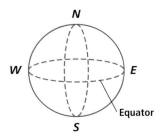

Example 1

Estimate the total surface area of Earth.

Solution

The formula for total surface area is $S.A. = 4\pi r^2$. Substitute 3,960 miles for r.

$$S.A. = 4\pi r^2$$
$$= 4\pi \cdot 3,960^2$$

Our calculator shows the following:

$$\approx 197,060,797.426 \text{ square miles}$$

This number is misleading because it has too many places with nonzero digits. The radius, 3,960 miles, is rounded. It could be anything from 3,955 to 3,965 miles, so we round the answer to a reasonable degree of accuracy:

$$\approx 197,000,000 \text{ square miles}.$$

GUIDED

Example 2

Table tennis rules stipulate that the ball must be spherical with a diameter of 40 millimeters. How much air is inside a table tennis ball?

Solution 1 Because we want the amount of air inside, we need to calculate volume. Let V be the volume. Because the diameter is 40 mm, the radius of the sphere is ___?___.

$$V = \frac{4}{3}\pi r^3$$
$$= \frac{4}{3} \cdot \pi \cdot \underline{\quad ? \quad}.$$
$$\approx \underline{\quad ? \quad} \text{ mm}^3$$

Solution 2 Because 10 mm = 1 cm, calculate the volume in cubic centimeters.

$$V = \frac{4}{3} \cdot \pi \cdot \underline{\quad ? \quad}.$$
$$\approx \underline{\quad ? \quad} \text{ cm}^3$$

Between ___?___ and ___?___ cubic centimeters of air are inside a table tennis ball.

► QY

Calculate the surface area and volume of a sphere with diameter 6.5 cm. Round your answers to the nearest hundredth of a unit.

 QY

It is usually correct to think of the surface area as the amount of material that covers a 3-dimensional figure. However, if the thickness of the surface needs to be used, then you need to subtract the volume without the material from the volume with the material.

GUIDED

Example 3

A tennis ball has a diameter of 6.6 cm but its shell is 0.3 cm thick. How much material is used in one tennis ball shell?

Solution

Drawing a picture of a tennis ball sliced in half shows the thickness of the shell.

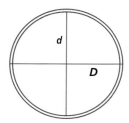

Call the outer diameter D and the inner diameter d.

$D =$ __?__ cm, $d =$ __?__ cm

Call the outer radius R and the inner radius r.

$R =$ __?__ cm, $r =$ __?__ cm

The amount of material in the shell is $\frac{4}{3}\pi R^3 -$ __?__ .

$\approx \frac{4}{3} \cdot 3.14 \cdot$ __?__ $^3 -$ __?__ .

$\approx$ __?__ cm^3

We found that the amount of material is about 37.4 cm^3. Your answer should agree.

Questions

COVERING THE IDEAS

1. What is a *sphere*?

2. Why is Earth not exactly a sphere?

3. Identify the formula for the total surface area of a sphere.

4. Calculate the total surface area of a sphere with radius 9 cm.

5. Identify the formula for the volume of a sphere.

6. Calculate the volume of a sphere with diameter 12 cm.

7. Who discovered the formulas for the surface area and volume of a sphere?

8. In the reading, it is noted that the radius of Earth is about 3,956 miles from its center to a pole and about 3,963 miles at the Equator. Calculate the volume of Earth if Earth were a sphere with each radius.

9. The moon is approximately a sphere with radius 1,080 miles.

   a. Estimate the total surface area of the moon to the nearest million square miles.

   b. The surface area of Earth is approximately how many times the surface area of the moon?

10. Suppose that a plastic beach ball is 0.008 inch thick when it is blown up to an outer diameter of 20 inches. How many cubic inches of plastic material are in the ball?

APPLYING THE MATHEMATICS

In 11–14, tell whether the idea is more like *surface area* or *volume*.

11. how much land there is in Asia

12. how much meat is in a meatball

13. how much material it takes to make a balloon

In 14 and 15, use this information. A bowling ball is approximately 8.6 inches in diameter.

14. How much surface does a bowling ball have? (Ignore the finger holes.)

15. How much material does it take to make a bowling ball? (Ignore the finger holes.)

16. A 20-centimeter diameter ball fits snugly in a box. What percent of the box is filled by the ball?

REVIEW

17. A cylindrical tube for mailing large pictures is $2\frac{15}{16}$ inches in inside diameter and 36 inches long. What is its volume, to the nearest cubic inch? **(Lesson 11-7)**

18. A prism has a right triangular base. The length of its legs are a and b and the height of the prism is h. **(Lessons 11-6, 11-3, 2-5)**

   a. Draw this prism.

   b. Draw a net for this prism.

   c. Find the surface area of this prism.

19. About 57,000,000 square miles of Earth's surface is land.
    (**Lesson 8-5**)
    a. What percent of Earth's surface is land? Answer to the nearest percent.
    b. The area of the United States is approximately 3,540,000 square miles. What percent of the total land area of Earth is in the United States?
    c. What percent of the total surface area of Earth is in the United States?

20. James and Ron live in apartment buildings facing each other across their street. They want to figure out how far apart they live. James lives on the fourth floor of his building and Ron on the second of his. Based on the measurements they made, how far apart are their apartments? (**Lessons 6-9, 2-5**)

21. **Multiple Choice** Which point is farthest from the point $(-5, 4)$? (**Lesson 6-9**)
    A $(-20, 16)$ B $(14, 4)$
    C $(-10, -18)$ D $(7, -8)$

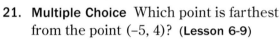

22. g is a whole number. The square root of g is between 10 and 11. The square root of $2g$ is between 15 and 16. g is a prime number. What is g? (**Lesson 3-8**)

EXPLORATION

23. Refer to Question 19.
    a. What three countries of the world have more land area than the United States? (Look in an almanac or at a globe for this information.)
    b. How much of the land area of Earth is occupied by these three countries?

24. Take a grapefruit and cut it in half across the center. Lay one of the halves cut side-down and trace four circles on a sheet of paper. Peel the grapefruit's outer rind and arrange the pieces of rind in the four circles. What do you observe? How does this activity relate to the formula for surface area of a sphere?

QY ANSWER

surface area: 132.73 cm²;
volume: 143.79 cm³

How Changing Dimensions Affects Area

> ▶ **BIG IDEA** If all dimensions of a figure are multiplied by k, the area of the figure is multiplied by k^2.

Here is a common mistake that people make when they are working with area.

Rosemary wants to triple the area of her herb garden, but keep it the same shape. It is currently rectangular with dimensions 2 feet by 3 feet. She tells her husband, Basil, to enlarge the garden to be 6 feet by 9 feet. Both Rosemary and Basil are surprised by the additional amount of work they have to do to keep up their garden.

In Lesson 9-8 you learned about situations that lend themselves to proportional thinking. Also in Lesson 9-9 you saw how proportions can be applied to similar figures to find missing side lengths. How do the areas of similar figures compare? Are the areas of similar figures in the same ratio as the sides?

Changing Dimensions and Area

In Lesson 9-7, you looked at the problem of changing map scales. When the scale was doubled, the area was not just doubled. The change in area is not proportional to the change in the side. This was seen in its graph, which was a curve. In the Activity, you will look at a triangle and its size-change image, measure and compare sides, and then measure and compare the areas.

Activity

Step 1 Create a slider labeled B on your DGS. On some DGS, you do this by drawing a horizontal line and measuring the distance between two points on the line.

(continued on next page)

Mental Math

Find the volume.

a.

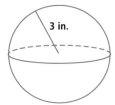

3 in.

b.

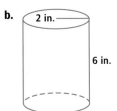

2 in.

6 in.

c.

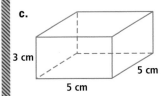

3 cm

5 cm

5 cm

d.

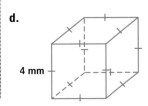

4 mm

Step 2 Create a point O and a triangle. Drag the point B to a value of 2. Then have your DGS construct the image of the triangle under a size change about O by a scale factor equal to the slider value.

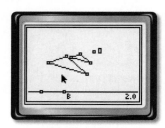

Step 3 Have the DGS measure the lengths of a pair of corresponding sides of the triangle and its image, and divide the image side length by the original length. The ratio should be equal to the slider value.

Step 4 Have the DGS measure the area of each triangle. Divide the area of the image by the area of the original triangle. Set up your screen like the one at the right, with the areas and their ratio separated from the sides and their ratio.

Step 5 Copy and complete the table below. You can change the scale factor by dragging point B. Note that you need to record only the slider value, the ratio of the image side to the original side, and the ratio of the image area to the original area. The first row is filled in for you.

Triangle Number	Slider Value	Image Side / Original Side	Image Area / Original Area
1	2.0	2.0	4.0
2	3.0	?	?
3	2.5	?	?
4	1.5	?	?
5	0.5	?	?
6	0.4	?	?

(continued on next page)

Step 6 Use the information in your table to complete the following pattern.

If you multiply the side length by 2, then you multiply the area by
<u> ? </u> = (2)².

If you multiply the side length by 3, then you multiply the area by
<u> ? </u> = (<u> ? </u>)².

If you multiply the side length by 1.5, then you multiply the area by
<u> ? </u> = (<u> ? </u>)².

If you multiply the side length by *k*, then you multiply the area by
<u> ? </u> = (<u> ? </u>)².

 QY

You should have noted that the pattern indicates that multiplication of each side length by a factor of *k* results in multiplication of the area by a factor of k^2. We can now explain what has happened with the herb garden.

▶ **QY**

Fill in the Blank If you multiply the side length of a square by 3.1, then you multiply the area by <u> ? </u>.

GUIDED

Example 1

Show Rosemary and Basil what happens to the area when the dimensions of their 2-foot-by-3-foot herb garden are tripled.

Solution

Area of old garden: $\ell \cdot w$ = <u> ? </u> ft • <u> ? </u> ft = <u> ? </u> sq ft

New dimensions: 3 • w = <u> ? </u> ft; 3 • w = <u> ? </u> ft

Area of new garden: $\ell \cdot w$ = <u> ? </u> ft • <u> ? </u> ft = 54 sq ft

Ratio of areas: $\frac{\text{Area of new garden}}{\text{Area of old garden}}$ = <u> ? </u>

We multiplied each dimension by <u> ? </u>, but the area was multiplied by <u> ? </u>. That is because when each dimension is multiplied by 3, the area is twice multiplied by 3, so it is multiplied by (<u> ? </u>)².

The general idea can be stated in terms of multiplication or in terms of division.

Size-Change Area Theorem

If a figure has been scaled by a size change with a factor *k*, then the area of the figure will be scaled by a size change with a factor k^2.

Or

If the dimensions of two figures are in the ratio *k*, then the ratio of their areas is k^2.

Example 2

Tup owns a small catamaran which is 16 feet long. It has a rainbow sail with an area of 112 square feet. He plans to make a model whose length will be 1 foot. He has about 0.5 square foot of striped cloth for the sail. Will that be enough?

Solution

The ratio of the lengths is $\frac{1}{16}$.

The ratio of the areas is $\left(\frac{1}{16}\right)^2$.

$\left(\frac{1}{16}\right)^2 = \frac{1}{256} \approx 0.0039$

The ratio of areas of the cloth he has to the area of the sail is $\frac{0.5}{112} \approx 0.0045$ square feet. Yes, he has enough cloth.

The Size-Change Area Theorem applies to surface area as well as to areas in a plane.

For example, if two similar figurines are 9 cm and 20 cm high, then the ratio of the surface area of the smaller to the surface area of the larger is $\left(\frac{9}{20}\right)^2$, or $\frac{81}{400}$, or 0.2025. So, even though the smaller figurine is almost half the height of the larger, its surface area is only about $\frac{1}{5}$ the surface area of the larger.

Questions

COVERING THE IDEAS

1. If the dimensions of a figure are multiplied by 25, then the area of the figure is multiplied by what number?

2. Refer to Rosemary and Basil's herb garden. Suppose they had multiplied each dimension of the garden by 2. By what would the area of the garden have been multiplied?

3. Suppose in Example 2 that the sail is a triangle with base length 16 feet and height 14 feet.
   a. What are the dimensions of the sail in the model?
   b. What is the area of the sail in the model?

In 4 and 5, two cubes have edges of 1 cm and 2 cm.

4. a. What is the surface area of the smaller cube?

    b. Find the surface area of the larger cube by adding the areas of its six faces.

    c. Find the surface area of the larger cube by using Part a and the Size-Change Area Theorem.

5. a. What are the volumes of the two cubes?

    b. Is the ratio of their volumes equal to the ratio of their surface areas?

6. Rosemary and Basil are planning to put a wooden border around their new garden.

    a. How long is the border of their current garden?

    b. If they multiply each dimension of their current garden by 3, how long will the border of their new garden be?

    c. Is the ratio of the perimeters of the two gardens equal to the ratio of their areas?

APPLYING THE MATHEMATICS

7. Begin with a square that has vertices $A = (0, 0)$, $B = (5, 0)$, $C = (5, 5)$, and $D = (0, 5)$.

    a. Find the coordinates of the vertices of its image under a size change with center $(0, 0)$ and magnitude 11.

    b. What is the area of $ABCD$?

    c. What is the area of its image?

    d. What is the perimeter of $ABCD$?

    e. What is the perimeter of its image?

8. Repeat Question 7 for the trapezoid $TRAP$ with vertices $T = (-4, 0)$, $R = (6, 0)$, $A = (8, 4)$, and $P = (-10, 4)$ under a size change with center $(0, 0)$ and magnitude 0.5.

9. Our moon has a mean radius of about 1,079 miles. Earth has a mean radius of about 3,960 miles. Calculate each value to the nearest percent.

    a. the ratio of the radius of the moon to the radius of Earth

    b. the ratio of the surface area of the moon to the surface area of Earth

10. About 29% of Earth's surface is land; the rest is water. The radius of Mars is about 2,100 miles, while the radius of Earth is about 3,960 miles. But virtually all of the surface of Mars is land. To the nearest percent, what is the ratio of the surface area of Mars to the land area of Earth?

REVIEW

11. A cylinder has radius 3 cm and height 8.7 cm.
    a. What is its volume?
    b. What is its total surface area? **(Lessons 11-7, 11-6)**

12. Some Swiss chocolate is sold in cartons that are prisms with an equilateral triangle having sides of length 3 cm as the base. The height of the prism is 21 cm. Draw a net for the carton in which the chocolate is sold. **(Lesson 11-3)**

13. Explain why a cube is a prism using the three characteristics of a prism mentioned in this chapter. **(Lesson 11-2)**

14. The diameter of the moon is about 3,500 kilometers. Find the approximate circumference of the Moon. **(Lesson 7-6)**

15. Shakespeare's sonnets typically contained fourteen lines of *iambic pentameter*. An *iamb* is a pattern of two syllables and a line of iambic pentameter contains five iambs. How many syllables are in an entire sonnet? **(Lesson 7-3)**

EXPLORATION

16. Rosemary and Basil wanted to triple the area of their herb garden, but their method resulted in an herb garden with 9 times the area. By what number could they have multiplied both dimensions of the garden and thus tripled the area of the garden?

QY ANSWER

3.1^2 or 9.61

How Changing Dimensions Affects Volume

Vocabulary

ratio of similitude

▶ **BIG IDEA**   If all three dimensions of a figure are multiplied by k, the volume of the figure is multiplied by k^3.

In Lesson 11-9, you saw that lengths and areas in similar figures are related in an interesting and simple way. If every length is multiplied by a number k, then the corresponding area is multiplied by k^2. You might wonder how volume is related to a change in length. Here is another problem which illustrates common mistakes people make with mathematics.

The Kewl family wanted a compact refrigerator in the shape of a cube for their new boat. They found one with a capacity of slightly less than 2 cubic feet, which fits easily under a counter. A friend recommended one in the shape of a cube with a capacity of 6 cubic feet. "Impractical!" said Wei Kewl, "I don't have the space under the counter for one that is three times as high."

Mental Math

a. How many nickels are in $5.00?

b. How many bagels are in 4 dozen?

c. There are 3 periods in a hockey game and 20 minutes in a period. How many hours are in 7 hockey games?

d. How many pens are in eight 15-packs?

Changing Only One Dimension

If only one length is multiplied by k, then the volume is multiplied by k. That is what happens in the following example.

GUIDED

Example

One box has dimensions 6 inches by 9 inches by 4 inches. A second box has dimensions 6 inches by 9 inches by 20 inches. What is the ratio of the volume of the larger box to the volume of the smaller box?

Solution 1   The volume of the larger box is __?__ • __?__ • __?__. (Do not carry out the multiplication.)

The volume of the smaller box is __?__ • __?__ • __?__.

The ratio of the volumes is $\dfrac{\text{?} \cdot \text{?} \cdot \text{?}}{\text{?} \cdot \text{?} \cdot \text{?}}$, which simplifies to __?__.

Solution 2   The volume of the larger box is __?__ • __?__ • __?__, which is __?__. (Multiply!)

The volume of the smaller box is __?__ • __?__ • __?__, which is __?__.

Comparing these volumes, we see that the ratio is __?__.

Changing All Dimensions

When two figures are similar, then *all* their corresponding lengths are in the same ratio. This ratio is known as **ratio of similitude,** and all their corresponding dimensions are in that ratio. In Lesson 11-9, you saw that the ratio of areas in similar figures is the square of that ratio. This Activity explores the ratio of volumes in similar figures.

Activity

Below is a table with lengths of edges and volumes of cubes. Some of the cells are filled in for you.

Step 1 Copy and complete the table.

			Comparing Volumes of Cubes			
	Preimage Edge	Preimage Volume	Size-Change Factor	Image Edge	Image Volume	Image Volume / Preimage Volume
a.	3 cm	27 cm³	2	6 cm	216 cm³	$\frac{216 \text{ cm}^3}{27 \text{ cm}^3} = 8$
b.	1.2 in.	1.728 in³	3	_?_	_?_	_?_ = 27
c.	15 units	_?_	$\frac{1}{3}$	5 units	_?_	_?_ = _?_
d.	300 ft	_?_	0.75	_?_	_?_	_?_ = _?_

When you complete the table, you should see that the relationship between the size-change factor for the edge and the scale factor for the volume follows a pattern.

Step 2 Use the following sentences to arrive at the general pattern.

a. When the edge is multiplied by 2, the volume is multiplied by 8 = (_?_)³.

b. When the edge is multiplied by 3, the volume is multiplied by _?_ = (_?_)³.

c. When the edge is multiplied by $\frac{1}{3}$, the volume is multiplied by _?_ = (_?_)³.

d. When the edge is multiplied by 0.75, the volume is multiplied by _?_ = (_?_)³.

e. When the edge is multiplied by *k*, the volume is multiplied by _?_.

The relationship that holds between changing linear measures and volume is much like the relationship between changing linear measures and area. This relationship that is true for cubes is true for any 3-dimensional figure which has been scaled.

Size-Change Volume Theorem

If a figure has been scaled by a size change with a factor k, then the volume of the figure will be scaled by a size change with a factor of k^3.

Or

If the dimensions of two figures are in the ratio k, then the ratio of their volumes is k^3.

The Size-Change Volume Theorem is true because in every volume formula, three dimensions are multiplied. If you multiply each of those dimensions by k, then the product is multiplied by k^3.

In this book, you have seen statements about ratios of lengths, areas, and volumes in similar figures. We show them all here.

Fundamental Theorem of Similarity

If two figures are similar with ratio of similitude k, then:

The ratio of corresponding side lengths or distances is k.
The ratio of corresponding areas is k^2.
The ratio of corresponding volumes is k^3.

Notice the pattern. The exponent of the ratio of similitude (the size-change factor) is the dimension of the measure. Length is 1-dimensional; area is 2-dimensional; volume is 3-dimensional. So if a model of a car is $\frac{1}{20}$ actual size in linear dimensions, then any surface area on the model of the car is $\left(\frac{1}{20}\right)^2$, or $\frac{1}{400}$, the surface area of the real car. The volume of the model is $\left(\frac{1}{20}\right)^3$, or $\frac{1}{8,000}$, the volume of the real car.

Now let us return to Wei Kewl's compact-refrigerator problem. Wei is thinking that a 6-cubic-foot refrigerator is 3 times all the dimensions of a 2-cubic-foot refrigerator. But if all the dimensions are multiplied by 3, then the volume (the number of cubic feet) would be multiplied by 3^3, or 27. If the height of the smaller refrigerator were multiplied by 3, then the 6-cubic-foot refrigerator would certainly not fit.

But these refrigerators are both cubes. So all three dimensions of the 2-cubic-foot refrigerator would be multiplied by some number k, so that k^3 is about 3. With a calculator, you can see that $1.4^3 = 2.744$ and $1.5^3 = 3.374$, and $1.45^3 = 3.048625$. So $k \approx 1.45$, and the 6-cubic-foot refrigerator would have dimensions about 1.45 times those of the 2-cubic-foot refrigerator. Wei might have room for the larger refrigerator under the counter.

Caution: The changes in this lesson and Lesson 11-9 involve multiplying dimensions by some number. When multiplying, you can predict what will happen to the volume of a figure. But these predictions do not work if you add the same number to all the dimensions. Area and volume are related to multiplication, not addition.

Questions

COVERING THE IDEAS

1. Two spheres have radii of 2 feet and 3 feet.
   a. What is the ratio of the diameter of the smaller sphere to the diameter of the larger sphere?
   b. What is the ratio of the surface area of the smaller sphere to the surface area of the larger sphere?
   c. What is the ratio of the volume of the smaller sphere to the volume of the larger sphere?
   d. How many times as much paint would you need to paint the larger sphere than the smaller sphere?

2. You have two similar cubes made of the same plastic. The edges of one cube are 1 cm long, and the edges of the other are 1 in. long. Remember that 1 in. = 2.54 cm.
   a. What is the ratio of the surface area of the centimeter cube to the surface area of the inch cube?
   b. What is the ratio of the volume of the centimeter cube to the volume of the inch cube?

3. Two similar dolls are 22 cm and 33 cm tall.
   a. What is a ratio of similitude of the dolls?
   b. What is the ratio of their volumes?
   c. What is the ratio of their surface areas?

4. A tree has been cut down and its trunk, a cylinder, is being further cut for logs. If the logs are the width of the tree and one log is 6" high and another is 8" high, how do the volumes of these logs compare?

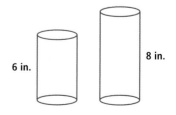

6 in.   8 in.

5. Suppose two boxes have the same height, 30 cm. The base of one box is a rectangle 20 cm by 30 cm. The base of the other box is a similar rectangle with shorter dimension 24 cm.

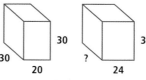

a. What is the third dimension of the other box?

b. What is the ratio of the volumes of the boxes?

6. The two water bottles at the right are similar. If the smaller bottle has a capacity of 24 ounces, what is the capacity of the larger bottle?

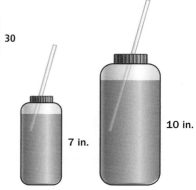

APPLYING THE MATHEMATICS

7. **Multiple Choice** A locomotive on a freight train is pulling cars of coal. If there are 80 full cars to pull, how many times as heavy is the load as it would be if there were 40 full cars to pull?

A 2 times   B 2^2 times   C 2^3 times   D 2^{40} times

8. Pictured below at the left is a wire frame of a cube. In the middle is an empty, closed cardboard cube. At the right is a solid cube made of wood. Suppose that each of these weighs 2 pounds. Now suppose that you have three cubes that are made with the same materials in the same thicknesses as these cubes; their dimensions are all 3 times the dimensions of these cubes.

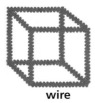

wire   cardboard   wood

a. What is the weight of the larger wire-frame cube?

b. What is the weight of the larger cardboard cube?

c. What is the weight of the larger wood cube?

9. A log is a cylinder 2 feet long with diameter 4 inches. A second log of the same length and kind of wood is a cylinder with diameter 6 inches.

a. Find the volume of the smaller log as a multiple of π.

b. Find the volume of the larger log.

c. What is the ratio of the volume of the larger log to the volume of the smaller log?

d. Why is the answer to Part c not equal to the ratio of diameters?

e. If the smaller log weighs 10 pounds, what would you expect the larger log to weigh?

How Changing Dimensions Affects Volume   **729**

10. In Philadelphia's International Sculpture Garden are two stones from Costa Rica, both made of the same material. The smaller stone has a diameter of 4 feet 6 inches. The larger stone has a diameter of 6 feet 6 inches. The smaller one weighs 9,000 pounds. Estimate the weight of the larger stone.

Philadelphia's International Sculpture Garden

11. **a.** Find the surface areas of the two boxes in the Guided Example.

    b. Why is the surface area of the larger box *not* 5 times the surface area of the smaller box?

REVIEW

12. A model airplane is 14 inches long and has a surface area of 98 square inches. If the actual airplane is 14 yards long, find its surface area. **(Lesson 11-9)**

13. A sphere's radius undergoes a size change by a factor m. If the original sphere had a radius of 3 cm, find the surface area of the new sphere. **(Lessons 11-9, 11-8)**

14. **a.** Find the exact volume of a cube with edge 5.15 feet.

    b. The correct answer to Part a is accurate to a millionth of a cubic foot. This is too precise for many uses. Round your answer to the nearest hundredth, the same precision as the original measure. **(Lesson 11-7)**

15. State the Algebraic Definition of Division. **(Lesson 9-3)**

16. Find the length of the left side of the trapezoid pictured at the right. **(Lesson 2-5)**

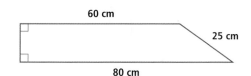

60 cm

25 cm

80 cm

17. Is the following statement *always, sometimes but not always,* or *never* true? If two lines are cut by a transversal, alternate exterior angles have the same measure. **(Lesson 6-6)**

EXPLORATION

18. Model airplanes come in various sizes compared to the originals. Find two typical scales of a model. Pick a particular airplane and compare the dimensions and weight of the original airplane to what the dimensions and weight would be for the model if the model were made of the same materials.

Chapter 11 Projects

1 Nets for Cubes

Two nets for a given 3-dimensional figure are considered to be the same if they are congruent. In this chapter, you have seen a number of different nets for cubes. There are 11 distinct nets for the cube. Draw as many of these 11 nets as you can, and show that each of them folds into a cube by numbering the six faces of each net so that the resulting cube looks like the one shown here with numbers on opposite faces adding to 7.

2 Will It Float?

An object will float in water if it weighs less than an amount of water occupying the same volume as the object. In other words, something will float if it has a lower *density* than water. The density of an object is its mass divided by its volume.

Water has a density of approximately 1 gram per cubic centimeter. Weigh five common objects that you can put into water, such as balls, cans, bottles, and pencils; use the formulas from this chapter to estimate their volumes. From this information, calculate their densities, compare them to water's density, and predict whether each object will float. Then test your predictions. Did any of your objects sink when they should have floated? Did they float when they should have sunk? Did any float for a time before sinking? Try to explain any differences from your predictions.

3 Surface Areas of Real Boxes

In this chapter, we have ignored overlaps in cardboard when calculating the total surface area of a box. Examine at least three real boxes. Look for boxes that have double bottoms or other interesting features. Calculate the actual amount of cardboard used to make the box. How does it compare to the total surface area?

4 Sponges and Filters

You've seen that the same volume can be enclosed by objects with very different surface areas. Research either sponges or air filters to find out how the relationship between surface area and volume helps these objects work. Write a short essay on what you find.

5 Constructing a Regular Dodecahedron

Many 3-dimensional figures can be constructed from nets. Below is a net for a *regular dodecahedron,* a figure whose twelve faces are all pentagons. A dodecahedron sometimes used as a calendar paperweight with each face having a calendar for one month of the year. Make a net like this with larger faces. Then fold and tape it into a regular dodecahedron.

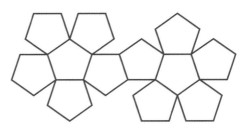

Chapter 11 Summary and Vocabulary

Vocabulary

11-1
parallel planes
skew lines
coplanar

11-2
face
box
edge
vertex of a prism
prism
base of a prism
right, rectangular, triangular, pentagonal, hexagonal prism
dimension
length, width, height, depth
isometric dot paper

11-3
lateral face
net
polyhedron (polyhedra)

11-4
views, elevations
pyramid
apex
square pyramid

11-5
surface area
volume, capacity
cubic units
cube
cubic centimeter

11-6
lateral area
cylinder

11-8
sphere
radius, diameter, center (of a sphere)
ball

11-10
ratio of similitude

- A **plane** is thought of as a flat surface that goes on forever in all directions. Exactly one plane is determined by three noncollinear points, which explains why tripods and tricycles make it hard for items they hold to tip over. If two points lie in a plane, then the line containing the points lies in the plane, explaining why a plane is flat. Two different planes are either parallel or intersect in a line. In contrast, lines may intersect in one point, be parallel, or be **skew**.

- Three common 3-dimensional shapes are examined in this chapter: **prisms** (including a special case—**boxes**), **cylinders**, and **spheres.** These and other figures are often described by drawing 2-dimensional **views** from the top, front, and sides. Prisms and cylinders can be made from 2-dimensional nets.

- The amount of surface of a 3-dimensional figure is measured by the **surface area** of that figure. The amount of space enclosed by the figure is measured by its **volume.** You should learn the formulas for the surface area and volume of a box, prism, cylinder, and sphere.

- If one dimension of a 2-dimensional figure is multiplied by k, then the area of the figure is multiplied by k. If one dimension of a 3-dimensional figure is multiplied by k, then the volume of the figure is multiplied by k. If all dimensions of a 3-dimensional figure are multiplied by k, resulting in a similar figure k times the size, then the surface area of the figure is multiplied by k^2 and the volume of the figure is multiplied by k^3.

Theorems and Properties

Box Volume Formula (p. 699)
Total Surface Area of a Prism or Cylinder (p. 705)
Volume Formula for a Prism (p. 709)
Volume Formula for a Cylinder (p. 710)
Surface-Area and Volume Formulas for a Sphere (p. 714)
Size-Change Area Theorem (p. 721)
Size-Change Volume Theorem (p. 727)
Fundamental Theorem of Similarity (p. 727)

Chapter

11 Self-Test

Take this test as you would take a test in class. You will need a calculator. Then use the Selected Answers section in the back of the book to check your work.

1. A cylinder has a diameter of 12 inches and a height of 17 inches.

   a. Find its total surface area.

   b. Find its volume.

2. Consider the prism below.

   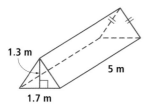

   a. Find its total surface area.

   b. Find its volume.

3. A sphere has radius 13 cm.

   a. Calculate its surface area.

   b. Calculate its volume.

4. a. Draw four points such that they determine exactly one plane.

   b. Move one point off the plane. Draw two new planes created by this move.

5. **True or False** It is possible for a prism to have three faces that are hexagons.

In 6 and 7, use the drawings of two similar square prisms below.

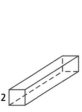

$S = 50$

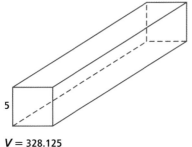

$V = 328.125$

6. Find the surface area of the larger prism.

7. Find the volume of the smaller prism.

8. Tell whether the following statement is *always, sometimes but not always,* or *never* true. The lateral faces of a prism are congruent rectangles.

9. A box of crackers is completely filled. Its dimensions are 3" by 4" by 10". A cylinder of crackers is completely filled. Its base has a diameter of 4" and its height is 9.5". Show your work.

   a. If both containers of crackers cost the same amount, which is the better value?

   b. Which container (including top and bottom) requires more material to make?

10. A jumbo granola bar comes in a container shaped like a triangular prism. It is 7.5 inches long. If the base of the container is an isosceles triangle with base 1 inch and height 0.8 inch, find the volume of the container.

11. A baseball has a radius of about 3.6 centimeters. The outer cover of a baseball is made from two equal-size pieces of leather. What is the area of each piece?

12. A farmer has 8 pigs in his pen. He wants to buy 8 more pigs, so he decides he should double the area of his pen. His current pen is enclosed by 100 feet of fencing, so the farmer reasons that he'll need 200 feet of fencing to build a new pen of the same shape. Is he correct? Explain your answer.

13. Draw a net for a box 3 meters by 5 meters by 5 meters. Label the measurement of each edge.

14. The drawing shown is a net for what figure?

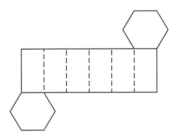

15. Draw top, front, and side views of the figure shown below.

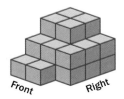

16. Draw the 3-dimensional figure shown in these 2-dimensional views.

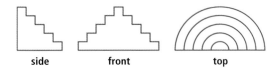

side   front   top

17. Two robots are similar in shape and made to look like humans. One robot is 3 feet tall while the other is 5 feet tall.

   a. what is the ratio of the volume of the smaller robot to the volume of the larger robot?

   b. What is the ratio of the surface area of the smaller robot to the surface area of the larger robot?

18. Draw a net for a cylindrical can of soup with diameter 4 inches and height of 6 inches.

Chapter 11

Chapter Review

SKILLS Procedures used to get answers

OBJECTIVE A Find the surface area and volume of cylinders and prisms. (Lessons 11-5, 11-6, 11-7)

1. A box is 18" high, 14" wide, and 12" deep. Find its surface area and volume.

2. Find the surface area and volume of a cube whose edges are 20 units long.

3. What is the surface area of a box with dimensions ℓ, w, and h?

4. The base of a right triangular prism has area 60 cm² and perimeter 100 cm. The height of the prism is 16 cm.

   a. Find the volume of the prism.

   b. Find the surface area of the prism.

5. Find the surface area and volume of a prism whose base is a right triangle with sides 13, 84, and 85, and whose height is 50.

6. Find the lateral surface area and volume of a 12-foot-long sewer pipe whose opening is a circle with radius 4 feet, as pictured here. Notice that both ends of the pipe are open.

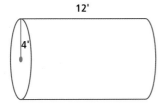

12'

4'

7. Which has more volume, a 20-cm-high cylinder with a radius of 15 cm, or a 15-cm-high cylinder with a radius of 20 cm? Explain your answer.

OBJECTIVE B Calculate the surface area and volume of a sphere. (Lesson 11-8)

In 8–11, given the radius r or the diameter d of a sphere, calculate...
a. the sphere's surface area.
b. the sphere's volume.

8. $r = 17$ cm

9. $r = 5.0 \cdot 10^{-3}$ mm

10. $d = \frac{1}{12}$ mi

11. $d = 12.4$ in.

PROPERTIES Principles behind the mathematics

OBJECTIVE C Apply properties of planes. (Lesson 11-1)

12. **True or False** Any three points determine a plane. Explain your answer.

13. **True or False** If two points lie in a plane, the line connecting the two points must lie entirely in the same plane.

14. Explain why parallel lines cannot be skew lines.

15. **Fill in the Blank** When two nonparallel planes intersect, their intersection is a ___?___.

OBJECTIVE D Apply the properties of prisms. (Lesson 11-2)

16. What three characteristics do prisms have?

17. Identify two ways in which a sphere differs from a prism.

18. Identify two ways in which a prism differs from a cylinder.

19. Draw a prism with six faces.

OBJECTIVE E From 2-dimensional views of a figure, determine properties of the 3-dimensional figure. (Lesson 11-4)

In 20–23, use these diagrams, which show views of a building.

right

front

top   front   right

20. How many stories tall is the building?

21. How long in sections is the building from front to back?

22. Draw a left-side view of the building.

23. Draw a 3-dimensional view of the building.

OBJECTIVE F Use the relationships among sides, areas, and volumes of similar figures to predict length, perimeter, area, and volume. (Lessons 11-9, 11-10)

In 24–28, the rectangular prisms are similar. Find the appropriate number.

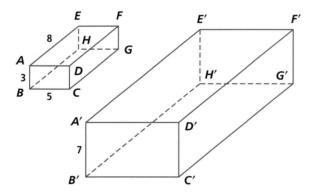

24. $A'D'$

25. area of $ABCD$

26. area of $A'B'C'D'$

27. volume of $A'B'C'D'E'F'G'H'$

28. Explain how to find the area of $A'B'C'D'$ without multiplying length and width.

29. If the length of a side of triangular prism T is three times the length of the corresponding side on a similar triangular prism P, then the volume of T is how many times the volume of P?

USES Applications of mathematics in real-world situations

OBJECTIVE G Find the volume and surface area of a rectangular solid in real-world situations. (Lesson 11-5)

30. A particular laptop computer is 1 inch high, 13.5 inches wide, and 9.5 inches deep. What is its volume?

31. How much cardboard is needed to make a rectangular box that is 30 cm high, 15 cm wide, and 6 cm deep?

32. A storage room is 12 feet high, 24 feet long, and 16 feet 9 inches wide.

    a. What is the volume of the room?

    b. If the walls and door are to be painted, how much surface will be painted?

OBJECTIVE H Find the volume and surface area of cylinders and prisms in real situations. (Lessons 11-6, 11-7)

33. A cylindrical silo has a base with diameter 25 feet and a height of 50 feet.

    a. What is its lateral area?

    b. What is its volume?

34. How much wood is contained in a cylindrical pencil 16 cm long and 6 mm in diameter if the lead is a cylinder 16 cm long and 1 mm in diameter?

35. A ruler is in the shape of a triangular prism, as shown below. If the ruler is 0.8″ high and its base is 1″ wide, then what is its volume?

OBJECTIVE I Use the formulas for the surface area and volume of a sphere in real-world situations. (Lesson 11-8)

36. What is the surface area of a basketball with a diameter of about 9.5 inches?

In 37 and 38, use the fact that the radius of the Sun is about 7×10^5 km.

37. What is its approximate surface area?

38. What is its approximate volume?

39. What is the volume of a bowling ball with diameter 8.55 inches?

OBJECTIVE J Use relationships among sides, areas, and volumes of similar figures in real-world situations. (Lessons 11-9, 11-10)

40. A diameter of a basketball is 25 cm. A diameter of a soccer ball is 22 cm.

    a. Find the ratio of their volumes.

    b. Find the ratio of their surface areas.

41. Jenny is making a miniature stop sign. She wants to make it exactly one-third the area of a regular octagonal stop sign that is 30 inches tall, how tall will her miniature stop sign be?

42. Ari is running on a circular track that encloses twice the area of the track that Tani is running on. Ari tells Tani that she has to run around her track twice as many times as Ari's in order to run the same distance. Is Ari right? Why or why not?

REPRESENTATIONS Pictures, graphs, or objects that illustrate concepts

OBJECTIVE K Draw and identify nets of prisms and cylinders. (Lesson 11-3)

43. Draw a net of a box 2 meters by 9 meters by 6.5 meters. Label each measurement.

44. Draw a net for this cylinder.

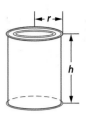

In 45–47, refer to this net.

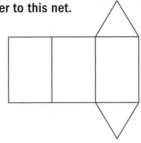

45. What type of prism will the net make?

46. Draw the prism.

47. Draw a second net for the prism.

48. Draw a cube.

49. Draw a pentagonal prism.

OBJECTIVE L Give views of a figure from the top, side, or front. (Lesson 11-4)

50. Draw the front, top, and side views of a school bus.

51. Draw an object that has the same view from the front, top, and sides.

52. Draw an object that has the same view from the front and top, but a different view from the side.

53. Draw the top, side, and front view of this object.

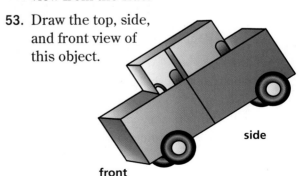

side

front

Chapter

12

Statistics and Variability

Contents

Statistics describe data that vary. People collect data for many reasons:

- to satisfy curiosity and learn about some area of interest;
- to have an historical record and make wise decisions based on what has happened in the past;
- to support a point of view;
- to compare what happens when something is done in different ways;
- to predict what might happen in the future;
- to discover relationships among quantities;
- to determine the best course of action.

The forms in which data are represented can help you to do all these things.

The table in the next column shows the number of babies (in thousands) born in the United States from 1964 to 2003.

Year	Births	Year	Births	Year	Births	Year	Births
1964	4,027	1974	3,160	1984	3,669	1994	3,953
1965	3,760	1975	3,144	1985	3,761	1995	3,900
1966	3,606	1976	3,168	1986	3,757	1996	3,891
1967	3,521	1977	3,327	1987	3,809	1997	3,881
1968	3,502	1978	3,333	1988	3,910	1998	3,942
1969	3,571	1979	3,494	1989	4,041	1999	3,959
1970	3,731	1980	3,612	1990	4,158	2000	4,059
1971	3,556	1981	3,629	1991	4,111	2001	4,026
1972	3,258	1982	3,681	1992	4,065	2002	4,022
1973	3,137	1983	3,639	1993	4,000	2003	4,090

The time-series graph of the ordered pairs (year, births) on the next page shows the change over time. The box plot to its right shows how much the numbers of births have varied over the years.

Births in the United States 1964–2003

Data like these help us know whether new schools need to be built, whether we can expect greater use of energy in the future, and how much food we will need to sustain the population. When we do not have appropriate and accurate statistics, we are more likely to make unwise decisions.

Look at the data in the table and graph. What are some things that you notice about the trends in U.S. births?

739

Lesson

12-1

Representing Categorical Data

Vocabulary

sample

data set

sample size

categorical data

▶ **BIG IDEA** Some bar graphs and circle graphs can distort the categorical data that they display.

The set of things about which you collect data is called a **sample.** The information you collect is called a **data set.** The size of the data set is called the **sample size.** For example, suppose there are 22 students in your class. If you find the eye color of the students in your class, then the sample is your class, the data set is the eye colors of the students in your class, and the sample size is 22.

When Do People Collect Data?

When people choose a sample to collect data, it is because there is some sort of *uncertainty* about the data. If you are sure of the data, then there is no need to collect them.

You would not ask students in your class whether they have a nose or whether they woke up this morning. But you might collect data on what color their eyes are or how much sleep they got last night. Rarely do all students in a class have the same eye color or sleep the same length of time each night. Data vary.

 QY1

Choosing a Data Representation

The type of data you have determines the possible ways to display them. When you ask people what their eye color is, the answers are sorted into categories. Data that can be sorted in this way are called **categorical data.** If you are collecting categorical data, you should make sure that every response falls into exactly one category.

 QY2

When the sample size is small, such as the 22 students in your class, you can list all the data. But if the sample size is large, data need to be summarized and displayed. Even if you knew the eye colors of everyone in a town or city, you could not list them. Most people would use percents to describe the number of people with "blue," "brown," or "green" eyes, and they would display the data in a graph.

Mental Math

Calculate.

a. $5 + 6 + 7 + 8 + 9$

b. $50 + 60 + 70 + 80 + 90$

c. $55 + 66 + 77 + 88 + 99$

d. $550 + 660 + 770 + 880 + 990$

▶ **QY1**

Multiple Choice Which of these varies?

  A the number of seconds in a minute

  B the number of minutes in an hour

  C the number of hours in a day

  D the number of days in a year

▶ **QY2**

You ask people what their favorite movie of all time is.

  a. What categories might you have?

  b. Why might there be a problem with any categories you might pick?

The table at the right shows the average amount of time per day that adults in the United States spent on various activities in 2005.

The two circle graphs at the right below represent the data in the table. The graph at the bottom is a 3-dimensional view of the circle graph at the top. The angled view in the 3-dimensional graph changes the angle measures of the sectors and distorts the areas of the sectors of the circle.

Activity	Hours
Personal Care (including Sleeping)	9.43
Eating and Drinking	1.24
Household Activities	1.82
Working and Work-Related Activities	3.69
Leisure and Sports	5.14
Other	2.68

Source: Bureau of Labor Statistics

Activity

Step 1 Use the table to calculate the percent of hours per day spent on each type of activity.

Step 2 **a.** Use a protractor to measure the angles at the center of the upper circle graph.

b. Do the angle measures agree with the percent you calculated in Step 1?

Step 3 Repeat Step 2 for the lower graph.

Step 4 **a.** If you want to argue that people in the United States do not spend much time on leisure and sports, which graph would you choose?

b. If you want to argue that people spend too much time eating and drinking, which graph would you choose?

Step 5 Explain how the lower graph has distorted the data.

Hours per day spent on activities, 2005 average

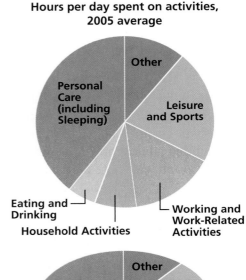

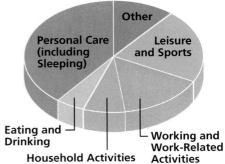

In the Activity, you saw that a view of a graph can cause it to be distorted. The graphs on the next page show a different type of distortion of the same data. The bar graph on the left is not distorted. On the right, the vertical scale of the bar graph is truncated so that it starts at 1 instead of 0. This causes the ratios of the lengths of the bars to be different from the ratios of the numbers in the data.

Representing Categorical Data   **741**

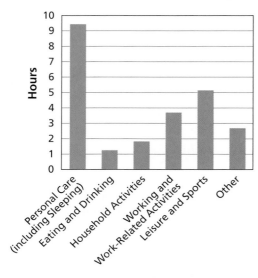

Hours per Day Spent on Activities, 2005 Average

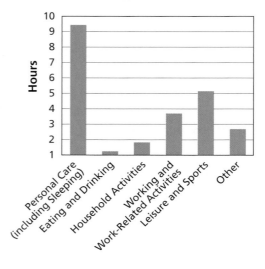

Hours per Day Spent on Activities, 2005 Average

Many published graphs have these and other distortions. For this reason, it is always important to examine the numbers being graphed. Do not let your eyes be influenced by the display. In examining a bar graph, look closely at the scale. In interpreting a circle graph, calculate percents if they are not shown.

Questions

COVERING THE IDEAS

In 1–4, use this information: Students in a class were given an assignment to cut out a triangle that would fit on their desk.
a. Tell whether it would be sensible to collect the given information.
b. Tell whether the data would be categorical or not.

1. the areas of the triangles

2. the sums of the measures of the angles of the triangles

3. whether the triangles were acute, right, or obtuse

4. the measures of the longest side in the triangles

5. Consider the U.S. time-usage data shown in the two bar graphs above. Let n = the amount of time spent on household activities. Let m = the amount of time spent eating and drinking.
   a. Calculate $\frac{m}{n}$ to the nearest hundredth.
   b. What is the ratio of the lengths of the bars that represent m and n in the left bar graph?
   c. What is the ratio of the lengths of the bars that represent m and n in the right bar graph?

d. Which ratio is closer to the answer to Part a?

e. What incorrect conclusion might a person make from this distortion?

APPLYING THE MATHEMATICS

In 6 and 7, use the table below, showing the percent of the U.S. population that was foreign born in various years.

Year	1900	1920	1940	1960	1980	2000
Percentage	13.6	13.2	8.8	5.4	6.2	10.4

Source: U.S. Census Bureau

Each year, more than 450,000 immigrants become U.S. citizens during naturalization ceremonies across the country.

Source: U.S. Citizenship and Immigration Services

6. Make a bar graph of these data.

7. Why is it inappropriate to make a circle graph of these data?

In 8–11, use the table from Questions 6 and 7. A person displays the percents of the U.S. population that were foreign born in 1960 and 2000. Examine the display. Does it distort the data? If so, how? If not, why do you think it does not distort the data?

8.

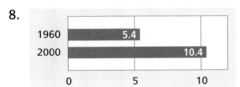

9.

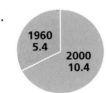

10.

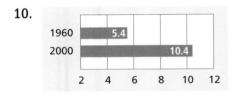

11.

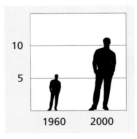

12. Here is a circle graph, viewed on an angle, of favorite colors of 232 people (both adults and children). Does the view distort the data? If so, in what way?

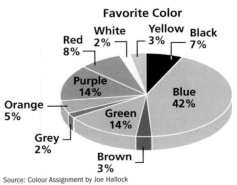

Favorite Color

Source: Colour Assignment by Joe Hallock

13. This bar graph displays the results of a 2004 telephone survey of more than 2,800 people who bought watermelon. Survey participants gave their reasons for buying watermelons.

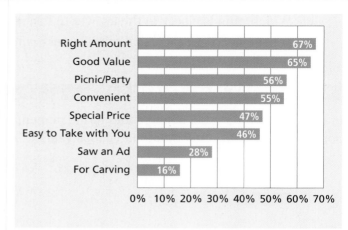

   a. Suppose a person made the bars in the bar graph vertical rather than horizontal. Would that distort the data? If so, why? If not, why not?

   b. Suppose a person deleted the "Picnic/Party" and "Saw an Ad" bars from the graph. Would that distort the data? Why or why not?

   Source: National Watermelon Promotion Board

   c. Suppose a person put these data into a circle graph with eight sectors. Would that distort the data? Why or why not?

REVIEW

14. Jenna needs a larger storage box for her sweaters. If she can fit 5 sweaters in the box she has, how many would she be able to fit in a new box with each dimension double the original? (Assume her sweaters are all the same size.) **(Lesson 11-10)**

15. The equatorial radius of Mars is 3,396 kilometers. Assume Mars is a sphere and calculate its surface area. **(Lesson 11-8)**

The radius of Earth is 6,378 km, nearly twice that of Mars.

Source: National Aeronautics and Space Administration

16. Which is larger: the volume of a cylinder with a base diameter d and height h or the volume of a box with a square base diagonal d and height h?

17. The sum of the integers 1 through n is given by the formula $S = \frac{n(n + 1)}{2}$.

   a. Graph the formula.

   b. Explain what the point (7, 28) on the graph represents. **(Lesson 10-8)**

18. In 2004, Joliet, Illinois, had a population of 129,519, while Las Vegas, Nevada, had a population of 534,847. Compare the populations (Joliet to Las Vegas and Las Vegas to Joliet), writing the answers as percents. **(Lesson 9-6)**

EXPLORATION

19. Copy a graph from a newspaper or magazine or print a graph from the Internet that you think distorts data in some way. Indicate why you think the graph distorts data.

QY ANSWERS

1. D

2. Answers vary. Sample:
   a. drama, action, comedy
   b. There could be overlap, so some movies may be both action and comedy.

Lesson
12-2
Histograms and Stem-and-Leaf Plots

Vocabulary

interval data

histogram

stem-and-leaf plot

stem

leaf

mode

range

▶ **BIG IDEA**   Interval data are most commonly displayed in histograms and are sometimes explored using stem-and-leaf plots.

It is relatively easy to describe categorical data. Suppose you ask people to tell you their favorite team, favorite color, or favorite singer. It is rather easy to summarize their responses. You can use a table, a circle graph, or a bar graph.

Temperature, income, distance, and many other types of data are examples of *interval data*. **Interval data** are data that are represented by measures or scale values. With interval data, there are too many different possible values to be individually graphed. For example, if you wanted to know the incomes of 20 people, you might get 20 different values. It would not help to create a circle graph with 20 different sectors or a bar graph with 20 bars. Data such as these are often put into intervals in order to make sense of them. Two types of graphs used for interval data are *histograms* and *stem-and-leaf plots*.

Histograms

A **histogram** is a special type of bar graph. It displays frequencies or relative frequencies in which the data are sorted into disjoint intervals and represented by bars placed next to each other.

Mental Math

a. Name six different numbers whose mean is 7.

b. Find the mean of {12, 14, 15, 11, 16, 10}.

c. If you score 74, 76, 78, and 80 on your first four tests, and you want the mean of your scores to be at least 80, what must you score on your fifth test?

d. What is the mean of a, $2a$, and $3a$?

Example 1

The test scores of 20 students were 80, 83, 91, 77, 65, 44, 93, 97, 62, 77, 84, 86, 88, 71, 92, 80, 84, 98, 79, and 69. Show the data in a histogram.

Solution

1. Decide how you want to split the data. Look for the minimum and maximum values. The minimum value is 44. The maximum value is 98. A convenient interval would be ten: $40 \leq x < 50$ for one bar, $50 \leq x < 60$ for the second bar, and so on. Notice that the right endpoint is not included on the interval. So, for example, a data value of 50 would belong to only the second interval.

(continued on next page)

2. Count to determine the length of each bar. The only score in the interval $40 \le x < 50$ is 44. There are no scores in the 50s. There are three scores in the interval $60 \le x < 70$, four in $70 \le x < 80$, seven in $80 \le x < 90$, and five in $90 \le x < 100$. The resulting histogram is shown at the right.

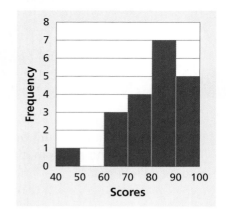

Notice two key characteristics of a histogram.

(1) There is a numerical axis on which the bars are placed.

(2) Frequencies or relative frequencies are measured on the other axis.

Many graphing calculators can display data as a histogram.

Activity

Use the following steps to make a histogram of the scores in Example 1. Your calculator may use slightly different steps.

Step 1 Clear all lists and enter the data into list L1.

Step 2 Press [2nd] [STAT PLOT] and make sure plots 2 and 3 are turned off. Turn on Plot1, and select the histogram type (the third icon on the top row).

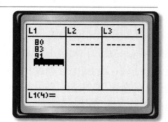

Step 3 Enter L1 as the Xlist to be graphed if it is not already selected.

Step 4 Select the frequency to be 1 if it is not already set to 1.

Step 5 Set up the viewing window to include all of the data. Note that the "Xscl" number determines the width of the intervals for each bar.

Step 6 Display the graph, and compare it to the graph in Example 1.

Stem-and-Leaf Plots

A **stem-and-leaf plot** is a display of every element of a numerical data set of numbers that are about the same size. To make a stem-and-leaf plot, you split each number at a specific decimal place. Depending on how much the data vary, 682 might be split as 6|82 or 68|2. The digits to the left of the vertical line form the **stem.** The digits to the right form the **leaf.** The main idea in this kind of display is that the stem is written only once, while the leaves are listed every time they appear. For instance, if both 682 and 683 appear and are split as 68|2 and 68|3, then you would write 68|2 3. If you made the split 6|82 and 6|83, then you would write 6|82 83.

One way to tell how difficult it might be to read a story is to look at the length of sentences in it. This is measured by the number of words in a sentence. The novel *The Adventures of Tom Sawyer* by Mark Twain was written for boys and girls. So it should be expected to have sentences of short length. Does it?

Example 2

The lengths of the first 40 sentences in Chapter 1 of *The Adventures of Tom Sawyer* are:

1, 2, 1, 2, 7, 2, 2, 24, 44, 20, 10, 30, 6, 9, 24, 2, 14, 2, 28, 1,
7, 6, 1, 1, 4, 5, 4, 4, 9, 14, 4, 10, 1, 4, 12, 15, 14, 8, 19, 9

a. Describe this set of numbers with a stem-and-leaf plot.

b. What does the display show?

Solution

a. A natural place to split the numbers is between the tens and ones. Think of a 1-digit number as having the digit 0 in the tens place. Because the greatest number is 44, which will be split as 4|4, the greatest possible stem is 4. List the possible stems in a vertical column.

```
0 |
1 |
2 |
3 |
4 |
```

"We could use up two Eternities in learning all that is to be learned about our own world and the thousands of nations that have arisen and flourished and vanished from it. Mathematics alone would occupy me eight million years." from Mark Twain's Notebook #22, Spring 1883–Sept. 1884

Now put the leaves into the display. The first value, 1, is treated as 01, 2 as 02, and so on, for the 1-digit numbers. For 24, a 4 goes to the right of the bar in the 2 row. For 44, a 4 goes to the right of the bar in the 4 row.

For 20, a 0 goes in the same row as 24. Proceed in this manner until all 40 values have been entered. Here is the finished display.

```
0 | 1 2 1 2 7 2 2 6 9 2 2 1 7 6 1 1 4 5 4 4 9 4 1 4 8 9
1 | 0 4 4 0 2 5 4 9
2 | 4 0 4 8
3 | 0
4 | 4
```

b. The display shows that shorter sentences are much more common. There are 26 sentences with fewer than 10 words. There are only 5 sentences with 20 or more words.

Stem-and-leaf plots were developed in the 1960s by John Tukey, a professor of statistics at Princeton University. Because stem-and-leaf plots are relatively new and this kind of display is primarily used to explore data, newspapers and magazines do not often use them to report data. But they are helpful in the study of some numerical information.

Why Is a Stem-and-Leaf Plot Useful?

Notice that the stem-and-leaf plot resembles a horizontal bar graph. But the stem-and-leaf plot shows all the original values. So you can gather more information about the sentence lengths from a stem-and-leaf plot than from a bar graph.

For example, the **mode** of a collection of objects is the object that appears most often. The stem-and-leaf plot shows six 1s and six 2s with the stem 0. No other leaf appears as often in a single stem. So the modes are 1 and 2. More sentences are 1 or 2 words long than any other length. From the stem-and-leaf plot, you can also identify the **range** of the data. This is the difference of the greatest and least numbers, $44 - 1$, or 43.

Questions

COVERING THE IDEAS

In 1–3, tell whether or not the data would be appropriate for a histogram.

1. a survey of eye color
2. a poll of people's favorite songs
3. a study of time to recover from knee surgery

In 4–6, refer to the histogram of Example 1. If the question can be answered using only the graph, then answer it. If not, indicate why.

4. If a score of 60 is passing, how many students passed?

5. How many more students scored in the 80s than in the 90s?

6. What was the mean score?

7. Here are the number of words in the first 40 sentences of the last chapter of *The Adventures of Tom Sawyer*:
   22, 12, 23, 39, 11, 59, 9, 23, 23, 19, 29, 9, 16, 90, 25, 9, 15, 41, 37, 39, 61, 14, 12, 17, 28, 26, 27, 18, 11, 2, 5, 11, 9, 13, 97, 10, 7, 28, 6, 6
   a. Create a stem-and-leaf plot from these data.
   b. Compare the stem-and-leaf plot you created in Part a with the plot in Example 2 . One of these chapters begins with Tom and his friend Huck talking to each other. Can you tell from the stem-and-leaf plot which chapter that is? Why or why not?

8. **a.** Create a histogram from the data of Example 2, using bars of interval 5.

   b. Why would using bars of width 5 be inappropriate for a histogram of the data for Question 7?

APPLYING THE MATHEMATICS

9. Here are the batting averages of the players with the highest batting average in the National League for each season from 1970 to 2006.

   1970s: .366, .363, .333, .338, .353, .354, .339, .338, .334, .344

   1980s: .324, .341, .331, .323, .351, .353, .334, .370, .313, .336

   1990s: .335, .319, .330, .370, .394, .368, .353, .372, .363, .379

   2000s: .372, .350, .370, .359, .362, .335, .344

   Source: The World Almanac and Book of Facts, 2007

   Tony Gwynn played 20 years for the San Diego Padres and had the highest batting average in the National League from 1984 to 1997. He was inducted into the National Baseball Hall of Fame in 2007.

   a. Put these data into a stem-and-leaf plot.

   b. What is the mode of the data?

   c. What is the range of the data?

   d. Is it true that a batting average of .350 would be the highest batting average most years?

   e. Use the stem-and-leaf plot to display the data in a histogram with bars representing .310–.319, .320–.329, and so on.

10. The great-great-grandparents of one of the authors of this book had 9 children and 53 grandchildren. An approximate year of birth is known for 47 of the grandchildren. Here are their birth years:

   1848, 1852, 1855, 1846, 1848, 1850, 1855, 1864, 1865, 1871, 1876, 1880, 1885, 1866, 1870, 1871, 1872, 1881, 1884, 1887, 1872, 1879, 1882, 1885, 1860, 1864, 1867, 1869, 1871, 1873, 1881, 1883, 1879, 1880, 1884, 1890, 1893, 1821, 1884, 1892, 1895, 1898, 1881, 1893, 1896, 1900, 1902

   a. Put these data into a stem-and-leaf plot.

   b. What is the mode of the data?

   c. What is the range of the data?

   d. If a grandfather of these grandchildren was born in 1805, how long would he have had to live to see the birth of the 25th of these grandchildren?

   e. Use the stem-and-leaf plot to display the data in a histogram with bars representing decades.

11. In 2004, the 50 movies that had the largest box-office gross
   sales in the United States ranged from a gross total of $436.7
   million to a gross total of $58.1 million. Here are the amounts
   grossed by these movies, in millions of dollars.
   436.7, 373.4, 370.3, 251.7, 249.4, 186.7, 176.1, 162.5, 160.8, 155.1,
   154.5, 144.8, 133.3, 120.8, 120.1, 119.1, 114.3, 114.2, 110.2, 107.0,
   100.2, 95.2, 94.6, 88.2, 87.9, 86.6, 86.1, 84.3, 84.2, 81.9, 81.0, 80.3,
   77.9, 77.1, 75.4, 73.9, 73.1, 71.6, 69.1, 67.3, 66.6, 66.2, 66.0, 65.1,
   64.4, 61.2, 59.5, 59.0, 58.9, 58.1
   Source: *Variety*

   a. Put these data into a histogram with intervals of width
      $50 million.

   b. Put these data into a histogram with intervals of width
      $100 million.

   c. Which histogram does a better job of displaying the data?

REVIEW

12. Karen surveyed students to find out why they took an art class
    at her college. The bar graph below shows the results.

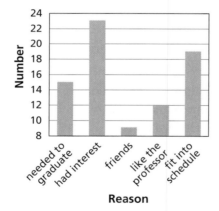

    Why is Karen's graph misleading? (**Lesson 12-1**)

13. Softball sizes are based on the circumference of the ball.
    Raphael argued that because a 16-in. ball is $\frac{4}{3}$ the size of a
    12-in. ball, the volume of the 16-in. ball is $\frac{4}{3}$ the volume of the
    12-in. ball.

    a. Prove or disprove his claim by calculating the two volumes.

    b. A roller hockey ball has a circumference of 23 cm. Is the
       volume of 12-inch softball more or less than $\frac{4}{3}$ of the volume of
       the roller hockey ball? (**Lessons 11-10, 11-8**)

14. Josefina bought two cylindrical cans of vegetables that had the same height but different-size bases. The diameter of the base of one can was half as much as the diameter of the other. If the larger can had a volume of 200π cubic centimeters, what was the volume of the smaller can? **(Lessons 11-9, 11-7)**

15. It takes Ericka 10 minutes to write a holiday card and 15 minutes to write a letter. She has 2 hours of free time. **(Lesson 10-3)**
    a. Write an inequality to describe the number of cards and letters Ericka can write.
    b. Graph the solutions to the inequality.

16. Rasheed and Crystal are earning money for a trip to Australia. Rasheed starts with $400 and earns $75 a week, while Crystal starts with $600 and earns $50 a week. After how many weeks will they have the same amount of money? **(Lesson 10-2)**

17. a. What is the winning percentage of a team that has won 13 of 30 games? (Give your answer as a decimal to three places.)
    b. If a team has a winning percentage of .300 and has played 30 games, how many games has it lost?
    c. If a team has won 20 games and has a winning percentage of .400, how many games has it played? **(Lesson 9-6)**

EXPLORATION

18. a. Find a histogram in a newspaper or magazine. Either cut it out or copy it.
    b. Does the histogram you found use intervals of the same width or of different widths?
    c. Summarize what the histogram tells about the data it displays.

Lesson 12-3

Properties of the Mean

Match the double inequality to the appropriate situation.

i. $63 < x < 78$

ii. $63 \leq x \leq 78$

iii. $63 \leq x < 78$

iv. $63 < x \leq 78$

a. On Saturday, there will be a high of 78 degrees and a low of 63 degrees. x is Saturday's temperature.

b. The school bus can hold as many as 78 students, teachers, and parents. There are 63 students on the bus who must be accompanied by at least one adult. x is the number of people on the bus.

c. A car was traveling between 63 and 78 miles per hour on the highway. x is the speed of the car.

d. There are at least 63 types of equipment in a hardware store, but fewer than 78. x is the number of types of equipment.

> ▶ **BIG IDEA** The mean (or average) of a data set is related to the sum of the numbers in the data set and is a balance point for the data set.

The Mean of 2, 3, and n Numbers

As you know, to find the mean of two numbers, you add them and divide the sum by 2. So, if the numbers are a and b and the mean is m, then

$$m = \frac{a + b}{2}.$$

For example, sometimes people average the high and low temperatures at a location on a particular day to estimate the mean temperature for the day. In January in Duluth, Minnesota, a typical high temperature is 18°F and a typical low temperature is –1°F. The mean of these numbers is

$$m = \frac{18 + (-1)}{2} = 8.5°F.$$

Notice that $2 \cdot 8.5 = 17$, the sum of the two temperatures.

To find the mean of three numbers, you add them and divide the sum by 3. If the numbers are a, b, and c, then

$$m = \frac{a + b + c}{3}.$$

For example, bowlers typically bowl 3 games in a match. If a bowler scores 153, 128, and 191 in the three games, then

$$m = \frac{153 + 128 + 191}{3} = \frac{472}{3} = 157.\overline{3}.$$

Notice that $3 \cdot 157.\overline{3} = 472$, the sum of the three scores.

To find the mean of 4 numbers, you add them and divide by 4. To find the mean of 5 numbers, you add them and divide by 5. There is a pattern that you can see from this. To find the mean of n numbers, add them and divide by n.

Example 1

Mykia has scored 86, 83, 91, and 75 on the first four tests in a class. What score does she need on the fifth test to average 85 for all five tests?

Solution The mean of five numbers is given by the sum of the five numbers, divided by 5. Here, four of the five values are known. **Let s stand for the fifth test score and m stand for the mean.**

$$m = \frac{86 + 83 + 91 + 75 + s}{5}$$

We know that Mykia's goal is to average 85, so substitute that value for *m*.

$$85 = \frac{86 + 83 + 91 + 75 + s}{5}$$

$$85 = \frac{335 + s}{5}$$

$$5 \cdot 85 = 335 + s$$

$$425 = 335 + s$$

$$90 = s$$

Mykia needs a score of 90 on the fifth test.

Check Enter the five scores into list **L1** on your calculator. Use the "mean" command to calculate the mean of the scores. The mean is 85. It checks.

Means and Sums

Start with the general formula for the mean of *n* numbers.

$$m = \frac{\text{sum of } n \text{ numbers}}{n}$$

Multiply both sides by *n*.

$$mn = \text{sum of } n \text{ numbers}$$

On the left side is the product of the mean and the number of numbers. On the right side is the sum of the numbers. This is a useful general property of means.

Means and Sums Property

In a collection of *n* numbers, the product of the mean of the numbers and *n* is the sum of the numbers.

▶ **QY1**

If you score a total of *P* points on *t* tests, what is your average score?

STOP QY1

In Example 1, the mean of the five numbers is 85, so the sum of the numbers must be 5 · 85, or 425.

Finding the Mean from a Display

You can sometimes find the mean of a data set from a display of the data.

Example 2

The bar graph below displays the frequencies of various numbers of children for the 42 U.S. presidents from George Washington to George W. Bush.

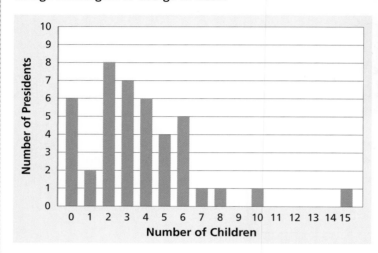

Woodrow Wilson had three daughters with his first wife, Ellen Louise Axson. After her death he remarried but had no additional children.

What is the mean number of children of a U.S. president?

Solution The mean is the total number of children divided by the number of presidents. From each bar we can obtain a number of children. For example, the bar above 6 tells us that 5 presidents had 6 children, so there are 5 · 6, or 30, children represented by that bar. Repeating this idea with every bar, the mean number of children is

$$\frac{6 \cdot 0 + 2 \cdot 1 + 8 \cdot 2 + 7 \cdot 3 + 6 \cdot 4 + 4 \cdot 5 + 5 \cdot 6 + 1 \cdot 7 + 1 \cdot 8 + 1 \cdot 10 + 1 \cdot 15}{42}$$

$$= \frac{153}{42} \approx 3.64.$$

A Geometric Property of the Mean

Here are the scores of ten students on a quiz: 100, 100, 100, 100, 90, 60, 60, 60, 50, 50. The sum of the scores is 770, so the mean is 77.

The dot plot shown at the right illustrates the distribution of scores on a number line.

If you placed equal weights on the number line for each score, the number line would balance at 77. The balance occurs because the sum of the distances from the dots to the mean on one side equals the sum of the distances from the dots to the mean on the other side.

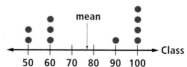

QY2

Balance Property of the Mean

Let m be the mean of a set of numbers. Then the sum of the distances to m from the numbers greater than m in the set equals the sum of the distances to m from the numbers less than m in the set.

▶ **QY2**

Use the quiz scores on the previous page. For each side of the mean, find the sum of the distances from the dots to the mean.

Example 3

Use the Balance Property of the Mean to answer the question in Example 1.

Solution The mean of the 5 numbers 86, 83, 91, 75, and s is 85. The numbers less than the mean are 83 and 75. Their distances from 85 are $85 - 83 = 2$ and $85 - 75 = 10$. The sum of these distances is $2 + 10$, or 12.

The numbers greater than the mean are 86 and 91. Their distances from 85 are $86 - 85 = 1$ and $91 - 85 = 6$. The sum of these distances is $1 + 6$, or 7.

These two sums need to be equal. Since $12 - 7 = 5$, we need another number greater than the mean and 5 away from it. So $s = 85 + 5 = 90$.

Questions

COVERING THE IDEAS

In 1–6, give the mean of the collection of values.

1. $102°$ and $71°$

2. 7, 8, 9, 10, 11, 12, 13

3. a, b, c

4. s, t, u, v

5. 50, x

6. 3 scores of 80 and 4 scores of 73

7. Dena ate $\frac{1}{2}$ of a sandwich one day, $\frac{2}{3}$ of a sandwich the next, and $\frac{1}{3}$ of a sandwich on a third day. On average, what fraction of a sandwich did she eat each day?

8. A class of 24 students took a survey of how many rooms were in each student's residence. The mean number of rooms was exactly 8.

   a. What was the total number of rooms in the residences?

   b. If the greatest number of rooms was 11 and the least number of rooms was 3, draw a possible bar graph of the numbers of rooms in the residences.

   c. State the median and the mode of the distribution in your bar graph for Part b.

9. Use the bar graph in Example 2. John Tyler, the 10th U.S. president, had the most children of any U.S. president through 2008.

   a. How many children did he have?
   b. If he and his children were removed from the frequency distribution in Example 2, what would be the new mean number of children of U.S. presidents?

10. The bar graph at the right displays a frequency distribution of the number of daughters of the 42 U.S. presidents. What is the mean number of daughters?

11. Ishi has a mean score of 57 on the first five of six tests she must take this semester. She wants to know what she has to score on the last test to average 60 for all six tests.

    a. Answer Ishi's question by solving an equation.
    b. Answer Ishi's question by calculating distances from the mean.

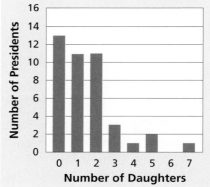

APPLYING THE MATHEMATICS

12. Let m be the mean of the measures of the three angles of a triangle.

    a. What is the greatest possible value of m?
    b. What is the least possible value of m?

13. Give an example of a data set of five different numbers whose mean is negative and whose mode is positive.

14. The mean of a and b is 45. The mean of a, b, and c is 48. What is the value of c?

REVIEW

In 15 and 16, use the histogram at the right, showing the heights of 32 students in Mr. Gauss's science class.

15. Within which interval is the value of the mode found? (**Lesson 12-2**)

16. **True or False** There are more students taller than 5'2" than there are shorter than 4'10". (**Lesson 12-2**)

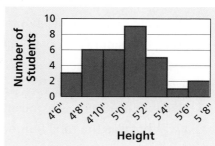

17. The following are elevations of summits (in feet) in the Presidential Range of the White Mountains in New Hampshire: 6,288; 5,712; 5,375; 5,584; 4,902; 5,249; 5,774; 5,492; 5,394; 5,532; 5,367; 5,089. Create a stem-and-leaf plot representing these data using a 2-digit stem. (**Lesson 12-2**)

18. Explain what it means if data are classified as categorical. (**Lesson 12-1**)

In 19 and 20, a sphere has a radius of x, a surface area of A, and a volume V. A second sphere has a radius of $5x$.

19. What is the volume of the second sphere? (**Lessons 11-10, 11-8**)

20. What is the surface area of the second sphere? (**Lessons 11-9, 11-8**)

In 21 and 22, solve. (**Lesson 10-4**)

21. $8f + 6.1 \geq -14f - 11.9$ 22. $0.06p - 4 < 0.05p + 26$

Multiple Choice For 23–25, use the choices below. What part of the indicated quadrant is covered by the graph of $y > 0.5x + 2$? (**Lesson 10-3**)

A   a bounded region of the quadrant

B   none of the quadrant

C   an unbounded region, but not all, of the quadrant

D   the entire quadrant

23. Quadrant I   24. Quadrant II   25. Quadrant IV

26. Dimitri is conducting an experiment to discover how hot a half-gallon of water gets when it boils with different amounts of salt dissolved in it. His results are shown in the table at the right. The temperature is rounded to the nearest degree.

Tablespoons of Salt	Boiling Temperature (°F)
0	212
1	214
2	215
3	217
4	218
5	220
6	221

a. Is there a pattern here? If so, describe the pattern using words or variables. (**Lesson 2-1**)

b. Create a scatterplot of this data on your graphing utility. (**Lesson 1-10**)

c. Is there a line that exactly fits these points? If not, is there a line that fits near these points? Experiment with your graphing utility and write the equation for such a line. (**Lesson 8-7**)

d. Suppose the formula for the temperature y to boil x ounces of water in Dimitri's kettle is of the form $y = ax + b$. Explain why Dimitri would not get the results in the table. (**Lesson 3-4**)

EXPLORATION

27. Let y be the mean of the integers from 1 to x. For instance, when $x = 2$, $y = \dfrac{1 + 2}{2} = 1.5$.

a. Graph the ordered pairs (x, y) for all values of x from 1 to 10.

b. Use your answer to Part a to find an expression for the mean of the integers from 1 to n.

QY ANSWERS

1. $\dfrac{P}{t}$

2. 105

Lesson

12-4

Deviations from the Mean

Vocabulary

measures of spread

mean absolute deviation
 (m.a.d.)

deviation

absolute deviation

▶ **BIG IDEA** The *mean absolute deviation* is a measure that indicates by how much data in a data set differs from the mean of the data set.

Here are the scores of the ten students mentioned in Lesson 12-3 and ten students from another class who took the same quiz.

The sum of the scores in each class is 770 and there are ten students in each class, so the mean of the scores in each class is 77.

Class 1	Class 2
100	100
100	90
100	90
100	85
90	80
60	75
60	70
60	70
50	60
50	50

Mental Math

Name a number that is 70 when rounded to the nearest ten, is divisible by 2 and 3, and whose digits added together make a perfect square.

Measures of Spread

Based on the mean, you might suppose that each class performed at about the same level. However, you can tell by looking at the table that the scores that contributed to each mean were very different. The dot plots at right illustrate the distribution of scores in each class.

The scores of Class 1 seem to be a little more spread out than the scores of Class 2. They vary from the mean a little more.

Quantities that measure the degree of variation in data are called **measures of spread.** One measure of spread is the *range* of a set of numbers. The range of a set of scores is the difference between the highest and lowest score. In both classes, the range is 100 − 50, or 50.

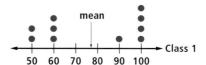

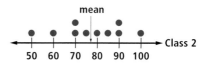

The Mean Absolute Deviation

Even though their means and ranges are equal, the distributions of scores in Classes 1 and 2 are quite different. Most of the scores in Class 1 are either much higher or much lower than the mean. In contrast, most of the scores in Class 2 are closer to the mean. A measure of spread that shows the difference between these distributions is called the **mean absolute deviation,** abbreviated **m.a.d.** Here is how to calculate the mean absolute deviation.

Activity

In this Activity, you will find the mean absolute deviation for the scores of Class 1. As its name suggests, you will calculate deviations, absolute deviations, and the mean of the absolute deviations.

Step 1	Calculate the mean of the scores of Class 1.
Step 2	Subtract the mean from each number in the distribution. This is the number's **deviation.** For example, the deviation of the first score is $100 - 77 = 23$.
Step 3	Take the absolute value of each number from Step 2. This is called the **absolute deviation.**
Step 4	Take the mean of the numbers found in Step 3. This is the mean absolute deviation. Compare your answer with those of other members in your class.

For large sets of data, calculating the mean absolute deviation by hand can be very time-consuming. A spreadsheet or graphing calculator can make the calculations much easier.

Example

Calculate the mean absolute deviation for the scores of Class 2.

Solution The steps you take to find the mean absolute deviation are almost the same whether you input the data into a spreadsheet or a calculator list.

Step	Spreadsheet	List
1. Organize the data.	After naming column A in cell A2, enter the 10 scores in cells A3 through 12.	Enter the 10 scores into L1, the first list on your calculator.
2. Calculate the mean.	Enter the formula "=average(A3:A12)" into cell A14 to find the mean. It is 77. Copy the mean into cells B3 through B12.	On the HOME screen enter mean (L1). It is 77.
3. Calculate the deviation of each value from the mean.	Enter the formula "=A3-B3" in cell C3 and copy down to C12 to complete the column.	Enter L1 − 77 in place of L2 at the top of the LIST screen. L2 will contain the deviations.
4. Find the absolute value of each deviation.	Recall that "abs(x)" is the calculator and computer symbol for absolute value of x. Enter "=abs(C3)" in cell D3 and copy down.	Enter abs (L2) for L3.
5. Calculate the mean absolute deviation.	Enter "=average(D3:D12)" into cell D14 to find the mean of the absolute deviations in column D. It is 12.	On the HOME screen, enter mean (L3). It is 12.

(continued on next page)

◇	A		B	C	D
1	Class 2 Quiz				
2	Score		mean score	score – mean	|score – mean|
3		100	77	23	23
4		90	77	13	13
5		90	77	13	13
6		85	77	8	8
7		80	77	3	3
8		75	77	-2	2
9		70	77	-7	7
10		70	77	-7	7
11		60	77	-17	17
12		50	77	-27	27
13					
14		77			12

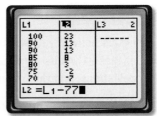

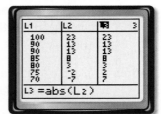

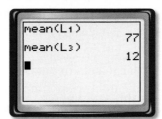

Another Property of the Mean

The steps in the calculation of the m.a.d. are usually simple calculations. Still, it is easy to make a careless error. You can check that your calculations of the deviations are correct by using the following property that follows from the Balance Property of the Mean: *The sum of the deviations of a set of numbers from the mean of the set is 0.*

Questions

COVERING THE IDEAS

1. **Multiple Choice** The m.a.d. is . . .

    A a number that measures the spread of a distribution.

    B a magazine.

    C a description of some hatters.

2. What does a higher m.a.d. for a data set indicate about that set?

In 3–6, a data set is given.

a. Find the range.

b. Find the sum of the deviations of the numbers from the mean of the numbers.

c. Calculate the m.a.d. for the collection.

3. bowling scores: 90, 85, 95

4. golf scores: 90, 97, 104, 95

5. low temperatures for Fairbanks, Alaska, in January:
   $-12°$F, $-20°$F, $-18°$F, $-17°$F

6. heights of 13-year-old quintuplets (in meters):
   1.60, 1.60, 1.60, 1.60, 1.60

Candlepin bowling, which is popular in Massachusetts, uses a ball that weighs no more than 2 pounds 7 ounces.

7. Carl has scored 45, 58, 37, 29, and 45 on the first five tests of the semester. What must he score on the sixth test to average 45?

8. **Multiple Choice** Suppose the mean of a set of numbers is A. Then the deviation of a number n in the set from the mean is which of the following?

   A $n - A$ **B** $A - n$ **C** $|n - A|$ **D** $|n| - |A|$

9. **Multiple Choice** Which of the choices in Question 8 is the absolute deviation of the number n from the mean?

APPLYING THE MATHEMATICS

10. Two people work in a candy store filling orders for people. The boss decides to check their work by weighing five 1-kilogram boxes of candy from each worker. Here are the weights.
    Worker A: 1.08, 1.04, 1.10, 1.01, 1.01
    Worker B: 1.00, 0.98, 1.02, 0.96, 1.03
    a. Use the m.a.d. to determine which worker is more consistent.
    b. In your opinion, who is the better worker?

11. The table at the right shows the normal mean temperatures °F for each month in San Francisco (SF) and Miami (M).
    a. Calculate the range of mean temperatures for each city.
    b. Use the m.a.d. to determine in which city the temperatures are more consistent.

In 12 and 13, choose the set of numbers that would probably have the smaller m.a.d.

12. temperatures in one place on the moon for a month; temperatures in one place on Earth for a month

13. guesses for the number of toy cars in a jar; guesses for the number of pennies in a jar of the same size

	SF	M
Jan.	49°	68°
Feb.	52°	69°
Mar.	54°	72°
Apr.	56°	76°
May	59°	80°
Jun.	61°	82°
Jul.	63°	84°
Aug.	64°	84°
Sept.	64°	82°
Oct.	61°	79°
Nov.	55°	74°
Dec.	50°	70°

REVIEW

14. Five friends are splitting a check at a restaurant. The total bill, including tip, comes to $128.00. One of the five has only $20 with him. On average, how much must each of the other four pay? (**Lesson 12-3**)

15. Set A is a set of twenty numbers with an average of g. Set B is a set of twenty numbers, and each number is 5.4 less than a corresponding number in Set A. What is the average of the numbers in Set B? (**Lesson 12-3**)

16. Why is it important to check the scale of a bar graph before drawing conclusions about a set of data? (**Lesson 12-1**)

17. A piece of clay is molded into a rectangular prism in order to be baked into a brick. It has a volume of 115 in³. During baking, the length, width, and height of the brick each shrank by 5%. What is the volume of the new brick? (**Lessons 11-10, 11-7, 7-7**)

18. Draw a net for a file pocket like the one shown at the right. (**Lesson 11-3**)

19. A coin sorter can sort dimes, nickels, pennies, and quarters. Arnold emptied a jar of coins into the sorter, and the machine reported the value of his change as $11.52. Write an equation describing how many of each coin he had. (**Lesson 10-5**)

20. a. Graph the intersection of the inequalities
    $y \geq -0.8x + 4$ and $y \leq 3x - 9$.
    b. At what point do the two boundary lines intersect?
    (**Lessons 10-3**)

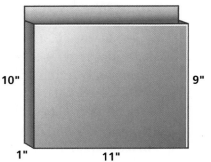

21. Central Middle School receives students from four schools: Northside, Eastside, Westside, and Southside. In grade 6, n students came from Northside, e from Eastside, w from Westside, and s from Southside.
    a. What is the ratio of grade 6 students from Northside to all the grade 6 students in Central Middle School?
    b. What is the ratio of students who came from Northside or Eastside to the students who came from Westside or Southside?
    c. There are 253 students in the 6th grade. Suppose 61 came from Northside, 46 from Westside, and 32 from Southside. To the nearest percent, what percent of students in grade 6 came from Eastside? (**Lesson 9-6**)

22. If tickets to a play cost $25 per person and seven friends plan on going, how much will they spend? (**Lesson 8-2**)

23. A number is rounded to the nearest 5% to give a result of 135%. What are the possible values of the number? (**Lesson 3-4**)

24. On a number line, graph a double inequality with a shaded region 4 units long, centered at 7.5. Write an expression for the double inequality. (**Lesson 2-8**)

EXPLORATION

25. Construct a set of 10 numbers with *all* of the properties.
    (**1**) The mean is 50.   (**2**) The range is 60.
    (**3**) The median is 40.   (**4**) The mean absolute deviation is 16.

Lesson
12-5

Medians and Box Plots

Vocabulary

median

quartile

first (lower) quartile, Q_1

second (middle) quartile, Q_2, med

third (upper) quartile, Q_3

five-number summary

box plot

interquartile range (IQR)

outlier

▶ **BIG IDEA** A convenient way of describing a data set is to use a five-number summary that can be pictured by a box plot.

The mean absolute deviation data set of Lesson 12-4 is a measure of spread of a data set based on its mean. A *box plot* pictures the measure of spread of a distribution based on its *median*.

Medians and Quartiles

Recall that the **median** of a data set is the middle number of the set when the data are ordered from least to greatest. If the data set has an odd number of elements, then the median is one of the elements of the set. For example, the median of the set {50, 90, 75, 12, 6} is 50. If the data set has an even number of elements, then the median is the mean of the two middle elements. For instance, the median of the set {1, 2, 3, 8, 12, 15} is 5.5, which is the mean of 3 and 8. Unlike the mean, the median is unaffected by one very large or very small number in a data set.

 QY

Quartiles are values that divide an ordered data set into four subsets of approximately equal size. (The word "quartile" has the same origin as the word "quarter.") There are three quartiles. The **first quartile (lower quartile)** is the median of the numbers below the median, and it is often written as Q_1. The **second (middle) quartile** is the median, often written as Q_2 or **med**. The **third (upper) quartile, Q_3,** is the median of the numbers above the median.

$$Q_1 \quad Q_2 \text{ or med} \quad Q_3$$
$$\bullet \; \blacklozenge \; \bullet \; | \; \bullet \; \blacklozenge \; \bullet$$

In the figure at the right, the dots represent numbers in increasing order. You can place vertical segments on the dots or between them to represent the median and quartiles.

The median is the mean of the values of the 3rd and 4th dots, so we have placed a vertical segment between them. The first quartile is the median of the numbers less than the median, so we place a vertical segment on the middle dot left of the median, which in this case is the 2nd dot from the left. Similarly, we place a vertical segment on the middle dot above the median, which in this case is the 5th dot from the left.

Mental Math

A deck of playing cards has four each of the numbers 1–13. A player draws one card at random.

a. What is the probability of picking a seven?

b. What is the probability of picking an odd card?

c. What is the probability of picking a double-digit card?

d. What is the probability of picking a prime card?

▶ **QY**

a. What is the median of {34, 56, 12, 78, 90}?

b. What is the median of {34, 56, 12, 78, 901}?

c. What is the median of {34, 56, 12, 78, 90, −200}?

GUIDED

Example 1

Trace the dots shown here and place vertical segments at the first, second and third quartiles.

• • • • • • • • • •

Solution

Step 1 There are __?__ dots, so the median is located ___?___. Place a vertical segment at the median.

Step 2 The first quartile, Q_1, is the median of the numbers left of the median, which in this case is located ___?___. Place a vertical segment to show Q_1.

Step 3 The third quartile, Q_3, is the median of the numbers right of the median, which in this case is located ___?___. Place a vertical segment to show Q_3.

The Five-Number Summary

Together with the minimum (least) and maximum (greatest) elements in a data set, the median and the first and third quartiles provide a **five-number summary** of the data.

Example 2

Create a five-number summary of the electoral votes each state and the District of Columbia will have had for the presidential elections of 2004 and 2008.

Total: 538; Majority needed to elect the U.S. President and Vice President: 270

Electoral Votes by State					
State	Number of Votes	State	Number of Votes	State	Number of Votes
Alabama	9	Kentucky	8	North Dakota	3
Alaska	3	Louisiana	9	Ohio	20
Arizona	10	Maine	4	Oklahoma	7
Arkansas	6	Maryland	10	Oregon	7
California	55	Massachusetts	12	Pennsylvania	21
Colorado	9	Michigan	17	Rhode Island	4
Connecticut	7	Minnesota	10	South Carolina	8
Delaware	3	Mississippi	6	South Dakota	3
District of Columbia	3	Missouri	11	Tennessee	11
Florida	27	Montana	3	Texas	34
Georgia	15	Nebraska	5	Utah	5
Hawaii	4	Nevada	5	Vermont	3
Idaho	4	New Hampshire	4	Virginia	13
Illinois	21	New Jersey	15	Washington	11
Indiana	11	New Mexico	5	West Virginia	5
Iowa	7	New York	31	Wisconsin	10
Kansas	6	North Carolina	15	Wyoming	3

Solution

Step 1 List the data from least to greatest. Here are the numbers arranged in ascending order.

3	3	3	3	3	3	3	3	4	4	4	4	4	5	5	5	5
5	6	6	6	7	7	7	7	8	8	9	9	9	10	10	10	10
11	11	11	11	12	13	15	15	15	17	20	21	21	27	31	34	55

Step 2 Determine the median of the data. The median is the middle number in the ordered list. Because there are 51 numbers in this set, the middle number is the 26th. So, the median is 8. Mark it as you did in Guided Example 1.

Step 3 Determine the first and third quartiles. There are 25 numbers below the median. So Q_1, the lower quartile, is in the 13th position: $Q_1 = 4$. There are 25 numbers above the median. So Q_3, the upper quartile, is the 13th value above the median: $Q_3 = 12$. Mark these in the ordered list.

Step 4 The quartiles, together with the minimum and the maximum of the data set, provide the five-number summary of the data: minimum $= 3$, $Q_1 = 4$, median $= 8$, $Q_3 = 12$, and maximum $= 55$.

Drawing a Box Plot

A **box plot,** or a box-and-whiskers plot, is a visual representation of the five-number summary of a data set. Box plots were invented in the 1970s by John Tukey. Here is how to construct a box plot by hand using the five-number summary of the electoral-vote data.

Step 1 Draw a number line with a scale including the minimum and maximum data values. Above the number line, draw line segments at the minimum value, Q_1, the median, Q_3, and the maximum value.

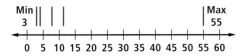

Step 2 Draw a rectangle with opposite sides (sometimes called *hinges*) that are the lower and upper quartiles of the data. This is the box of the box plot.

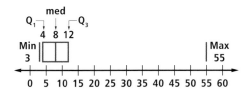

John Tukey, inventor of the stem-and-leaf plot and the box plot, was home schooled and did not begin formal education until he entered Brown University in Providence, Rhode Island.

Medians and Box Plots **765**

Step 3 Draw segments from the midpoints of the hinges to the minimum and maximum values. Identify these values. These segments are called *whiskers*. The finished product looks like the graph below.

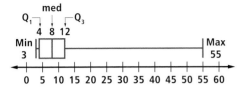

A box plot graphically splits the data set into four subsets of about equal size. About 25% of the data lie from the minimum to Q_1. About 50% are from Q_1 to Q_3, with 25% on each side of the median. And about 25% of the data lie from Q_3 to the maximum. So, from the box plot you can see that about 75% of the states have fewer than 12 electoral votes. You can also see that there are about as many states with 4 to 8 electoral votes as there are with 8 to 12 electoral votes. You can also get a sense of how unusual it is for a state to have 55 electoral votes.

Activity

Use a calculator or a computer to draw a box plot of the electoral vote data and read the five-number summary.

Step 1 Enter the numbers into a list.

Step 2 Find what plots can be made from the list and choose box plot. On some calculators, the screen may look like the one at the right.

Step 3 Choose an appropriate window and graph the box plot.

Step 4 Trace the box plot to view the five-number summary.

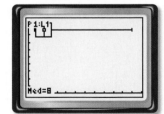

$0 \le x \le 60$; x-scale: 5

The Interquartile Range and Outliers

The difference, $Q_3 - Q_1$, between the third quartile and the first quartile is called the **interquartile range,** or **IQR.** It is the length of the box in the box plot. Specifically, it gives an interval in which you will find the middle 50% of the data. For the electoral-vote data set, $IQR = Q_3 - Q_1 = 12 - 4 = 8$.

An **outlier** in a distribution is a number that is more than 1.5 times the length of the box away from either the first or third quartiles. Specifically, if a number is less than $Q_1 - 1.5 \cdot IQR$ or greater than $Q_3 + 1.5 \cdot IQR$, then it is an outlier.

GUIDED

Example 3

Find all outliers in the electoral-vote data set.

Solution

Step 1 Determine Q_1, Q_3, and the IQR to calculate how large or small the outliers have to be. For the electoral votes, we have already determined that $Q_1 = \underline{?}$, $Q_3 = \underline{?}$, and IQR $= \underline{?}$.

Step 2 Calculate $Q_1 - 1.5 \cdot$ IQR to see if there are any outliers on the small side. $\underline{?} - 1.5 \cdot \underline{?} = \underline{?}$
A small outlier has to be less than $Q_1 - 1.5 \cdot$ IQR. There are $\underline{?}$ outliers to the left of the box.

Step 3 A large outlier has to be greater than $Q_3 + 1.5 \cdot$ IQR. Calculate $Q_3 + 1.5$ IQR.
$\underline{?} + 1.5 \cdot \underline{?} = \underline{?}$
A large outlier has to be more than $Q_1 + 1.5 \cdot$ IQR. There are $\underline{?}$ outliers to the right of the box.

You should have found that $\underline{?}$, $\underline{?}$, $\underline{?}$, and $\underline{?}$ are outliers.

Outliers in a distribution are often looked at individually because they are so special.

 GAME Now you may play *Let's Data Deal*. The directions for this game are on pages G19 and G20 at the back of your book.

Questions

COVERING THE IDEAS

In 1–3, trace the dots. Mark the first, second, and third quartiles with vertical segments.

1. • • • • • • • • •

2. • • • • • • • • • •

3. • • • • • • • • • • •

4. Create a five-number summary of the set {40, 41, 42,..., 80}, the integers from 40 to 80.

5. Trace the box plot at the right. Locate each of the following on the diagram.
   a. maximum value
   b. minimum value
   c. whiskers
   d. median
   e. first quartile
   f. second quartile
   g. third quartile

6. The box plot in this lesson summarizes the number of electoral votes for each state and the District of Columbia. The number of representatives of each state in Congress can be found by subtracting 2 from its number of electoral votes and ignoring the District of Columbia. Create a box plot of the number of representatives of the 50 states.

7. Use these box plots of the number of home runs hit by home-run leaders in the American and National Leagues from 1901 to 1920.

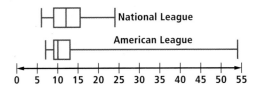

Sam Crawford was the home-run leader in 1901.

a. Estimate the five-number summary for each league.

b. Estimate the range for the highest home run total for each league from 1901 to 1920.

c. **True or False** More National League (NL) home-run leaders hit at least 12 home runs than did American League (AL) home-run leaders. Explain your answer.

d. Here are the numbers that went into making these two box plots. Are there any outliers? Explain your answer.

NL	16	6	9	9	9	12	10	12	7	10
	21	14	19	19	24	12	12	9	12	15
AL	13	16	13	10	8	12	8	7	9	10
	9	10	13	9	7	12	9	11	29	54

APPLYING THE MATHEMATICS

8. Copy this dot plot. Then place vertical segments to locate the first, second, and third quartiles.

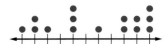

9. The table at the right shows the number of hurricanes that have struck the U.S. mainland in each decade since 1850.

a. Create a five-number summary of the number of hurricanes in each decade.

b. Create a box plot of these data.

Decade	Hurricanes
1851–1860	12
1861–1870	15
1871–1880	20
1881–1890	22
1891–1900	21
1901–1910	18
1911–1920	21
1921–1930	13
1931–1940	19
1941–1950	24
1951–1960	17
1961–1970	14
1971–1980	12
1981–1990	15
1991–2000	14

10. There are 24 states west of the Mississippi and 26 states east of the Mississippi. But over $\frac{2}{3}$ of the land area of the United States is west of the Mississippi. Therefore, you might expect that, because the states are larger, they have more counties. Is this true? Here are the numbers of counties in each state.

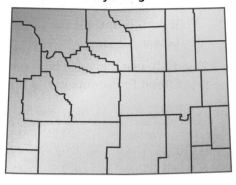

Wyoming

West of the Mississippi		East of the Mississippi	
State	Number of Counties	State	Number of Counties
Alaska	27 (divisions)	Alabama	67
Arizona	15	Connecticut	8
Arkansas	75	Delaware	3
California	58	Florida	67
Colorado	64	Georgia	159
Hawaii	5	Illinois	102
Idaho	44	Indiana	92
Iowa	99	Kentucky	120
Kansas	105	Maine	16
Louisiana	64 (parishes)	Maryland	23
Minnesota	87	Massachusetts	14
Missouri	114	Michigan	83
Montana	56	Mississippi	82
Nebraska	93	New Hampshire	10
Nevada	16	New Jersey	21
New Mexico	33	New York	62
North Dakota	53	North Carolina	100
Oklahoma	77	Ohio	88
Oregon	36	Pennsylvania	67
South Dakota	66	Rhode Island	5
Texas	254	South Carolina	46
Utah	29	Tennessee	95
Washington	39	Vermont	14
Wyoming	23	Virginia	95
		West Virginia	55
		Wisconsin	72

Maryland

The land area of Wyoming is about 10 times the land area of Maryland.

a. Create a box plot of the numbers of counties for states west of the Mississippi.

b. Using the same number line and scale, create a box plot of the numbers of counties for states east of the Mississippi.

c. From your box plots, would you say that states west of the Mississippi tend to have more counties than states east of the Mississippi?

REVIEW

11. What does it mean if the sum of the deviations for a data set is 0? (**Lesson 12-4**)

In **12** and **13**, use the table below showing the names and heights of the first fifteen Presidents of the United States.

Name	Height	Name	Height
George Washington	6'1.5"	William Henry Harrison	5'8"
John Adams	5'7"	John Tyler	6'0"
Thomas Jefferson	6'2.5"	James Polk	5'8"
James Madison	5'4"	Zachary Taylor	5'8"
James Monroe	6'0"	Millard Fillmore	5'9"
John Quincy Adams	5'7"	Franklin Pierce	5'10"
Andrew Jackson	6'1"	James Buchanan	6'0"
Martin Van Buren	5'6"		

James Buchanan was the only U.S. president to not marry.

12. Calculate the mean height and the mean absolute deviation. (**Lesson 12-4**)

13. If the sixteenth and seventeenth Presidents, Abraham Lincoln and Andrew Johnson, are added to the above group, the average height of the seventeen presidents is 0.4" greater than the average height of the first fifteen. Abraham Lincoln was 6'4". How tall was Andrew Johnson? (**Lesson 12-3**)

14. Copy the dot plot at the right and show where the mean occurs to balance the data. (**Lesson 12-3**)

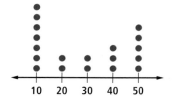

15. To get to school, Talika travels in one direction. She walked 3 blocks in 6 minutes at a constant rate to the train station. She waited there for 5 minutes for a train and then got on board. The train traveled at a constant rate for 20 minutes for 30 blocks, and then Talika walked 2 more blocks in 5 minutes. Graph her distance from home over time, beginning with when she left home. (**Lesson 10-7**)

16. **Multiple Choice** What inequality is graphed at the right? (**Lesson 10-3**)

    A $y \geq 5 - x$ **B** $y < x + 5$

    C $y = y + 5$ **D** $y \geq 5 + x$

17. Solve $\frac{6}{k} = \frac{-15}{11}$. (**Lesson 9-7**)

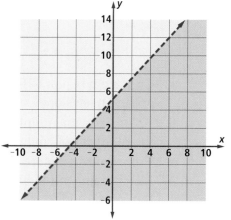

18. Suppose the temperature of an oven is 400°F and cools off at a rate of 5 degrees per minute. A foaming oven cleaner cannot be used until the temperature of the oven is below 100°F. Write and solve an inequality describing how long it will be before the oven can be cleaned. **(Lesson 8-9)**

19. A trapezoidal nature preserve has an area of 45 square miles and a height of 4.5 miles. The length of one of its bases is 7 miles. What is the length of the other base? **(Lesson 7-5)**

20. In the figure at the right, m∠2 + m∠3 = 262°. Find m∠4. **(Lessons 6-8, 6-5)**

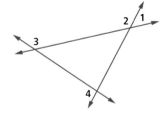

21. What is the difference between probability and relative frequency? **(Lesson 3-9)**

EXPLORATION

22. Create a box plot of the land areas of the 50 states of the United States. Identify all outliers.

Lesson

12-6 Describing Tolerance

Vocabulary

tolerance

▶ **BIG IDEA** The allowable interval in a measurement, the *tolerance,* can be described mathematically by a double inequality, using absolute value, or with a ± sign.

In any natural population, there may be outliers. Sometimes, an outlier, such as an unusually large gem, may be desired. At other times, outliers are not desired and are avoided. In manufacturing, a company will not be able to use parts that do not meet certain specifications. The button you press on a cell phone, for example, cannot be too large or too small.

width 0.375 in.

Suppose the button is nearly a prism that is to be $\frac{3}{8}$ inch (0.375") in width. Buttons that are manufactured cannot all be exactly 0.375". So a specification to the manufacturer includes some *tolerance,* perhaps 0.002 inch either way. This means that a button with a width from 0.375" − 0.002" to 0.375" + 0.002" is acceptable.

You can write these acceptable widths w as the double inequality
$$0.375" - 0.002" \leq w \leq 0.375" + 0.002",$$
$$\text{or } 0.373" \leq w \leq 0.377".$$

Here is a picture of this interval. Notice that 0.375 is its mean.

0.373   0.375   0.377 w

In manufacturing, this interval is written 0.375" ± 0.002", read "three hundred seventy-five thousandths of an inch *plus or minus* two thousandths," or, informally, "three hundred seventy-five thousandths of an inch *give or take* two thousandths." The number 0.002" is called the **tolerance.** All pieces that are manufactured must be within the interval determined by the tolerance. Anything outside that interval cannot be used and must be discarded.

Another way to describe this interval is to use deviation. The absolute deviation of a button's width w from 0.375" is given by the expression $|w - 0.375|$. Because that deviation cannot be more than 0.002", $|w - 0.375| \leq 0.002$.

Mental Math

a. How many feet tall is a person who is 71 inches tall?

b. How many inches tall is a person who is 5'2"?

c. How many cups are in one gallon?

d. How many gallons are in one pint?

Example

Write the interval from 6 to 6.5

a. as a double inequality.

b. using $\pm$ notation.

c. using absolute value.

Solution

a. Let x be a number in the interval. The numbers in the interval are greater than or equal to 6, and they are less than or equal to 6.5. So the double inequality is $6 \leq x \leq 6.5$.

b. To find the tolerance, first find the middle of the interval. This is the mean of 6 and 6.5, which is 6.25. Now subtract either number from the mean to get the tolerance. In this case, the tolerance is $6.25 - 6 = 0.25$. So the interval is 6.25 ± 0.25.

c. The absolute deviation of the number x in the interval from the middle, 6.25, must be less than or equal to the tolerance. So the interval can be written as $|x - 6.25| \leq 0.25$. You could also write $|6.25 - x| \leq 0.25$.

 QY

> ▶ **QY**
>
> Write the interval from 2.535 cm to 2.545 cm
>
> a. as a double inequality.
>
> b. using $\pm$ tolerance.
>
> c. using absolute value.

When Length Is Given by an Interval, So Is Area

When there is an interval for a length, then any calculation based on that length cannot be exact. For example, the width of a cell phone button was described as

$$0.373" \leq w \leq 0.377".$$

Suppose the button's height h, which should be 0.25", also has a tolerance of 0.002", so that

$$0.248" \leq h \leq 0.252".$$

Then the button's top (which looks like a rectangle) has a surface area that can be any of the values attainable by hw. The smallest possible value of hw is $0.373 \cdot 0.248$, or 0.092504 square inch. The largest possible value of hw is $0.377 \cdot 0.252$, or 0.095004 square inch. So the area can be described by the interval

$$0.0925 \text{ in}^2 \leq hw \leq 0.0950 \text{ in}^2.$$

We have rounded the decimals to three places starting with the 9 because the given dimensions have three places.

Although 0.0925 and 0.0950 square inch are reasonably close to each other, if you are manufacturing millions of phones, the difference in material can be quite costly.

Questions

COVERING THE IDEAS

1. The interval $3.95 \leq L \leq 4.05$ can be written as $4 \pm t$, where t is what number?

2. The interval $4 \leq x \leq 8$ can be written as $|x - 6| \leq d$, where d is what number?

3. a. Write the values satisfying $|y - 0.1| \leq 3.5$ as a double inequality.
   b. Write the values satisfying $|y - 0.1| \leq 3.5$ using $\pm$ tolerance.

4. A poll reports that 52% of the people favored Candidate A, but with a 6% tolerance or margin of error. Write the possible percentage of people favoring Candidate A . . .
   a. as a double inequality.   b. using $\pm$ tolerance.
   c. using absolute value.

In 5–8, write these specifications for a tennis ball, set by the International Tennis Federation

a. as a double inequality.

b. using $\pm$ tolerance.

c. using absolute value.

5. The diameter must be more than $2\frac{1}{2}''$ and less than $2\frac{5}{8}''$.

6. The weight must be more than 2 ounces and less than $2\frac{1}{16}$ ounces.

7. When dropped onto a concrete surface from 100 inches, the ball should bounce more than 53" and less than 58".

8. The stiffness of a fast-speed tennis ball, defined by how much it deforms (curve in or out) at 18 pounds of pressure, must be more than 0.195" and less than 0.235".

In 9–10, the length ℓ of a rectangle is in the interval 16.35 cm $\leq$ $\ell \leq$ 16.45 cm and the width w of the rectangle is in the interval 6.15 cm $\leq w \leq$ 6.25 cm.

9. What is the largest possible area of the rectangle?

10. What is the smallest possible area of the rectangle?

APPLYING THE MATHEMATICS

11. The surface area $S.A.$ of a sphere with diameter d is given by the formula $S.A. = \pi d^2$. Use the information from Question 5 to determine the largest and smallest possible surface areas of a tennis ball that meets the specifications of the International Tennis Federation.

12. A telephone button has a width w in the interval
    $0.373" \le w \le 0.377"$. The button's height h is in the interval
    $0.248" \le h \le 0.252"$. Suppose the button is a prism with depth d
    in the interval $0.421" \le d \le 0.425"$.

    a. What is the smallest possible amount of plastic needed to
       make the button?

    b. What is the largest possible amount of plastic needed to
       make the button?

    c. If you are making 1 million phones, each with 12 of these
       buttons, how much of a difference (in cubic inches of plastic)
       is there between the largest and smallest possible amounts
       of plastic you could use?

13. In a table of estimated populations of the American Colonies of
    England from 1630 to 1776, the population of New Hampshire
    in 1630 is given as 0.5 thousand and the population of Virginia
    in 1630 is given as 2.5 thousand. These numbers have been
    rounded to the nearest 0.1 thousand.

    a. Write 0.1 thousand in base 10.

    b. Write the possible populations of New Hampshire in 1630 as
       an interval in base 10.

    c. Write the possible populations of Virginia in 1630 as an
       interval in base 10.

    d. If you take the populations as given in the table to be
       exact, Virginia had how many times the population of
       New Hampshire in 1630?

    e. If you take the populations as given in the table to be better
       described by intervals, Virginia had how many times the
       population of New Hampshire in 1630? (Your answer should
       be an interval.)

14. If you count days from January 1, 2001, the first day of the
    21st century, then the year 2001 is the interval $1 \le d \le 365$. The
    year 2002 is the interval $366 \le d \le 730$, and so on. Consider leap
    years in your answers to these questions.

    a. What interval would describe the year 2005?

    b. What interval would describe the year 2010?

    c. What are the greatest and least number of days apart two
       babies could be if they were born in the years 2011 and 2012?

15. Find the two solutions to the equation $|x - 453| = 261$.

REVIEW

In 16 and 17, use the table below, which lists the average number of vacation days per year in selected countries.

Country	Italy	France	Germany	Brazil	United Kingdom	Canada	Korea	Japan	United States
Days	42	37	35	34	28	26	25	25	13

16. Create a five-number summary of these data. (**Lesson 12-5**)

17. **a.** Calculate the IQR.
    b. Are there any outliers in this distribution? If so, list them. (**Lesson 12-5**)

18. Use the table at the right showing the total number of points scored by the two teams that played in each of the first 20 Super Bowls. (**Lessons 12-5, 12-4**)
    a. Create a box plot of these data. Be sure to label the values for the median, first and third quartiles, and the minimum and maximum.
    b. How many outliers are greater than the median?
    c. How many outliers are less than the median?
    d. Calculate the mean and the mean average deviation for the scores.
    e. In Super Bowl XXI, New York defeated Denver 39–20. How did the mean total points for all Super Bowls up to this time change as a result of this score?

19. Consider the following statement:
    "Doubling each value in a set doubles the mean of the set."
    a. Rewrite this statement in if-then form.
    b. Is the statement true? Why or why not?
    c. Write the converse of your answer to Part a and explain whether or not it is true. (**Lessons 12-3, 4-4**)

20. Draw a prism with eight faces. (**Lesson 11-2**)

Super Bowl	Total Number of Points
I	45
II	47
III	23
IV	30
V	29
VI	27
VII	21
VIII	31
IX	22
X	38
XI	46
XII	37
XIII	66
XIV	50
XV	37
XVI	47
XVII	44
XVIII	47
XIX	54
XX	56

In 21 and 22, use the time-distance graph shown below. Scales on the axes have purposely been omitted.

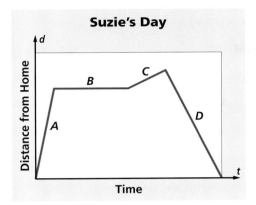

Suzie's Day

21. During which segment, *A, B, C,* or *D,* was Suzie traveling fastest? **(Lesson 10-7)**

22. **Multiple Choice** Which is a possible scenario that could account for the graph?
    A   Suzie walked to the store, shopped, and stopped to talk to a neighbor on her way home.
    B   Suzie drove to school, realized she forgot something, and went back home before returning to school.
    C   Suzie drove to work. After working for a little while, she drove to the grocery store farther away before heading home.
    D   Suzie jogged to the park. After resting she ran part of the way home, then walked the rest of the way. **(Lesson 10-7)**

In 23 and 24, solve. **(Lessons 10-2, 10-4)**

23. $18x - 45 = -3.6x + 12$

24. $-\frac{4}{5}n + 3 < \frac{-n}{10} - 17$

25. Millie has a ruler that measures to the nearest eighth of an inch. If she measures something that is *exactly* 5.8 centimeters long, what will be the reading on Millie's ruler? **(Lesson 3-4)**

EXPLORATION

26. Find the specifications that involve intervals for some pieces of equipment used in a sport other than tennis.
    a. Write down exactly how the specifications are described in the source you locate.
    b. Describe each interval you find as a double inequality, using the ± sign, and using absolute value.

QY ANSWERS

a. $2.535 \leq x \leq 2.545$

b. 2.54 ± 0.005

c. $|x - 2.54| \leq 0.005$

Lesson

12-7 Time Series

Vocabulary

time series

line graph

rates of change

▶ **BIG IDEA** When a set of numerical data is collected at regular time intervals, it can be conveniently displayed in a line graph on a coordinate grid.

Many quantities change over time, including populations of people or animals, the temperature and other climate variables, a person's height and weight, the sales in a business, and a family's savings.

When a quantity is measured in regular time intervals, the data collected are called a **time series.** Examples are U.S. census data (collected every 10 years), temperatures (recorded every hour), a person's height (measured in a doctor's office perhaps every year), and daily or monthly business sales. In this book, you first saw a time series in Chapter 1 with the graph of yearly snowfall in Philadelphia.

Another Example of a Time Series

Here are a table and a graph of the mean height of 14-year-old boys in Japan every 5 years from 1950 to 2000. Because the data points are connected with line segments, the graph is called a **line graph.**

Year	Height (cm)
1950	147.3
1955	151.7
1960	155.1
1965	158.3
1970	160.5
1975	162.2
1980	163.6
1985	163.8
1990	164.5
1995	165.1
2000	165.5

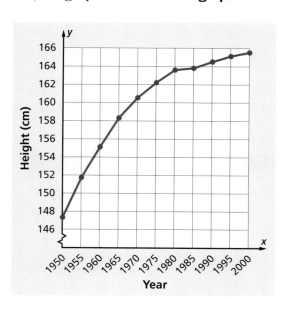

Mental Math

Find the area of the figure.

a.

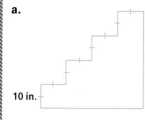

10 in.

b.

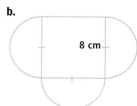

8 cm

c.

13 cm

9 cm 2 cm   5 cm

d. 1 mm

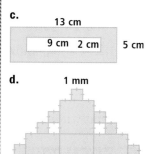

With time-series data such as these, there are natural questions to ask.

1. *What are the maximum value, minimum value, and range of the quantity being examined?*

The quantity being examined is the mean height of 14-year-old boys in Japan. The maximum value is 165.5 cm. The minimum value is 147.3 cm. The range is 18.2 cm.

2. *Are there any trends in the data?*

There is an obvious trend. The mean height of 14-year-old boys in Japan has been increasing. You can see this because the graph rises as you go to the right.

3. *How fast has the quantity being measured changed from one time to the next?*

In 1950 the mean height of a Japanese 14-year-old boy was 147.3 cm, and in 1970 the mean height was 160.5 cm. In those 20 years, the mean height increased by 13.2 cm. The increase was thus $\frac{13.2 \text{ cm}}{20 \text{ yr}}$, or 0.66 centimeter per year. This number is a *rate of change*. A formula for calculating rate of change involves subtraction (because there are changes) and division (because there is a rate).

> **Rate of Change of a Quantity between Time 1 and Time 2**
>
> $$\text{rate of change} = \frac{\text{quantity at time 2} - \text{quantity at time 1}}{\text{time 2} - \text{time 1}}$$

We calculated the rate of change of mean height of 14-year-old boys between 1950 and 1970 above

$$\frac{160.5 \text{ cm} - 147.3 \text{ cm}}{1970 - 1950} = \frac{13.2 \text{ cm}}{20 \text{ yr}} \approx 0.66 \text{ cm/year}$$

 QY

▶ **QY**

What is the average rate of change of mean height of 14-year-old Japanese boys between 1970 and 2000?

4. *Can we make any predictions for times not in the data?*

Even though mean height is increasing, the growth in mean height is steadily decreasing, so we could probably fill in years between 1950 and 2000. We might guess that the mean height in 2005 would be a little more than 165.5 cm but less than 166.0 cm.

Some questions about the data cannot be answered by mathematics. Why has the mean height increased? This increase in height is usually attributed to a change in diet in Japan during this period.

Activity 1

Use the height data on page 778 to make a line graph on your calculator. On some calculators you may need to choose the line graph option in the statplot menu as shown at the right. Be careful to set an appropriate window so that your graph looks similar to the one at the beginning of this lesson.

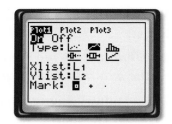

Time Series in Bar Graphs

Here is the percent of small, midsize, large, and luxury cars sold in the United States in certain years.

	Type of Car (Percent of Total Car Sales)			
Year	Small	Midsize	Large	Luxury
1975	42.1	29.2	31.0	5.8
1980	38.5	32.3	22.4	6.8
1985	37.9	42.1	9.8	10.2
1990	35.2	42.8	9.5	12.5
1995	27.1	48.5	10.8	13.6
2000	29.7	46.1	7.0	17.4

Source: 2006 World Almanac, p. 115
http://www.senate.michigan.gov/sfa/Publications/Issues/MOTORVEH/MOTORVE1.html

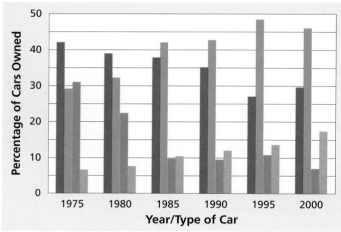

Bar graphs for each year can show trends.

Activity 2

Work with a partner or a group to answer these questions.

Step 1 What are the maximum values, minimum values, and ranges of each of the four quantities being examined in the data above?

Step 2 Describe the trends in the data.

Step 3 a. How fast has each percentage changed from 1975 to 2000?
b. Which **rates of change** are positive?
c. Which rates of change are negative?

Step 4 Are any predictions possible for times in between the years shown on the bar graph?

It is fitting that the topic of time series is the last in this book. We hope that your knowledge of mathematics has increased this year and that it continues to increase in following years as shown in the graph at the right.

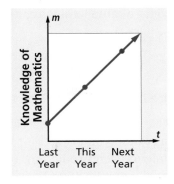

We also hope that you have found it interesting to learn more mathematics and that you will enjoy using the mathematics you have learned.

Questions

COVERING THE IDEAS

1. Give an example of a quantity which changes over time that is not mentioned in the reading.

2. Refer to the table and graph of mean heights of 14-year-old boys in Japan over time.
   a. What was the mean height of a Japanese 14-year-old boy in 1980?
   b. What was the rate of change in mean height of a Japanese 14-year-old boy from 1980 to 2000?
   c. If the rate of change in Part b continued until the year 2100, what would the mean height of a 14-year-old Japanese boy be then?
   d. Do you think that the answer to Part c is possible?

In 3–8, use the data at the right of the mean height of 14-year-old Japanese girls from 1950 to 2000.

3. What are the maximum value, minimum value, and range of mean heights?

4. a. Make a line graph using these data.
   b. From the graph, how can you determine the minimum value?

5. Are there any trends in the data?

6. How quickly did the mean height change from 1950 to 1965?

7. How quickly did the mean height change from 1970 to 2000?

8. Do you think any predictions are possible for the years 2005 and 2010?

Year	Height (cm)
1950	146.6
1955	148.9
1960	150.7
1965	152.5
1970	154.2
1975	155.0
1980	156.0
1985	156.3
1990	156.4
1995	156.7
2000	156.8

In 9–11, use the data of percents of small, midsize, large, and luxury cars sold in the United States.

9. What is the rate of change from 1990 to 2000 in the percents of large cars sold?

10. What is the rate of change from 1990 to 2000 in the percents of luxury cars sold?

11. Based on the graph, what would you predict for the values of the four percents in 2005? Defend each prediction. (*Caution:* The total of the four percentages must be 100%.)

APPLYING THE MATHEMATICS

12. a. Use the data on page 778 and in Questions 3–8 to calculate the difference in the mean heights of Japanese 14-year-old boys and girls from the years 1950 to 2000.
    b. What trends, if any, are there in these differences over time?
    c. What is the rate of change of the difference in mean heights from 1950 to 2000?

In 13–16, use this table of sales (in millions of dollars) of music cassettes and CDs in the United States for each two-year period from 1987 to 2003.

Year	1987	1989	1991	1993	1995	1997	1999	2001	2003
CD	1,594	2,588	4,338	6,511	9,402	9,915	12,816	12,909	11,233
Cassette	2,960	3,346	3,020	2,916	2,304	1,523	1,062	363	108

Cassette tapes passed 8-track tapes in popularity because they were smaller and allowed you to cue up specific tracks. With CDs, song selection is almost instantaneous.

13. a. Create a line graph showing the number of CDs sold over time.
    b. On the same graph, using another color or shade, plot the number of cassettes sold over the same period of time.

14. In dollars, what were the sales of CDs in 2003?

15. a. Describe the trend in the sales of CDs over this time.
    b. Describe the trend in the sales of cassettes over this time.
    c. What happened to cause these trends?

16. What would you predict for the dollar sales of CDs and cassettes in 2005?

17. Examine the graph of the mean heights of Japanese 14-year-old boys, shown on page 778.
    a. What in the graph tells you the time interval when the rate of change was the greatest?
    b. When was the rate of change the greatest? What is that rate?

REVIEW

18. A bathroom scale has a tolerance of 2 pounds. Manuel steps on the scale and reads a measurement of 175 pounds. **(Lessons 12-6, 8-9)**

a. Write a double inequality for the range of Manuel's possible weight.

b. What percentage more is the maximum weight than the minimum?

19. The mean low monthly temperatures of Helsinki, Finland, are shown in the table at the right. Create a box plot from these values. **(Lesson 12-5)**

20. Is it possible to have a set of ten numbers such that (i) the interquartile range equals the mean absolute deviation, and (ii) not all members of the set have the same value? If it is possible, give an example of such a set, indicating the m.a.d. and the interquartile range. **(Lesson 12-5, 12-4)**

21. The mean of the lengths of the four sides of a parallelogram is 13.4 cm. One side measures 8 cm. Find the lengths of the other three sides. **(Lessons 12-3, 6-7)**

22. Debbie has borrowed $2,700, and will pay $75 every month until she has repaid that amount. Paul has borrowed $3,000 and will pay $100 every month.

a. Write and solve an inequality showing how many months it will be until Paul owes less than Debbie.

b. Will Paul owe less than Debbie before the loans are repaid in full? **(Lesson 10-5)**

23. What is the magnitude of rotation that the *hour* hand of an analog clock makes in 17 hours? **(Lesson 5-2)**

24. If T = the set of all prime numbers and J = {4, 8, 17, 19, 21, 34, 76} what is $T \cap J$? **(Lesson 4-4)**

Month	Temperature (°C)
January	−11
February	−11
March	−7
April	−1
May	4
June	9
July	11
August	11
September	6
October	2
November	−3
December	−8

EXPLORATION

25. What is meant by *extrapolation?* Perform extrapolation on one of the data sets presented in this lesson.

26. There is an error in the data presented in the table of car sales on page 780. This error was in the original data source. Where is the error?

QY ANSWER

$0.1\overline{6} \frac{cm}{year}$

Chapter 12 Projects

Cy Young

1 Displays in Newspapers

Obtain a large city's Sunday newspaper. Cut out every mathematical display in the newspaper. Organize the displays in some fashion, giving the purpose of each display.

2 Display of Temperature

Keep track of the high and low temperatures where you live each day for a week. Display the data in a coordinate graph. Summarize in writing what the temperature has been like for the week.

3 Displays of the Tchokwe

The design below comes from the Tchokwe people of northeast Angola, in the southwestern part of Africa. The Tchokwe draw in the sand and tell stories about what they draw. These drawings almost always begin with setting down a collection of equally spaced points. Then curves are added through and around the points. The drawing below represents a leopard with five cubs. Copy this design and decide where you think the leopard and its five cubs are. Make two more designs of this type and write a short story for each.

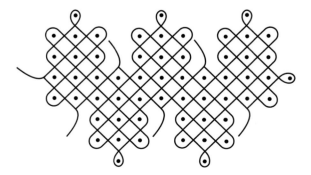

4 Cy Young Award

The Cy Young Award in Major League Baseball is given to the best pitcher in each league (National League and American League), and is decided by vote of the Baseball Writers Association of America. As such, there is no single statistic that will guarantee a pitcher the award for a season. For example, a pitcher may have the lowest earned run average (ERA) and have the most strikeouts but have a losing record, which may take him out of the running for the award. Find the number of strikeouts, the ERA, and the number of wins that each Cy Young winner in the National League had from 1967 to the present day and plot these statistics on three separate histograms. Find the mean, median, and range for each data set. Which of these statistics would you say is the best predictor of who wins the Cy Young Award? Why?

5 Birthday Poll

Poll your classmates to find out their birth dates.

a. Organize the birth dates by month in a bar graph and a circle graph. Describe any trends in the data.

b. Calculate how old each of your classmates is in days. (Don't forget leap years!) Create a box plot for this data and a five-number summary for the box plot. Are there any outliers?

Chapter 12 Summary and Vocabulary

- Data can vary for a number of reasons. Some data, such as population or money earned or spent, vary over time. By graphing the data or by examining a table, you can see trends over time. You can also calculate the rate at which a quantity has increased or decreased.

- Other data vary because things cannot be measured exactly. If many people try to measure the same thing or if objects are manufactured or appear to be alike, there still may be differences. A particular measurement is likely to be in an interval. The interval from a to b (for example, from 380 to 400) can be described in various ways:

	in general	specific example
using a double inequality:	$a \le x \le b$	$380 \le x \le 400$
using $\pm$:	$m \pm \left(\dfrac{b-a}{2}\right)$, where $m = \dfrac{a+b}{2}$	390 ± 10
using absolute value:	$\left\lvert x - \dfrac{a+b}{2}\right\rvert \le \left(\dfrac{b-a}{2}\right)$	$\lvert x - 390\rvert \le 10$

- You are familiar with the use of the mean to describe a distribution of data with a single number. A statistic based on the mean that describes the spread in a distribution is the mean absolute deviation. This is the mean of the absolute value of the deviations of all the numbers in the distribution.

- Another of the many ways to describe a distribution of data is with a box plot. A box plot is based on five numbers: the minimum value of the distribution, the first quartile, the median, the third quartile, and the maximum value.

- Graphing a distribution of data that vary over time helps you to see trends, to determine whether something is generally increasing or decreasing, and to estimate values in between known values.

Vocabulary

12-1
sample
data set
sample size
categorical data

12-2
interval data
histogram
stem-and-leaf plot
stem
leaf
mode
range

12-4
measures of spread
mean absolute deviation (m.a.d.)
deviation
absolute deviation

12-5
median
quartile
first (lower) quartile, Q_1
second (middle) quartile, Q_2, med
third (upper) quartile, Q_3
five-number summary
box plot
interquartile range (IQR)
outlier

12-6
tolerance

12-7
time series
line graph
rates of change

Theorems and Properties

Means and Sums Property (p. 753)
Balance Property of the Mean (p. 755)

Chapter 12   Self-Test

Take this test as you would take a test in class. You will need a calculator. Then use the Selected Answers section in the back of the book to check your work.

1. Find the mean absolute deviation of this set of numbers: 3, 9, 27, 81.

2. Calculate the five-number summary of this set of numbers.
   19, 23, 29, 31, 37, 41, 43, 50, 55, 60

3. Write the interval $3.6 \leq J \leq 3.7$
   a. using absolute values.
   b. using the $\pm$ sign.

4. The interval $-4 \leq x \leq 12$ can be written as $|x - 4| \leq y$, where y is what number?

5. Find the mean absolute deviation of the following times, in seconds, for solving the Rubik's Cube for the 2005 Rubik's Cube champion, Jean Pons: 15.62, 15.87, 13.81.

6. **True or False** The sum of the deviations of n numbers from their mean *must* equal 0.

7. The mean of six numbers is 18. When a seventh number is added to these six, the mean decreases by 2. What is the value of the seventh number?

In 8 and 9, refer to the following data on the minimum wage in the United States at different times.

Year	1980	1985	1990	1995	2000
Wage	$3.10	$3.35	$3.80	$4.25	$5.15

8. What trend do you notice in the data?

9. Between which two years in the data is there the greatest rate of change?

10. A manufacturing company produces boxes that must have a width between 11 and 12 inches, a length between 13 and 15 inches, and a height between 4 and 6 inches. Calculate the interval for the possible volume of the box.

11. A store in the United States advertises that it sells pants between 27 and 42 inches in the waist. A store in Europe advertises that it sells pants between 61 and 90 cm in the waist. One inch = 2.54 cm. Find the interval for waist sizes (in inches) that are sold in *both* stores.

In 12–14, use the data below showing the median family incomes of seven states in 2004.

State	Income
Alabama	$45,768
Alaska	$66,254
Arizona	$48,995
Arkansas	$39,945
California	$58,327
Colorado	$58,849
Connecticut	$73,458

12. Give a five-number summary of these data.

13. Construct a box plot for the data.

14. Name all the states that are outliers with respect to median family incomes.

In 15 and 16, use the data below on the percent of U.S. homes with a personal computer.

Year	Percent
1985	8.2
1990	15.0
1994	22.8
1995	24.1
1998	36.6
1999	42.1
2001	51.0
2002	56.5

15. Create a time series coordinate graph of the data.

16. If the increase from 2001–2002 were to continue at the same rate, in which year would over 70 percent of U.S. homes have a computer?

17. In order to qualify for a promotion, James needs to sell an average of 4.5 cars per day. On the first 20 days of the month, he sold 115 cars. How many cars does he need to sell for the last 10 days?

In 18 and 19, Graham kept note of the number of books about travel he sold at his store each day and came up with this list: 5, 11, 23, 17, 31, 16, 14, 24, 20, 7, 12, 17, 26, 9.

18. Make a stem-and-leaf plot of these data.

19. Use your plot to determine the median number of travel books sold.

20. The heights of the 26 tallest buildings (in meters) in Vancouver, Canada, are: 150, 149, 146, 142, 141, 141, 140, 140, 138, 138, 127, 122, 120, 117, 116, 111, 109, 109, 109, 108, 108, 106, 106, 106, 104, 104.

   a. Construct a histogram for these data with intervals of length 5.

   b. Which interval has the most buildings?

21. Refer to the circle graph below.

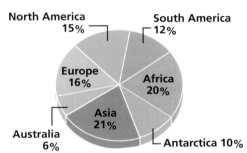

Continiental Land Area

   a. What is the measure of the angle for Asia?

   b. Explain why this graph is a distortion of the data.

Chapter 12 Chapter Review

SKILLS
PROPERTIES
USES
REPRESENTATIONS

SKILLS Procedures used to get answers

OBJECTIVE A Calculate the mean absolute deviation of a set of numbers. (Lesson 12-4)

In 1 and 2, find the mean absolute deviation of the set of numbers, which is the number of points a college basketball team scored in its first six games of the 2006–2007 season.

1. Villanova University: 97, 81, 66, 89, 70, 72

2. University of Missouri-Kansas City: 85, 97, 68, 70, 70, 79

3. **Multiple Choice** Given a set of data, the mean absolute deviation is a measure of

   A center.   **B** spread.

   C range.   **D** frequency.

4. If a set of 5 numbers has a mean absolute deviation of 16, and a set of 50 numbers has a mean absolute deviation of 18, which set of numbers deviates less from the mean? Explain your answer.

OBJECTIVE B Calculate the five-number summary of a distribution of numbers. (Lesson 12-5)

5. What values of a five-number summary does each of a, b, c, d, and e on this box plot represent?

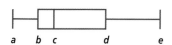

6. Find the interquartile range of these data: 43, 52, 25, 98, 81, 43, 55, 37, 73.

In 7 and 8, calculate the five-number summary of the set of numbers.

7. 13, 5, 26, 310, 512, 54, 58, 7, 86, 90

8. 211, 210, 212, 218, 220, 215, 219, 221, 224

OBJECTIVE C Write intervals using double inequalities, the ± sign, and absolute value. (Lesson 12-6)

In 9 and 10, write the interval using the ± sign.

9. $7.6 \leq p \leq 8.4$ 10. $18.7 \leq x \leq 29.1$

In 11 and 12, write the interval using absolute value.

11. 5 ± 2.1 12. $13 \leq q \leq 15.4$

In 13 and 14, write the interval using a double inequality.

13. $|x - 5| < 3$ 14. $|y - 3| < 0.4$

15. The interval $82 < p < 88$ can be written as $|p - 85| < m$. What is the value of m?

16. The interval $0.15 \leq c \leq 0.25$ can be written as $0.2 \pm k$. What is k?

PROPERTIES Principles behind the mathematics

OBJECTIVE D Apply the Means and Sums Property and the Balance Property of the Mean. (Lesson 12-3)

17. Show that the sum of the deviations of 25, 43, and 52 from their mean is 0.

18. On the first 3 tests, Carmen had a mean of 7 correct. On the next 5 tests, Carmen had scores of 10. What was Carmen's mean score for the 8 tests?

19. **a.** Find $(8 - 5) + (7 - 5) + (2 - 5) + (3 - 5) + (5 - 5)$.

    b. Based on your answer to Part a, what is the mean of 8, 7, 2, 3, and 5?

20. Casey has an expense account that entitles him to average $25 per day. On the first four days of his trip he spent $24, $28, $32, and $21. What is the maximum he can spend on his fifth and last day?

USES Applications of mathematics in real-world situations

OBJECTIVE E Interpret information displayed in bar graphs, circle graphs, histograms, and stem-and-leaf displays. (Lessons 12-1, 12-2)

In 21, use the histogram displaying the frequency of different amounts of monthly rainfall in Seattle, taken from averaged data from 1961 to 1990.

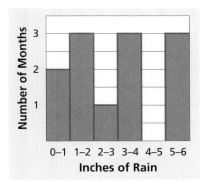

21. Why can you not compute the mean monthly rainfall in Seattle from this histogram?

In 22 and 23, Julie measured the rainfall in millimeters every day for two weeks. Her results are in stem-and-leaf displays.

```
0 | 4 6 0 0 0 7 2 1
1 | 8 0 3
2 | 3
3 | 1 7
```

22. What is the median amount of rain that fell during this period?

23. On how many days did it

    a. rain more than 1.5 centimeters?

    b. not rain at all?

In 24 and 25, consider the two circle graphs and two bar graphs, all showing household incomes in the United States in 2005.

U.S. Household Income 2005

U.S. Household Income 2005

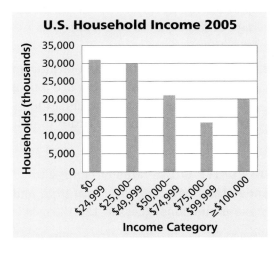

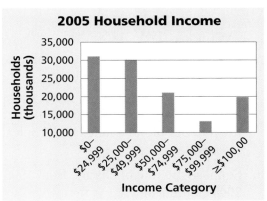

24. Suppose you want to argue that not many households in the United States earned from $75,000 to $99,999 per year.

    a. Which circle graph would you choose?

    b. Which bar graph would you choose?

25. Which of the four graphs distorts the data? Justify your answer.

OBJECTIVE F Use the properties of means to find values in real-world situations. (Lesson 12-3)

26. Tonya has scored 12, 16, 8, 23, and 19 points in her first five games. How many points must she score in the next two games to average at least 17 points per game?

27. Theo's grandfather is 86 years old. The average age of Theo, his sister, and his parents is 31 years. What is the mean age of Theo's family including his grandfather?

28. It is recommended that an elevator hold a maximum of 850 lb. If there are 5 people riding at once, what is the most their average weight can be in order to not overload the elevator?

OBJECTIVE G Use rates of change to understand how data vary over time and to make predictions. (Lesson 12-7)

In 29 and 30, use the data for the number of recorded Atlantic hurricanes and tropical storms.

Year	1965	1975	1985	1995	2005
Storms	6	9	11	19	31

29. Between which two of the given years was there the greatest rate of change in the number of hurricanes and tropical storms?

30. Suppose the rate of change from 1995 to 2005 continues.

    a. How many storms would you predict in 2015?

    b. In what year would you first expect more than 100 storms?

In 31 and 32, Michael estimated the length of his pet piranha Oscar over several months.

Age	Length
1 month	4 cm
3 months	6 cm
5 months	7.5 cm
7 months	9 cm
9 months	10 cm

31. Compare the rate of change between each estimation. Did Oscar grow faster or slower as he aged?

32. If Oscar continues to grow at the rate of change between 7 and 9 months, at what month will he be more than half the length of his 30-cm-long tank?

OBJECTIVE H Use tolerance to determine the interval of a measurement that is based on measures that are themselves in an interval. (Lesson 12-6)

33. If the length ℓ of one side of a square is said to be 5 feet $\pm$ 6 inches, describe an interval for the area A of the square using a double inequality.

34. Suppose 25 to 30 schools are involved in a citywide competition and 15 to 20 students per school are allowed to participate. Find the maximum and minimum of the total number of students that could participate.

35. In 2006, the population of China was estimated as 1.3 billion. India's population was estimated as 1.1 billion. These numbers are rounded to the 0.1 billion. Use absolute value to describe the interval for the total population of China and India combined.

REPRESENTATIONS Pictures, graphs, or objects that illustrate concepts

OBJECTIVE I Represent numerical data in a stem-and leaf plot. (Lesson 12-2)

In 36 and 37, use the following data, which is a list of interest rates available for 1-year certificates of deposit at various banks.

4.82%, 5.29%, 5.40%, 5.00%, 5.03%, 5.03%, 5.15%, 5.42%, 4.98%

36. Construct a stem-and-leaf plot of these data using

   a. a two-digit stem and a one-digit leaf.

   b. a one-digit stem and a two-digit leaf.

37. Which of the stem-and-leaf plots in Question 36 is more useful? Explain.

OBJECTIVE J Represent numerical data in a histogram. (Lesson 12-2)

In 38 and 39, Billie read 17 novels last summer. She made a list of the number of pages in each: 425, 318, 501, 138, 128, 211, 401, 373, 96, 448, 402, 117, 384, 285, 441, 102, 452.

38. a. Make a histogram using intervals with a length of 50 pages.

   b. Which interval has the most books?

39. a. Make a histogram using intervals with a length of 100 pages.

   b. Which interval has the most books?

   c. How could you answer Part b using just the histogram in Question 38?

40. The following data are the number of games played by individual pitchers on the Cleveland Indians in the 2006 season: 32, 33, 29, 31, 14, 14, 38, 51, 50, 39, 34, 29, 17, 9, 10, 8, 15, 14, 13, 24, 18, 9, 9.

   a. Give an appropriate window for displaying these data in a calculator histogram.

   b. What does the tallest bar represent?

OBJECTIVE K Draw and interpret a box plot of given data. (Lesson 12-5)

In 41–43, use the data from Questions 38 and 39, the number of pages of the novels Billie read.

41. Identify the maximum, minimum, and median of the data.

42. Construct a box plot of the data.

43. What novels are outliers in terms of length?

OBJECTIVE L Represent trends in data over time. (Lesson 12-7)

	Nelia	Lorena
1 hour	2.5 miles	2 miles
2 hours	4 miles	4 miles
3 hours	4.5 miles	6 miles
4 hours	6 miles	8 miles
5 hours	7 miles	9 miles

In 44–46, Nelia and Lorena are participating in a walk-a-thon to raise money for charity. They plan to walk for 5 hours (including short breaks) and keep track of how far they have gone each hour. The results are listed in the table above.

44. Construct a time-series line graph showing Nelia's progress.

45. Construct a time-series line graph showing Lorena's progress.

46. Compare the two graphs. Whose progress is steadier?

A Guide to Games

 Games

Throughout the year, you will play games that help you practice important math skills in a way that is different and enjoyable. We hope that you will play often and have fun!

In this Appendix, you will find the directions for each game. The numbers in most games are generated randomly, so that the games can be played over and over without repeating the same problems.

Many students have created their own variations to these games to make them more interesting. We encourage you to do this too.

Materials

You will need a deck of number cards for many of the games. You can use a UCSMP Math Deck, a deck of regular playing cards, or make your own deck out of index cards.

A UCSMP Math Deck includes 54 cards. There are four cards each for the numbers 0–12, and there are two blank cards.

You can also use a deck of regular playing cards after making a few changes. A deck of playing cards includes 54 cards (52 regular cards, plus 2 jokers). To create a deck of number cards, use a permanent marker to mark the cards in the following ways:

- Mark each of the four aces with the number 1.
- Mark each of the four jacks with the number 11.
- Mark each of the four queens with the number 12.
- Mark each of the four kings with the number 0.
- Discard the two jokers.

For some games you will have to make a gameboard, a score sheet, or a set of cards that are not number cards. The instructions for doing these things are included with the game directions. More complicated gameboards and card decks are available from your teacher.

Build-It

Materials	1 *Build-It* Gameboard for each player (Game Master 1, p. GM3)
	1 *Build-It* Card Deck (blue UCSMP card deck or Game Masters 2 and 3, pp. GM4 and GM5)
	calculator (optional)
Players	2
Skill	Comparing and ordering fractions
Objective	To be the first player to arrange five fraction cards in order from least to greatest

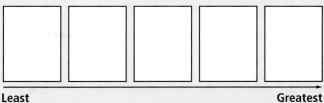

Least   Greatest

***Build-It* Gameboard**

Directions

1. Shuffle the fraction cards with a block in the upper left corner. Deal one card number-side down on each of the five spaces on the two *Build-It* gameboards.

2. Put the remaining cards number-side down for a *draw pile*.

3. Turn over the 5 cards on each gameboard. Do not change the order of the cards at any time during the game.

4. Take turns. When it is your turn:
   - Take the top card from the draw pile.
   - The card must replace one of the five cards on your *Build-It* gameboard. Put the replaced card on a discard pile.

5. If all the cards in the draw pile are used, shuffle the cards in the discard pile. Place them number-side down in a draw pile.

6. The winner is the first player to have all five cards on his or her gameboard in order from the least to greatest.

Variation

Play a version of the game using the cards with a hex nut in the upper left corner. These cards have negative and improper fractions and fractions not in lowest terms.

$\frac{1}{3}$	$\frac{2}{3}$	$\frac{1}{4}$	$\frac{3}{4}$
$\frac{1}{5}$	$\frac{3}{5}$	$\frac{1}{6}$	$\frac{5}{6}$
$\frac{4}{7}$	$\frac{3}{8}$	$\frac{7}{8}$	$\frac{2}{9}$
$\frac{3}{10}$	$\frac{5}{12}$	$\frac{11}{12}$	$\frac{19}{20}$

***Build-It* Cards**

$\frac{5}{2}$	$\frac{1}{3}$	$-\frac{4}{3}$	$-\frac{2}{5}$
$-\frac{5}{6}$	$\frac{7}{6}$	$\frac{6}{7}$	$-\frac{6}{8}$
$\frac{4}{10}$	$\frac{20}{10}$	$\frac{9}{12}$	$\frac{10}{12}$
$\frac{16}{12}$	$\frac{8}{18}$	$\frac{18}{27}$	$\frac{150}{600}$

***Build-It* Cards (Variation)**

GAME Top-It: Fraction Addition

Materials	number cards 1–10 (four of each, except 7s and 9s)
	calculator (optional)
Players	2
Skill	Adding and subtracting fractions
Objective	To collect the most cards

Directions

1. Shuffle the cards and place them number-side down on the table.

2. Each player turns over four cards. The card numbers are used to form two fractions.

   ■ The first card drawn is placed number-side up on the table. This card number is the numerator of the first fraction.

   ■ The second card drawn is the denominator of the first fraction and is placed number-side up directly below the first card. The third and the fourth cards drawn form the other fraction.

3. Each player calculates the sum of his or her two fractions. The player with the greatest sum takes all the cards. Players may use a calculator to compare their sums.

4. In case of a tie for the greatest sum, each player repeats Steps 2 and 3. The player with the greatest sum takes all the cards from both plays.

5. The game ends when there are not enough cards left for each player to have another turn. The player with the most cards wins. If the players are tied, repeat Steps 1–4 once more. The player with the greater sum wins.

Example

Amy turns over the following cards in order: 3, 2, 5, and 1.
Roger turns over the following cards in order: 4, 10, 2, and 8.

Amy's sum is $\frac{3}{2} + \frac{5}{1} = 6\frac{1}{2}$.

Roger's sum is $\frac{4}{10} + \frac{2}{8} = \frac{26}{40} = \frac{13}{20}$.

Amy's sum is greater, so she takes all of the cards.

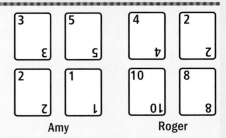

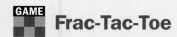

Frac-Tac-Toe

Materials	1 *Frac-Tac-Toe* Gameboard (Game Master 4, p. GM6)
	1 *Frac-Tac-Toe* Number-Card Board (Game Master 5, p. GM7)
	number cards 0–10 (four of each)
	counters (two colors), or pennies (one player using heads, the other using tails)
	calculator (optional)
Players	2
Skill	Finding fraction, decimal, and percent equivalents
Objective	To cover three squares in a row, in any direction (horizontal, vertical, or diagonal)

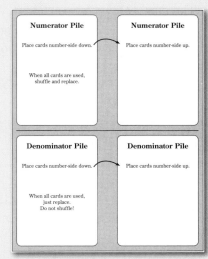

Frac-Tac-Toe **Number-Card Board**

Advance Preparation

Separate the cards into two piles on the Number-Card Board: a numerator pile and a denominator pile. Place two each of the 1, 2, 3, 4, 5, 6, 8, and 10 cards in the denominator pile. All other cards are placed in the numerator pile.

Shuffle the cards in each pile. Place the piles number-side down in the left-hand spaces. After all of the cards in the numerator pile have been flipped number-side up, reshuffle that pile, and place it number-side down in the left-hand space. When the denominator pile is completely used, turn it over and place it number-side down in the left-hand space without reshuffling it.

Directions

1. Take turns. When it is your turn:
   - Turn over the top card from each pile to form a fraction (numerator card above denominator card).
   - Try to match the fraction shown with one of the grid squares on the gameboard. If a match is found, cover that grid square with your counter, and your turn is over. If no match is found, your turn is over.

2. To change the fraction shown by the cards to a decimal, players may use either a calculator or the table of decimal and percent equivalents for fractions on pages 163 and 170.

3. The first player to cover 3 squares in a row in any direction (horizontal, vertical, or diagonal) is the winner of the game.

> 1.0	0 or 100%	> 2.0	0% or 1	> 100%
10% or 0.9	0.2 or 12.5%	25% or 0.3	30% or 0.375	0.4
> 150%	0.5 or 0.16	> 2.5	50% or 0.83	> 1.5
60%	70% or 0.625	0.75 or $66\frac{2}{3}\%$	0.8 or 87.5%	0.1 or 90%
> 100%	0 or 1	> 200%	0% or 100%	> 1.0

Frac-Tac-Toe **Gameboard**

(continued on next page)

Example 1

The cards show the fraction $\frac{4}{5}$, which is equivalent to the decimal 0.8. The player may cover the square labeled "0.8 or 87.5%" unless that square has already been covered.

Example 2

The cards show the fraction $\frac{0}{5}$. The player may cover any one of the four squares labeled "0 or 1," "0 or 100%," "0% or 1," or "0% or 100%" that has not already been covered.

Example 3

The cards show the fraction $\frac{4}{2}$. The player may cover any square labeled "> 1.0," "> 100%," "> 1.5," or "> 150%" that has not already been covered. The player may not cover a square labeled "> 2.0," "> 2.5," or "> 200%" because $\frac{4}{2}$ is equal to but not greater than 2.

GAME

Shape Capture: Polygons

Materials	1 set of *Shape Capture: Polygons* Picture Cards (green UCSMP card deck or Game Master 6, p. GM8)
	1 set of *Shape Capture: Polygons* Property Cards (green UCSMP card deck or Game Master 7, p. GM9)
Players	2 or two teams of 2
Skill	Identifying properties of polygons
Objective	To capture the most polygons

Directions

1. Randomly spread out the picture cards picture-side up on the table. Shuffle the Property Cards and place them writing-side down in a pile on the table.

2. Players take turns. When it is your turn:
   - Draw the two top cards from the pile of Property Cards.
   - Take all of the polygons that have *both* of the properties shown on the Property Cards in your hand.
   - If there are no polygons with both properties, your turn ends and the other player's turn begins.
   - At the end of a turn, if you have not captured a polygon that you could have taken, the other player may capture it.
   - At the end of a turn, if you have captured a polygon that you should *not* have taken, the other player may capture it.
   - Keep the used Property Cards separate from the original pile.

3. When all the Property Cards in the pile have been drawn, reshuffle all of them. Place them writing-side down in a pile, and continue playing.

4. The game ends when there are fewer than three polygons left or when there is a winner no matter how many polygons remain.

5. The winner is the player who has captured the most polygons.

Example

Letti has these Property Cards: "a polygon with at least two right angles" and "a parallelogram." She can take all the rectangles (*hint:* a square is a rectangle), so she has captured these polygons.

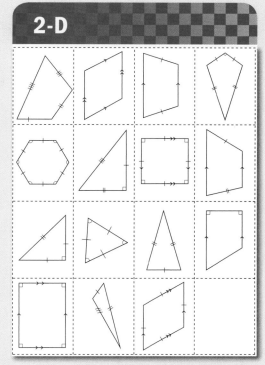

2-D

Shape Capture: Polygons
Picture Cards

2-D

a regular polygon	a trapezoid	a triangle
a scalene triangle	a rectangle	a polygon with no acute angles
a parallelogram	a quadrilateral	a polygon with no two sides the same length
a polygon with a pair of sides that are the same length	an isosceles triangle	a right triangle
a polygon with at least one right angle	an equilateral polygon	a polygon with at least two right angles
a polygon with no right angles	an equiangular polygon	a rhombus
a polygon with a pair of opposite sides parallel	a polygon with no obtuse angles	an equilateral triangle
a square	a polygon with at least one acute angle	a polygon with at least one obtuse angle

Shape Capture: Polygons
Property Cards

GAME Top-It: Integer Addition

Materials	1 complete deck of number cards
	calculator (optional)
Players	2 to 4
Skill	Adding and subtracting integers
Objective	To collect the most cards

Directions

The color of the number on each card tells you if a card is a positive number or a negative number.

- Black cards (spades and clubs) are *positive numbers.*
- Red cards (hearts and diamonds) or blue cards (UCSMP Math Deck) are *negative numbers.*

1. Shuffle the deck and place it number-side down.

2. Each player turns over two cards and calls out the sum of the numbers. The player with the greatest sum takes all the cards.

3. In case of a tie, each tied player turns over two more cards and calls out the sum of the numbers. The player with the greatest sum takes all the cards from both plays. If necessary, check answers with a calculator.

4. The game ends when there are not enough cards left for each player to have another turn. The player with the most cards wins.

Example

Kasha turns over a blue 3 and a black 6.

$$-3 + 6 = 3$$

Ted turns over a blue 2 and a blue 5.

$$-2 + (-5) = -7$$
$$3 > -7$$

Kasha takes all four cards because 3 is greater than –7.

Variation (Addition with Three Cards)

Each player turns over three cards and finds the sum.

GAME

Top-It: Integer Subtraction

Materials	1 complete deck of number cards
	calculator (optional)
Players	2 to 4
Skill	Adding and subtracting integers
Objective	To collect the most cards

Directions

The color of the number on each card tells you if a card is a positive number or a negative number.

- Black cards (spades and clubs) are *positive numbers*.
- Red cards (hearts and diamonds) or blue cards (UCSMP Math Deck) are *negative numbers*.

1. Shuffle the deck and place it number-side down.

2. Each player turns over two cards, one at a time, and subtracts the second number from the first number. The player with the greatest answer takes all the cards.

3. In case of a tie, each tied player turns over two more cards and calls out the difference of the numbers. The player with the greatest answer takes all the cards from both plays. If necessary, check answers with a calculator.

4. The game ends when there are not enough cards left for each player to have another turn. The player with the most cards wins.

Example

Kasha turns over a black 2 first and then a blue 3.

$$+2 - (-3) = 5$$

Ted turns over a blue 5 first and then a black 8.

$$-5 - (+8) = -13$$
$$5 > -13$$

Kasha takes all four cards because 5 is greater than −13.

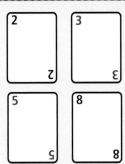

Variation (Subtraction with Three Cards)

Each player turns over three cards, subtracts the second number from the first number, and then subtracts the third number.

GAME **Match-It: Transformations**

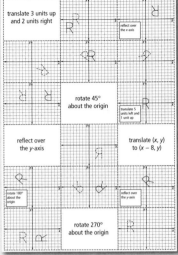

Materials | 1 set of *Match-It: Transformations* Transformation Cards (green UCSMP card deck or Game Master 8, p. GM10)

Players | 2

Skill | Identifying transformations of figures

Objective | To collect the most transformation cards

Directions

1. Shuffle the Transformation Cards.

2. Place them facedown on the table in any order.

3. Players take turns. When it is your turn:

   ■ Turn over two cards.

   ■ If the cards "match" (that is, if the two cards describe an entire transformation with pre-image, rule, and image), then take the two cards.

   ■ If there is no match, turn the cards facedown.

   ■ Your turn is over after you either make a match or do not match one set of two cards.

4. The game ends when there are not enough cards for each player to have another turn. The player with the most cards wins.

Match-It: Transformations
Transformation Cards

Example

Ben turns over the two cards shown at the right. Because the rule on the first card is shown by the image and pre-image on the second card, the cards match. So he takes both cards.

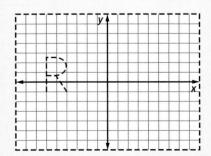

reflect over
the *y*-axis

Annie turns over the two cards shown at the right. Because the two cards are both images, the cards do not match. So she turns the cards facedown.

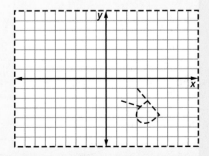

Top-It: Fraction Multiplication

Materials	number cards 1–12 (four of each)
	calculator (optional)
Players	2
Skill	Multiplication of fractions
Objective	To collect the most cards

Directions

1. Shuffle the cards and place them number-side down on the table.

2. Each player turns over four cards. The card numbers are used to form two fractions.

   - The first card drawn is placed number-side up on the table. This card is the numerator of the first fraction.

   - The second card drawn is the denominator of the first fraction and is placed number-side up directly below the first card.

   - The third and the fourth cards drawn form the second fraction.

3. Each player calculates the product of their fractions and calls it out. The player with the greatest product takes all the cards. Players may use a calculator to compare their products.

4. In case of a tie for the greatest product, each player repeats Steps 2 and 3. The player with the greatest product takes all the cards from both plays.

5. The game ends when there are not enough cards left for each player to have another turn. The player with the most cards wins.

Example

Kenny turns over the following cards in order: 1, 2, 4, and 8.

Liz turns over the following cards in order: 2, 3, 5, and 5.

Kenny's product is $\frac{1}{2} \cdot \frac{4}{8} = \frac{4}{16} = \frac{1}{4}$.

Liz's product is $\frac{2}{3} \cdot \frac{5}{5} = \frac{10}{15} = \frac{2}{3}$.

Liz's product is greater, so she takes all the cards.

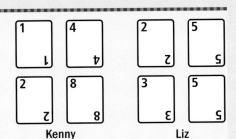

X-Tac-Toe

There are four variations of *X-Tac-Toe*. The materials and directions that are used in all four variations are listed below. The materials and directions that are specific to each variation will be listed with each variation.

Materials	*X-Tac-Toe* Outer Number-Card Board (Game Master 9, p. GM13)
	X-Tac-Toe Inner Number-Card Board (Game Master 10, p. GM14)
	number cards: Look at the variation you are playing to determine which number cards to use.
	counters (two colors) or pennies
	calculator (optional)
Players	2 or two teams of 2
Objective	To cover three squares in a row, in any direction (horizontal, vertical, or diagonal)

Directions

If you use a standard deck of playing cards:

- Use Aces as ones (1).
- Discard Jacks, Queens, and Kings.

If you use a UCSMP Math Deck, discard the 0 cards and cards greater than 10.

The color of the number on each card tells you if a card is a positive number or a negative number.

- Black cards (spades and clubs) are *positive numbers.*
- Red cards (hearts and diamonds) or blue cards (UCSMP Math Deck) are *negative numbers.*

If you use coins as counters, one player is HEADS and the other player is TAILS.

1. Shuffle the deck of cards.

2. Place the deck facedown in a pile on the table.

3. Look at the variation you are playing for Direction 3.

4. When there are no cards left in the draw pile, shuffle the cards in the discard pile to make a new draw pile.

5. The first player to cover three squares in a row in any direction (horizontal, vertical, and diagonal) is the winner of the game.

X-Tac-Toe: $ax + b = c$

Materials	*X-Tac-Toe* Equation Gameboard (Game Master 11, p. GM15)
	number cards 1–10 (four of each)
Skill	Solving equations of the form $ax + b = c$

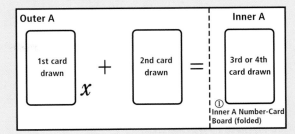

Advance Preparation

Set up the *X-Tac-Toe* Number-Card Board by folding the outer and inner boards as marked on Game Masters, pages G14 and G15. Slide the folded inner board inside the folded outer board so that the A sides are facing up, and it looks like the diagram above at the right.

Directions

For steps 1, 2, 4, and 5, refer to the directions on page G12.

3. Players take turns. When it is your turn:

- Draw three cards from the deck and place them face up on the Number-Card Board in the sequence they were drawn. The numbers on these cards are the values for *a*, *b*, and *c*, respectively, in the equation $ax + b = c$.

- Solve the equation.

- Try to match the solution with an interval that contains it on the Equation Gameboard. If a match is found, cover that grid square with your counter and your turn is over. If no match is found, your turn is over.

- If a player puts his or her counter on an incorrect square, the other player may place his or her counter on a correct square. The counter on the incorrect square should then be removed.

$0 \le x < 1$	$-2 \le x < -1$	$0 \le x < \frac{1}{2}$	$-5 \le x < -3$	$-1 \le x < 0$
$3 \le x < 5$	$\frac{1}{2} \le x < 1$	$2 \le x < 3$	$-1 \le x < -\frac{1}{2}$	$-3 \le x < -2$
$-\frac{1}{2} \le x < 0$	$1 \le x < 2$	$x < -5$ or $x \ge 5$	$1 \le x < 2$	$-\frac{1}{2} \le x < 0$
$-3 \le x < -2$	$-1 \le x < -\frac{1}{2}$	$2 \le x < 3$	$\frac{1}{2} \le x < 1$	$3 \le x < 5$
$-1 \le x < 0$	$-5 \le x < -3$	$0 \le x < \frac{1}{2}$	$-2 \le x < -1$	$0 \le x < 1$

Equation Gameboard

Example

Jeff turns over a black 2, then a blue 5, and then a black 4. His equation is $2x + -5 = 4$. He gets a solution of $\frac{9}{2}$ or 4.5. He can place his counter on any one of the squares labeled $3 \le x < 5$.

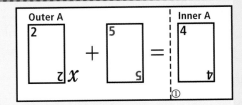

GAME

X-Tac-Toe: $ax + b < c$

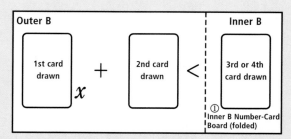

Materials	X-Tac-Toe Inequality Gameboard (Game Master 12, p. GM16)
	number cards 1–10 (four of each)
Skill	Solving inequalities of the form $ax + b < c$

Advance Preparation

Set up the *X-Tac-Toe* Number-Card Board by folding the outer and inner boards as marked on Game Masters, pages G14 and G15. Slide the folded inner board inside the folded outer board so that the B sides are facing up and it looks like the diagram above at the right.

Directions

For steps 1, 2, 4, and 5, refer to the directions on page G12.

3. Players take turns. When it is your turn:

- Draw three cards from the deck and place them face up on the Number-Card Board in the sequence they were drawn. The numbers on these cards are the values for *a*, *b*, and *c*, respectively, in the inequality $ax + b < c$.

- Solve the inequality.

- Try to match the solution with a number on the Inequality Gameboard that is contained in that interval. If a match is found, cover that grid square with your counter and your turn is over. If no match is found, your turn is over.

- If a player puts his or her counter on an incorrect square, the other player may place his or her counter on the correct square. The counter on the incorrect square should then be removed.

4	−2.2	$\frac{7}{8}$	$\frac{1}{3}$	3
$-1\frac{1}{2}$	1	$\frac{1}{2}$	−2	$\frac{1}{5}$
0.9	$-\frac{3}{4}$	0	$\frac{3}{4}$	−3.3
$-\frac{11}{5}$	2	−0.5	−1	$\frac{2}{3}$
−3	−2.5	$-\frac{5}{4}$	$1\frac{3}{8}$	−4

Inequality Gameboard

Example

Trent turns over a black 2, then a blue 5, and then a black 4. His equation is $2x + -5 < 4$. He gets a solution of $x < \frac{9}{2}$ or $x < 4.5$. He can place his counter on any one of the squares labeled with a number less than 4.5, such as −2.2 or $\frac{3}{4}$. On a gameboard with all of the spaces available, Trent could put his counter on any square.

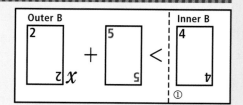

GAME

X-Tac-Toe: $ax + b = cx + d$

Materials	*X-Tac-Toe* Equation Gameboard (Game Master 11, p. GM15)
	number cards 1–10 (one of each color)
Skill	Solving equations of the form $ax + b = cx + d$

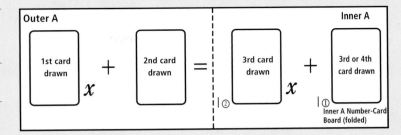

Advance Preparation

Set up the *X-Tac-Toe* Number-Card Board by folding the inner and outer boards as marked on Game Masters, pages G14 and G15. Slide the folded inner board inside the folded outer board so that the A sides are facing up and it looks like the diagram above at the right.

Directions

For steps 1, 2, 4, and 5, refer to the directions on page G12.

3. Players take turns. When it is your turn:

   - Draw four cards from the deck and place them face up on the Number-Card Board in the sequence they were drawn. The numbers on these cards are the values for *a*, *b*, *c*, and *d*, respectively, in the equation $ax + b = cx + d$.

   - Solve the equation.

   - Try to match the solution with an interval that contains it on the Equation Gameboard. If a match is found, cover that grid square with your counter and your turn is over. If no match is found, your turn is over.

   - If a player puts his or her counter on an incorrect square, the other player may place his or her counter on a correct square. The counter on the incorrect square should then be removed.

$0 \le x < 1$	$-2 \le x < -1$	$0 \le x < \frac{1}{2}$	$-5 \le x < -3$	$-1 \le x < 0$
$3 \le x < 5$	$\frac{1}{2} \le x < 1$	$2 \le x < 3$	$-1 \le x < -\frac{1}{2}$	$-3 \le x < -2$
$-\frac{1}{2} \le x < 0$	$1 \le x < 2$	$x < -5$ or $x \ge 5$	$1 \le x < 2$	$-\frac{1}{2} \le x < 0$
$-3 \le x < -2$	$-1 \le x < -\frac{1}{2}$	$2 \le x < 3$	$\frac{1}{2} \le x < 1$	$3 \le x < 5$
$-1 \le x < 0$	$-5 \le x < -3$	$0 \le x < \frac{1}{2}$	$-2 \le x < -1$	$0 \le x < 1$

Equation Gameboard

Example

Yolanda turns over a black 2, then a blue 5, then a blue 4, and then a black 10. Her equation is $2x + -5 = -4x + 10$. She gets a solution of $\frac{15}{6}$ or 2.5. She can place her counter on any one of the squares labeled $2 \le x < 3$.

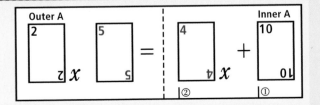

GAME

X-Tac-Toe: $ax + b < cx + d$

Materials	*X-Tac-Toe* Inequality Gameboard (Game Master 12, p. GM16)
	number cards 1–10 (one of each color)
Skill	Solving inequalities of the form $ax + b < cx + d$

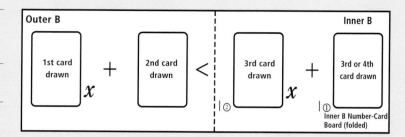

Advance Preparation

Set up the *X-Tac-Toe* Number-Card Board by folding the inner and outer boards as marked on Game Masters, pages G14 and G15. Slide the folded inner board inside the folded outer board so that the B sides are facing up and it looks like the diagram above at the right.

Directions

For steps 1, 2, 4, and 5, refer to the directions on page G12.

3. Players take turns. When it is your turn:

- Draw four cards from the deck and place them face up on the Number-Card Board in the sequence they were drawn. The numbers on these cards are the values for *a, b, c,* and *d,* respectively, in the inequality $ax + b < cx + d$.

- Solve the inequality.

- Try to match the solution with a number on the Inequality Gameboard that is contained in that interval. If a match is found, cover that grid square with your counter and your turn is over. If no match is found, your turn is over.

- If a player puts his or her counter on an incorrect square, the other player may place his or her counter on a correct square. The counter on the incorrect square should then be removed.

4	-2.2	$\frac{7}{8}$	$\frac{1}{3}$	3
$-1\frac{1}{2}$	1	$\frac{1}{2}$	-2	$\frac{1}{5}$
0.9	$-\frac{3}{4}$	0	$\frac{3}{4}$	-3.3
$-\frac{11}{5}$	2	-0.5	-1	$\frac{2}{3}$
-3	-2.5	$-\frac{5}{4}$	$1\frac{3}{8}$	-4

Inequality Gameboard

Example

Kiki turns over a blue 2, a blue 5, a black 4, and then a black 10. Her inequality is $-2x + -5 < 4x + 10$. She gets a solution of $x > -\frac{15}{6}$ or $x > -2.5$. She can place her counter on any one of the squares labeled with a number larger than -2.5, like 4 or $-\frac{5}{4}$. On a gameboard with all of the spaces available, Kiki would have 22 squares from which to choose.

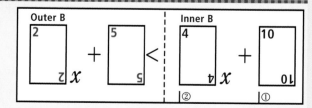

GAME

Match-It: Fraction Division

Materials	*Match-It: Fraction Division* Division Cards (blue UCSMP card deck or Game Masters 13–15, pp. GM17–GM19)
	calculator
Players	2
Skill	Dividing fractions
Objective	To collect the most fraction cards

Directions

1. Shuffle the Level 1 *Match-It: Fraction Division* Cards, page GM17.

2. Place them facedown on the table in a rectangular array in any order.

3. Players take turns. When it is your turn:
   - Turn over two cards.
   - If the cards "match," that is, if one card is a division expression and the other card is the solution to that expression, then take the two cards.
   - If there is no match, turn the cards facedown.
   - Your turn is over after you either match or don't match two cards.

4. Check answers using a calculator.

5. The game ends when there are not enough cards left for each player to have another turn. The player with the most cards wins.

＊

$\frac{18}{25} \div \frac{9}{5}$	$\frac{3}{4} \div \frac{9}{8}$	$\frac{\frac{1}{5}}{\frac{2}{9}}$	$\frac{3}{\frac{4}{3}}$	$\frac{\frac{15}{17}}{\frac{15}{17}}$
$\frac{10}{3} \div \frac{3}{10}$	$1\frac{2}{3} \div \frac{2}{3}$	$\frac{3}{\frac{16}{2}}$	$\frac{3}{14} \div \frac{1}{7}$	$\frac{\frac{8}{7}}{\frac{5}{7}}$
$\frac{3}{32}$	$\frac{2}{5}$	$\frac{5}{2}$	$\frac{100}{9}$	$\frac{9}{10}$
$\frac{8}{5}$	1	$\frac{2}{3}$	$\frac{3}{2}$	$\frac{9}{4}$

Level 1

Example

Danelle turns over two cards as shown at the right. Because $\frac{3}{14} \div \frac{1}{7} = \frac{3}{2}$, the cards match, and Danelle takes the two cards.

Mark turns over two cards as shown at the right. Because $\frac{100}{9} \neq \frac{9}{4}$, the cards do not match, so he turns the cards facedown.

$\frac{3}{14} \div \frac{1}{7}$	$\frac{3}{2}$
$\frac{100}{9}$	$\frac{9}{4}$

Variation (Levels 2 and 3)

The players must match a division expression to its answer or to another division expression with the same answer.

Level 2

Level 3

GAME Shape Capture: 3-D

Materials	*Shape Capture: 3-D* Shape Cards (green UCSMP card deck or Game Master 16, p. GM20)
	Shape Capture: 3-D Property Cards (green UCSMP card deck or Game Master 17, p. GM21)
Players	2 or two teams of 2
Skill	Identifying properties of 3-D shapes
Objective	To collect the most Shape Cards

Directions

1. Randomly spread out the Shape Cards picture-side up on the table. Shuffle the Property Cards and place them writing-side down in a pile on the table. Consider nets as representatives of 3-D shapes.

2. Players take turns. When it is your turn:

   ■ Draw the 2 top cards from the pile of Property Cards.

   ■ Take all the Shape Cards that have *both* of the properties shown on the Property Cards.

   ■ If there are no Shape Cards with both properties, your turn ends and the other player begins their turn.

   ■ At the end of a turn, if you have not taken a Shape Card that you could have taken, the other player may name and take it.

   ■ At the end of a turn, if you have taken a Shape Card that you should *not* have taken, the other player may take it.

   ■ Keep the used Property Cards separate from the original pile.

3. When all of the Property Cards in the pile have been drawn, shuffle *all* of the Property Cards. Place them writing-side down in a pile. Continue to play.

4. The game ends when there are fewer than three Shape Cards left or when one player has more Shape Cards than the remaining amount available.

5. The winner is the player with the most Shape Cards.

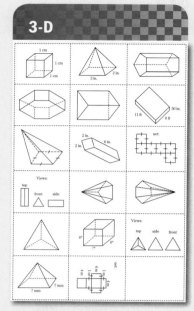

Shape Capture: 3-D
Shape Cards

Shape Capture: 3-D
Property Cards

GAME

Let's Data Deal

Materials	complete deck of number cards (View all cards as positive.)
	one set of Range, Median, and Mode *Let's Data Deal* Landmark Cards for each player (green UCSMP card deck or Game Master 18, p. GM22)
	Let's Data Deal Score Sheet (score pad or Game Master 19, p. GM23)
Players	2 to 4
Skill	Finding the range, mode, median, and mean
Objective	To score the most points by finding data measures

Directions

1. To play a round:

- Shuffle the number cards and deal five to each player number-side down.
- Players order their cards from least to greatest without revealing them.
- There are three ways players may score points using their five cards:

Range: The player's score is the range of the five numbers.
Example

Brady's hand:    Range = 12 − 1 = 11
points scored = 11

Median: The player's score is the median of the five numbers.
Example

Letti's hand:    Median = 9
points scored = 9

Mode: The player must have at least two cards with the same number. The player's score is found by multiplying the mode of the five numbers by the number of modal cards. If there is more than one mode, the player uses the mode that will produce the most points.

Example

Jerome's hand:    Mode = 8
points scored = 2 · 8 = 16

GAME
Let's Data Deal (continued)

2. Each player decides which data measure will yield the highest score for his or her hand. A player indicates his or her choice by placing one of the three *Let's Data Deal* Landmark Cards (Range, Median, or Mode) on the table. The player must use this data measure to calculate his or her score for the round.

3. Players can try to improve their scores by exchanging up to three of their cards for new cards from the deck. However, the *Let's Data Deal* Landmark Card stays the same.

Examples

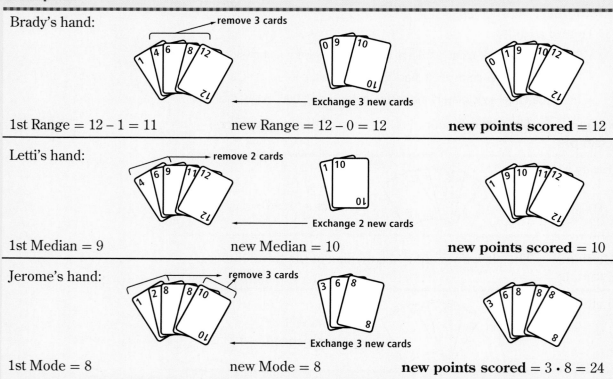

Brady's hand: remove 3 cards   Exchange 3 new cards

1st Range = 12 − 1 = 11   new Range = 12 − 0 = 12   **new points scored = 12**

Letti's hand: remove 2 cards   Exchange 2 new cards

1st Median = 9   new Median = 10   **new points scored = 10**

Jerome's hand: remove 3 cards   Exchange 3 new cards

1st Mode = 8   new Mode = 8   **new points scored = 3 · 8 = 24**

4. Players lay down their cards and record their points scored on the score sheet.

5. **Bonus Points:** Each player calculates the mean of their card numbers to the nearest tenth, and adds it to the points from their hand. Each player's score for the round is the sum of their points scored plus any bonus points.

6. Repeat Steps 1–5 for each round. The winner is the player with the highest score after five rounds.

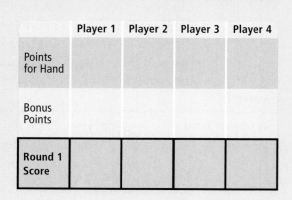

	Player 1	Player 2	Player 3	Player 4
Points for Hand				
Bonus Points				
Round 1 Score				

Selected Answers

Chapter 7

Lesson 7-1 (pp. 430–437)

Guided Example 2: Solution 1: Step 2: 25'; 30'; 41'; 41';
$AE + EB = AB$ because of the Putting-Together Model for
Addition; $41' - 25' = 16'$ **Step 3:** $30 \cdot 25$; 750 ft²; $16 \cdot 30$;
240 ft²; $750 + 240$; 990 **Solution 2: Step 3:** $30 \cdot 41$; 1,230 ft²;
$\frac{1}{2} \cdot 30 \cdot 16$; 240 ft²; $1{,}230 - 240$; 990

Questions: 1.

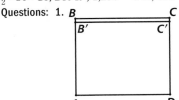

3. square feet
5. 120 m² **7. a.** 4
b. 12 **c.** 48
9. a. 3; 2.4 **b.** $\frac{1}{2}$; 6
c. n; p

11. a.

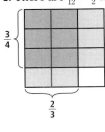

b. 11 mm, 60 mm **c.** 61 mm **d.** 330 mm²
e. 132 mm **13. a.** $246.7 \cdot \left(8 \cdot \frac{1}{4}\right) = 493.4$
b. $(246.7 \cdot 8) \cdot \frac{1}{4} = 493.4$ **15.** Associative
Property of Multiplication **17.** both
19. Answers vary. Sample: 5 inches by
5 inches; 25 inches by 1 inch
21. a. 10 inches by 4 inches **b.** 40 in²
23. 72 cm² **25.** The area becomes 16
times as large. Instances vary. Sample:
$(1 \cdot 4)(2 \cdot 4) = 32 = 16(1 \cdot 2)$, $(3 \cdot 4)(4 \cdot 4) = 192 = 16(3 \cdot 4)$, $(8 \cdot 4)(5 \cdot 4) = 640 = 16(8 \cdot 5)$ **27.** $\sqrt{8}$ units
29. a. Commutative Property of Addition **b.** Addition
Property of Equality **c.** Associative Property of Addition

Lesson 7-2 (pp. 438–443)

1. There are $\frac{6}{12} = \frac{1}{2}$ double-shaded squares.

3. A unit fraction is a fraction with
1 in the numerator and a positive
integer in its denominator. **5.** $\frac{1}{5y}$
7. $\frac{1}{4}$ **9.** The double-shaded area
represents $\frac{3}{12} = \frac{1}{4}$ of a square mile.

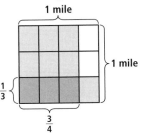

11. $\frac{1}{41}$ **13.** $\frac{ax}{by}$ **15.** $\frac{4}{13}$ **17.** $\frac{8}{9}$ **19. a.** $\frac{1}{6}$ **b.** $\frac{1}{360}$ **c.** $\frac{1}{8,640}$
21. Answers vary. Sample: A reciprocal of zero would

have to equal 1 when multiplied by 0, but any number
times 0 equals 0. **23.** 5 **25.** $\frac{16}{3}$ or $5\frac{1}{3}$ **27.** $\frac{5}{17} \cdot \frac{17}{5} = \frac{5 \times 17}{5 \times 17} = 1$
29. 6,144 pixels **31.** Answers vary. Sample:

Lesson 7-3 (pp. 444–449)

Guided Example 1: $3.35; $1.75; 6; $5.10; 6; $30.60
Questions: 1. $30 \cdot 25\frac{3}{4} - 30 \cdot 12\frac{1}{2}$ in²; $30\left(25\frac{3}{4} - 12\frac{1}{2}\right) = $
397.5 in²

3.

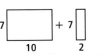

5. a. true **b.** false
7. $3ab - ac$; Check: let $a = 5$,
$b = 4$, $c = 3$; $a(3b - c) = $
$5(3 \cdot 4 - 3) = 5 \cdot 9 = 45$;
$3ab - ac = 3 \cdot 5 \cdot 4 - 5 \cdot 3 = $
$60 - 15 = 45$ **9.** $6p - 4q$;
Check: let $p = 24$, $q = 20$;
$8\left(\frac{3}{4}p - \frac{1}{2}q\right) = $
$8\left(\frac{3}{4} \cdot 24 - \frac{1}{2} \cdot 20\right) = $
$8(18 - 10) = 8 \cdot 8 = 64$; $6p - 4q = 6 \cdot 24 - 4 \cdot 20 = 144 - $
$80 = 64$ **11.** $12(1 - 0.01) = 12 - 0.12 = 11.88$ **13.** 100
15. Answers vary. Sample: If $a = 2$, $b = 3$, and $c = 5$, then
$a(b \cdot c) = 30$ and $ab \cdot ac = 60$. **17.** $0.2(100 - 0.25) = $
$20 - 0.5 = $19.95 **19.** $3a$ **21.** 30 square inches
23. $10n + z$ **25.** 60 square units **27.** True; vertical
angles are congruent.

Lesson 7-4 (pp. 450–455)

Guided Example: Solution 2: $\triangle DKR$; KY; KR; 4; 11; 4; 3; 22;
6; 16
Questions: 1. a. area of $\triangle MNI$ = area of $\triangle MNA$ + area of
$\triangle MTI$. **b.** area of $\triangle MNI = \frac{1}{2}$ area of $TINA$

3.

5. He forgot to distribute the one-half;
it should be $\frac{1}{2}(35 \cdot 12 + 5 \cdot 12)$.
7. 22.5 square units **9.** 390 square
inches **11.** blue: 299.25 in²; green:
299.25 in²; red and white: 199.5 in²
13. 9 square units **15.** 6 square units

17. a.

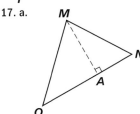

b. For sample drawn:
$AM = \frac{29}{32}$ in., $ON = 1\frac{1}{2}$ in.
c. $\frac{87}{128}$ or 0.7 in² **19.** $7x$
21. $11v - 4w$ **23.** $\frac{1}{9}$
25. 2.04 **27.** $\frac{1}{nm}$
29. a. 0.096 **b.** 135,000

Lesson 7-5 (pp. 456–462)

Guided Example: 310; 210; 520; 310; 730; 155; 730; 113,150
Questions: 1. false **3.** false **5. a.** 18 units, 15 units

b. 16 units c. 264 square units   7. $\frac{1}{2}k(m+n)$ 9. 320 in^2
11. 53,240 square miles   13. 32 square units   15. 6 square
units   17. a. 120 square units b. Since $120 = bh,$ and $b = 10,$
then $AT = h = 12.$ 19. 54 square units   21. C   23. 4, 5, 7
25.

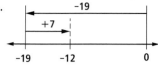

Lesson 7-6 (pp. 463–469)
Guided Example 3: $A = \pi r^2;$ ≈ 113.10 in^2; ≈ 84.82 in^2
Questions: 1. a. Answers vary. Sample: $\overline{AB}, \overline{AC}$ **b.** Answers
vary. Sample: $\overset{\frown}{DC}, \overset{\frown}{BC}, \overset{\frown}{DBC}$ **c.** $\overline{DB}$ **d.** Answers vary.
Sample: sector $CAB,$ sector DAC **3. a.** estimate **b.** 3.14
c. 3.142   **5.** πn m, 3.1n m   **7.** $2\pi m$ ft, 6.3m ft   **9.** 49π cm^2,
153.9 cm^2 **11.** πr **13.** $0.79r^2$ **15.** 142.56π cm^2 or about
447.87 cm^2 **17. a.** 289π cm^2 **b.** 34π cm **c.** 4 times **d.** 2
times **e.** No; answers vary. Sample: Doubling r always
quadruples $r^2,$ so the circumference is always doubled
while the area is always quadrupled.   **19. a.** $5\pi \approx 15.71$ ft
b. $25 - 6.25\pi$ ft$^2 \approx 5.37$ ft^2 **21. a.** true **b.** true
c. Commutative Property of Multiplication
23.   **25.** always

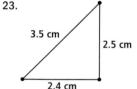

Lesson 7-7 (pp. 470–476)
Guided Example 1: Step 1: 1.5 **Step 2:** 8.5; 1.5; 12.75 **Step 3:**
When she works overtime, Megan makes $12.75 per hour,
which is 1.5 times her original wage of $8.50 per hour.
Questions: 1. a. 1.5 **b.** expansion **c.** $13.50   **3. a.** $P' = (0, 2.5),$
$O' = (2.5, 2.5), I' = (2.5, 0), N' = (7.5, 0), T' = (7.5, 2.5),$
$E' = (10, 2.5), R' = (5, 7.5)$ **b.** $P^* = (0, 0.8), O^* = (0.8, 0.8),$
$I^* = (0.8, 0), N^* = (2.4, 0), T^* = (2.4, 0.8), E^* = (3.2, 0.8),$
$R^* = (1.6, 2.4)$ **5.** (kx, ky) **7.** contraction   **9.** a and e
are expansions, b and d are contractions, and c is neither.
11. $5.25   **13.** 0.75 inch   **15. a.** 8 inches by 6.4 inches
b. 6.4 inches by 5.12 inches **c.** 64%   **17. a.** A **b.** A
19. about 4 inches   **21.** False; The other angle must be

acute so that their sum will equal 180°.   **23.** 20 minutes
25 seconds

Chapter 7 Self-Test (p. 479)
1. The area covered by the sprinkler is a circle with radius
15 feet, so the area covered is $(15^2)\pi$ square feet, which
is approximately 707 ft^2.   **2.** $28m + 14 - 70n$ **3.** $x + 6z$
4. $5x$ **5.** 817,518 mi^2 **6.** $\frac{5}{12} \cdot \frac{3}{4} = \frac{15}{48} = \frac{3 \times 5}{3 \times 16} = \frac{5}{16}$
7. $360\left(\frac{1}{2} + \frac{1}{3}\right) = 180 + 120 = 300$
8.

The number of double-shaded
squares is 15. The total number
of squares is $4 \cdot 12 = 48,$ so the
fraction of double-shaded squares
is $\frac{15}{48} = \frac{5}{16}$.   **9.** A right triangle with base b and height h
has the area of half a rectangle, or $\frac{1}{2}bh$. The triangle is
the sum of two right triangles, both with height $h,$ and
with bases b_1 and b_2 such that $b_1 + b_2 = b$. So, its area
is $\frac{1}{2}(b_1)(h) + \frac{1}{2}(b_2)(h) = \frac{1}{2}(b_1 + b_2)h = \frac{1}{2}bh$.   **10.** The town
is $2(10,000) = 20,000$ in. away, which is $\frac{20,000}{12} \approx 1,667$ ft.
11. Since $50\pi = 2\pi r =$ circumference, $r = 25$. Thus, the
circle's area is $\pi(25^2) \approx 1,963.5$ units^2.   **12.** True, since
area is determined uniquely determined by the two bases
and the height if the two trapezoids have the same bases
and height, they have the same area.   **13.** False, knowing
the bases and height does not give information about the
length of the other one or two sides, so the two trapezoids
may have different perimeters.   **14.** The auditorium has
$12(24) + 6(28) = 456$ seats.
15.

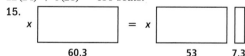

The areas of the two smaller rectangles are $53x$ and $7.3x$.
The area of the large rectangle is $(53 + 7.3)x = 60.3x$. The
areas of the two small rectangles sum to the area of the
large rectangle, so $53x + 7.3x = 60.3x$.   **16.** Answers vary.
Sample: If someone has $\frac{1}{4}$ of his week's pay unspent
and deposits $\frac{1}{3}$ of that into a savings account, he deposits
$\frac{1}{4}\left(\frac{1}{3}\right) = \frac{1}{12}$ of his week's pay.   **17.** Yes, they have the same
height and will have the same area if the bases are equal
(if $AB = EF$). Since $AB = DC$ and $EF = DC, AB = EF.$ So,

The chart below keys the **Self-Test** questions to the objectives in the **Chapter Review** on pages 480–483 or to the **Vocabulary**
(**Voc**) on page 478. This will enable you to locate those **Chapter Review** questions that correspond to questions missed on the
Self-Test. The lesson where the material is covered is also indicated on the chart.

Question	1	2	3	4	5	6	7	8	9	10
Objective(s)	I	E	E	E	G	C	C	K	A	J
Lesson(s)	7-6	7-1, 7-3	7-1, 7-3	7-1, 7-3	7-1	7-2	7-2	7-1, 7-2	7-1, 7-4	7-7

Question	11	12	13	14	15	16	17	18	19	20
Objective(s)	D	B	F	G	L	C	H	M	M	A
Lesson(s)	7-6	7-1, 7-5	7-1, 7-6	7-1	7-3	7-2	7-4, 7-5	7-7	7-7	7-1, 7-4

the two parallelograms have the same area. **18.** It is an expansion, since $2.5 > 1$.

19.

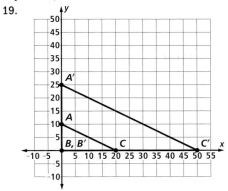

20. The area of $\triangle ABC = \frac{1}{2}bh = \frac{1}{2}(20)(10) = 100$ square units. The area of $\triangle A'B'C' = \frac{1}{2}(50)(25)$, or 625 square units.

Chapter 7 Chapter Review (pp. 480–483)

1. 60 square units **3.** 36 square units **5.** 96 square inches or $\frac{2}{3}$ square feet **7.** 75 square units **9.** 1,200 square units **11.** $\frac{1}{6}$ **13.** $9\frac{4}{13}$ **15.** 2 **17.** $23\frac{1}{5}$ **19.** 4.2 miles; 1.4 square miles **21.** $3x + 3y$ **23.** $6c - \frac{9}{2}d + \frac{3}{4}$ **25.** $3x$ **27.** $3a + b$ **29.** Multiply $30.00 by 6 and then subtract the product of $0.01 and 6 to get $179.94. **31.** Commutative Property of Multiplication **33.** Use the Associative Property to switch the parentheses and use the Commutative Property to change the order so the expression becomes $\left(\frac{1}{2} \cdot 2\right) \cdot \left(\frac{1}{7} \cdot 7\right) \cdot \left(\frac{5}{8} \cdot \frac{8}{5}\right) = 1 \cdot 1 \cdot 1 = 1$ **35.** The area of a trapezoid is $\frac{1}{2}h(b_1 + b_2)$. In trapezoid $ABCD$, $b_1 = BC$ and $b_2 = AD$. So, the area is $\frac{1}{2}h(BC + AD)$. **37.** A **39.** perimeter **41.** 3,145,728 pixels **43.** 15 ft^2 **45.** 1,100,000 km^2 **47.** 255π square feet or about 801 square feet **49.** 1,152 feet **51.** about 2,398,000 **53.** The area of the enlarged picture will be 1.69 times the area of the original. **55.** $3,328 **57.** Both $\frac{87}{97}$ and $\frac{67}{77}$ are less than 1, and the product of any two numbers that are less than 1 is also less than 1. **59.** The two rectangles are congruent, so they have the same area.

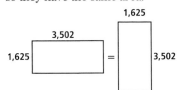

61.

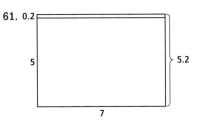

63.

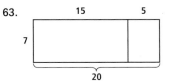

65.

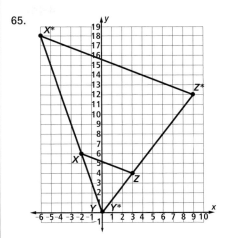

67. $(10x, 10y)$ **69.** The sides of $Q'U'A'D'$ are $\frac{1}{2}$ as long as the corresponding sides of $QUAD$;

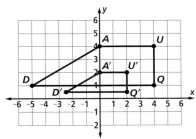

Chapter 8

Lesson 8-1 (pp. 486–492)

1. a. $0.25 + $0.25 + $0.25 + $0.25 + $0.25 + $0.10 + $0.10 + $0.10 = $1.55 **b.** $5 \times $0.25 + 3 \times $0.10 = $1.55 **3.** $2\ell + 2w$ **5.** $4a + 2b + 2c + d$ **7. a.** $x + x + x + x + x + x + x + x + x + x - x = 9x$ **b.** $(10 - 1)x = 9x$ **9.** $8C + 5D + 9$ **11.** $\frac{6}{5}n$ **13.** $-39x - 4y$ **15. a.** $-\frac{3}{5} + -\frac{3}{5} + -\frac{3}{5} + -\frac{3}{5} + -\frac{3}{5}$ **b.** -3 **17.** $(19.3h + 4s)$ cm^2 **19.** Monica is correct; use repeated addition to write $5m - m$. **21.** $7a$ **23.** $3x$ **25.** $6k + 6j$ **27.** $k < -8$ **29. a.** 12 **b.** 5,280 **c.** 3 **d.** 1,760

Lesson 8-2 (pp. 493–499)

Guided Example 2: a. Step 1 3.499 / gallon
Step 2 $\frac{\$3.499}{\text{gallon}} \cdot 10.2$ gallons **Step 3** $35.69 **b. Step 2** $n \cdot c = T$
Questions: 1. a. Only 6 tickets per student are available for the graduation ceremony. **b.** 6 tickets/student **c.** $6 \frac{\text{tickets}}{\text{student}}$
3. a. 1.99 **b.** $\frac{\text{dollars}}{\text{can}}$ **c.** Answers vary. Sample: Peas cost

$1.99 per can, and Sean needs to buy 4 cans of peas. How much money will Sean spend? **d.** $n \cdot c = T$; n is the number of cans, c is the price per can, and T is the total cost.
5. 15 apples   **7.** $600   **9. a.** 1.89 miles **b.** Answers vary. Sample: If Addy jogs 10,000 ft every morning, and there are 5,280 ft in 1 mile, how many miles does Addy jog?
11. a. 3,200 words **b.** For t = time in minutes, w = number of words typed, and r = words typed per minute, $w = r \cdot t$.   **13.** $\approx$ 23.6 inches   **15.** $7.86
17. about 487 kilometers   **19.** $40.5r$; $8.1r + 8.1r + 8.1r + 8.1r + 8.1r$ **21.** $\frac{3}{2}hx$ square units
23. a.

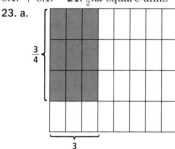

b. Answers vary. Sample: A plot of land is $\frac{3}{4}$ mile long and $\frac{3}{8}$ mile wide. What is the area of this plot of land?
25. Answers vary. Sample: $5 + (-5) = 0$
27. a. Answers vary. Sample: $(8 + 4) \cdot (3 \div (6 - 4)) = 18$; $8 + ((4 \cdot 3) \div (6 - 4)) = 14$ **b.** $-\frac{2}{3}$; $((8 + (4 \cdot 3)) \div 6) - 4$

Lesson 8-3 (pp. 500–506)

1. a. –235 feet/hour **b.** –0.05 point/minute   **3. a.** $-3 \cdot -5$ **b.** 15; the person weighed 15 more pounds 5 months ago.
5. 0   **7.** –13   **9.** 47.972   **11. a.** 44 **b.** 56   **13.** Negative; Answers vary. Sample: There is an odd number of negative numbers and there is no 0 in the multiplication. Therefore, the product must be nonzero and negative.   **15.** (–18, 6)
17.

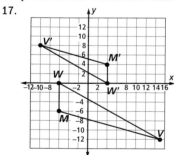

19. 21   **21.** $x = -1$
23. a. D
b. $-3{,}000 - m \cdot 250$
25. true
27. Quadrant II
29. a. 1,800 mm/hr
b. 9 m
31. hexagon

Lesson 8-4 (pp. 507–512)

Guided Example 1: Solution 1: $\frac{2}{3} \cdot \frac{1}{3} = \frac{2}{9}$ **Solution 2:** $\frac{2}{9}$
Questions: **1.** Events are independent if the outcome of one event does not affect the probability of the other event(s).
3. (b); Answers vary. Sample: Best friends often do things and go places, like concerts, together. Therefore, the probability of one friend going will influence the decision of the other friend, changing the probability that the second friend would go.   **5.** (b); Answers vary. Sample: The weather of one day is closely related to the weather of the next day.   **7.** (a); Answers vary. Sample: It is not likely

that the winning performances of Jayla's team and her brother's team are connected.   **9. a.** $\frac{2}{5}$ **b.** $\frac{3}{5}$ **c.** $\frac{4}{25}$ **d.** $\frac{9}{25}$ **e.** $\frac{6}{25}$
f. $\frac{16}{625}$ **11. a.** 36% **b.** 16% **c.** about 18 times   **13.** $\frac{1}{32}$
15. 125 times   **17.** 6 in.   **19. a.** 6 lines of symmetry **b.** 8 lines of symmetry **c.** n **21.** 2 inches taller

Lesson 8-5 (pp. 513–518)

Guided Example 2: 0.7 P; 80; 80; 70; 70; 80; 70; 0.8; 0.7; 0.56; 44%
Guided Example 4: 110; 90; 110; 0.9; 1.1; 0.99; 1
Questions: **1. a.** $53.00 **b.** $32.50 **c.** $34.45 **d.** $1.06P$; $0.65P$; $0.689P$ **3.** $20.86   **5.** 29.6   **7.** $105.45   **9. a.** $495,000
b. 160.5%   **11.** 300%   **13.** $2.59P$ **15.** $\frac{1}{216}$
17. $5 \cdot (12 + 8) = 100$ pages; $12 + 8 + 12 + 8 + 12 + 8 + 12 + 8 + 12 + 8 = 100$ pages   **19.** $1 - x + y$

Lesson 8-6 (pp. 519–523)

Guided Example 2: Solution: $-\frac{4}{7}$; $-\frac{3}{14}$; $-\frac{7}{4}$; $-\frac{4}{7}$; $-\frac{7}{4} \cdot \left(-\frac{4}{7}m\right) =$ $-\frac{7}{4} \cdot -\frac{3}{14}$; $1 \cdot m = \frac{21}{56}$; $m = \frac{3}{8}$ **Check:** $-\frac{4}{7} \cdot \frac{3}{8} = -\frac{12}{56} = -\frac{3}{14}$; yes
Guided Example 3 101.2% $\cdot p$; 1.012p; 101.2%; 1.012p = 36.94
$\left(\frac{1}{1.012}\right)1.012p = 36.94\left(\frac{1}{1.012}\right)$ Multiply both sides by $\frac{1}{1.012}$.
$p = 36.50$; $36.50
Questions: **1. a.** 100; w; 50g **b.** $w = 0.5g$ **3.** $\frac{1}{a}(ax) = \frac{1}{a} \cdot b$
5. $\frac{1}{a} \cdot (ax) = \left(\frac{1}{a} \cdot a\right)x$ **7.** $x = \frac{b}{a}$ **9.** $8.00   **11.** $f = 54\%$
13. $w = -1.5$ **15.** $b = 900$ **17.** $75.00   **19.** about 1,016,000 people   **21.** about $3.40   **23.** 180°   **25.** false

Lesson 8-7 (pp. 524–531)

Questions
1. a. Answers vary. Sample:

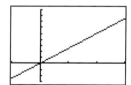

b. Answers vary. Sample: $t \approx 1.5$

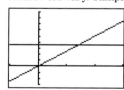

c. $t = 1.4$ **d.** the time it takes to walk 3.5 miles at 2.5 mph
3. Answers vary. Sample: (1, –2) and (3, –12)

5.

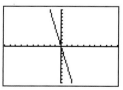

7.

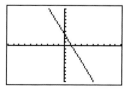

9. A

11. a.

b. 110 minutes c. 160 minutes

13. a.

d (days)	L (minutes)
1	580
2	560
3	540
4	520
5	500

b. **Gabriel's Phone Minutes**

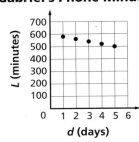

c. $L = 600 - 20d$
d. Yes, after 3 weeks he'll have 180 minutes left. **15.** $w = 9$
17. 8.1 inches
19. 51 hours 56 minutes 31 seconds + 6 hours 4 minutes 38 seconds < 51 hours 57 minutes 40 seconds

+ 6 hours 4 minutes 38 seconds

Lesson 8-8 (pp. 532–537)

Guided Example 3 Step 1: Addition Property of Equality
Step 2: Arithmetic **Step 3:** Multiplication Property of Equality
Step 4: Arithmetic
Guided Example 4 Step 1: $2x$; -4; 5; -4 **Step 2:** 4; 5; -4; 4; 54; 5
Step 3: $\frac{1}{5}$; 54; $\frac{1}{5}$; 5; 10.8 **Check:** 10.8; 10.8
Questions:

1. a.

b.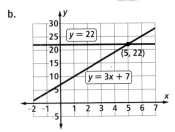

3. a. combine like terms b. Answers vary. Sample:
$24 - 24 + 12y = 60 - 24$
$12y = 36$; $y = 3$
5. a. Answers vary. Sample:
$(-14) + 14 + 5x = -21 + (-14)$
$5x = -35$; $x = -7$

b.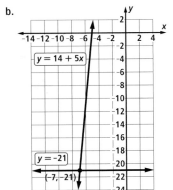

7. a. $a = 5$, $b = -13$, $c = 132$ b. $y = 29$ 9. $y = 38$
11. $B = -8$ 13. a. $\$1,500 + \$90n$ b. about 11 days
15. a. 640 b. $34\frac{6}{11}$

17.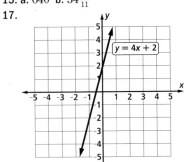

19. $\frac{2}{3}$ 21. -1
23. 240 minutes, or 4 hours

Lesson 8-9 (pp. 538–544)

Guided Example 1 $0.08P$; $\frac{1}{0.08} \cdot 0.08P \geq 22 \cdot \frac{1}{0.08}$; $1P \geq 22 \cdot \frac{1}{0.08}$; $P \geq 22 \cdot \frac{1}{0.08}$; $P \geq 275$
Guided Example 3 -420; -420; 380; $\frac{1}{11}$; positive; $\frac{1}{11}$; 380; $\frac{1}{11}$; $34\frac{6}{11}$ or $34.\overline{54}$; 34
Questions: 1. a. $-2 < 3$ b. $3 < 10.5$ c. $-4 > -14$ **3.** $6x \leq 180$; $x \leq 30$; She paid at most \$30 for each sweater.
5. $x > 2$: a, d, e, f; $x < 2$: b, c, g, h 7. 35 french fries or more 9. $x \geq 92$ 11. $a > \frac{1}{2}$ 13. a. $(100 - 5x)$

b.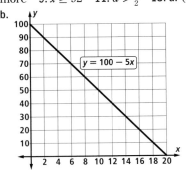

c. at most 16
d. $100 - 5x \geq 20$
15. $85g \leq 12,000$; 141 guests
17. $n \geq -5$
19. $x > -\frac{1}{3}$
21. 20 minutes
23. 1.6 km

Chapter 8 Self-Test (p. 548)

1. a. There are 10 addends, so the sum can be written as the product $10 \cdot 13.8$. b. 138 2. a. There are four addends,

so the sum can be written $4 \cdot (-2.5)$. **b.** -10 **3. a.** Each value being added is multiplied by -4, so the expression can be rewritten $(-4) \cdot (-6 + 11 + 17) = (-4) \cdot 22$. **b.** -88
4. 10% of 60% of 12 m is $0.10 \cdot 0.6 \cdot 12 = 0.72$ m , 10% of 60% of 13.5 m is $0.10 \cdot 0.6 \cdot 13.5 = 0.81$ m, so the smallest carpet is 0.72 meters by 0.81 meters. **5.** 112% of $156 = 1.12 \cdot 156 = 174.72$, so Tim is 174.72 centimeters.
6. This can be solved using units and rate factors: $24 \frac{\text{hours}}{\text{day}} \cdot 365 \frac{\text{days}}{\text{year}} = 8{,}760 \frac{\text{hours}}{\text{year}}$. **7.** $-1 \cdot 20 \cdot ab = -1 \cdot 20 \cdot (-1)(-9) = -1 \cdot 20 \cdot 9 = -180$ **8.** $(a+b)^2 + (a-b)^2 = (-1 + -9)^2 + (-1 - -9)^2 = (-10)^2 + 8^2 = 100 + 64 = 164$. **9.** $1{,}121 = 19r; \left(\frac{1}{19}\right)1{,}121 = \left(\frac{1}{19}\right)19r; 59 = r$ **10.** $2\frac{3}{4} = \frac{11}{12}b + 1\frac{3}{4};$ $2\frac{3}{4} - 1\frac{3}{4} = \frac{11}{12}b + 1\frac{3}{4} - 1\frac{3}{4}; 1 = \frac{11}{12}b; \left(\frac{12}{11}\right)1 = \left(\frac{12}{11}\right)\frac{11}{12}b; \frac{12}{11} = b$
11. $8v + v + v = 921; 10v = 921; \left(\frac{1}{10}\right)10v = \left(\frac{1}{10}\right)921; v = 92.1$ **12.** $42.7 \geq 6.1w; \left(\frac{1}{6.1}\right)42.7 \geq \left(\frac{1}{6.1}\right)6.1w; 7 \geq w$
13. $-7p + 5 < 54; -7p + 5 + (-5) < 54 + (-5); -7p < 49;$ $\left(-\frac{1}{7}\right)(-7p) < \left(-\frac{1}{7}\right)49; p > -7$ **14. a.** $\frac{9}{4}k = y; (4)\frac{9}{4}k = (4)y;$ $9k = 4y$ **b.** Multiplication Property of Equality **15.** Ines runs d miles every weekday and e miles on the weekend, so she runs $d + d + d + d + d + e$ miles or $5d + e$ miles in one week. In four weeks Ines runs $(5d + e) + (5d + e) + (5d + e) + (5d + e), 4(5d + e)$ or $20d + 4e$ miles.
16. $20d + 4e = 20(3) + 4(5) = 60 + 20 = 80$ **17.** If we let $P(F)$ be the probability that Brian forgets to brush his teeth on one day, then because the brushing on different days is independent we know $P(F \text{ and } F \text{ and } F) = P(F) \cdot P(F) \cdot P(F)$. We know $P(F) = \frac{1}{10}$, so $P(F \text{ and } F \text{ and } F) = P(F) \cdot P(F) \cdot P(F) = \frac{1}{1{,}000}$. **18.** If we let $P(C)$ be the probability that Colin's coin lands heads, $P(J)$ be the probability that Jun's die lands on an even number, and $P(L)$ be the probability that Luanda's die lands on an odd number, then because the events are all independent we know $P(C \text{ and } J \text{ and } L) = P(C) \cdot P(J) \cdot P(L)$. We know $P(C) = \frac{1}{2}, P(J) = \frac{1}{2}$, and $P(L) = \frac{1}{2}$, so $P(C \text{ and } J \text{ and } L) = P(C) \cdot P(J) \cdot P(L) = \frac{1}{8}$. **19.** $\$914.06 \cdot \frac{1}{14 \text{ calculators}} = 65.29 \frac{\text{dollars}}{\text{calculator}}$ **20.** $8.50 \frac{\text{dollars}}{\text{hour}} \cdot x \geq \$114;$

$\left(\frac{1}{8.50} \frac{\text{hour}}{\text{dollar}}\right) \cdot 8.50 \frac{\text{dollars}}{\text{hour}} \cdot x \geq \left(\frac{1}{8.50} \frac{\text{hours}}{\text{dollar}}\right) \cdot \$114; x \geq 13.42$ hours **21.** $0.44x + 10 < 405; 0.44x + 10 + (-10) < 405 + (-10); 0.44x < 395; \left(\frac{1}{0.44}\right)0.44x < \left(\frac{1}{0.44}\right)395; x < 897.73$

22.

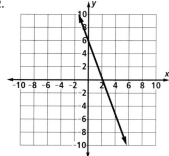

23.

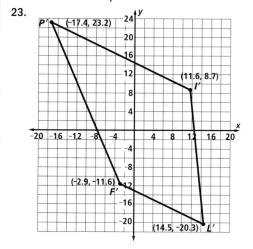

P' $(-17.4, 23.2)$
$(11.6, 8.7)$ I'
$(-2.9, -11.6)$ F'
$(14.5, -20.3)$ L'

Chapter 8 Chapter Review

1. 99 **3.** 144 **5. a.** 16 **b.** $-\frac{16}{9}$ **7.** -150 **9.** $A = \frac{1}{4}$
11. $c = \frac{11}{13}$ **13.** $m = \frac{36}{35}$ **15.** $j = 13$ **17.** $g = 569$
19. $H = 3$ **21.** $x = 28.25$ **23.** $r \leq 8; 5 \cdot 8 = 40; 5 \cdot 7 < 40$
25. $v < -9; -9 \cdot 9 = -81; -10 \cdot 9 < -81$ **27.** $r > -0.875;$
$4 \cdot -0.875 + 9 = 5.5; 4 \cdot -0.5 + 9 > 5.5$ **29.** $k < 576;$
$-\frac{576}{21} + 27 = -\frac{3}{7}, \frac{-570}{21} + 27 > -\frac{3}{7}$ **31.** 0 **33.** 0 **35.** $-1;$

The chart below keys the **Self-Test** questions to the objectives in the **Chapter Review** on pages 549–551 or to the **Vocabulary (Voc)** on page 547. This will enable you to locate those **Chapter Review** questions that correspond to questions missed on the **Self-Test**. The lesson where the material is covered is also indicated on the chart.

Question	1	2	3	4	5	6	7	8	9	10
Objective(s)	D	D	D	I	I	G	A	A	B	B
Lesson(s)	8-1, 8-3	8-1, 8-3	8-1, 8-3	8-5	8-5	8-6	8-3	8-3	8-6, 8-8	8-6, 8-8
Question	11	12	13	14	15	16	17	18	19	20
Objective(s)	B	C	C	E	F	F	J	J	G	H
Lesson(s)	8-6, 8-8	8-9	8-9	8-6, 8-9	8-2	8-2	8-4	8-4	8-6	8-9
Question	21	22	23							
Objective(s)	C	L	K							
Lesson(s)	8-9	8-7	8-3							

Multiplication Property of –1   **37.** 0; Multiplication Property of 0   **39.** A   **41.** Ted multiplied both sides of the equality by 5.   **43.** $54q < 540$ **45. a.** 455 miles **b.** Answers vary. Sample: If Petey can get $26 \frac{\text{miles}}{\text{gallon}}$ in his luxury sedan and he used up 17.5 gallons, how far did he drive?   **47.** $9 \frac{\text{dollars}}{\text{hour}} \cdot 7 \frac{\text{hours}}{\text{day}} \cdot 5 \frac{\text{days}}{\text{week}} \cdot 8 \text{ weeks} = \$2,520$ **49.** 25.83 miles per hour   **51.** $24 \frac{\text{hours}}{\text{day}} \cdot 60 \frac{\text{minutes}}{\text{hour}} \cdot 60 \frac{\text{seconds}}{\text{minute}} = 86,400 \frac{\text{seconds}}{\text{day}}$ **53.** $2,640x = 1,200 \cdot 43,560 = 52,272,000;$ $x = 19,800$ feet   **55.** $5 \cdot 12q = 100; q = 1.67$ pounds **57.** at most $7\frac{1}{3}$ years   **59.** 7.5 days   **61.** \$16.32   **63.** 42% **65.** $\frac{343}{5,832}$ **67.** $\frac{7}{250}$, or 0.028   **69.** $\frac{161}{500}$, or 0.322

71.

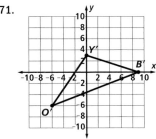

73.

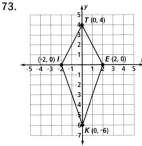 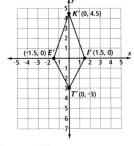

75. 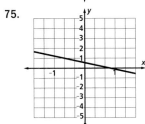   **77.**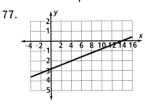

Chapter 9

Lesson 9-1 (pp. 554–561)

Questions: 1. a. 13.125 **b.** quotient 13, remainder 1   **3.** B **5. a.** 8 buses **b.** 7 buses **c.** 9 people   **7.** $A = BC + D$ **9.** Answers vary. Sample: **a.** A seafood restaurant serves 7 shrimp per dinner. If the restaurant has 50 shrimp, how many shrimp dinners can it serve? **b.** Mary made 50 cookies. She gave as many cookies as she could to each of her 7 friends so that they each had the same number of cookies. Mary ate the leftovers. How many cookies did each of Mary's friends receive and how many cookies did

Mary eat? **c.** A school uses 7-passanger vans to transport students. If 50 students sign up for a field study, how many vans does the school need?   **11. a.** 27 years and 145 days **b.** 21,921 days   **13. a.** No, the 0.36 means she receives 0.36 of \$50, not 36 cents. **b.** five \$50 bills, one \$10 bill, one \$5 bill, three \$1 bills   **15.** Yes, this is possible; $x = 54$. **17.** $x < -\frac{2}{3}$ **19. a.** $\frac{499}{500}$ **b.** $\frac{1}{125,000,000}$ **21.** C and E **23.**

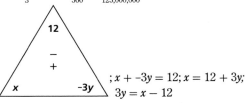

; $x + -3y = 12; x = 12 + 3y;$ $3y = x - 12$

Lesson 9-2 (pp. 562–566)

Guided Example 2. $\approx 0.98; \approx 0.80; 12$ **Questions: 1.** If a and b are quantities with different units, then $\frac{a}{b}$ is the amount of quantity a per quantity b. **3.** $40.2 \frac{\text{scores}}{\text{minute}}$ **5.** $\frac{50}{p}$ questions per page   **7.** 31 books with 1 left over   **9. a.** 8 cobblers **b.** 4 peaches   **11. a.** $0.125 \frac{\text{mi}}{\text{min}}$ **b.** $7.5 \frac{\text{mi}}{\text{hr}}$ **13. a.** $\frac{h}{m}$ beats per minute **b.** $60\frac{h}{s}$ beats per minute   **15.** Answers vary. Sample: If a person runs 2 miles in 20 minutes, and another runs 2 miles in 15 minutes, the person who ran 2 miles in 20 minutes ran at a slower rate. This corresponds to $\frac{a}{b} < \frac{a}{c}$.   **17.** 680 **19.** 31   **21.** No, division by zero is undefined.

Lesson 9-3 (pp. 567–571)

Guided Example 2. $\frac{2}{7}; 3; \frac{2}{7}; \frac{1}{3}; \frac{2}{21}$ **Questions: 1.** 4   **3.** \$6.80/hour   **5.** $\frac{2}{35}$ **7.** $\frac{25}{9}$ **9. a.** 1.25 **b.** $4\frac{1}{4} > 3\frac{2}{5}$ **11. a.** 2 miles **b.** Answers vary. Sample: multiplied $\frac{1}{3}$ by 6   **13.** $\frac{2y}{x}$ **15.** 50   **17.** $1.7 \frac{\text{shots}}{\text{minute}}$ **19.** $n = -\frac{233}{165} \approx -1.41$ **21.** $\frac{27}{4}$ **23.** –1

Lesson 9-4 (pp. 572–577)

Guided Example 2 $\frac{-1+5+1+-2+-6}{5} = -\frac{3}{5} = -0.6$ **Questions: 1.** –60   **3.** 0   **5.** Negative; for any a and b, $b \neq 0$, $\frac{-a}{b} = -\frac{a}{b}$ is negative.   **7.** Positive; for any a and b, $b \neq 0$, $\frac{-a}{-b} = \frac{a}{b}$ is positive.   **9. a.** \$3.75 per day **b.** $\frac{-7.50}{2} = -3.75$ **c.** 2; 7.50; more **d.** $\frac{7.50}{-2} = -3.75$ **11.** You can change subtraction to addition and division to multiplication or think of a real situation using negative numbers. Answers vary; some will find one method easier than the other. **13.** $x + y = 10; x - y = -6; xy = 16; \frac{x}{y} = \frac{1}{4}$ **15.** $x + y = -3;$ $x - y = -\frac{8}{3}; xy = \frac{17}{36}; \frac{x}{y} = 17$ **17.** $C = -40$ **19.** $-\frac{25}{2}$ **21.** $\frac{1}{288}$ **23.** the 16-ounce jar   **25.** $g = 368$ **27.** $\frac{1}{2}$; Store-brand prices are being compared to name brand prices. **29.** $\frac{672}{1,000}$; The volleyball team's wins are being compared to total games played.

Lesson 9-5 (pp. 578–582)

Guided Example 1 $\frac{6.78w}{6.78} = \frac{16.95}{6.78}$; 2.5; I bought about 2.5 pounds of coffee.

Questions: 1. $n = \frac{20}{3}$ **3.** $F = -72$ **5.** Question 3; Multiplication is easier when the coefficient is a fraction. **7.** $m \leq 7.5$ **9.** $y < 1$ **11.** > 280 pages **13.** $b - 3 = 19$ **15.** about 5.3 hours **17.** $x = -\frac{37}{320}$; $x \approx -0.116$ **19.** $p \leq \frac{3}{16}$ **21.** $-9.6 \times \frac{1}{3} = -3.2$ **23.** $-\$15 \times \frac{1}{3} = -\$5$ **25.** 10 pieces; one 6-inch piece **27. a.** 4.875 inches **b.** 28°, 152°, 152°

Lesson 9-6 (pp. 583–588)
Guided Example 1: .09; 9%; 9%; 9; 9
Questions: 1. $\frac{4}{3}$ **3.** 57.1% **5.** 6% **7.** 6 **9.** 10 **11.** $\frac{1}{2}$ **13. a.** South Africa produced about 133.41% of the gold produced by Australia. Australia produced about 74.96% of the gold produced by South Africa. **b.** about 25.41% **15. a.** 36% **b.** 64% **17. a.** London **b.** York **19.** Saturn **21.** B **23.** $-32 \cdot \frac{x}{5} = -19.2$; $\frac{-19.2}{\frac{x}{5}} = -32$; $\frac{-19.2}{-32} = \frac{x}{5}$; $x = 3$ **25.** C **27.** $\frac{1}{LH}$

Lesson 9-7 (pp. 589–595)
Guided Example 1 4; 8
Guided Example 3
Step 1: x; 8 **Step 2:** $5x = 56$ **Step 3:** $x = 11.2$
Guided Example 4
$6\frac{3}{4}$ inches; 200 miles; $6.75x = 200 \cdot 28.75$; $6.75x = 5,750$; 6.75; $851.\overline{851}$; 850
Questions: 1. A proportion is an equation stating that two ratios are equal. **3. a.** 1,800 **b.** $\frac{300}{10} = \frac{1,800}{60}$ **5.** C **7.** Answers vary. Sample: If you need 2 scoops of lemonade mix for 3 cups of water, then you would need 6 scoops of lemonade mix for 9 cups of water. **9.** $A = 3.5$ **11.** $C = 8$ **13.** \$4.55 **15.** 675 miles **17.** 24 matches **19. a.** sometimes but not always **b.** sometimes but not always **c.** always **d.** sometimes but not always **21.** 3 teaspoons **23.** 3 more cages **25.** 1.16% **27.** 312 km **29.** 0.0045 second

Lesson 9-8 (pp. 596–600)
Guided Example 2
Solution 1: 5; 1,150; 5,750

Solution 2: 4; 1,150; 20; $4 \cdot s = 20 \cdot 1,150$; 5,750; 5,750
Questions: 1. The sense to recognize situations in which setting up a proportion is a way to find an answer, and the ability to get or estimate an answer to a proportion without solving an equation. **3.** 8.6; As the percentage doubles, the amount doubles. **5.** A restaurant can cook more than one pizza at a time. **7.** People tire as they walk faster. **9.** about 120 times; 114 times **11. a.** 4 and 5 **b.** $4\frac{4}{9}$ hours **13.** 4,687.5 square miles **15.** 118.75 miles **17.** 12 cakes **19.** false **21.** \$69,054.05 **23.** $\frac{2}{3}$ **25. a.**

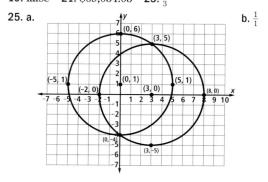

b. $\frac{1}{1}$

Lesson 9-9 (pp. 601–606)
Guided Example 3
$\frac{9 \text{ feet}}{17 \text{ mm}} = \frac{L}{60}$; 9; 60; 17; 31; 9
Questions: 1. The ratios of the corresponding lengths are equal. **3.** $31\frac{7}{9}$ **5.** 7.5 **7.** No; the ratios of corresponding sides are not proportional. **9.** 9 cm, 12 cm **11. a.** 15 cm long and 11.25 cm wide **b.** yes **c.** yes **13.** 47.14 miles **15.** 8.75 **17.** C **19.** $2\frac{4}{9}$ miles per hour **21.** 114.125

Chapter 9 Self Test (p. 610)
1. $13 \div \frac{2}{3} = 13 \cdot \frac{1}{\frac{2}{3}} = 13 \cdot \frac{3}{2} = \frac{39}{2}$

2. $-\frac{\frac{6}{5}}{\frac{9}{15}} = -\frac{6}{5} \cdot -\frac{1}{\frac{9}{15}} = -\frac{6}{5} \cdot -\frac{15}{9} = 2$

The chart below keys the **Self-Test** questions to the objectives in the **Chapter Review** on pages 611–613 or to the **Vocabulary (Voc)** on page 609. This will enable you to locate those **Chapter Review** questions that correspond to questions missed on the Self-Test. The lesson where the material is covered is also indicated on the chart.

Question	1	2	3	4	5	6	7	8	9	10
Objective(s)	A	B	A	H	G	I	C	C	C	C
Lesson(s)	9-3	9-4	9-3	9-2	9-1	9-6	9-5	9-5	9-5	9-5
Question	11	12	13	14	15	16	17	18	19	20
Objective(s)	K	K	E	E	F	H	H	D	J	I
Lesson(s)	9-4	9-4	9-7	9-7	9-4	9-2	9-2	9-4	9-7, 9-8	9-6
Question	21	22								
Objective(s)	J	L								
Lesson(s)	9-7, 9-8	9-9								

3. $\dfrac{5\frac{4}{9}}{12\frac{1}{3}} = \dfrac{\frac{49}{9}}{\frac{37}{3}} = \dfrac{49}{9} \cdot \dfrac{1}{\frac{37}{3}} = \dfrac{49}{9} \cdot \dfrac{3}{37} = \dfrac{49}{3} \cdot \dfrac{1}{37} = \dfrac{49}{111}$ **4.** 81 miles

per hour is equivalent to $\dfrac{81 \text{ miles}}{60 \text{ minutes}} = \dfrac{27}{20} = 1.35$ miles.

5. a. $\dfrac{390 \text{ oranges}}{\frac{35 \text{ oranges}}{1 \text{ crate}}} = 390 \cdot \dfrac{1}{35} = \dfrac{390}{35} = \dfrac{78}{7} = 11\frac{1}{7}$, so 11 crates

would be filled. **b.** $390 - 11(35) = 5$ oranges remain
6. Marla is $4(12) + 2 = 50$ inches tall. Geoff is
$6(12) + 3 = 75$ inches tall. Geoff is $\dfrac{75 \text{ inches}}{50 \text{ inches}} = \dfrac{3}{2} = 1.5$ times
as tall as Marla. **7.** $\dfrac{12p}{12} = \dfrac{96}{12} = 8 = p$ **8.** $12d < -18 + 7$,
$\dfrac{12d}{12} < \dfrac{-18 + 7}{12}, d < -\dfrac{11}{12}$ **9.** $21k = 1.05 + 4.3, 21k = 5.35, \dfrac{21k}{21} =$
$\dfrac{5.35}{21} = 5.35 \cdot \dfrac{1}{21} = \dfrac{107}{420}, k = \dfrac{107}{420}$ **10.** $\dfrac{1}{900} \cdot -900p \le 360 \cdot \dfrac{1}{900}$,
$p \ge -0.4$ **11.** $x = 72 \div -\dfrac{8}{9}, 72 \div x = -\dfrac{8}{9}, x \cdot -\dfrac{8}{9} = 72$
12. $x = 72 \div -\dfrac{8}{9}, 72 \div -\dfrac{1}{\frac{8}{9}} = 72 \cdot -\dfrac{9}{8} = -\dfrac{648}{8} = -81$

13. $10w = 9 \cdot 15, \dfrac{10w}{10} = \dfrac{9 \cdot 15}{10} = \dfrac{135}{10}, w = 13.5$ **14.** $245r =$
$350 \cdot 7, \dfrac{245r}{245} = \dfrac{350 \cdot 7}{245} = \dfrac{2450}{245}, r = 10$ **15.** false; By the
Algebraic Definition of Division, for any numbers a and b,
$b \ne 0, a \div b = a \cdot \dfrac{1}{b}$. If b is negative, $\dfrac{1}{b}$ will also be negative.
Since the product of two negative numbers is positive,
$a \cdot \dfrac{1}{b} = a \div b$ will also be positive. **16.** $\dfrac{32 \text{ problems}}{20 \text{ minutes}} = \dfrac{8}{5} =$
1.6 math problems per minute **17.** $\dfrac{26.2}{6 + \frac{23}{60}} = \dfrac{26.2}{\frac{383}{60}} = 26.2 \cdot \dfrac{1}{\frac{383}{60}} =$
$26.2 \cdot \dfrac{383}{60} = \dfrac{1,572}{383} = 4.1$ miles per hour **18.** $7p \div 34 = 129$,
$7p = 129 \cdot 34, 7p \div 129 = 34$ **19.** 114 dollars $\div \dfrac{8.5 \text{ dollars}}{1 \text{ hour}} =$
$114 \cdot \dfrac{1}{8.5} = \dfrac{228}{17} = 13\frac{7}{17}$ hours, so she must work 14 hours.
20. $0.44x = 405, \dfrac{0.44x}{0.44} = \dfrac{405}{0.44} = 920.4\overline{5}$, so there are 920 or
921 students in the school. **21.** $\dfrac{5}{9} = \dfrac{7}{x}, 5 \cdot x = 9 \cdot 7, \dfrac{5x}{5} =$
$\dfrac{9 \cdot 7}{5} = \dfrac{63}{5}, x = 12.6$ inches **22.** $\dfrac{t}{3.5} = \dfrac{5}{8}, 8t = 5 \cdot 3.5, \dfrac{8t}{8} = \dfrac{17.5}{8}$,
$t = 2.1875$

Chapter 9 Chapter Review (pp. 611–613)
1. 21 **3.** $\dfrac{147}{4}$ **5.** $\dfrac{ws}{2jq}$ **7.** -2 **9.** -15 **11.** $-\dfrac{33}{14}$ **13.** $t = -\dfrac{1}{3}$
15. $p = 4.859$ **17.** $p > -10$ **19.** $2\frac{53}{120} < j$ **21.** C
23. $k = \dfrac{36}{0.9}, 0.9 = \dfrac{36}{k}, k = 40$ **25.** $7x$ **27.** B **29.** negative
31. a. $35 \div 4 = x$ remainder y, where x is the number
of times he can use the machine and y is the number
of quarters he has left. **b.** 8 times and 3 quarters left
over **33. a.** $223 \div 15 = x$ remainder y, where x is the
number of full teams, and y the number of students left
over. **b.** 14 teams and 13 students left over **35.** $4\frac{1}{6}$ oz
of lettuce per salad **37.** about 834 people per square
mile **39.** Answers vary. Sample: If Blanca paid by check,
what was the average daily impact of the car rental on her
checking account? (Answer: –$54.17) **41.** about 15.6%
43. 1.9 **45.** $6\frac{1}{4}$ cups **47.** $\dfrac{16}{k}$
49. a.   **b.** $n = -3\frac{11}{15}$ **51.** 17.1

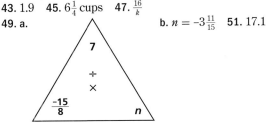

Chapter 10

Lesson 10-1 (pp. 616–621)
Questions: **1.** $t = 150$ seconds, $d = 600$ feet **3.** \$62
5. $A = 50 + 3.5w$ **7. a.** \$54.95 **b.** (5, 54.95) **9.** Evaluate
which graph is higher at the point $m = 120$.
11. $80 + 0.59m = 50 + 0.99m$ **13. a.** $P = 12,900 + 24.1g$
                                                              c. $P = 6,307 + 31.4g$
b.

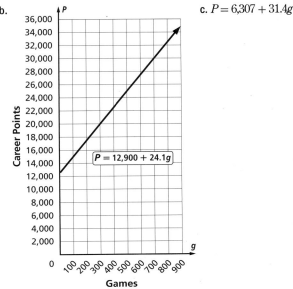

d.

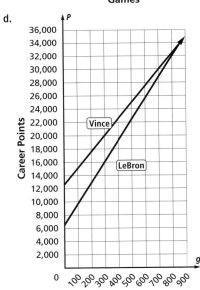

e. about 900 games
f. $12,900 + 24.1g = 6307 + 31.4g$
15. 75 minutes
17. D

19.

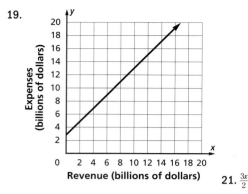

y-axis: Expenses (billions of dollars), values 2, 4, 6, 8, 10, 12, 14, 16, 18, 20
x-axis: Revenue (billions of dollars), values 0, 2, 4, 6, 8, 10, 12, 14, 16, 18, 20

21. $\frac{3x}{2}$

Lesson 10-2 (pp. 623–628)

Guided Example 2:

Step 2: $-4x$; $-4x$

Step 3: $9x$

Step 4: -30; -30

Step 5: -18; $9x$

Step 6: -2; 2

Check: -2; -2

Guided Example 3:

1. 17   **2.** 23

Check: 23; 23

Questions: **1.** Answers vary. Sample: add -46 to both sides, then add $4x$ to both sides; add $-8x$ to both sides, then add -13 to both sides.   **3. a.** $5t$ **b.** $t = 30$ **5.** $p = \frac{1}{6}; \frac{1}{6} +$
$3\left(\frac{1}{6}\right) - 5 = -2\left(\frac{1}{6}\right) - 4; \frac{2}{3} - 5 = -\frac{1}{3} - 4; -\frac{13}{3} = -\frac{13}{3}$
7. $m = 1$; $99 + 19(1) = 99(1) + 19$;
$99 + 19 = 99 + 19$; $118 = 118$ **9.** $x = -\frac{1}{7}$;
$36 - 42\left(-\frac{1}{7}\right) = 6\left(7\left(-\frac{1}{7}\right) + 8\right); 36 + 6 = 6(-1 + 8); 42 = 6(7)$;
$42 = 42$ **11.** $x = -\frac{209}{51}$ **13.** $d = \frac{27}{2}; 48 + \frac{27}{2} +$
$2\left(30 - 4\left(\frac{27}{2}\right)\right) = \frac{27}{2}; 48 + \frac{27}{2} + 60 - 8\left(\frac{27}{2}\right) = \frac{27}{2}; 108 - 7\left(\frac{27}{2}\right) =$
$\frac{27}{2}, \frac{216}{2} - \frac{189}{2} = \frac{27}{2}; \frac{27}{2} = \frac{27}{2}$ **15.** $y = \frac{9}{20}; \frac{7}{12}\left(\frac{9}{20}\right) + \frac{3}{4} = 2\left(\frac{9}{20}\right) + \frac{9}{20}\over 4$;
$\frac{21}{80} + \frac{3}{4} = \frac{9}{10} + \frac{9}{80}; \frac{21 + 60}{80} = \frac{72 + 9}{80}; \frac{81}{80} = \frac{81}{80}$ **17. a.** Step 3
b. $x = 3.5$ **19. a.** 17.67% **b.** \$288.67   **21.** $y + x = 180 -$
$133 = 47$

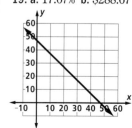

23. a. $\left(\frac{3}{4} \text{ mi}\right) \cdot \left(\frac{7}{4} \text{ mi}\right)$

b. $\frac{21}{16}$ mi

Lesson 10-3 (pp. 629–634)

Guided Example 3

Step 1: Answers vary. Sample: $(3, 0), (6, 2); \frac{2}{3}x - 2$ will be an integer if x is a multiple of 3.

Step 2: solid

Step 3:

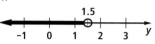

$y \geq \frac{2}{3}x - 2$

Step 4: Answers vary. Sample: $(0, 0), 0 > \frac{2}{3}(0) - 2$

Questions: 1. $a = b$ **3.** $a < b$ **5.** less than π or greater than π

7. a.

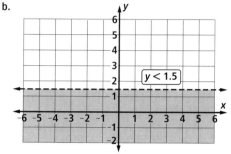

number line with point at 1.5, open circle; values $-1, 0, 1, 2, 3$; y

b.

graph $y < 1.5$

9. $x \leq 3$

11.

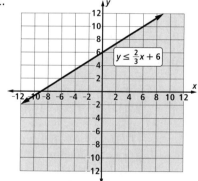

graph $y \leq \frac{2}{3}x + 6$

13. iii; Only iii has a graph of the equation of $y = \frac{1}{2}x + 3$.
15. ii; Only ii shows values above the line $y = x - \frac{3}{4}$.
17. iv; Only iv has a graph of the equation $y = -4$.
19. $t = \frac{200}{99}$ sec; $d = \frac{1{,}000}{99}$ m   **21. a.** 7,625 square units
b. 14,563 square units

23. a.

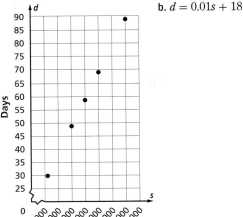

b. $d = 0.01s + 18$

Lesson 10-4 (pp. 635–640)

Guided Example 3
$>$; 0.40; $>$; 0.40; $>$; 30; $>$; 75; 75

Questions: 1. a. $\$(37.14 + 2.3w)$ **b.** $\$(46.35 + 1.95w)$
c. after 27 weeks **3. a.** $-3z - 5 > 11$; $z < -\frac{16}{3}$
b. $-5 > 3z + 11$; $-\frac{16}{3} > z$ **c.** Answers vary. Some students
prefer Part b because it does not involve division by a
negative number, some prefer Part a because it places the
variable on the left. **d.**

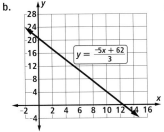

5. $1.5 < q$ **7.** $21 \geq x$
9. $50 > 80 - 0.40m$,
$m > 75$
11. a. $3.95 + 0.19m >$
$4.95 + 0.16m$, where
m is the number of
minutes **b.** $m > 33\frac{1}{3}$
13. 2014 **15.**
17. a. 5
b. $x = -23{,}987$
c. $\frac{845}{12}$

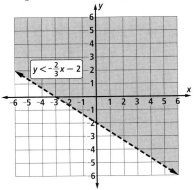

Lesson 10-5 (pp. 641–646)

Guided Example 1 $3n$; $4w$; $3n$; $4w$
Questions: 1. x; y **3.** 2.5 **5.** Yes, let $n = 10$, then
$3 \cdot 10 + 4w = 206$, so $4w = 176$, and $w = 44$.
7. a. $0.05n + 0.1d + 0.25q$ **b.** Answers vary. Sample:
$(20, 0, 0)$, $(5, 5, 1)$, $(10, 0, 2)$ **9. a.** $n + 5f + 10t + 20w$

b. $5f + 20w = 85$ **11. a.** $2.35 = 0.1m + 0.25b$ **b.** Answers
vary. Sample: $m = 1, b = 9$ **13.** yes **15.** $1{,}000T + 100h +$
$10t + u$ **17.** $30{,}000 + 3{,}000t = 45{,}000 + 1{,}500t$ **19.** $5x +$
$(-5x) + 14 \geq 8x - 25 + 5x$; $13x - 25 \leq 14$; $25 + 13x -$
$25 \leq 14 + 25$; $13x \leq 39$; $x \leq 3$ **21.** 2.1048

Lesson 10-6 (pp. 647–653)

Questions: 1. a. 25 **b.** $n = 9$ boxes of nuts, $w = 25$ rolls
of wrapping paper. **3.** A **5.** E **7.** The point $(-4, 15)$
satisfies the equation $y = \frac{18 - 3x}{2}$. **9. a.** $y = \frac{3}{2}x - 3$
b.

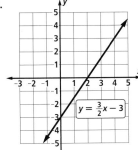

11. D **13.** B
15. changing $<$ to $\leq$ or
changing $>$ to $\geq$
17. a. $5x + 3y = 62$, where
x is the number of times
the beanbag landed in
the bucket and y is the
number of times it landed
on the rim or against the
bucket.

c. $(1, 19)$; $(4, 14)$; $(7, 9)$

b.

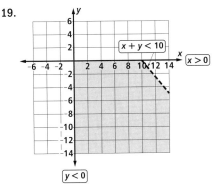

19.

21. a. 17 **b.** $+ 0.17$ **23. a.** $9.71 \frac{m}{sec}$ **b.** 165.7 seconds
25. Let z be the length of the third side; then
$z < 8x - y$, $z > 3y - 2x$, $z > 2x - 3y$.

Lesson 10-7 (pp. 654–658)

Questions: 1. At 40 minutes, Bick was 1.6 miles from home.
3. The length of time that was spent at the library 1.6 miles
away from home was 13 minutes. **5.** C **7.** Slope. $\overline{EF}$ is
steeper than $\overline{AB}$. So Bick biked faster on the way home.
9. One hour after the graph begins, the train is 35 miles
west of the station.

11.

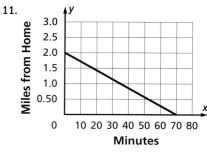

13. Answers vary. Sample: Rico takes a trip to see his friend Phil. Phil lives 10 miles away, and it takes Rico one hour to run there.

He stays for 3 hours, walks 5 miles back in an hour, and stops for 30 minutes to get a hamburger. Then Rico walks the remaining 5 miles back home in 45 minutes.

15. a. $8x + 5y = 52$ **b.** No, a ring is either hit or is not hit.

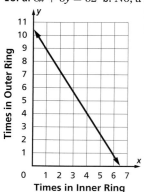

17. $C = 0.49n$ **19. a.** 20 **b.** 2 **c.** 80 **21.** C

Lesson 10-8 (pp. 659–665)

Questions: 1. a. d **b.** C **3.** Answers vary. Sample: $(3, 9.425)$ **5.** parabola **7. a.** The graph of $y = x^2$ includes points with negative x-coordinates. **b.** The two graphs are the same for positive values of x.

9. a.

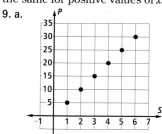

b.

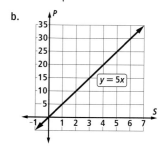

c. Answers vary. Sample: The graph is a line that intersects the point $(0, 0)$ and has a slope of 5.

11.

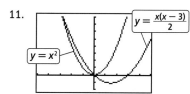

Answers vary. Sample: Both graphs contain the points $(0, 0)$ and $(-3, 9)$, but the graph of $y = x^2$ contains only positive values of y and is narrower than the graph of $y = \frac{x(x-3)}{2}$.

13. a. Answers vary. Sample: $(0, 0)$, $(-1, 1)$, $(2, 2)$, $(-4, 4)$, $(5, 5)$, $(7, 7)$

b.

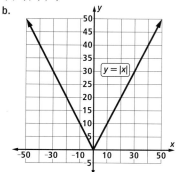

15.

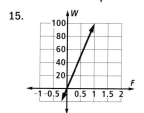

17. a.

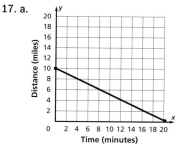

b. 0.85 ounce per minute **19.** 0.077 square mile **21.** 7

Chapter 10 Self-Test (p. 668)

1. $3y - 12 - 3y = 4y + 88 - 3y$; $-12 = y + 88$; $y = -100$

2. $8a - 1.5 - 3a = 3a - 7 - 3a$; $5a - 1.5 = -7$; $5a = -5.5$; $a = -1.1$ **3.** $\frac{3}{2}x + 2 + \frac{1}{2}x \le -\frac{1}{2}x - 2 + \frac{1}{2}x$; $2x + 2 \le -2$; $2x \le -4$; $x \le -2$ **4. a.** Let x represent a quantity of walnuts in pounds. Then for the store to be more economical, $3x + 0 > 2x + 10.95$ or $3x > 2x + 10.95$. **b.** $3x - 2x > 2x + 10.95 - 2x$; $x > 10.95$ pounds

5.

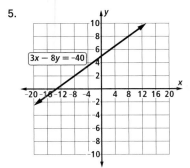

$3x - 8y = -40$

6.

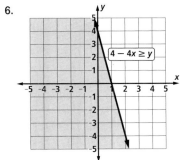

$4 - 4x \geq y$

7.

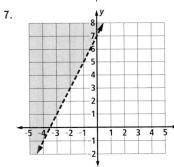

8. This situation fits the form $Ax + By = C$, where A, B, and C are amounts in dollars and x and y are quantities of baked goods sold. The appropriate sentence is $12m + 10n = 480$. **9.** This situation fits the form $Ax + By \leq C$, where A, B, and C are mass in kilograms and x and y are quantities of furniture loaded onto the elevator without exceeding the weight limit. The appropriate inequality is $4c + 22d \leq 4,000$. **10. a.** Answers vary.

Sample: Use values of r between 0 and 5, with r changing by 0.5 each time, and substitute them into the equation to get values for V.

r	$V = \frac{5}{3}\pi r^2$	r	$V = \frac{5}{3}\pi r^2$
0	0	3	47.124
0.5	1.309	3.5	64.141
1	5.236	4	83.776
1.5	11.781	4.5	106.03
2	20.944	5	130.90
2.5	32.725		

b. Graph V on the y-axis and r on the x-axis:

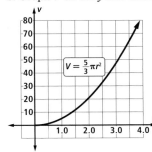

$V = \frac{5}{3}\pi r^2$

11. $5.5 - 0.5r + 0.5r > \frac{2}{5} + 2r + 0.5r$; $2.5r < 5.5 - 0.4$; $r < 2.04$ **12.** $0.08d + 0.09 - 0.08d = 0.09d + 0.08 - 0.08d$; $0.09 = 0.08 + 0.01d$; $0.01d = 0.01$; $d = 1$ **13.** $\frac{2h}{7} - \frac{3}{14} + \frac{4h}{7} < -\frac{4h}{7} - 66 + \frac{4h}{7}$; $\frac{6h}{7} - \frac{3}{14} < -66$; $6h - 1.5 < -66(7)$; $6h < -462 + 1.5$; $6h < 460.5$; $h < -76.75$

14. Graph the equations $y = 20x$ and $y = 18x + 100$ for Lorraine and Nell respectively, where x represents time in seconds, and y represents distance run in feet.

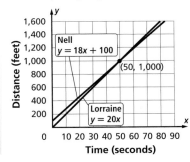

Nell
$y = 18x + 100$
(50, 1,000)
Lorraine
$y = 20x$

15. $20x + 0 = 18x + 100$ **16.** From the graph, we see that the lines intersect at $x = 50$ seconds and $y = 1,000$ ft.

The chart below keys the **Self-Test** questions to the objectives in the **Chapter Review** on pages 669–671 or to the **Vocabulary (Voc)** on page 667. This will enable you to locate those **Chapter Review** questions that correspond to questions missed on the **Self-Test**. The lesson where the material is covered is also indicated on the chart.

Question	1	2	3	4	5	6	7	8	9	10
Objective(s)	A	A	B	C	F	E	E	D	D	H
Lesson(s)	10-2	10-2	10-4	10-1, 10-2, 10-4	10-6	10-3	10-3	10-5	10-5	10-7

Question	11	12	13	14	15	16	17
Objective(s)	B	A	B	G	C	A	H
Lesson(s)	10-4	10-2	10-4	10-7	10-1, 10-2, 10-4	10-2	10-8

17.

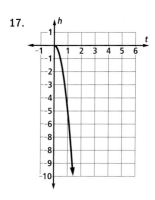

Chapter 10 Chapter Review (pp. 669–671)

1. $x = 23$ **3.** $g = -4$ **5.** $\ell = \frac{39}{10}$ **7.** $q > -\frac{5}{2}$ **9.** $s \leq 65$

11. $n \geq \frac{567}{11}$ **13. a.** $0.05m + 25{,}000 = 0.16m + 20{,}000$

b. $m \approx 45{,}455$ **15. a.** $0.4g + 30 > 0.2g + 55$ **b.** $g > 125$

17. a. $3.00f + 2 > 2.95f + 20$ **b.** $f > 360$

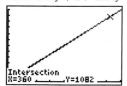

19. $15a + 10c = 265$

21. $15d + 5m \leq 150$

23. $7t + 3f = 43$

25.

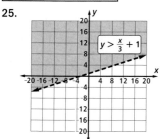

27.

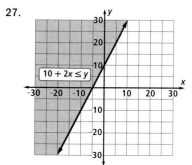

29.

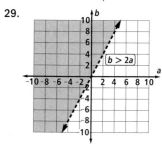

31.

33.   **35.**

37.   **39.**

41.

43.

45. a.   **b.**

47. a.   **b.**

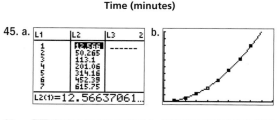

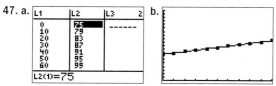

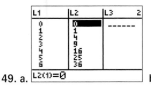

49. a. 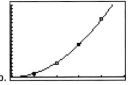 b.

Chapter 11

Lesson 11-1 (pp. 674–679)

Questions: 1. Answers vary. Sample: tabletop **3.** plane, plane **5.** $\overrightarrow{PQ}$ **7.** Q, P, H **9.** Answers vary. Sample: $\overleftrightarrow{RH}$ **11.** They are skew lines. **13.** always

15.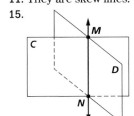

17. Answers vary. Sample: plane *BAEF* and plane *CBFG*
19. Answers vary. Sample: $\overrightarrow{BC}$ intersects plane *CDHG* only at *C.* **21.** Answers vary. Sample: $\overleftrightarrow{AB}$ and $\overleftrightarrow{FG}$ **23.** If two different planes intersect, then their intersection is a line.

25. a. yes **b.** yes **27. a.** *H* **b.** *F* **c.** *D* **29. a.** 18.34, 12.6, 12.04, 4.9, 4.06, 15.4, 5.6, 9.52, 15.4, 10.64 **b.** 7.86, 5.4, 5.16, 2.1, 1.74, 6.6, 2.4, 4.08, 6.6, 4.56 **31.** Yes; by the Pythagorean Theorem, the diagonal is about 36.37 cm, which is about 14.32 inches.

Lesson 11-2 (pp. 680–685)

Questions: 1. true **3. a.** triangles *ABC* and *DEF,* quadrilaterals *BCFE, ABED, ACFD* **b.** *A, B, C, D, E, F* **c.** $\overline{BE}, \overline{ED}, \overline{AD}, \overline{AB}, \overline{BC}, \overline{CF}, \overline{DF}, \overline{EF}, \overline{AC}$ **5.** prism **7.** not a prism, the base (a circle) is not a polygon **9.** triangular prism **11.** hexagonal prism **13.** length, width, height

15.

17. pencil **19.** I and II; opposite sides are parallel and translation images of each other. Figure II has only one base shaded.

21. 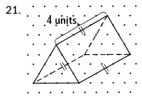 23.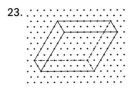

25. always **27.** They can intersect at one point, at infinitely many points, or never intersect.

29. a.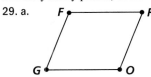

b. Opposite sides are parallel and equal in length. **c.** Opposite angles have equal measure, and consecutive angles are supplementary.

31. a. Answers vary. Sample: the length of the crust of a 10" pizza **b.** Answers vary. Sample: the ratio of boys to girls in a class **c.** Answers vary. Sample: the low temperature in Barrow Alaska, on January 7 **d.** Answers vary. Sample: the number of sides of a Yield sign

Lesson 11-3 (pp. 686–690)

Questions: 1. triangle **3.** 9 **5.** 6

7.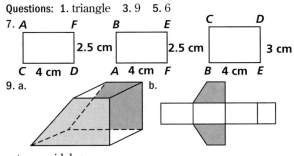

9. a. 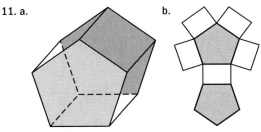 b.

c. trapezoidal

d.
Faces	Edges	Vertices
6	12	8

11. a. 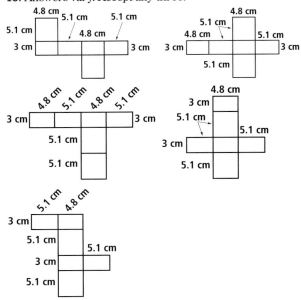 b.

c. pentagonal

d.
Faces	Edges	Vertices
7	15	10

13. Answers vary. Accept any three.

15. false **17.** false **19.** triangular prism **21.** no

23. Yes, 6-3, 2-5, 1-4 would face each other. **25.** Yes, the figure has two pentagons as its bases, which are congruent and lie in parallel planes.

27.

8.5 ft

40 ft

8 ft

29. $j = 28.75$

Lesson 11-4 (pp. 691–695)

Questions: 1. different 2-D views of the structure

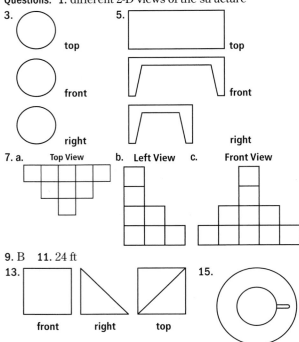

3. top, front, right

5. top, front, right

7. a. Top View **b.** Left View **c.** Front View

9. B **11.** 24 ft

13. front, right, top **15.**

17. No, the definition must specify that the congruent faces are polygons and that they lie in parallel planes. If the congruent faces lie along an edge (adjacent in 3-D space), the figure may not be a prism. A cylinder has two congruent faces, but it is not a prism. **19.** 1: 800,000 **21.** 20 fl oz

Lesson 11-5 (pp. 696–702)

Guided Example

Step 1: top dimensions: 4×8
front dimensions: $2\frac{2}{3} \times 8$
right dimensions: $2\frac{2}{3} \times 4$

Step 2: 4, 32; 8, $21\frac{1}{3}$; 4, $10\frac{2}{3}$

Step 3: 32; $21\frac{1}{3}$; $10\frac{2}{3}$; 64

Questions: 1. the amount of space inside of a 3-dimensional figure **3.** A **5.** B **7.** B **9. a.** 17.5 in. by 12 in. by 15.25 in. **b.** 1,319.75 in^2 **c.** 3,202.5 in^3

11. a. 3 in.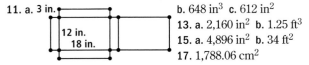

12 in.
18 in.

b. 648 in^3 **c.** 612 in^2
13. a. 2,160 in^2 **b.** 1.25 ft^3
15. a. 4,896 in^2 **b.** 34 ft^2
17. 1,788.06 cm^2

19. Front: **Top:** **Left:**

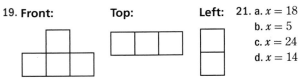

21. a. $x = 18$
b. $x = 5$
c. $x = 24$
d. $x = 14$

23. a. $2.25\pi \approx 7.07$ in^2 **b.** $0.5625\pi \approx 1.77$ in^2 **c.** $1.6875\pi \approx 5.30$ in^2 **d.** $3\pi \approx 9.42$ in. **25.** Answers vary. Sample: $\triangle SOX, \triangle SXO, \triangle OXS$

Lesson 11-6 (pp. 703–708)

Guided Example 2

a. $\pi(2.5)(3.75) \approx 29.5$ in^2; 29.5 in^2; **b.** 1.25 in.; (1.25); 4.9; 4.9; 9.8 in^2; $S.A \approx 29.5$ in^2 + 9.8 in$^2 \approx 39.3$ in^2; 39.3 in^2

Guided Example 3

Step 1 $2\pi(20) \cdot 15 \approx 1,885$ cm^2

Step 2 $\pi \cdot 20^2 \cdot 2 \approx 2,513$ cm^2

Step 3 1,885 cm^2 + 2,513 cm^2 = 4,398 cm^2

Questions: 1. triangular prism **3.**

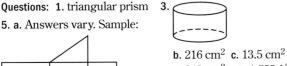

5. a. Answers vary. Sample:

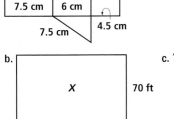

12 cm

7.5 cm 6 cm

7.5 cm 4.5 cm

b.

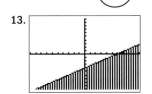

X

70 ft

35 ft

13.

b. 216 cm^2 **c.** 13.5 cm^2
d. 243 cm^2 **7.** 1,755 ft^2
9. a. 47.1 in^2 **b.** 14.1 in^2
11. a. circle

c. 7,696.9 ft^2 **d.** 52 gallons

15. 741 ft **17.** 1.25 square miles **19.** 8 **21.** $x > -2$

Lesson 11-7 (pp. 709–713)

Guided Example 2

Step 2. 10.24π cm$^2 \approx 32.17$ cm^2

Step 3. 122.88π cm$^3 \approx 386.04$ cm^3

Step 4. Volume is expressed in cubic centimeters.

Questions: 1. 1,440 cubic units **3.** 62.8 in^3 **5. a.** rectangle **b.** 125 in^3 **7.** Erica got the better deal. She paid $10.25 for $18\pi \approx 57$ in^3 of cheese, whereas Elena paid $8.25 for 28 in^3 of cheese. Therefore, Elena got about half of the volume of cheese that Erica got, but she paid more than half of Erica's price. **9.** 1,800,000 cm^3 **11.** 255.84 cm^2

13. 25 in.   15. The area of a circle is based on the square of its radius, and $\left(\frac{26.5}{2}\right)^2$ is more than double $\left(\frac{17.91}{2}\right)^2$.
17. $w = 284$ 19. a. 0.1% b. $\frac{1}{1000}$ 21. a. 116.$\overline{6}$% b. $\frac{7}{6}$

Lesson 11-8 (pp. 714–718)
Guided Example 2 Solution 1: 20 mm; 20^3; 33,510
Solution 2: 2^3; 33.5; 33; 34
Guided Example 3 $D = 6.6$ cm, $d = 6$ cm; $R = 3.3$ cm, $r = 3$ cm; $\frac{4}{3}\pi r^3$; 3.3, $\frac{4}{3} \cdot 3.14 \cdot 3^3$; 37.4
Questions: 1. A sphere is a set of points in space at a given distance from a given point.   3. $S.A. = 4\pi r^2$ 5. $V = \frac{4}{3}\pi r^3$
7. Archimedes   9. a. 15,000,000 square miles b. 13.13
11. surface area   13. surface area   15. about 333 in^3
17. 244 in^3 19. a. 29% b. about 6.32% c. about 1.80% 21. C

Lesson 11-9 (pp. 719–724)
Guided Example
1. 2, 3, 6; 6, 9; 6, 9; 9; 3, 9, 3
Questions: 1. 625   3. a. 1 ft by $\frac{7}{8}$ ft b. $\frac{7}{16}$ ft^2 5. a. 1 cm^3 and 8 cm^3 b. no   7. a. $A' = (0, 0)$, $B' = (55, 0)$, $C' = (55, 55)$, $D' = (0, 55)$ b. 25 units^2 c. 3,025 units^2 d. 20 units
e. 220 units   9. a. 27% b. 7%   11. a. $78.3\pi \approx 245.99$ cm^3
b. $70.2\pi \approx 220.54$ cm^3 13. The two bases are squares that are congruent polygons and lie in parallel planes. Points on any line connecting any two corresponding points on the bases are contained in the cube.
15. 140 syllables

Lesson 11-10 (pp. 725–730)
Guided Example Solution 1: 6 in.; 9 in.; 20 in.; 6 in.; 9 in.; 4 in.; $\frac{6\text{ in.} \cdot 9\text{ in.} \cdot 20\text{ in.}}{6\text{ in.} \cdot 9\text{ in.} \cdot 4\text{ in.}}$, 5
Solution 2: 6 in.; 9 in.; 20 in.; 1,080 in^3; 6 in.; 9 in.; 4 in.; 216 in^3; 5
Questions: 1. a. $\frac{2}{3}$ b. $\frac{4}{9}$ c. $\frac{8}{27}$ d. 2.25 as much paint   3. a. $\frac{2}{3}$
b. $\left(\frac{2}{3}\right)^3 = \frac{8}{27}$ c. $\left(\frac{2}{3}\right)^2 = \frac{4}{9}$ 5. a. 36 cm b. 1.44 7. A
9. a. 96π in^3 b. 216π in^3 c. 2.25 d. Because the volume of a cylinder changes as the square of the diameter, so the ratio of volumes is equal to the square of the ratio of the diameters. e. 22.5 pounds   11. a. The smaller box has surface area 228 in^2, and the larger box has surface area 708 in^2 b. The surface areas of the boxes are sums of the areas of different sides and only the measurements of two pairs of sides were different.   13. $36\pi m^2$ 15. For any numbers a and b, $b \neq 0$, $a \div b = a \cdot \frac{1}{b}$.   17. sometimes but not always

Chapter 11 Self-Test (pp. 733–734)
1. a. $SA = \pi dh + 2\pi\left(\frac{d}{2}\right)^2 = \pi(12 \cdot 17) + 2\pi\left(\frac{12}{2}\right)^2 = 204\pi + 72\pi = 276\pi \approx 867$ in^2 b. $V = \pi\left(\frac{d}{2}\right)^2 h = \pi\left(\frac{12}{2}\right)^2 \cdot 17 = 612\pi \approx 1{,}923$ in^3 2. a. $SA = 2 \cdot \frac{1.7 \cdot 1.3}{2} + 5 \cdot \left(1.7 + 2\sqrt{1.3^2 + \left(\frac{1.7}{2}\right)^2}\right) \approx 26.24$ m^2 b. $V = \frac{1.7 \cdot 1.3}{2} \cdot 5 = 5.525$ m^3 3. a. $SA = 4\pi r^2 = 4\pi \cdot 13^2 = 676\pi \approx 2{,}124$ cm^2
b. $V = \frac{4}{3}\pi r^3 = \frac{4}{3}\pi \cdot 13^3 = \frac{8788}{3}\pi \approx 9{,}203$ cm^3

4. a. 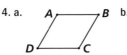 b.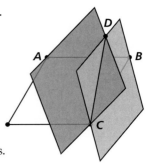

5. False, a hexagonal prism has only two faces that are hexagons. The other faces are rectangles.   6. Area is measured in square units. The ratios of the two prisms should be $\frac{2^2}{5^2} = \frac{50}{SA}$, so $SA = 50 \cdot \frac{25}{4} = 312.5$ square units.   7. Volume is measured in cubic units, so the ratios we are comparing should be $\frac{2^3}{5^3} = \frac{V}{328.125}$, so $V = \frac{8}{125} \cdot 328.125 = 21$ cubic units.   8. sometimes but not always
9. a. The box is a better value; $V_{box} = 3 \cdot 4 \cdot 10 = 120$ in^2, $V_{cyl} = 2^2\pi \cdot 9.5 = 4\pi \cdot 9.5 \approx 119.381$ in^2 b. The box requires more material to make; $SA_{box} = 3 \cdot 4 \cdot 2 + 4 \cdot 10 \cdot 2 + 3 \cdot 10 \cdot 2 = 164$ in^2; $SA_{cyl} = 2^2\pi \cdot 2 + 4\pi \cdot 9.5 = 46\pi \approx 144.513$ in^2 10. $V = 1 \cdot \frac{0.8}{2} \cdot 7.5 = 3$ in^3 11. $\frac{1}{2}S = \frac{1}{2} \cdot 4 \cdot \pi \cdot 3.6^2 = 25.92\pi \approx 81.4$ cm^2 12. No, the area of a shape and the perimeter of the shape are not directly related. So doubling the perimeter may not double the area. For example, if his current pen is 40 ft by 10 ft, he only needs 100 feet of fencing to cover 400 ft^2 of area. Now say he decides to use his 200 feet of fencing to build a pen of 99 ft by 1 ft, the area covered in this is only 99 ft^2, which is actually smaller than the area covered by 100 feet of fencing.

13.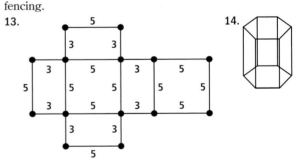

14.

15. Front: Top: Right: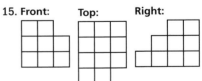

16.

17. a. $\left(\frac{3}{5}\right)^3 = 0.216$ b. 0.36

The chart below keys the **Self-Test** questions to the objectives in the **Chapter Review** on pages 735–737 or to the **Vocabulary (Voc)** on page 732. This will enable you to locate those **Chapter Review** questions that correspond to questions missed on the **Self-Test**. The lesson where the material is covered is also indicated on the chart.

Question	1	2	3	4	5	6	7	8	9	10
Objective(s)	A	A	B	C	C	A	A	D	G	H
Lesson(s)	11-5, 11-6, 11-7	11-5, 11-6, 11-7	11-8	11-1	11-1	11-5, 11-6, 11-7	11-5, 11-6, 11-7	11-2	11-5	11-6, 11-7

Question	11	12	13	14	15	16	17	18
Objective(s)	I	F	K	K	L	E	J	K
Lesson(s)	11-8	1-9, 11-10	11-3	11-3	11-4	11-4	11-9, 11-10	11-3

18.

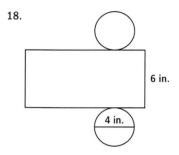

6 in.

4 in.

Chapter 11 Chapter Review (pp. 735–737)

1. $SA = 1,272$ in^2; $V = 3,024$ in^3 3. $2\ell w + 2\ell h + 2hw$
5. $SA = 10,192$ units^2; $V = 27,300$ units^3 7. A 15-cm high cylinder with a radius of 20 cm has more volume: A 20-cm high cylinder with a radius of 15 cm has a volume of $15^2\pi \cdot 20 = 4,500\pi$, while a 15-cm high cylinder with a radius of 20 cm has a volume of $20^2\pi \cdot 15 = 6,000\pi$.
9. a. 0.0001π mm^2 b. 0.00000016π mm^3 11. a. 153.76π in^2
b. $\frac{119,164}{375}\pi$ in^3 13. True. It is an assumed property that if two points lie in a plane, the line containing them lies in the plane.   15. line   17. Answers vary. Sample answer: Spheres have no edges or polygonal bases.
19.

21. 3 sections

23.

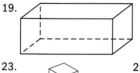

25. 15   27. $1,524\frac{4}{9}$
29. 27 times   31. 1,440 cm^2
33. a. $1,250\pi \approx 3,926.99$ ft^2
b. $7,812.5\pi \approx 24,543.69$ ft^3
35. 4.8 in^3 37. 6.16×10^{12} km^2
39. about 327.26 in^3
41. 17.32 in.

43.

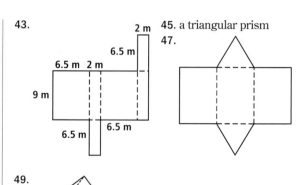

2 m   45. a triangular prism
47.
6.5 m
6.5 m 2 m
9 m
6.5 m
6.5 m

49.

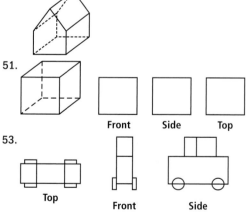

51.

Front   Side   Top

53.

Top   Front   Side

Chapter 12

Lesson 12-1 (pp. 740–744)

Questions
1. a. Yes b. No   3. a. Yes b. Yes   5. a. 0.68 b. about 0.67 c. about 0.25 d. Part b e. That the overall amount of time spent on household activities is much larger, in proportion, to the overall amount of time spent eating and drinking than it really is.   7. This is time-series data, it does not represent percent of a total population.   9. Yes, a circle graph's percents must sum to 100.   11. Yes, since the graph is both wider and taller for 2000 than

for 1960. **13. a.** No, switching the axes does not distort data. **b.** Yes, because it would be removing options that were given in the survey. **c.** Yes. The fact that the percents add up to more than 100 shows that people could pick more than one reason for buying watermelon. Thus, some people's responses fall into more than one category, so a circle graph would not accurately represent the data.

15. ≈ 144.9 million km²

17. a.

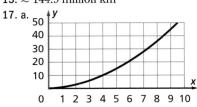

b. The sum of the integers 1 through 7 is 28.

Lesson 12-2 (pp. 745–751)

Questions

1. The data would not be appropriate for a histogram.

3. The data would be appropriate for a histogram.

5. 2 more students

7. a.

0	9 9 9 2 5 9 7 6 6
1	2 1 9 6 5 4 2 7 8 1 1 3 0
2	2 3 3 3 9 5 8 6 7 8
3	9 7 9
4	1
5	9
6	1
7	
8	
9	0 7

b. Chapter 1 because the stem-and-leaf plot for Chapter 1 begins with many short sentences that are common for dialogue.

9. a.

.31	3 9
.32	4 3
.33	3 8 9 8 4 1 4 6 5 0 5
.34	4 1 4
.35	3 4 1 3 3 0 9
.36	6 3 8 3 2
.37	0 0 2 9 2 0
.38	
.39	4

b. 353 and .370 **c.** .081 **d.** It would be the highest in just over half the years.

e.

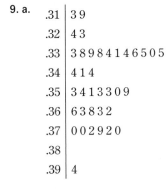

11. a.

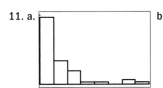

b.

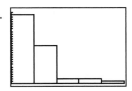

c. The first histogram does a better job of picturing the data. **13. a.** The volume of the 16 in. ball is about 69.17 in³ and the volume of the 12 in. ball is about 29.18 in³, so Raphael's claim is wrong. **b.** more

15. a. $10c + 15\ell \le 120$ **b.** all points with integer coordinates in the shaded region **17. a.** 0.433

b. 21 games **c.** 50 games

Lesson 12-3 (pp. 752–757)

Questions: 1. 86.5° **3.** $\frac{a+b+c}{3}$ **5.** $\frac{50+x}{2}$ **7.** $\frac{1}{2}$ a sandwich
9. a. 15 children **b.** 3.37 **11. a.** solve $\frac{(57 \cdot 5) + x}{6} = 60$;
$x = 75$ **b.** The sum of the distances from the mean of her five tests is 15 below, so her final test must be 15 above, or
75. **13.** Answers vary. Sample: –10, –6, 1, 1, 4; mean: –2; mode: 1 **15.** 5'0"–5'2"

17. Answers vary. Sample:

62	88
61	
60	
59	
58	
57	12, 74
56	
55	32, 84
54	92
53	67, 75, 94
52	49
51	
50	89
49	02

19. $125V$ **21.** $f \ge -\frac{9}{11}$ **23.** C **25.** B

Lesson 12-4 (pp. 758–762)

Questions: 1. A **3. a.** 10 **b.** 0 **c.** $3.\overline{3}$ **5. a.** 8 **b.** 0
c. 2.375 **7.** 56 **9.** C **11. a.** SF = 15, M = 16 **b.** San Francisco **13.** toy car guesses **15.** $g - 5.4$ **17.** 98.60 cubic inches **19.** $0.25q + 0.1d + 0.05n + 0.01p = \$11.52$
21. a. $\frac{n}{n+s+e+w}$ **b.** $\frac{n+e}{s+w}$ **c.** 45% **23.** $132.5\% \le x \le 137.5\%$

Lesson 12-5 (pp. 763–771)
Guided Example 1
Step 1. 9, at the fifth dot
Step 2. between the second and third dots
Step 3. between the seventh and eighth dots
Guided Example 3
Step 1. 4; 12; 8
Step 2. 4; 8; –8; 0
Step 3. 12; 8; 24; 4; California (55), Florida (27), New York (31), and Texas (34)
Questions:
1.

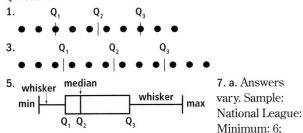

3.

5.

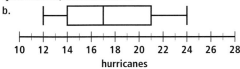

7. a. Answers vary. Sample: National League: Minimum: 6; First quartile: 8; Second quartile: 12; Third quartile: 16; Maximum: 24; American League: Minimum: 7; First quartile: 9; Second quartile: 10; Third quartile: 13; Maximum: 54 b. Answers vary. Sample: National League: 18; American League: 47 c. True, the median for the National League is 12 while the median for the American League is 10. Since the sample size is the same, more National League players hit 12 or more home runs. d. 29 and 54 are outliers in the American League because they are greater than 19, and $Q_3 + 1.5 \cdot IQR = 13 + 1.5 \cdot (4) = 19$. 9. a. minimum: 12; first quartile: 14; median: 17; third quartile: 21; maximum: 24
b.

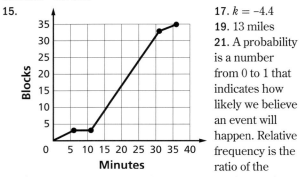

hurricanes

11. It means that your calculations of the deviations are correct. 13. 5'10"
15.

17. $k = -4.4$
19. 13 miles
21. A probability is a number from 0 to 1 that indicates how likely we believe an event will happen. Relative frequency is the ratio of the number of times a certain outcome occurs to the number of total outcomes.

Lesson 12-6 (pp. 772–777)
Questions: 1. 0.05 3. a. $-3.4 \le y \le 3.6$ b. 0.1 ± 3.5
5. a. $2.5 < x < 2.625$ b. 2.5625 ± 0.0625
c. $|x - 2.5625| < 0.0625$ 7. a. $53 < x < 58$ b. 55.5 ± 2.5
c. $|x - 55.5| < 2.5$ 9. 102.8125 cm² 11. approximately $19.635 \le S.A. \le 21.648$ square inches 13. a. 100 b. 450 $\le$ New Hampshire population ≤ 550 c. $2,450 \le$ Virginia population $\le 2,550$ d. 5 times e. $4.45 \le x \le 5.67$
15. $x = 714$ or 192 17. a. 11 b. There are no outliers in the distribution. 19. a. If you double each value in a set, then you double the mean of the set. b. Yes, multiplying each term of the calculation of the mean will double the mean. c. If you double the mean of the set, then you double every value of the set. This is not true; one or a few elements of the set could be significantly altered, doubling the mean without doubling every term. 21. A
23. $x = 2.63\overline{8}$ 25. $2\frac{2}{8}$ inches $\le x \le 2\frac{3}{8}$ inches

Lesson 12-7 (pp. 778–783)
Questions: 1. Answers vary. Sample: Number of pizzas eaten in New York. 3. Maximum: 156.8 cm, Minimum: 146.6 cm, Range: 10.2 cm 5. Yes, the mean height slowly increases over time. 7. $0.08\overline{6}$ cm per year
9. –0.25 percent/year 11. Answers vary. Sample: 32% small, as it enjoyed a small increase from 1995 until 2000, and they tend to get better gas mileage; 45% midsize, it seems to be stabilizing toward this percent; 3% large, as large cars seem to slowly but continually be decreasing in popularity; 20% luxury, as it has enjoyed a slow but steady increase. 15. a. It has increased drastically. b. Although it initially increased, it has decreased drastically. c. Answers vary. Sample: CD players decreased in price and CDs are more durable than cassettes. 17. a. the steepest line between two points b. 1950 to 1955, 0.88 cm a year
19.

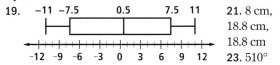

21. 8 cm, 18.8 cm, 18.8 cm 23. 510°

Chapter 12 Self-Test (pp. 786–787)
1. The mean of these numbers is 30. The deviations are $3 - 30 = -27$, $9 - 30 = -21$, $27 - 30 = -3$, and $81 - 30 = 51$. The mean of the absolute values of these deviations is 25.5. So the mean absolute deviation of this set is 25.5.
2. There are 10 numbers in the set. The minimum is 19; Q_1 is the median of the first five numbers, so $Q_1 = 29$; the median is the mean of the fifth and sixth numbers, so the median is 39; Q_3 is the median of the last five numbers, so $Q_3 = 50$; the maximum is 60. 3. a. The mean of 3.6 and 3.7 is 3.65, and $3.7 - 3.65 = 0.05$. $|x - 3.65| \le 0.05$
b. 3.65 ± 0.05 4. $y = 12 - 4 = 8$ 5. The mean of these times is 15.1 seconds. The deviations are $15.62 - 15.1 = 0.52$, $15.87 - 15.1 = 0.77$, and $13.81 - 15.1 = -1.29$.

The mean of the absolute values of these deviations is 0.86. So the mean absolute deviation of the times is 0.86 second.   **6.** True; this statement is the same as the Balance Property of the Mean.   **7.** Since the mean of the six numbers is 18, by the Means and Sums Property, the sum of these six numbers is $18 \cdot 6 = 108$. If x is the seventh number, then $\frac{108 + x}{7} = 18 - 2 = 16$. Multiplying both sides of this equation by 7 gives $108 + x = 112$. So $x = 4$.   **8.** The minimum wage increases over time. **9.** rate of change from 1980 to 1985: $0.05 per year; 1985 to 1990: $0.09 per year; 1990 to 1995: $0.09 per year; 1995 to 2000: $0.18 per year. The rate of change is largest between 1995 and 2000.   **10.** The least possible volume is $11 \cdot 13 \cdot 4 = 572$ cubic inches. The greatest possible volume is $12 \cdot 15 \cdot 6 = 1{,}080$ cubic inches. So the volume is in the interval $572 \text{ in}^3 \leq V \leq 1{,}080 \text{ in}^3$ **11.** 61 cm $\approx$ 24.02 inches; 90 cm $\approx$ 35.43 inches. So the sizes that are sold in both stores are approximately those in the interval 24 in. $\leq w \leq$ 35.43 in.   **12.** There are 7 numbers in this set. In order, they are $39,945, $45,768, $48,995, $58,327, $58,849, $66,254, $73,458. The minimum is $39,945; Q_1 is the median of the first three numbers, so $Q_1 = $45,768; the median is the fourth number, so the median is $58,327; Q_3 is the median of the last three numbers, so $Q_3 = $66,254; the maximum is $73,458.

13.

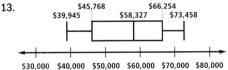
$39,945 $45,768 $58,327 $66,254 $73,458

$30,000 $40,000 $50,000 $60,000 $70,000 $80,000

14. The interquartile range is $66,254 - $45,768 = $20,486. So $1.5 \cdot$ IQR is more than $30,000. Since no states are more than $30,000 more than Q_3 or less than Q_1, there are no outliers.

15.

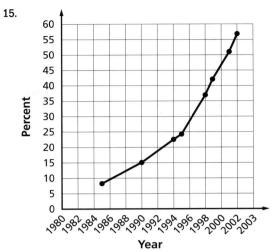

16. The rate of change from 2001 to 2002 is 5.5% per year. At this rate, the percentage will be 62% in 2003, 67.5% in 2004, and 73% in 2005, so 2005 is the first year in which more than 70% of U.S. homes would have a personal computer.   **17.** Let x be the number of cars James sells in the last 10 days. Then $\frac{115 + x}{30} = 4.5$. Multiplying both sides of the equation by 30 gives $115 + x = 135$. So $x = 20$. James must sell 20 cars in the last 10 days.

18.

0	5 7 9
1	1 2 4 6 7 7
2	0 3 4 6
3	1

19. There are fourteen numbers, so the median is the mean of the seventh and eighth, which are 16 and 17. So the median is 16.5 books.

The chart below keys the **Self-Test** questions to the objectives in the **Chapter Review** on pages 788–791 or to the **Vocabulary (Voc)** on page 785. This will enable you to locate those **Chapter Review** questions that correspond to questions missed on the **Self-Test**. The lesson where the material is covered is also indicated on the chart.

Question	1	2	3	4	5	6	7	8	9	10
Objective(s)	A	B	C	C	A	D	D	G	G	H
Lesson(s)	12-4	12-5	12-6	12-6	12-4	12-3	12-3	12-7	12-7	12-6

Question	11	12	13	14	15	16	17	18	19	20
Objective(s)	H	B	K	K	L	G	F	I	E	J
Lesson(s)	12-6	12-5	12-5	12-5	12-7	12-7	12-3	12-2	12-1, 12-2	12-2

Question	21
Objective(s)	E
Lesson(s)	12-1, 12-2

20. a.

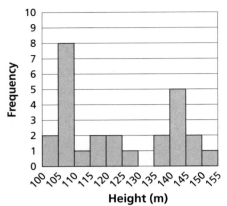

Heights of the 26 Tallest Buildings in Vancouver

b. 105–109

Chapter 12 Chapter Review (pp. 788–791)

1. $9.8\overline{3}$ **3.** B   **5.** minimum: a; first quartile: b; second quartile/median: c; third quartile: d; maximum: e
7. minimum: 5; first quartile: 13; second quartile/median: 56; third quartile: 90; maximum: 512   **9.** 8 ± 0.4
11. $|x - 5| \le 2.1$ **13.** $2 < x < 8$ **15.** $m = 3$ **17.** The mean of 25, 43, and 52 is 40. $(25 - 40) + (43 - 40) + (52 - 40) = 0$.   **19. a.** 0 **b.** 5   **21.** Because the rainfall is given in ranges instead of exact values.   **23. a.** 4 days **b.** 3 days   **25.** Answers vary. Sample: The second graph of each type distorts the data. On the 3-D graph, the sectors in the front appear larger and the ones in the back appear smaller than they really are. The vertical scale on the second bar graph has been chopped so that the ratio of one bar to another is greater.   **27.** 42 yr   **29.** 1995–2005
31. slower   **33.** $20.25 \le A \le 30.25$ **35.** $|p - 2.4| < 0.1$
37. The first is more useful for seeing a greater breakdown in the 5% values
39. a.

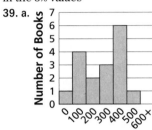

Number of Pages

b. The 400–499 page interval has the most books. **c.** By combining the number of books in the 0–49 and 50–99 intervals, the 100–149 and 150–199 intervals, the 200–249 and 250–299 intervals, the 300–349 and 350–399 intervals, the 400–449 and 450–499 intervals, and the 500–549 interval and finding the largest number.   **41.** minimum: 96; median: 373; maximum: 501   **43.** There are no outliers.
45.

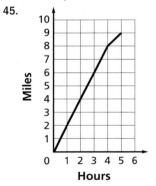

Glossary

A

absolute deviation The absolute value of the deviations in a data set. (**759**)

absolute value The distance between a number n and 0 on a number line. (**285**)

active cell The cell that is highlighted in a spreadsheet. (**104**)

acute angle An angle whose measure is greater than 0° and less than 90°. (**240**)

Adding (or Subtracting) Fractions Property To add (or subtract) fractions with the same denominator, add (or subtract) the numerators and keep the denominator the same. That is, for $x \neq 0$, $\frac{n}{x} + \frac{m}{x} = \frac{n+m}{x}$ and $\frac{n}{x} - \frac{m}{x} = \frac{n-m}{x}$. (**147**)

Addition Counting Principle Suppose A and B are finite sets. Then the number of elements in $A \cup B$ is the sum of the number of elements in A and the number of elements in B minus the number of elements in $A \cap B$. (**330**)

Addition Property of Equality For all real numbers a, b, and c, if $a = b$, then $a + c = b + c$. (**306**)

Addition Property of Inequality For any real numbers a, b, and c, if $a < b$, then $a + c < b + c$. (**314**)

additive identity The number zero. (**211**)

Additive Identity Property of Zero For any real number n, $n + 0 = n$. (**211**)

additive inverse The number y such that $x + y = 0$, written $-x$, also called *opposite*. (**213**)

Additive Inverse Property See *Property of Opposites*. (**213**)

Add-Op Property See *Algebraic Definition of Subtraction*. (**295**)

adjacent angles Two nonstraight and nonzero angles that share a side that is interior to the angle formed by the non-common sides. (**280**)

Algebraic Definition of Division For all real numbers a and nonzero real numbers b, $a \div b = \frac{a}{b} = a \cdot \frac{1}{b}$. (**440, 567**)

Algebraic Definition of Subtraction For any numbers x and y, $x - y = x + (-y)$. Also called the *Add-Op Property*. (**295**)

algebraic expression An expression that contains a variable alone or variables with numbers and operation symbols. (**76**)

alternate exterior angles Angles formed by two lines and a transversal that are on opposite sides of the transversal and not between the two given lines, such as angles 1 and 2 shown below. (**395**)

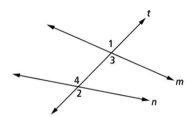

alternate interior angles Angles formed by two lines and a transversal that are between the two given lines and are on opposite sides of the transversal, such as angles 3 and 4 shown above. (**395**)

altitude (**A**) The perpendicular segment from the vertex of a triangle to the opposite side of the triangle. (**B**) The length of that segment. Also called *height*. (**450**)

angle The union of two rays with the same endpoint. (**238**)

Angle-Addition Property If $\overrightarrow{OB}$ is in the interior of $\angle AOC$, then $m\angle AOB + m\angle BOC = m\angle AOC$. (**280**)

antecedent See *hypothesis*. (**216**)

apex The vertex of a pyramid or cone that is not on its base. (**692**)

arc A part of a circle that connects two points on the circle. (**336, 463**)

area A measure that indicates how much space is inside a plane figure. (**430**)

Area Formula for a Right Triangle The area A of a right triangle with legs a and b is $A = \frac{1}{2}ab$. (**432**)

Area Model for Multiplication The area of a rectangle with length ℓ units and width w units is $\ell \cdot w$ or ℓw square units. (**431**)

Area of a Circle Formula Let A be the area of a circle with radius r. Then $A = \pi r^2$. (**466**)

array See *rectangular array*. (**431**)

Associative Property of Addition For any real numbers a, b, and c, $(a + b) + c = a + (b + c)$. (**288**)

Associative Property of Multiplication For any numbers a, b, and c, $(ab)c = a(bc)$. (**433**)

average The sum of a group of numbers divided by the number of numbers in the collection. Also called *mean*. (**40**)

B

Balance Property of the Mean Let m be the mean of a set of numbers. Then the sum of the distances to m from the numbers in the set greater than m equals the sum of the distances to m from the numbers in the set less than m. (**755**) The sum of the deviations of a set of numbers from the mean of the set is 0. (**760**)

ball The union of a sphere and the set of all points inside it. (**714**)

base (**A**) In the power x^y, x is the base. (**23**) (**B**) A side to which an altitude of a triangle is drawn. (**450**) (**C**) One of the parallel sides of a trapezoid. (**458**) (**D**) The face of a pyramid or cone that does not contain the apex. (**692**) (**E**) Either of the two parallel faces of a prism or cylinder whose points are connected by lateral edges. (**680**)

base 10 system See *decimal system*. (**6**)

baseline A segment on a protractor that marks off $0°$ and $180°$. It is placed over one side of an angle that is being measured with its midpoint at the vertex of the angle. (**239**)

Betweenness Property If point B is between points A and C on line segment $\overline{AC}$, then $AB + BC = AC$. (**279**)

bisector A line, ray, or line segment that intersects a line segment at its midpoint. (**367**)

boundary A line that separates a plane into two half-planes. Also called *edge*. (**630**)

boundary point On a number line, a point that separates solutions from nonsolutions. (**314**)

box A three-dimensional figure with six faces that are rectangles. (**680**)

box plot A visual representation of the five-number summary of a data set. (**765**)

C

capacity The amount of space inside a three-dimensional figure. Also called *volume*. (**698**)

categorical data Data that can be sorted into categories or groups. (**740**).

cell The intersection of a row and a column in a spreadsheet. (**104**)

center (**A**) The middle point of the baseline of a protractor. The center is placed over the vertex of the angle being measured. (**239**) (**B**) A point in a plane that is fixed under a rotation. (**288, 376**) (**C**) The point in the plane of a circle equidistant from all the points of the circle. (**463**) (**D**) The point equidistant from all the points of a sphere. (**714**)

center of symmetry The center of a rotation. (**376**)

circle The set of points that are all the same distance (the radius) from a fixed point (the center). (**463**)

circumference The perimeter of a circle. In a circle with diameter d and circumference C, $C = \pi d$. (**464**)

coefficient A numerical value by which a variable is multiplied. (**489, 642**)

collecting like terms Using the Distributive Property to write the sum or difference of multiples of the same number as a single multiple of that number. (**489**)

collinear Points that lie on the same line. (**241**)

column A vertical arrangement of items in a spreadsheet. (**104**)

common denominator A nonzero number that is a multiple of the denominators of two or more fractions. (**148**)

Commutative Property of Addition For any numbers a and b, $a + b = b + a$. (**282**)

Commutative Property of Multiplication For any real numbers a and b, $ab = ba$. (**431**)

Comparison Model for Subtraction $x - y$ is how much more x is than y. (**294**)

complement (**A**) For any event E, the set of those outcomes that are *not* in E. (**329**) (**B**) One of two angles that are complementary. (**251**)

complementary angles Two angles whose measures have a sum of $90°$. (**251**)

conclusion The clause following *then* in an if-then statement. Also called *consequent*. (**216**)

congruent figures Two figures with the same size and shape. (**360**)

consecutive angles Two angles whose vertices are the endpoints of the same side of a polygon. (**401**)

consecutive sides In a polygon, two sides with a common endpoint. (**401**)

consequent See *conclusion*. (**216**)

contraction A size change in which the final quantity is smaller than the original quantity. (**471**)

converse An if-then statement in which the hypothesis and the conclusion are switched. (**218**)

Converse of the Pythagorean Theorem If a triangle has side lengths a, b, and c, and $a^2 + b^2 = c^2$, then the triangle is a right triangle. (**219**)

conversion factor A rate factor that equals 1. (**494**)

coplanar Points or lines that lie in the same plane. (**679**)

corresponding angles Any pair of angles in similar locations in relation to a transversal intersecting two lines. (**394**)

counterexample A specific instance for which a statement is not true. (**204**)

cube A box in which each face is a square. (**698**)

cubic units Units that measure the volume of a three-dimensional figure. (**698**)

cylinder (circular cylinder) A cylindrical solid whose bases are circles. (**704**)

D

data set A set of information collected for statistical analysis. (**740**)

decagon A polygon with ten sides. (**242**)

decimal notation A system of notation in which a number is written in the decimal system. (**6**)

decimal system A system of writing numbers based on the number 10. Also called *base 10 system*. (**6**)

deductive reasoning (deduction) To reason logically from some things that you assume true or know to be true. (**407**)

degree A unit of measure for angles, arcs, and rotations. (**238**)

denominator The divisor of a fraction; the b in $\frac{a}{b}$. (**140**)

dependent variable A variable whose value relies on the value of at least one other variable. (**105**)

depth One of the dimensions of a box, often designating the distance front to back or top to bottom of a box. (**681**)

deviation The difference between a data value and the mean of its data set. (**759**)

diagonal In a polygon, a segment that connects two vertices of the polygon but is not a side of the polygon. (**249, 661**) The number d of diagonals of a polygon with n sides is given by $d = \frac{n(n-3)}{2}$. (**662**)

diameter (**A**) A segment connecting two points of a circle and containing the center of the circle. (**463**) (**B**) The length of that segment. (**463**) (**C**) A segment from one point on a sphere to another point on the sphere that contains the center of the sphere. (**714**) (**D**) The length of that segment. (**714**)

dimensions The lengths of the sides of a rectangle or a box. (**430, 681**)

disjoint sets Two sets that have no elements in common. (**206, 226**)

Distributive Property of Multiplication over Addition For any real numbers a, b, and x, $ax + bx = (a + b)x$ and $x(a + b) = xa + xb$. (**445**)

Distributive Property of Multiplication over Subtraction For any real numbers a, b, and x, $ax - bx = (a - b)x$ and $x(a - b) = xa - xb$. (**446**)

dividend The number in a quotient that is being divided. In $a \div b$ or $\frac{a}{b}$, a is the dividend. (**161**)

Division Property of Equality If $a = b$ and $c \neq 0$, then $\frac{a}{c} = \frac{b}{c}$. (**578**)

Division Property of Inequality For any real numbers x and y: If $x < y$ and a is positive, $\frac{x}{a} < \frac{y}{a}$; if $x < y$ and a is negative, $\frac{x}{a} > \frac{y}{a}$. (**580**)

divisor The number by which you divide. In $a \div b$ or $\frac{a}{b}$, b is the divisor. (**161**)

double inequality An expression of an inequality in which two or more inequality symbols of the same form (is less than or is greater than but not both) are present. (**13**)

E

edge (**A**) The side of a face of a three-dimensional geometric figure. (**680**) (**B**) See also *boundary*.

elements The objects of a set. Also called *members*. (**205**)

elevation See *view*. (**691**)

empty set The set with no elements, represented by the symbol Ø. Also called *null set*. **(226)**

endpoints The points at the ends of a line segment. **(233)**

Equal-Fractions Property If the numerator and denominator of a fraction are both multiplied or divided by the same nonzero number, then the resulting fraction is equal to the original one. If $k \neq 0$, then $\frac{a}{b} = \frac{ka}{kb} = \frac{a \div k}{b \div k}$. **(141)**

equation A mathematical sentence with an equal sign (=). **(91, 110)**

equation of the form $x + a = b$ On one side of the equation is a single number. On the other side of the equation, a number is being added to a variable. **(306)**

equation of the form $ax + b = c$ A type of linear equation in which x is the unknown and a, b, and c are constants. **(533)**

equiangular polygon A polygon in which the measures of all angles are equal. **(248)**

equilateral polygon A polygon in which the lengths of all sides are equal. **(248)**

equilateral triangle A triangle in which the lengths of all sides are equal. **(256)**

evaluating an expression Carrying out the operations in a numerical expression to find the value of the expression. **(34)**

event A set of outcomes from the same experiment. **(190)**

example A true instance of a general statement. **(204)**

expansion A size change in which the final quantity is larger than the original quantity. **(471)**

exponent In the power x^y, y is the exponent. **(23)**

exponential form A number that is written as a power. **(23)**

exterior angles When transversal x intersects lines m and n, angles outside lines m and n are exterior angles. **(393)** See *alternate exterior angles*.

extremes In the proportion $\frac{a}{b} = \frac{c}{d}$, the numbers a and d. **(591)**

F

face A side of a three-dimensional figure. **(680)**

factor A number that divides into another number without a remainder. **(142)**

fact triangle A diagram to show related facts for addition and subtraction, or for multiplication and division. **(300, 568)**

figure A set of points. **(231)**

first quartile (Q_1) The median of the numbers below the median of a data set. **(763)**

five-number summary A series of five numbers that summarize the data in a data set: the minimum (least) and maximum (greatest) elements in a data set, the median, and the first and third quartiles. **(764)**

formula An equation in which one variable is given in terms of other variables or numbers. **(91)**

fraction bar The horizontal line in a fraction that indicates division. **(161)** Also called *vinculum*.

frequency In probability, the number of times an outcome occurs. **(187)**

full turn See *revolution*. **(289)**

Fundamental Property of Rotations If a rotation of measure x is followed by a rotation of measure y, the result is a rotation of measure $x + y$. **(289)**

Fundamental Property of Similar Figures If two figures are similar, then ratios of corresponding lengths are equal. **(602)**

fundamental region (shape) Smallest figure whose congruent images make up a tessellation. **(380)**

Fundamental Theorem of Arithmetic Every positive integer greater than 1 is a prime number or can be represented as a product of two or more prime numbers. This factoring can be done in exactly one way except for the order of the factors. **(143)**

Fundamental Theorem of Similarity If two figures are similar with ratio of similitude k, then (1) the ratio of corresponding side lengths or distances is k; (2) the ratio of corresponding areas is k^2; and (3) the ratio of corresponding volumes is k^3. **(727)**

G

greatest common factor (GCF) The largest number that is the factor of all numbers in a given set. **(142)**

grouping symbol Symbols such as parentheses that indicate that certain arithmetic operations should be done before others in an expression. **(39)**

H

half-plane The region on either side of a line in a plane. **(630)**

height (A) One of the three dimensions of a box. It describes how tall a box is. **(681) (B)** See also *altitude*. **(450)**

heptagon A polygon with seven sides. **(242)**

hexagon A polygon with six sides. **(242)**

hexagonal prism A prism that has hexagons as its bases. **(681)**

hierarchy A system for organizing things. **(253)**

histogram A special type of bar graph that displays frequencies or relative frequencies in which the data are sorted into disjoint intervals and represented by bars placed next to each other. **(745)**

hypotenuse The longest side of a right triangle. **(96)**

hypothesis The clause following *if* in an if-then statement. Also called *antecedent*. **(216)**

I

independent variable A variable whose value does not rely on the values of other variables. **(105)**

if-then statement A sentence with an *if* clause and a *then* clause. **(216)**

independent events See *probability of independent events*. **(508)**

inequality A sentence with one of the following symbols: $\neq, <, \leq, >,$ or $\geq$. **(110)**

inequality symbols Any one of the symbols $\neq, <, \leq, >,$ or $\geq$ used to compare two numbers. **(12)**

infinite repeating decimal A decimal that forever repeats a fixed set of numbers to the right of the decimal point. **(162)**

instance A special case of a general pattern. **(70)**

integer A number that is a whole number or the opposite of a whole number (e.g., one of . . . –3, –2, –1, 0, 1, 2, 3, . . .). **(12)**

integer division An integer a divided by an integer b in which there is an integer quotient q and a remainder r with $a = bq + r$ and $0 \leq r < b$. **(554)**

interest The amount a financial institution pays on money in an account. It is based on a percentage of the principal. **(176)**

interior angles When transversal x intersects lines m and n, angles between lines m and n are interior angles. **(393)** See *alternate interior angles.*

interquartile range (IQR) The difference between the third quartile and the first quartile of a data set: $Q_3 - Q_1$. **(766)**

intersection of sets The set of elements in both set A and set B, written as $A \cap B$. **(223)**

interval The set of numbers between two numbers, perhaps including the numbers. **(132)**

interval data Data that are represented by measures or scale values. **(745)**

irrational number A number that is not rational. A real number that cannot be written as a simple fraction. **(182)**

isometric dot paper Paper with dots in an equilateral triangular pattern. **(682)**

isosceles triangle A triangle in which the lengths of at least two sides are equal. **(256, 369)**

is parallel to (||) See *parallel lines.* **(395)**

L

lateral area The area of the surface of a three-dimensional figure excluding its bases. **(703)**

lateral face The face of a prism that is not a base. **(686)**

leaf The digits to the right of the vertical line in a stem-and-leaf plot. **(746)**

least common denominator (LCD) The least common multiple of the denominators of a group of fractions. **(148)**

least common multiple (LCM) The smallest number that is a multiple of every number in a set. **(148)**

legs The two sides of a right triangle that are on the sides of the right angle. **(96)**

length One of the three dimensions of a box. **(681)**

ℓ-by-w (ℓ × w) rectangle A rectangle with dimensions ℓ and w. **(431)**

like terms Terms that contain the same variables raised to the same powers but may have different coefficients. **(489)**

line properties Through two distinct points, there is exactly one line. Every real number corresponds to a point on a number line, and every point on a number line can be represented by a real number. Two lines are either identical, intersect at exactly one point, or have no points of intersection. **(232)**

linear combination The sum or difference of multiples of variables to the first power that are not multiplied or divided by each other. **(642)**

linear equation An equation that can be written as $y = ax + b$. An equation of the form $ax + b = cx + d$. **(533)**

linear pair Two angles that share a common side and whose noncommon sides are opposite rays. **(387)**

line graph The resulting graph when data points are connected by line segments. **(778)**

line of symmetry A line over which the reflection image of a figure coincides with its preimage. **(368)**

line segment A subset of a line consisting of two different points on a line and all the points between them. **(233)**

lower quartile See *first quartile* (Q_1). **(763)**

lowest terms A fraction in which both the numerator and denominator have no common factors, other than 1. **(142)**

M

magnitude A measurement of how much a figure has turned (rotated) and in what direction. **(288)**

mean The sum of a group of numbers divided by the number of numbers in the collection. Also called *average*. **(40)**

mean absolute deviation (m.a.d.) In a data set, the mean of the absolute deviations of the elements of the set from the mean of the set. **(758–759)**

means In the proportion $\frac{a}{b} = \frac{c}{d}$, the numbers b and c. **(591)**

Means and Sums Property In a collection of n numbers, the product of n and the mean of the numbers is the sum of the numbers. **(753)**

Means-Extremes Property In any true proportion, the product of the means equals the product of the extremes: In $\frac{a}{b} = \frac{c}{d}$, $ad = bc$. **(591)**

measure of an angle A number indicating the amount you have to turn one side to get to the other side. **(238)**

measures of spread Quantities that measure the degree of variation in data. **(758)**

median The middle number of a data set when the data are ordered from least to greatest. **(763)**

members See *elements*. **(205)**

middle quartile See *second quartile* (Q_2). **(763)**

midpoint The point of a line segment that is equidistant from its endpoints. **(367)**

mode The element that appears most often in a data set. **(748)**

Multiplication of Fractions Property For all real numbers a and c and nonzero real numbers b and d, $\frac{a}{b} \cdot \frac{c}{d} = \frac{ac}{bd}$. **(440)**

Multiplication of Unit Fractions Property For all nonzero numbers a and b, $\frac{1}{a} \cdot \frac{1}{b} = \frac{1}{ab}$. **(439)**

Multiplication Property of Equality For all real numbers a, x, and y, if $x = y$, then $ax = ay$. **(520)**

Multiplication Property of Inequality For any real numbers x and y: If $x < y$ and a is positive, then $ax < ay$. If $x < y$ and a is negative, then $ax > ay$. **(539)**

Multiplication Property of -1 For any number x, $(-1) \cdot x = -x$. **(502)**

Multiplication Property of Zero For any number x, $x \cdot 0 = 0$. **(502)**

Multiplicative-Identity Property of 1 For any number x, $1 \cdot x = x$. **(487)**

multiplicative inverses See *reciprocals*. **(441)**

mutually exclusive events Events that cannot occur at the same time. **(328)**

N

negative integers Integers less than or equal to -1. **(12)**

negative number The opposite of a positive number. **(12)**

nested parentheses Parentheses inside of parentheses. **(39)**

net A connected two-dimensional pattern of polygons that folds to form a three-dimensional object. **(687)**

n-fold rotation symmetry n is the fewest number of rotations of the smallest positive magnitude less than 360° that will rotate a figure to its original position. **(376)**

n-gon A polygon with n sides. **(242)**

nonagon A polygon with nine sides. **(242)**

null set See *empty set*. **(226)**

numerator The dividend of a fraction; the a in $\frac{a}{b}$. **(140)**

numerical expression A combination of symbols for numbers and operations that stands for a number. **(34)**

O

oblique line A line that is neither horizontal nor vertical. (**631**)

obtuse angle An angle whose measure is greater than 90° and less than 180°. (**240, 259**)

octagon A polygon with eight sides. (**242**)

open sentence A sentence that contains one or more variables and may be either true or false, depending on what is substituted for the variables. (**110**)

opposite angles In a quadrilateral, two angles that do not share a side. (**401**)

Opposite of Opposite (Op-Op) Property For any real number n, $-(-n) = n$. (**212**)

opposite rays Two rays that have the same endpoint and whose union is a line. (**387**)

opposite sides In a quadrilateral, two sides that do not share a vertex. (**401**)

ordinal number A number that designates a place (as in first, second, third, etc.) in a number sequence. (7)

origin The point $(0, 0)$ where the x-axis and the y-axis intersect. (**52**)

outlier A number in a distribution that is more than 1.5 times the width of the box less than the first quartile or greater than the third quartile. (**766**)

overlap (overlapping sets) Two sets in which some (but not all) elements of each set are in the other set. (**206**)

P

parabola A curve that is defined by an equation of the form $y = ax^2$, where $a \neq 0$. (**660**)

parallel lines Two or more lines that lie in the same plane but have no points of intersection. (**233**) If m is parallel to n, this is written as $m \parallel n$. (**395**)

parallel planes Two or more planes that have no points in common. (**676**)

parallelogram A quadrilateral with two pairs of parallel sides. (**254**)

Parallelogram Area Formula Let A be the area of a parallelogram with base b and height h. Then $A = bh$. (**458**)

pattern A general idea for which there may be many instances. (**70**)

pentagon A polygon with five sides. (**242**)

pentagonal prism A prism that has pentagons as its bases. (**681**)

percent A number written with a % sign, meaning to multiply the number preceding it by one hundredth. (**167**)

perpendicular Rays, line segments, or lines that intersect at right angles to each other. (**367**)

perpendicular bisector A line that intersects a line segment at its midpoint, forming a right angle. (**367**)

plane A set of points thought of as a flat surface, like a tabletop. (**233**)

point The fundamental object in geometry. It indicates a precise location and has no thickness and no dimensions. (**231**)

polygon A union of segments in a plane in which each segment intersects exactly two others, one at each of its endpoints. (**241, 247**)

polyhedron (polyhedra) A closed three-dimensional figure whose faces are polygons. (**687**)

positive integers Integers greater than or equal to 1. (**12**)

positive numbers The positive integers and 0 and all numbers between them. (**12**)

power The result of x^y. (**23**)

preimage A figure to which a transformation is applied. It is the original image before the transformation is applied. (**359**)

prime factorization Expressing a number as a product of its prime numbers. (**143**)

prime number A positive integer other than 1 that is divisible only by itself and 1. (**142**)

principal The amount of money you put into a savings account or other investment. (**176**)

prism A three-dimensional figure with the following characteristics: It consists of two bases that are polygons and that are translation images of each other in space. It contains all the points of the bases and the points on the line segments connecting corresponding points of the bases. (**680**)

probability A number from 0 to 1 that indicates how likely an event will happen. (**188**) A situation has N equally likely possible outcomes and an event includes E of these. Then the probability P that the event will occur is $P = \frac{E}{N}$. (**190**)

Probability of a Complement Property If E is any event, then the probability of *not E* is $1 - P(E)$. **(329)**

probability of (A or B) (general case) If A and B are events, then $P(A \text{ or } B) = P(A) + P(B) - P(A \cap B)$. **(330)**

probability of (A or B) (mutually exclusive case) If A and B are mutually exclusive events, then $P(A \text{ or } B) = P(A) + P(B)$. **(328)**

probability of independent events Two events A and B are independent events if and only if $P(A \text{ followed by } B) = P(A) \cdot P(B)$. **(508)**

property A characteristic of a set that is true for all members of the set. **(205)**

Property of Opposites For any real number n, $n + (-n) = 0$. Sometimes called the Additive Inverse Property. **(213)**

Property of Reciprocals For any nonzero real number a, a and $\frac{1}{a}$ are reciprocals if $a \cdot \frac{1}{a} = 1$. **(441)**

proportion An equation stating that two fractions are equal. **(589)**

proportional thinking The ability to obtain an answer to a proportion without solving an equation. **(596)**

protractor A common instrument used for measuring angles, based on a semicircle or circle. **(239)**

Putting-Together Model for Addition Suppose a count or measure x is put together with a count or measure y with the same units. If there is no overlap, then the result has count or measure $x + y$. **(278)**

pyramid A three-dimensional shape formed by connecting a polygonal base with a point (the apex) not in the plane of the base, called the apex. **(692)**

Pythagorean Theorem If the legs of a right triangle have lengths a and b and the hypotenuse has length c, then $a^2 + b^2 = c^2$. **(97)**

Q

quadrant One of the four regions on a coordinate graph determined by the x-axis and the y-axis. **(53)**

quadrilateral A polygon with four sides. **(242)**

Quadrilateral-Sum Property The sum of the measures of the angles of a quadrilateral is $360°$. **(382)**

quartile One of three values that divide an ordered data set into four subsets of approximately equal size. **(763)**

quotient The result of a division operation. **(161)**

quotient-remainder form The result of integer division expressed as an integer quotient and an integer remainder. Dividend = divisor · integer quotient + remainder. **(555–556)**

R

radical sign The symbol for a square root ($\sqrt{}$). **(41)**

radius **(A)** A segment that connects the center of a circle to any point on the circle. **(B)** The length of that segment. **(463)** **(C)** A segment that connects the center of a sphere to any point on the sphere. **(D)** The length of that segment. **(714)**

random When all outcomes of an experiment, such as tossing a coin or tossing a 6-sided die have the same probability, the outcomes are called random. **(190)**

range The difference between the greatest and least elements in a data set. **(748)**

rate The quotient of two quantities with different units. **(17)**

rate factor Rate used in multiplication. **(494)**

Rate-Factor Model for Multiplication The product of $(a \; unit_1)$ and $\left(b\dfrac{unit_2}{unit_1} \right)$ is $(ab \; unit_2)$, signifying the total amount of $unit_2$ in the situation. **(494)**

Rate Model for Division If a and b are quantities with different units, then $\frac{a}{b}$ is the amount of quantity a per quantity b. **(563)**

rate of change Rate of change = the difference in quantity between time 2 and time 1 divided by the difference between time 2 and time 1: $\dfrac{\text{quantity at time 2} - \text{quantity at time 1}}{\text{time 2} - \text{time 1}}$. **(779)**

rate unit The unit for a given rate. **(17)** Rate units may be written with a slash (/) or a horizontal bar (—). **(493)**

ratio A quotient of two quantities with the same unit. **(18)**

Ratio-Comparison Model for Division If a and b are quantities with the same units, then $\frac{a}{b}$ compares a to b. **(583)**

rational number A number that can be written as a fraction with integers in its numerator and denominator. **(19)**

ratio of similitude The ratio of any two corresponding lengths in similar figures. **(726)**

ray A point and all the points of a line on one side of that point. (**234**)

real number Any number that can be represented as a decimal. (**211**)

real number division Dividing the real number a by the nonzero real number b is the single real number quotient $\frac{a}{b}$. (**554**)

reciprocals Two numbers whose product is 1. Also called *multiplicative inverses*. (**441**)

rectangle A quadrilateral with four right angles. (**254**)

rectangular array An arrangement of objects in rows and columns. (**431**)

rectangular prism A prism in which the bases are rectangles. (**681**)

reflection image of A over m A is a point and m is a line. If A is not on m, then the reflection image of A over m is the point A' so that m is the perpendicular bisector of $\overline{AA'}$. If A is on m, then A coincides with its reflection image. (**368**)

reflection-symmetric (reflection symmetry) The property that a figure coincides with its reflection image over a line (a line of symmetry). (**368**)

regular polygon A polygon that is both equiangular and equilateral. (**248**)

related facts for addition and subtraction For any three numbers x, y, and z, if $x + y = z$, then $y + x = z$, $z - x = y$, and $z - y = x$. (**301**)

relative frequency The frequency of a particular outcome (F) divided by the total number of times an experiment is performed (N): $\frac{F}{N}$. (**187**)

relatively prime Two integers whose greatest common factor is 1. (**144**)

Repeated-Addition Property of Multiplication If n is a positive integer, $nx = x + x + \ldots + x$. There are n addends. (**487**)

repetend The digits that repeat in an infinitely repeating decimal. (**162**)

revolution A full turn (rotation) of $360°$. (**289**)

rhombus A quadrilateral with all sides the same length. (**254**)

right angle An angle whose measure is $90°$. (**240**)

right prism A prism in which the lateral edges are perpendicular to the base. (**681**)

right triangle A triangle in which one angle has measure $90°$. (**96**)

rotation The transformation that yields a rotation image. Also called *turn*. (**288**)

rotation image Let A and P be points. Under a rotation with center A and magnitude $x°$, the rotation image P' of P is the point P with $PA = P'A$ and $m\angle PAP' = x°$. If x is positive, measure from $\overrightarrow{AP}$ to $\overrightarrow{AP'}$ in a counterclockwise direction. If x is negative, measure from $\overrightarrow{AP}$ to $\overrightarrow{AP'}$ in a clockwise direction. (**375**)

rotation symmetry The property that a figure coincides with its own image under a rotation of less then $360°$. (**376**)

rounding A type of approximating that substitutes a more precise value with a number that is easier to work with. (**154**)

rounding down Rounding to an equal or a lower value. (**154**)

rounding to the nearest Rounding to the same or closer value. (**154**)

rounding up Rounding to an equal or a higher value. (**154**)

row A horizontal arrangement of items in a spreadsheet. (**104**)

S

sample A set of things about which you collect data. (**740**)

sample size The size of a data set. (**740**)

scalene triangle A triangle in which all sides are different lengths. (**256**)

scatterplot A coordinate graph of individual data points. (**57**)

scientific notation A notation in which a number is expressed as a number greater than or equal to 1 and less than 10 multiplied by an integer power of 10. The form $decimal \times 10^{exponent}$ with $1 \leq decimal < 10$. (**45**)

second quartile (Q_2) The median of a data set. (**763**)

sector A region bounded by two radii of a circle and an arc of the circle. (**463**)

sentence A statement of numbers, variables, or operations that contains a verb. (**110**)

set A collection of objects called elements or members. (**205**)

side (A) Either of two rays that form an angle. (**238**) (B) Any one of the line segments whose union is a polygon. (**242**)

simple fraction A fraction with an integer as its numerator and a nonzero integer as its denominator. (**142**)

simple interest The amount earned by money on deposit. A formula for calculating simple interest is $I = prt$, where $I =$ the interest earned, $p =$ the principal, $r =$ the annual interest rate, and $t =$ the time in years. (**176**)

Size-Change Area Theorem If a figure has been scaled by a size change with a factor k, then the area of the figure will be scaled by a size change with a factor k^2. Alternatively, if the dimensions of two figures are in the ratio k, then the ratio of their areas is k^2. (**721**)

Size-Change Volume Theorem If a figure has been scaled by a size change with a factor k, then the volume of the figure will be scaled by a size change with a factor of k^3. Alternatively, if the dimensions of two figures are in the ratio k, then the ratio of their volumes is k^3. (**727**)

size-change factor The number k by which the size of a quantity is multiplied. (**471**)

Size-Change Model for Multiplication Let k be a nonzero number without a unit. Then ka is the result of a applying a size change of magnitude k to the quantity a. (**472**)

skew lines Two lines that are not in the same plane and do not intersect. (**677**)

slash The symbol / used to indicate division. (**161**)

slide See *translation*. (**358**)

Slide Model for Addition If a slide x is followed by a slide y, the result is a slide $x + y$. (**281**)

Slide Model for Subtraction If a quantity x is decreased by an amount y, the resulting quantity is $x - y$. (**295**)

solution A value of a variable that makes the sentence true. (**110**)

sphere The set of points in *space* at a given distance (its radius) from a given point called the center. (**714**)

spreadsheet A table or computer program used to organize information. (**104**)

square A rectangle with all sides the same length or a rhombus with four right angles. (**254**)

square pyramid A pyramid whose base is a square. (**692**)

square root If $x^2 = y$, then x is a square root of y. (**41**)

squaring Multiplying a value by itself or raising the value to the power of 2. (**41**)

stem The digits to the left of the vertical line in a stem-and-leaf plot. (**746**)

stem-and-leaf plot A display of every element of a numerical data set. Each stem is written once, and the leaves are listed every time they appear. (**746**)

straight angle An angle with measure $180°$. (**240**)

subset A set whose elements are all elements of another set. (**206**)

Substitution Principle If two numbers are equal, then one can be substituted for the other in any computation without changing the results of the computation. (**170**)

supplement One of two angles that are supplementary. (**249, 389**)

supplementary angles Two angles whose measures have a sum of $180°$. (**249, 389**)

surface area The total area of the surface of a three-dimensional figure. (**696**)

T

Take-Away Model for Subtraction If a quantity y is taken away from an original quantity x with the same units, the quantity left is $x - y$. (**294**)

term A number, variable, or product of numbers and variables. (**489**)

tessellation A filling up of a two-dimensional space by congruent copies of a figure that do not overlap. (**380**)

theorem A statement that follows logically from other statements known or assumed to be true. (**98**)

third quartile (Q_3) The median of the numbers greater than the median of the whole data set. (**763**)

tick marks Marks on a number line that divide a number line into parts. (**132**)

time-distance graph A graph of the distance traveled over time. (**655**)

time series A quantity that is measured in regular time intervals. (**778**)

tolerance The specific amount that manufactured parts are allowed to vary from an accepted standard value. (**772**)

total surface area The sum of the areas of each face of a rectangular solid. (**696**) The total surface area (S.A.) of any prism or cylinder is the sum of its lateral area (L.A.) and twice the area B of a base: S.A. = L.A. + 2B. (**705**) The total surface area of a sphere with radius r is S.A. = $4\pi r^2$. (**714**)

transformation A one-to-one correspondence between a first set of points (the preimage) and a second set of point (its image). (**366**)

translation A transformation in which every point in the image of a figure is at the same distance in the same direction from its corresponding point in the figure. Also called *slide*. (**358**)

translation image In a coordinate plane, the result of adding a number h to each first coordinate and a number k to each second coordinate of all the points of a figure. (**359**) Under a translation h units horizontally and k units vertically, the translation image of any point (x, y) is $(x + h, y + k)$. (**361**)

transversal A line that intersects at least two other lines. (**393**)

trapezoid A quadrilateral with at least one pair of parallel sides. (**256**)

Trapezoid Area Formula Let A be the area of a trapezoid with bases b_1 and b_2 and height h. Then the area of a trapezoid is one half the product of its height and the sum of the lengths of its bases: $A = \frac{1}{2}h(b_1 + b_2)$. (**457**)

triangle A polygon with three sides. (**242**)

Triangle Area Formula Let b be the length of a side of a triangle with area A. Let h be the length of the altitude drawn to that side. Then $A = \frac{1}{2}bh$. (**451**)

Triangle Inequality If A, B, and C are any three points, then $AB + BC \geq AC$. If A, B, and C are vertices of a triangle, then $AB + BC > AC$. (**341**)

Triangle Sum Property The sum of the measures of the three angles of any triangle is 180°. (**407**)

triangular prism A prism that has triangles as its bases. (**681**)

Trichotomy Property Given two numbers, either the numbers are equal, the first is greater than the second, or the second is greater than the first and no two of these statements can be true at the same time. If a and b are real numbers, then $a = b$, $a > b$, or $a < b$, and no two of these can happen at the same time. (**629**)

truncating Discarding all digits to the right of a particular decimal place. (**157**)

Two-Dimensional Size-Change Model for Multiplication Under a size change of magnitude $k \neq 0$, the image of (x, y) is (kx, ky). (**474**)

U

union of sets The set of all elements in either set A or set B (or in both), written as $A \cup B$. (**225**)

unit fraction A fraction with 1 in its numerator and a positive integer in its denominator. (**439**)

unit square Any square that measures 1 unit on each side. (**430**)

unknown A variable in an open sentence for which the sentence is to be solved. (**111**)

upper quartile See *third quartile* (Q_3). (**763**)

V

value The result of carrying out the operations in a numerical expression. (**34**)

variable A letter or other symbol that can stand for any one of a set of numbers or other objects. (**70**)

Venn diagram A diagram that uses circles or ovals to represent sets. The positions of the ovals indicate the relationships among the sets. (**206**)

vertex (A) The common endpoint of two rays that make up an angle. (**238**) (B) A point common to two sides of a polygon. (**242**) (C) A point where three or more faces of a polyhedron intersect. (**680**)

vertical angles Two angles in which the opposite rays of the sides of one angle are the sides of the other angle. (**388**)

Vertical Angle Theorem Vertical angles have the same measure. (**388**)

view A two-dimensional drawing that represents a three-dimensional object, such as a building as seen from a particular point p. (**691**)

volume (A) A measure of the space inside a three-dimensional or solid figure. Also called *capacity*. (**698**) (B) The volume V of a box or a rectangular solid with dimensions a, b, and c is $V = abc$. (**699**) (C) The volume V of a prism with height h and a base with area B is given by $V = Bh$. (**709**) (D) The volume of a circular cylinder with height h and base with radius r is given by $V = Bh = \pi r^2 h$. (**710**) (E) The volume of a sphere is $V = \frac{4}{3}\pi r^3$. (**714**)

W

whole numbers Any of the numbers 0, 1, 2, 3, ... **(6)**

width One of three dimensions of a box. **(681)**

window The part of the coordinate plane that is being viewed on a graphing utility. **(57)**

X

x-axis The horizontal number line on a coordinate graph. **(52)**

x-coordinate The first coordinate of a point designated by an ordered pair. **(52)**

Y

y-axis The vertical number line on a coordinate graph. **(52)**

y-coordinate The second coordinate of a point designated by an ordered pair. **(52)**

Index

Photo Credits

Volume 2 Chapters 7–12

Cover: ©Kevin Summers/Photographer's Choice/Getty Images, cover **front, back**.

©AFP/Getty Images, p. **749**; ©age fotostock/SuperStock, pp. **638, 685**; ©Glenn Allison/Getty Images, p. **692**; ©Ty Allison/Taxi/Getty Images, p. **653**; ©Angilla S./Shutterstock, p. **454**; ©AP/Wide World Photos, pp. **569, 573, 593, 621, 624**; ©Arco Images/Alamy, p. **574**; ©ARTEKI/Shutterstock, p. **461** *top*; ©Yann Arthus-Bertrand/Corbis, p. **461** *bottom*; ©Atlantide Phototravel/Corbis, p. **492** *top*; ©Wm. Baker/GhostWorx Images/Alamy, p. **711**; ©Bettmann/Corbis, pp. **600, 754**; ©bluliq/Shutterstock, p. **443**; Courtesy Bowers and Merena Auctions, p. **644**; ©Brand X Pictures/PunchStock, p. **722**; ©The Bridgeman Art Library/Getty Images, p. **607** *right*; ©Michelle D. Bridwell/PhotoEdit, p. **571**; ©Trevor Bryan/Alamy, p. **524**; ©Chris Cheadle/Photographer's Choice/Getty Images, pp. **484-485**; ©Corbis, p. **448**; ©Gary Crabbe/Alamy, p. **476**; ©Steve Crise Photoproduction/scrise.com, p. **606**; ©Custom Medical Stock Photo/Alamy, p. **565**; ©Digital Vision/Getty Images, pp. **738-739**; ©Digital Vision/PunchStock, p. **690** *top*; Courtesy Eisenhower Junior High School, Taylorsville, Utah, p. **521**; ©Alfred Eisenstaedt/Time & Life Pictures/Getty Images, p. **765**; ©Eyewire (Photodisc)PunchStock, p. **586**; ©David R. Frazier Photolibrary, Inc./Alamy, p. **762**; ©Bill Freeman/PhotoEdit, p. **511**; ©Tony Freeman/PhotoEdit, p. **701**; ©Galleria Nazionale d'Arte Moderna, Rome, Italy/The Bridgeman Art Library, p. **607** *bottom left*;©Ilya Genkin/Shutterstock, p. **661**; ©Lowell Georgia/Corbis, p. **599**; ©Getty Images News/Getty Images, p. **743**; ©Steve Gooch, p. **585**; ©The Granger Collection, New York, p. **770**; ©Neil Gray, p. **506**; ©Stuart Gregory/Photographer's Choice/Getty Images, p. **607** *top left*; ©Jeff Gynane/iStockphoto, p. **491**; ©Rab Harling/Alamy, p. **728**; ©G.K. & Vikki Hart/Getty Images, p. **575**; ©Hemera Technologies/Jupiterimages, p. **674** *bottom*; ©Brandon Holmes/Shutterstock, p. **553** *bottom*; ©Steven Hunt/Riser/Getty Images, p. **587**; ©Ed Isaacs/Shutterstock, p. **713**; ©iStock International, Inc., p. **453**; ©Stephanie Jackson, p. **576**; ©Jerzyworks/Masterfile, p. **516**; ©JustASC/Shutterstock, p. **773**; ©Hobart M. King/Geology.com, p. **466**; ©Richard Laird/Taxi/Getty Images, pp. **552-553** *top*; ©Bobbi Lane/Beateworks/Corbis, p. **461** *middle*; Courtesy Library of Congress, p. **747**; ©Misha Logvinov, p. **594**; ©Renee Lynn/Stone/Getty Images, p. **558**; ©Ilene MacDonald/Alamy, p. **645**; ©Joe McBride/Stone/Getty Images, pp. **614-615**; ©Gary McKinnis, p. **730** *top*; ©Ryan McVay/Stone/Getty Images, p. **781**; ©Menna/Shutterstock, p. **782**; ©Doug Menuez/Getty Images, p. **433**; ©Paul Merideth/Stone/Getty Images, p. **577**; ©Leo Meyer/Painet Inc., p. **504**; ©MLB Photos via Getty Images, pp. **768, 784**; ©Jeff Morgan/Alamy, p. **700**; ©Juriah Mosin/Shutterstock, p. **656**; ©Museum of Science and Industry, Chicago, p. **475** *bottom*; Courtesy NARA, p. **475** *top*; Courtesy NASA, p. **744**; Courtesy NASA/JPL, p. **492** *bottom*; Courtesy NASA/JPL-Caltech, p. **462**; Courtesy of the National Park Service, p. **708**; ©Michael Newman/PhotoEdit, p. **564**; ©John Nordell/Christian Science Monitor/Getty Images, p. **752**; ©North Wind/North Wind Picture Archives, p. **690** *bottom*; ©Photodisc/PunchStock, p. **579**; ©Tim Platt/Iconica/Getty Images, p. **446**; ©polartern/Shutterstock, pp. **428-429**; ©Paul Poplis/Jupiterimages, p. **536**; ©Pradeep/Hornbil Images Pvt./hornbil.com., p. **529**; ©Louie Psihoyos/Science Faction/Getty Images, p. **658**; ©Punchstock, pp. **544, 637, 707** *top*, **715, 717**; ©Donovan Reese/Getty Images, p. **640**; ©Roger Ressmeyer/Corbis, p. **523**; ©Reunion des Musees Nationaux/Art Resource, NY, p. **634**; Courtesy RoadWorks Mfg., p. **657**; ©Elena Rooraid/PhotoEdit, p. **622**; ©Antonio M Rosario/Stone/Getty Images, pp. **672-673**; ©Tom Rosenthal/SuperStock, p. **627**; ©Royalty-Free/Corbis, pp. **440, 467, 608, 712**; ©Rich Rushton/Rushton-Chartock Architects, Fairfax CA., p. **450**; ©James Salzano, p. **595**; ©Joel Sartore/National Geographic/Getty Images, p. **526**; ©2006 SASI Group (University of Sheffield) and Mark Newman (University of Michigan)/http://www.worldmapper.org, p. **666** *left, right*; ©Chuck Savage/Corbis, p. **497**; ©Martin Shields, p. **534**; ©SIME s.a.s./eStock Photo, p. **674** *top*; ©ML Sinibaldi/Corbis, p. **477**; ©Richard Hamilton Smith/Corbis, p. **707** *bottom*; ©Paul A. Souders/Corbis, p. **582**; ©Stockdisc/Getty Images, p. **730** *bottom*; ©Stockdisc/Stockdisc Classic/Getty Images, p. **439**; ©SuperStock, Inc./SuperStock, p. **555**; ©Swerve/Alamy, p. **760**; ©Kuni Takahashi, p. **779**; ©Christophe Testi/Shutterstock, p. **495**; ©ThinkStock LLC/Index Stock Imagery, p. **444**; Courtesy TVA, p. **545**; Courtesy USDA, p. **557**; ©Steve Vidler/eStock Photo, p. **695**; ©Kristin Wheeler/Shutterstock, p. **774**;

Illustrations: Garry Nichols

Symbols

$<$	is less than	$0.\overline{a}$	repetend bar
$>$	is greater than	$\ldots$	continuing pattern
$\leq$	is less than or equal to	$\cap$	intersection
$\geq$	is greater than or equal to	$\cup$	union
$=$	is equal to	$\{\,\}, \varnothing$	empty set
$\neq$	is not equal to	$\overleftrightarrow{AB}$	line through A and B
$\approx$	is approximately equal to	$\overrightarrow{AB}$	ray with endpoint A containing B
$+$	plus sign	$\overline{AB}$	segment with endpoints A and B
$-$	minus sign	$\overset{\frown}{AB}$	arc AB
$\pm$	plus or minus	AB	length of segment from A to B, distance from A to B
$\times, \cdot, *$	multiplication signs	$n°$	n degrees
$\overline{)}, \div, /, :$	division signs	$\angle ABC$	angle ABC
$\dfrac{a}{b}$	a divided by b	$m\angle ABC$	measure of angle ABC
$a^b, a{\wedge}b$	a to the bth power	$\triangle ABC$	triangle ABC
$-x$	opposite of x	$\perp$	is perpendicular to
$\%$	percent	$//$	is parallel to
π	pi	$\llcorner$	right angle symbol
$|n|$	absolute value of n	(x, y)	ordered pair
$(\ )$	parentheses	A'	image of point A
$[\ ]$	brackets	b_1	subscripted variable ("b sub 1")
$\{\ \}$	braces	$P(E)$	probability of event E
$\sqrt{}$	radical sign	Q_1, Q_2, Q_3	first, second, and third quartiles